# TRANSITIONAL JUSTICE IN BRAZIL

SERIES ON TRANSITIONAL JUSTICE

The *Series on Transitional Justice* offers a platform for high-quality research within the rapidly growing field of transitional justice. The research is, of necessity inter-disciplinary in nature, drawing from disciplines such as law, political science, history, sociology, criminology, anthropology and psychology, as well as from various specialised fields of study such as human rights, victimology and peace studies. Furthermore, the research is international in outlook, drawing on the knowledge and experience of academics and other specialists in many different regions of the world.

Established in 2007 as the first of its kind, this series is aimed at a variety of audiences who are either working or interested in fields such as crime and justice; human rights; humanitarian law and human security; conflict resolution and peace building. These audiences include academics, researchers, students, policy makers, practitioners, non-governmental organisations and the media.

All books published within the series are subject to a double-blind peer review by recognised authorities in the field.

The General Editors of the Series are:
- Prof. Stephan Parmentier (KU Leuven, Belgium)
- Prof. Jeremy Sarkin (NOVA University of Lisbon, Portugal)
- Dr. Mina Rauschenbach (KU Leuven, Belgium)

The general editors receive support from an Advisory Board, consisting of internationally renowned academics and practitioners.

Published titles within this Series:

12. Anne-Marie de Brouwer, Charlotte Ku, Renée Römkens and Larissa van den Herik (eds.), *Sexual Violence as an International Crime: Interdisciplinary Approaches* (2012), 978-1-78068-002-6
13. Estelle Zinsstag and Martha Albertson Fineman (eds.), *Feminist Perspectives on Transitional Justice: From International and Criminal to Alternative Forms of Justice* (2013), 978-1-78068-142-9
14. Josep M. Tamarit Sumalla, *Historical Memory and Criminal Justice in Spain: A Case of Late Transitional Justice* (2013), 978-1-78068-143-6
15. Catherine Jenkins and Max du Plessis (eds.), *Law, Nation-Building & Transformation: The South African Experience in Perspective* (2014), 978-1-78068-184-9
16. Susanne Buckley-Zistel and Stefanie Schäfer (eds.), *Memorials in Times of Transition* (2014), 978-1-78068-211-2
17. Nico Wouters (ed.), *Transitional Justice and Memory in Europe (1945–2013)* (2014), 978-1-78068-214-3
18. Agata Fijalkowski and Raluca Grosescu (eds.), *Transitional Criminal Justice in Post-Dictatorial and Post-Conflict Societies* (2015), 978-1-78068-260-0
19. S. Elizabeth Bird and Fraser M. Ottanelli (eds.), *The Performance of Memory as Transitional Justice* (2014), 978-1-78068-262-4
20. Bo Viktor Nylund, *Child Soldiers and Transitional Justice* (2016), 978-1-78068-394-2
21. Peter Malcontent (ed.), *Facing the Past: Amending Historical Injustices through Instruments of Transitional Justice* (2016), 978-1-78068-403-1
22. Francesca Capone, *Reparations for Child Victims of Armed Conflict: State of the Field and Current Challenges* (2017), 978-1-78068-438-3
23. Cheryl S. White, *Bridging Divides in Transitional Justice: The Extraordinary Chambers in the Courts of Cambodia* (2017), 978-1-78068-440-6
24. Jeremy Sarkin (ed.), *The Global Impact and Legacy of Truth Commissions* (2019), 978-1-78068-794-0
25. Camila de Gamboa Tapias and Bert van Roermund (eds.), *Just Memories: Remembrance and Restoration in the Aftermath of Political Violence* (2020), 978-1-78068-908-1
26. Grazyna Baranowska, *Rights of Families of Disappeared Persons* (2021), 978-1-83970-137-5
27. Elin Skaar, Eric Wiebelhaus-Brahm and Jemima García-Godos, *Exploring Truth Commission Recommendations in a Comparative Perspective: Beyond Words Vol. I* (2022), 978-1-83970-178-8
28. Elin Skaar, Eric Wiebelhaus-Brahm and Jemima García-Godos (eds.), *Latin American Experiences with Truth Commission Recommendations: Beyond Words Vol. II* (2022), 978-1-83970-179-5

For previous volumes in the series, please visit https://www.larcier-intersentia.com/en/series/series-transitional-justice.html

TRANSITIONAL JUSTICE IN BRAZIL

Walking the Tightrope

Lucia Elena Arantes Ferreira Bastos

Cambridge – Antwerp – Chicago

Intersentia Ltd
8 Wellington Mews
Wellington Street | Cambridge
CB1 1HW | United Kingdom
Tel: +44 1223 736 170
Email: contact@larcier-intersentia.com
www.larcier-intersentia.com

Distribution for the UK and
Rest of the World (incl. Eastern Europe)
NBN International
1 Deltic Avenue, Rooksley
Milton Keynes MK13 8LD
United Kingdom
Tel: +44 1752 202 301 | Fax: +44 1752 202 331
Email: orders@nbninternational.com

Distribution for Europe
Lefebvre Sarrut Belgium NV
Hoogstraat 139/6
1000 Brussels
Belgium
Tel: +32 (0)2 548 07 13
Email: contact@larcier-intersentia.com

Distribution for the USA and Canada
Independent Publishers Group
Order Department
814 North Franklin Street
Chicago, IL 60610
USA
Tel: +1 800 888 4741 (toll free) | Fax: +1 312 337 5985
Email: orders@ipgbook.com

Transitional Justice in Brazil. Walking the Tightrope
© Lucia Elena Arantes Ferreira Bastos 2023

The author has asserted the right under the Copyright, Designs and Patents Act 1988, to be identified as author of this work.

No part of this book may be reproduced, stored in a retrieval system, or transmitted, in any form, or by any means, without prior written permission from Intersentia, or as expressly permitted by law or under the terms agreed with the appropriate reprographic rights organisation. Enquiries concerning reproduction which may not be covered by the above should be addressed to Intersentia at the address above.

Artwork on cover: Author Jan Jordaan, title 'Hurt', medium Linocut, 1999. From the Universal Declaration of Human Rights – International Print Portfolio, Article 5, published by Art for Humanity, South Africa, 1999.

ISBN 978-1-83970-327-0
D/2023/7849/9
NUR 828

British Library Cataloguing in Publication Data. A catalogue record for this book is available from the British Library.

FOREWORD

This book concerns a topic that is almost taboo in Brazilian political culture and the Brazilian political system: Transitional Justice. In the last 50 years, different societies whose citizens have lived under the dominion of authoritarian regimes and civil–military dictatorships have gone through specific processes as they transitioned to democratic regimes. In some of them, the transition resulted in the cessation of repressive policies directed at the opposition and contesting movements. In many cases, the transition was initiated by the ruling elite itself, in an attempt to maintain control of the transition process and to avoid being held directly responsible for the human rights violations that took place during the authoritarian regime. In such cases, the assurances of a transition to democracy were accompanied by commitments to forget the recent past, a kind of full-stop before beginning a new history and new agreements aimed at reconstructing existing institutions through reform or the passage of a new Constitution. Though at first those agreements seemed to represent an advance over the atrocities and violence committed against everyday citizens in the past – especially those with ties to opposition parties – subsequently dissatisfaction came to the fore and demands for justice, accountability, and criminal prosecution of the violators were more frequent.

In other societies, however, the scenarios were very different. The transition processes were accompanied by what is recognized as Transitional Justice. This is a series of political and institutional procedures capable of preventing serious human rights violations from being forgotten and of promoting a permanent policy of collective memory of past events – real policies which institute specific rules for the judgment of the crimes committed and for holding the perpetrators accountable, while simultaneously fostering mechanisms for reconciliation and reparations. Such procedures seek to keep group resentment from remaining just below the surface, capable of manifesting itself in a moment of political crisis and endangering the perpetuation of democratic life. Thus, there arises a minimum degree of consensus at the core of public opinion with respect to the fundamental values underlying the culture and protection of human rights. Among those points of consensus is the refusal to accept practices that were common during the dictatorship, such as torture, persecution, and the suppression of basic civil and public rights and liberties. In most societies emerging out of autocratic and authoritarian regimes, the consolidation of such points of consensus has worked to ensure the stability of their political systems and to preserve democracy.

Foreword

In focusing on the unique aspects of the transition process and the consolidation of democracy in Brazil, this book explores an intermediate model, situated somewhere between the two poles mentioned above. On the one hand, it cannot be said that the transition process was initiated by the military or political elites in power at the time of the civil–military dictatorship, as has been shown by historical and sociological studies. On the other hand, this process did not embrace Transitional Justice, a fact which has shown itself to be a great challenge to the process of democratic consolidation.

Since the *coup* in 1964, the regime was challenged in a multitude of ways, initially through street protests, in the press, by the student movement, by intellectuals and opinion makers, and even by legislators. The regime responded immediately by revoking legislative mandates, censoring the press and the media, suspending elections, and persecuting students, teachers, researchers, writers, journalists, workers, union organizers, political party leaders and all who openly opposed it. The target of these repressive actions was principally the various stripes of the political left, as the regime considered them to be representatives of foreign interests interested in the implementation of communism in the country. The conflict became more vigorous. Part of the opposition went in the direction of armed struggle and was forced underground or into exile. A minority of the opposition persisted in discrete actions calling for the return of the Rule of Law. The response of the State was ever more violent and cruel repression, mainly through the issuance of extraordinary "normative acts" (*atos normativos*) cancelling all constitutional guarantees and legalizing, if one can use that word in such a context, the exercise of arbitrary power.

By the end of the 1970s, the progressive deterioration of the economy and the capitalist market was evident, in contrast to surprising rates of growth and wealth creation at the height of the democratic regime. This deterioration was accompanied by high rates of inflation, concentration of income in the upper levels of the social pyramid, and the resulting worsening of social inequality and poverty among wide swathes of low-income urban workers directly or indirectly tied to industry or the service sector. Living under precarious conditions in terms of urban infrastructure and services, concentrated on the margins of metropolitan regions, in all of the country – but principally in Rio de Janeiro and São Paulo – such workers formed the social basis for the rebirth of the labor movement, the formation of new, modern political parties (including the Workers Party), the burgeoning of Church-sponsored communities inspired by Liberation Theology, and the intensification of social movements in defense of social rights, including civil rights such as freedom of expression, the right to come and go, and the right to political association. This social dynamic contributed to intensifying conflicts at the highest levels of the civil–military power structure. Conflicts within the Armed Forces also became more intense, between those who envisioned a gradual and restricted transition and those who sought to harden the political regime. In the political-institutional and legislative spheres, the profile of the opposition – until then controlled by the military through a division of power between a pro-government party (ARENA) and a tolerated opposition party (MDB) – tended to change. The Brazilian Democratic Movement (known by its Portuguese initials, MDB) became a pole for the flagrant dissatisfaction and began to lead the transition process from a civil–military dictatorship to a State under the Democratic Rule of Law.

Thus, the transition process was not the exclusive result of an initiative by the military rulers through their associations with representatives of business interests and the capitalist market. Rather, it was the result of the dynamic formed by a rising opposition putting an end to the authoritarian regime. Nevertheless, those in power did impose conditions on the process. The transition which was the object of so much hope and anticipation after 21 years of a "state of exception" came about due to an agreement not from on high, but through the intervention of skilled political actors of recognized legitimacy, among which were large parts of institutions such as the liberal press (which had originally supported the *coup* in 1964), unions, center-left political parties, universities, and artists and intellectuals, with the noticeable participation of the Brazilian Bar Association (OAB).

This aim of this book is to precisely explore the reasons why Transitional Justice was not possible in Brazil. In the first chapter, a careful and detailed reconstruction of the political history of Brazilian society from the start of republican government in 1889 until the present time – with special emphasis on the recurring alternations between periods of authoritarian and democratic regimes – establishes the social basis for the conservatism and authoritarianism that persisted for more than a century. This basis is to be found in the almost complete control of the levers of power by alliances between the business, industrial, and commercial classes, landowners, the Church, sectors of the professional middle classes, and the Armed Forces. Despite changes which occurred in the formation and structure of the various social classes, power remained concentrated in the hands of these elites. Even in periods of political agitation and worker uprisings, the struggle of the working class to enlarge their political and social rights, and by extension their civil rights, was insufficiently robust to produce any profound ruptures in the structures of political and social power. The economic cycles of expansion and contraction did not produce any lasting effects in the distribution of wealth. Structural inequalities remained resistant to change, sometimes more so, sometimes less. Not coincidentally, suspicions arose during the political transition that human rights for all citizens, independent of their class, gender, age, power, or wealth, were not to be had. In fact, such rights were simply not destined for all.

It is against this background that the book reconstructs the myriad facts, events, dilemmas, paradoxes, and processes, as well as the political culture and their actors and agencies, which culminated in the impediments to the implementation of effective Transitional Justice in Brazil. Each chapter concentrates on a specific set of questions. After a more detailed examination of the setting in which the demands for this modality of justice arose, the book considers the Special Commission on Political Deaths and Disappearances and the Amnesty Commission, demonstrating that there were demands for both monetary as well as symbolic reparations. Following that is an analysis of the role of the judiciary, the Federal Prosecutor's Office (*Procuradoria Geral da União*), and the Inter-American Court of Human Rights in establishing the existence of serious violations of human rights and holding the perpetrators responsible, a topic currently of undeniable relevance. This chapter also contains a thorough examination of the Amnesty Law of 1979.

Following this, the focus shifts to the institutional conditions that preceded the creation of the National Truth Commission from 2012–2014, as well as the procedures and steps it took to place in evidence the authoritarian legacy and the culture of impunity that persisted over the last three decades of Brazilian society. Subsequently, attention is paid to the role of civil society and non-governmental organizations (NGOs) in their struggles, successes, and failures in the process of uncovering the truth about the violations of human rights committed during the rule of the civil–military dictatorship and in promoting justice and reparations to guarantee one of the most fundamental rights, the right to memory. This right is basic to avoiding a repeat of ruptures in constitutional, republican, and democratic norms, as highlighted by the famous report Brazil: Never Again (*Brasil: Nunca Mais*). In this context, the chapter references and examines some of the events with enormous repercussions, such as the opening of clandestine mass graves (notably in the Perus district of the City of São Paulo), where the fatalities among the victims of the dictatorship's dungeons were buried. It also looks at the efforts of the families of victims and those who were politically persecuted to discover the whereabouts of the disappeared.

Two subsequent chapters constitute innovations in the treatment of the question. The first concerns the serious violations committed against the rights of indigenous people during the dictatorship. This is a particularly relevant issue, not only because of the current state of affairs or the on-going violations of this nature, but also due to the fact that it directs attention to a population which is frequently forgotten or ignored by the public in general and by the authorities charged with protecting it from the constant attacks on its lands and reservations. The next chapter focuses on the role of women in constructing their own path to Transitional Justice. Women played a strategic role in the organization of civil society movements, in the preparations for street demonstrations, in the political maneuvering to obtain justice, and in laying the groundwork for, reconstituting, and preserving collective memory. The transition was not the exclusive result of the concerted actions of men of different political ideologies and party affiliations. Rather, it was also the fruit of the participation of women who succeeded in placing questions of gender and the advancement of women's rights on the broader human rights agenda.

Foreword

The following chapter returns to some of the questions addressed in the initial chapter of the book, but from a more refined and closely examined perspective as it attempts to clarify the complicity of certain companies and private citizens in the 1964 *coup* and in the history of the dictatorship up until the promulgation of the 1988 Constitution.

The development and conclusions of the book's analysis point to the possibilities for a reconciliation capable of ensuring permanent respect for human rights and the stability of a democratic political regime, and the book ends with a reflective and prospective chapter regarding the limits of democratic political culture and the role the law has played in the Brazilian context over the last three decades.

This book has many qualities. It is the result of minutious, careful, and exhaustive bibliographic and documentary research. It was written for the purpose of illustrating the everyday reality of a society that ambiguously and paradoxically combines both conservative and authoritarian roots with a certain democratic political culture. For those who lived through the events discussed, for all or at least part of the period from the 1964 *coup* until today, it is inevitable that it will evoke memories of moments of fear, uncertainty, and anguish, but also of the joy resulting from resistance to oppression, the hopes for a democratic future, and the hard-won democracy achieved in the constitutional pact, even if the task of sustaining and consolidating it remains before us and unfinished.

In particular, the book has two outstanding merits. First, there is its balanced analysis that seeks to describe and understand the facts and events of the time, *sine ira et studio* in the words of Weber's celebrated formula, but with solid arguments clearly laid out so that both the specialized and the ordinary reader may understand the recent history of Brazilian society. Second, in an internally consistent and articulate narrative, it has the merit of uniting the social and institutional conditions, the facts, and the initiatives that allow Transitional Justice in Brazil to be seen as a project still to be pursued.

Sérgio Adorno, Scientific Coordinator of NEV-CEPID/USP
May 2023

ACKNOWLEDGMENTS

In 2016, when my sabbatical period had just started, I chose to spend some time outside Brazil, and I took a decision that could affect my research, as well as my personal and professional life. By August of 2016, I had decided that the time had come to end my cycle of studies on Transitional Justice, which had begun with my PhD research at the University of São Paulo in 2004. That research was about amnesties and international law, and had extended into post-doctorate research (2006–2010). Finally, as a sabbatical goal, I had planned to make room for the new, freeing my mind up for different facets of my field of study.

However, I absolutely did not follow through with that plan. On the contrary, I soon realized that there were still many activities and developments left unexplored, while Brazil was still progressing on its journey towards Transitional Justice. Thus, I gradually came to terms with the fact that I could not go through with my plans to change perspective. While I was abroad and debating with foreign researchers, I noticed that, while there was truly quite an awareness of Brazil, actual knowledge was still sparse and separated by a wall of major research themes and the knowledge that did exist was poorly interconnected. It seemed as if the "eyes" of history had still not addressed the concerns arising from law and that the underlying motivation and "hands" of sociology had not entered into dialogue with the legal and economic foundations. However, Transitional Justice requires multidisciplinary thinking, and it was with this inglorious target in mind that I began my thoughts. As a result, I felt that a mapping of the facts and an exposition of the paths followed by Brazil in the field of Transitional Justice was still an urgent project, a tool that might encourage further dialogue.

At the height of my restlessness, between 2017 and 2018, I approached the Editorial Board of the Intersentia Series on Transitional Justice to start a conversation about the Brazilian case, and I am grateful to them for always listening to me and being available to discuss the manuscript. They certainly knew how to encourage me to move forward, even when the intellectual crossroads kept multiplying.

From the beginning of this project, I have leaned into the subject over and over. At several moments I felt like the figure in Paul Klee's painting entitled "*Angelus Novus*",[1] which Walter Benjamin described as the "Angel of History":[2]

---

[1] KLEE, Paul, *Angelus Novus*. Israel Museum. Jerusalem. Painted 1920.
[2] BENJAMIN, Walter, *Obras escolhidas, Magia e técnica, arte e política: Ensaios sobre literatura e história da cultura*, vol. 1, São Paulo, Brasiliense, 1987, pp. 222–232.

that creature who looks in fear to the catastrophe of the past, who accumulates ruins, gathers fragments, and is finally trapped by a storm without ever seeing the future. However, putting aside this melancholy view of the historical process as an incessant cycle of despair, sometimes I was astonished and at other times totally shocked with the phases of recent Brazilian history and how legal mechanisms affected decision-making in each decade, from the 1980s until now. Yes, I looked to the past with all its afflictions, but I also sought to learn and develop an overview of the pillars of Transitional Justice in the Brazilian context.

After I had gazed into the past with all its nuances, I finally completed a project that lasted almost five years, one which included both mental and physical comings and goings, the beginning and end of my sabbatical, and my eventual return to Brazil during the global pandemic. Certainly, a project like this implies focus and, to maintain the energy required, I mixed my daily and incessant reflections with other activities. This strategy paid off as many insights came to me while I was serving as a volunteer in a refugee camp, as I watched my kids grow up, and while I was practicing yoga to get away from other pressures.

Over these five years, I realized that a book cannot be born only from the effort and love of its author, but is also the result of the environment in support of its development. Evoking Virginia Woolf's essay in "A Room of One's Own",[3] in which the author analyzes the intellectual production and material conditions of nineteenth-century women writers, I recognize that I needed a break or a hiatus in my life to dedicate myself to writing. I also needed a degree of isolation for reflection and, consequently, this required me to obtain both emotional and economic support. I required, first, having a "roof" and second an empowering environment that would give me enough time and the proper atmosphere to write. For this I thank my husband and my children who welcomed my ideas, understood my concerns, and supported me throughout this process. I also thank my parents (*in memoriam*) for raising me to be an independent and daring person, always with the courage to dream.

The ways of thinking and the strategy to write this book, especially the chapters on the history and dilemmas of amnesty and judicial accountability, including national and international trials, are the results of the academic environment that shaped me – the Faculty of Law of the University of São Paulo (FADUSP); the Post-Graduate Program in Latin American Integration at the University of São Paulo (PROLAM/USP) and the Center for the Study of Violence at the University of São Paulo (NEV/USP) – all of which I would like to thank through my former Supervisors and Professors Sérgio Adorno, Cláudia Perrone-Moisés, Umberto Celli Jr., Maria Cristina Cacciamali, and Amaury Patrick Gremaud.

---

[3] WOOLF, Virginia, *Um Teto Todo Seu*, trans. Bia Nunes de Sousa and Glauco Mattoso, São Paulo, Tordesilhas, 2014 [1929].

At various stages of the manuscript, I benefitted from profitable dialogues related to Brazil and Transitional Justice for which I am very grateful, namely the *2017 Summer School on Epistemologies of the South* organized by the Center for Social Studies of the University of Coimbra (CES/UC). The thoughts of Professor Boaventura de Sousa Santos regarding the sociological aspects of indigenous rights, invisibility, and the role of civil society in activism were precise and greatly contributed to this book.

In addition, in the field of symbolic reparations and transformative justice, I would like to highlight the relevant discussions at the February 2018 Seminar on *Gender, Symbolic Reparations and the Arts: Exploring and Disrupting Narratives of Gender Based Violence within Transitional Justice*, which took place at the University of Cape Town (South Africa), under the organization of Professors Jelke Boesten (King's College London) and Helen Scanlon (University of Cape Town), whom I wish to thank for several suggestions concerning the chapter on gender and Transitional Justice. In addition, regarding the studies on women's reparations, I wish to acknowledge the huge contribution of Brazilian Federal Judge Inês Virgínia Prado Soares, who has been an impressive research partner and enthusiastic supporter of my beliefs for more than a decade.

Likewise, on the topic of Transitional Justice and women's rights, I am grateful for the conversations enhanced by the *XX Annual Conference on Women in Spanish, Portuguese and Latin American Studies* (WISPS), held at Maynooth University (Ireland), in 2019, under the coordination of Professor Mirna Vohnsen (Technological University Dublin/Ireland). I also must recognize the feedback I received about my research on the truth-telling processes and the work of truth commissions during the *2019 Annual Conference of the Alliance for Historical Dialogue and Accountability* (AHDA), organized by the Institute for the Study of Human Rights at Columbia University (New York).

During the years 2016, 2017 and 2018, I also attended the 5th, 6th and 7th *United Nations Forums on Business and Human Rights* in Geneva, and the resulting lively atmosphere from the gathering of all those stakeholders, ranging from civil society and non-governmental organizations to State actors, was of great value to my research regarding the complicity of corporations and private actors during the dictatorship, as well as the links between repression and its financing.

Moreover, many close friends of many years have helped me with the essence of this work, both by listening to what I had to say and by calling my attention to aspects I had overlooked. I am grateful to them all for those gestures and the time they made available to me which were vital to my own path and work.

For all those who could no longer stand me saying that I was writing a book that seemed to never end, I confess that, at certain times, I did not want to finish it myself. New events were adding up day after day, and I felt a lot of pressure as the work became ever more relevant with the most recent developments. But, besides the puzzle that insisted on growing in front of me, some things have not changed, and it seems to me that Brazil continues to walk a tightrope.

Therefore, this book ends without Brazil having completed the crossing of this imaginary canyon that might be capable of leading us to the consolidation of democracy. But then again, I believe it is time to share this unfinished history, so that the knowledge contained herein can continue to be developed as well as scrutinized. After all, calls to look into the past, reflect on the present and envisage the future are the types of call we should always heed.

Lucia Elena Arantes Ferreira Bastos
May 2023

CONTENTS

Foreword v
Acknowledgments xi
List of Acronyms and Abbreviations xix

Chapter 1. Introduction: Historical Perspectives from the Brazilian Dictatorship and Transitional Justice Measures 1

1.1. From Historical Perspectives to the Early Years of the Transition to Democracy. 4
1.2. A General Overview of Transitional Justice Mechanisms Implemented in Brazil. 20

PART I. THE INTERSECTION BETWEEN AMNESTY, THE RULE OF LAW, AND AUTHORITARIAN LEGACIES

Chapter 2. Options for Impunity and Amnesty: Forgetting the Past 27

2.1. The Amnesty Law's Overview: Context, Scope and Legitimacy. 29
    2.1.1. The Scenario in which the Amnesty Law was Adopted 29
    2.1.2. The Scope and Legitimacy of the Amnesty Law 34
2.2. Dilemmas of the Amnesty Law: Connected Crimes and the Two-Sided Law Theory. 37
    2.2.1. The Theory of Connected Crimes 37
    2.2.2. The Two-Sided Law Theory 39
2.3. Conclusions 42

PART II. STEPS TOWARDS REPARATIONS, ACCOUNTABILITY, AND TRUTH

Chapter 3. Victims' Reparations Program 47

3.1. The Special Commission for Political Deaths and Disappearances 50
3.2. The Amnesty Commission and Amnesty Caravans: Compensation, Rehabilitation, Acknowledgment 56
3.3. Monuments, Memorials and Commemorative Practice 67
3.4. Conclusions 76

Contents

Chapter 4. Criminal Justice and Judicial Accountability 81

4.1. National Trials 81
    4.1.1. The STF's Judgment on the Legality of the 1979 Amnesty Law:
         Continuity with the Past 81
    4.1.2. Criminal Trials and the Work of the Federal Public Prosecutor's
         Office 84
4.2. International Trials 90
    4.2.1. The *Araguaia Case* and the Inter-American Conventionality
         Control Doctrine: Clash of Jurisdictions 92
    4.2.2. The *Herzog Case* 96
4.3. Conclusions 99

Chapter 5. The Truth-Telling Process 107

5.1. The Long Road to a National Truth Commission 108
5.2. The Relevant Steps Taken by the National Truth Commission 111
    5.2.1. Highlights and Recommendations 114
    5.2.2. The Creation of an Extensive Network of Local Truth
         Commissions as a Positive Effect of the NTC 115
5.3. The NTC's Work on the Effect of the Brazilian Dictatorship
    on the LGBTI Population 118
5.4. The NTC's Failure to Address Accountability for Violations
    of Economic and Social Rights 121
5.5. The NTC's Failure to Catalyze Changes in the Country 126
5.6. General Assessments of the National Truth Commission:
    The Hidden Cases 132
5.7. Authoritarianism's Legacies and the Culture of Impunity 134
5.8. Conclusions 138

PART III. COMPLEX FORMS OF REPARATIONS, ACCOUNTABILITY, AND TRUTH-SEEKING: ACTORS BEYOND AGENTS OF THE STATE

Chapter 6. The Role of Civil Society and NGOs in the Quest for Truth, Justice, and Memory 145

6.1. From the Amnesty Movement to the Drafting of "Brazil: Never Again"
    and Discovery of the Mass Grave in Perus 149
6.2. Activisms and Strategies During the 2000s: From Claims for Justice
    to the "*Escrachos*" 159
6.3. Conclusions 166

Chapter 7. Redressing Violations of Indigenous Rights................171

7.1. The Invisibility of Indigenous People 171
    7.1.1. Indigenous People and Legal Protection During the Mid-Twentieth Century 172
    7.1.2. Indigenous Tribes and the Dictatorship Period (1964–1985)...176
7.2. The Challenges of Collective Reparations 184
    7.2.1. Obstacles to Land Recovery 186
    7.2.2. Obstacles to Collective Reparations 192
    7.2.3. Challenges to Judicial and Administrative Measures 195
7.3. Conclusions 202

Chapter 8. A Gendered Approach to Brazilian Transitional Justice 205

8.1. Women's Participation in the Anti-Dictatorship Movement..........205
8.2. Official Symbolic Reparations to Women 213
    8.2.1. The Book *Luta, Substantivo Feminino* (Fight: A Feminine Noun)...213
    8.2.2. The Work of the Amnesty Commission: "Amnesty Caravans" and the "Stamps of Memory" Project 214
    8.2.3. The Final Report of the National Truth Commission (NTC) and Gender..218
    8.2.4. The Symbolic Reparation to Women at the Memorial of the Resistance of São Paulo 221
8.3. Struggles to be Faced...223
    8.3.1. Emblematic Setback: The *Inês Etienne Case*.................223
    8.3.2. Normalization of Violence against Women: Continuums and Inequalities 227
    8.3.3. Gender Identity and Transitional Justice: Beyond the Binary Perspective 232
8.4. Conclusion: The Need for More Critical Interventions and Fewer Representations of Suffering....................................236

Chapter 9. The Complicity of Corporations and Private Actors During the Dictatorship..241

9.1. Introduction 241
9.2. The Links between Repression and its Financing...................246
    9.2.1. The *OBAN Case* 246
    9.2.2. The *"Black Lists" Case* 249
9.3. The Propositions of the Truth Commissions Regarding Corporate Complicity 254

9.4. The Intricate Way to Connect Corporate Complicity within the
 Transitional Justice Framework................................. 258
9.5. Conclusions 263

Chapter 10. Final Remarks: The Limits and Possibilities of Transitional Justice in Brazil 267

Bibliography... 275
Index... 297

LIST OF ACRONYMS AND ABBREVIATIONS

ABAP	*Associação Brasileira de Anistiados Políticos* (Brazilian Association of Political Amnesty Recipients)
ADCT	*Ato das Disposições Constitucionais Transitórias* (List of Transitory Constitutional Provisions)
ADNAM	*Associação Democrática e Nacionalista de Militares* (National Democratic Military Association)
ADPF/ADFP	*Argüição de Descumprimento de Preceito Fundamental* (Allegation of Disobedience of a Fundamental Precept)
AI-5	*Ato Institucional no. 5* (Institutional Act no. 5)
AJD	*Associação Juízes para a Democracia* (Association of Judges for Democracy)
ALICE	*Agência Livre para a Informação, Cidadania e Educação* (Free Agency for Information, Citizenship and Education)
ARENA	*Aliança Renovadora Nacional* (National Alliance for Renewal)
BNM	*Brasil: Nunca Mais* (Brazil: Never Again)
CATJ	Corporate Accountability and Transitional Justice
CBA	*Comitê Brasileiro pela Anistia* (Brazilian Committee for Amnesty)
CEJIL	Center for Justice and International Law
CFMD	*Comissão dos Familiares dos Mortos e Desaparecidos Politicos* (Commission of the Families of the Dead and Disappeared)
CIMI	*Conselho Missionário Indígena* (Indian Missionary Council)
CPMVJ	*Comitê Paulista pela Memória, Verdade e Justiça* (*Paulista* Committee for Memory, Truth and Justice)
DEOPS/SP	*Departamento Estadual de Ordem Política e Social de São Paulo* (São Paulo State Department of Political and Social Order)

List of Acronyms and Abbreviations

DOI/CODI	*Destacamentos de Operações de Informações – Centros de Operações de Defesa Interna* (Department of Information Operations – Center for Internal Defense Operations)
DOPS	*Departamento de Ordem Política e Social* (Department of Political and Social Order)
EAFF	*Equipo Argentino de Antropología Forense* (Group of forensic archeology, Argentina)
ESCR	Economic, Social and Cultural Rights
FDDD	*Fundo de Defesa dos Direitos Difusos* (Fund for the Defense of Diffuse Rights)
FIESP	*Federação de Indústria do Estado de São Paulo* (São Paulo State Federation of Industry)
FUNAI	*Fundação Nacional do Índio* (National Indigenous Foundation)
GGI	Gender Gap Index
GRIN	*Guarda Rural Indígena* (Indigenous Rural Guard)
HIJOS	*Hijas y Hijos por Identidad y Justicia y Contra el Olvido y Silencio* (Daughters and Sons for Identity and Justice and Against Silence and Forgetting, Argentina)
IACHR	Inter-American Commission on Human Rights/Inter-American Court of Human Rights
IBAD	*Instituto Brasileiro de Ação Democrática* (Brazilian Institute for Democratic Action)
IBAMA	*Instituto Brasileiro do Meio Ambiente e dos Recursos Naturais Renováveis* (Brazilian Institute of Environment and Natural Resources)
ICMP	International Commission of Missing Persons
ICTJ	International Center for Transitional Justice
IPES	*Instituto de Pesquisas e Estudos Sociais* (Institute for Social Studies Research)
JK	President Juscelino Kubitschek
LGBTI	Lesbian, Gay, Bisexual, Transgender and Intersex
MBL	*Movimento Brasil Livre* (Free Brazil Movement)
MDB	*Movimento Democrático Brasileiro* (Brazilian Democratic Movement)

List of Acronyms and Abbreviations

MFPA	*Movimento Feminino pela Anistia* (Women for Amnesty Movement)
MPF	*Ministério Público Federal* (Federal Public Prosecutor's Office)
NGOs	Non-governmental organizations
NTC	National Truth Commission
OAB	*Ordem dos Advogados do Brasil* (Brazilian Bar Association)
OAS	Organization of American States
OBAN	*Operação Bandeirante* (Operation *Bandeirantes*)
OHCHR	Office of the United Nations High Commissioner of Human Rights
PCB	*Partido Comunista Brasileiro* (Brazilian Communist Party)
PGR	*Procuradoria Geral da República* (Office of the Prosecutor General)
PMDB	*Partido do Movimento Democrático Brasileiro* (Brazilian Democratic Movement Party)
POLOP	*Política Operária* (Worker's Policy)
PT	*Partido dos Trabalhadores* (Workers' Party)
SCPDD	*Comissão Especial de Mortos e Desaparecidos Políticos* (Special Commission of Political Deaths and Disappearances)
SPI	*Serviço de Proteção ao Índio* (Indigenous Protection Service)
STF	*Supremo Tribunal Federal* (Brazilian Federal Supreme Federal Court)
STJ	*Superior Tribunal de Justiça* (High Court of Justice)
STM	*Superior Tribunal Militar* (Superior Military Court)
TRC	Truth and Reconciliation Commission, South Africa
UNICAMP	*Universidade de Campinas* (University of Campinas)
UNIFESP	*Universidade Federal de São Paulo* (Federal University of São Paulo)
VAR-Palmares	*Vanguarda Armada Revolucionária – Palmares* (Revolutionary Armed Vanguard – *Palmares*)

CHAPTER 1

INTRODUCTION

Historical Perspectives from the Brazilian Dictatorship and Transitional Justice Measures

In October 2018, at an event celebrating the 30th anniversary of the 1988 Constitution, a justice of the Brazilian Supreme Court said that, currently, he no longer preferred to call what happened in 1964 a *coup d'état*, but rather a "movement",[1] which is a multi-sense word that could apply to a whole spectrum of political actions, since in politics almost anything might be termed a "movement". Moreover, using a word with such a generic meaning for something so concrete might in fact be seen as a way of hiding or obscuring the reality that a President was overthrown, thousands of Brazilians were exiled or had their political rights suspended, thousands more were tortured, and more than 400 people were killed or were the victims of forced disappearances.

Likewise, when one says "movement" instead of dictatorship or *coup d'état*, the perception of political evil is affected, and the past that once was real becomes another phenomenon, another experience. Indeed, this past became so different and unusual that, in December 2018, during a truckers' strike that threatened to stop the country, it was possible to see posters in the streets calling for military intervention and dictatorship.[2] Similarly, in April 2020, during a rally, protesters also carried signs demanding military intervention and called for Brazil's Congress and Supreme Court to be shut down, making allusion to the restoration of legislation commonly issued by the Brazilian dictatorship to close the parliament and restrict civil liberties (like the Decree "AI-5").[3] Unsurprisingly, those facts are a definite sign that the project to create an anti-authoritarian culture in Brazil may have failed.

---

[1] FELIPPE, Marcio Sotelo, "A Ditadura Despertada", *Revista Cult*, October 22, 2018, https://revistacult.uol.com.br/home/a-ditadura-despertada/.

[2] FAVARO, Cristian, "Brasil Falhou em Não Criar Cultura Contra o Autoritarismo", *Agência Estado*, December 10, 2018, https://noticias.uol.com.br/ultimas-noticias/agencia-estado/2018/12/10/brasil-falhou-em-nao-criar-cultura-contra-o-autoritarismo-diz-maria-do-rosario.htm.

[3] *Deutsche Welle*, "Brazilian President Bolsonaro Sides with Anti-Democracy Protesters", April 24, 2020, https://www.dw.com/en/brazilian-president-bolsonaro-sides-with-anti-democracy-protesters/a-53235241.

This and many stories related to the 1964–1985 period that have lately emerged[4] serve to demonstrate that this is an opportune time to study Transitional Justice mechanisms and how they have been implemented over the more than 30 years since democracy and the Rule of Law returned to Brazil. It is also a time to assess whether all that has been done has in fact been able to restructure the country, especially at a time when the Inter-American Commission on Human Rights has stated that Brazil is backsliding in the promotion of human rights.[5] This is also a moment when Brazilian politicians feel free to treat their rivals as enemies ripe for intimidation and act on the assumption that a new type of martial law may soon be imposed, just like the scenario during the '60s and '70s.[6] Finally, it is a time when recent decisions – including the President's changing of members of a commission[7] – threaten to reject the results of work by a special commission appointed to implement Transitional Justice measures and reparations programs.[8]

So, not surprisingly, the title of this book ("Walking the Tightrope") resembles one of the classic lyrics of the so-called "openings songs" phase in Brazil. Beginning in 1979, those songs indicated a new historical era, which it was between the trauma of the dictatorship and the dream of a future democracy. So, this book was inspired by some verses of the song "*O Bêbado e a Equilibrista*"

---

[4] Just to mention but one: the idea to "celebrate" the 1964 *coup d'état* that was proposed by President Bolsonaro during 2019. See: LEITE, Marcelo, "Juíza Proíbe Celebrar 1964; Gilmar Nega Pedido de Vítimas da Ditadura", *Uol Notícias*, March 29, 2019, https://noticias.uol.com.br/politica/ultimas-noticias/2019/03/29/juiza-cita-violencia-e-estado-de-excecao-e-proibe-uniao-de-celebrar-golpe.htm. In fact, however, such initiative was not new among retired military personnel, since on various occasions over the years the *Clube Militar*, located in the city of Rio de Janeiro, has organized gatherings to celebrate the 1964 *coup d'état*. See: RÖTZSCH, Rodrigo, "Clube Militar Celebra Golpe com Críticas à Comissão de Verdade", *Folha de São Paulo*, March 25, 2011, https://m.folha.uol.com.br/poder/2011/03/894120-clube-militar-celebra-golpe-com-criticas-a-comissao-da-verdade.shtml. *Terra Notícias*, "Militares da Reserva Comemoram 48 anos do Golpe Militar no Rio", March 31, 2012, https://www.terra.com.br/noticias/brasil/politica/militares-da-reserva-comemoram-48-anos-do-golpe-militar-no-rio,431a0a43aa1da310VgnCLD200000bbcceb0aRCRD.html.

[5] BARBON, Júlia, "Brasil Vive Retrocesso nos Direitos Humanos, diz OEA em Visita ao País", *Folha de São Paulo*, November 12, 2018, https://www1.folha.uol.com.br/poder/2018/11/brasil-vive-retrocesso-nos-direitos-humanos-diz-oea-em-visita-ao-pais.shtml.

[6] PHILLIPS, Tom, "Brazilian President's Son Suggests Using Dictatorship-Era Tactics on Leftist Foes", *The Guardian*, November 1, 2019, https://www.theguardian.com/world/2019/nov/01/brazili-president-son-jair-eduardo-bolsonaro-dictatorship-era-tactics-leftist-foes.

[7] *Correio Braziliense*, "Bolsonaro Troca Integrantes da Comissão de Mortos e Desaparecidos Políticos", August 1, 2019, https://www.correiobraziliense.com.br/app/noticia/politica/2019/08/01/interna_politica,800677/bolsonaro-troca-integrantes-da-comissao-de-mortos-e-desaparecidos-poli.shtml.

[8] *Agência Brasil*, "Damares Anuncia Auditoria em Atos da Comissão da Anistia", *Isto É*, March 27, 2010, https://istoe.com.br/damares-anuncia-auditoria-em-atos-da-comissao-de-anistia/.

(The Drunk and the Tightrope Walker) by João Bosco and Aldir Blanc (1979) and recorded by Elis Regina (Album named "*Elis, Essa Mulher*").

In particular, the song "*O Bêbado e a Equilibrista*" offered a reflection about the social context of that time and also called for the return of political exiles. The song ended up by encouraging those who were feeling like tightrope walkers to stay confident and wait for better days, even if this would entail many risks, with this remarkable verse:

> But I know, that such a stinging pain/ Will not be useless/ Hope dances on the tightrope with an umbrella/ And in every step of that line it can get hurt/ Bad luck/ The tightrope walker, Hope, knows that every artist's show must go on.[9]

By studying not only the past atrocities but also researching how Brazil has dealt with them – how the country has given voice to the victims and relatives (or not), how society has perceived the need for reconstruction and healing the wounds of the past, what has exceed expectations and what has gone very wrong – we may reach some understanding about the present situation, since lately it has seemed that Brazilians are living a moment when the buffers of democracy are being weakened in silence[10] and we continue to walk on a tightrope from the perspective of human rights' protection.

Apropos of this possible democratic erosion, it is appropriate to cite Levitsky and Ziblatt[11] when they comment that democracies do not die at the hands of men with guns anymore, as they did during the Cold War, when *coups d'état* accounted for nearly three out of every four democratic breakdowns. Nowadays, there are other ways to disrupt democracy in barely visible steps, sometimes even at the hands of elected leaders. There are no tanks in the streets. Presidents are not being killed, imprisoned, or sent into exile. The Constitution is not suspended, and democratic institutions remain in place. People still vote. While a veneer of democracy is still maintained, its very substance is nevertheless slowing deteriorating. And this situation causes public confusion, since citizens do not immediately realize what is really happening.

---

[9] Free translation of: "*Mas sei, que uma dor assim pungente/ Não há de ser inutilmente/ A esperança dança na corda bamba de sombrinha/ E em cada passo dessa linha pode se machucar/ Azar/ A esperança equilibristas Sabe que o show de todo artista tem que continuar*". For more details, see: SILVA, Fernando Lopes, "O Poético e o Factual na Narrativa da Canção O Bêbado e a Equilibrista", *Alpha Revista*, vol. 17(1)/2016, pp. 115–127.

[10] CHADE, Jamil, "Bolsonaro Enfraquece Consenso Democrático Já Fraco no Brasil, Diz Levitsky", *Uol Notícias*, November 20, 2019, https://noticias.uol.com.br/colunas/jamil-chade/2019/11/20/bolsonaro-enfraquece-o-consenso-democratico-diz-autor-de-best-seller.htm.

[11] LEVITSKY, Steven and ZIBLATT, Daniel, *How Democracies Die*, New York, Crown Publishing, 2018.

1.1. FROM HISTORICAL PERSPECTIVES TO THE EARLY YEARS OF THE TRANSITION TO DEMOCRACY

Some brief historical context surrounding the analysis of Transitional Justice measures in the country is in order.[12] It is important to remember that Brazil has been an independent nation since 1822 and a republic governed by a federalist constitution since 1889. The transition from the Empire of Brazil[13] to the Republic was characterized by a period of great uncertainty, since there were different interests and conceptions of how the Republic should be organized. The Brazilian Republic was idealized by a group of military officers who were antagonistic to the civilian elite of the Empire and who were disappointed with the country's situation and their own political status.[14] But these officers were also unable to agree on the meaning of republicanism itself and on the purposes of the new regime. Even so, the defenders of a liberal Republic were in a hurry to guarantee the convening of a Constitutional Assembly, as they feared extending the near dictatorship that prevailed under the command of Marshall Deodoro da Fonseca from 1889–1891.

It was against this background that the first Constitution of the Brazilian Republic was promulgated, in February 1891. Inspired by the US Constitution, the 1891 Constitution envisioned Brazil as a liberal, federal republic, with a system of presidential government. It included direct elections and universal suffrage for all male citizens over the age of 21, except for certain categories such as illiterates, beggars, and some members of the military. No reference was made to voting rights for women, but it was implicitly considered that they were prevented from voting.[15]

This period, from 1889 to 1930, is commonly known as the "First Republic" or as the "Republic of Colonels", in reference to the colonels of the former National Guard, mostly rural landowners with considerable local influence and power. In fact, this so-called *coronelismo* represented a variant of a sociopolitical relationship called "clientelism", which ended up existing both in the countryside and in urban areas. This clientelism or patronage was the result of

---

[12] For this historical analysis see: SCHWARCZ, Lilia M. and STARLING, Heloisa M., *Brasil: Uma Biografia*, São Paulo, Companhia das Letras, 2015. GASPARI, Elio, *A Ditadura Escancarada*, São Paulo, Companhia das Letras, 2002. GASPARI, Elio, *A Ditadura Envergonhada*, São Paulo, Companhia das Letras, 2002. FLEISCHER, David, *Countries at the Crossroads 2012: Brazil*, available at https://freedomhouse.org/sites/default/files/Brazil%20-%20FINAL.pdf.

[13] Formed in 1822 and comprising territories from modern-day Brazil and Uruguay, ruled successively by Emperors Dom Pedro I and Dom Pedro II.

[14] FAUSTO, Boris, *História Concisa do Brasil*, São Paulo, EDUSP, 2015, pp. 139–141.

[15] SCHWARCZ, Lilia M. and STARLING, Heloisa M., *Brasil Uma Biografia*, São Paulo, Companhia das Letras, 2015, pp. 319–322.

social inequality – namely, the impossibility for citizens to enforce their rights, as well as the precarious or non-existent social assistance network at the time. Though these characteristics existed during the colonial period, the conditions under the Republic allowed local political leaders to concentrate power even further and to use it as a bargaining chip to favor their own interests. Electorally, local colonels controlled voters in their area of influence and exchanged votes for favors such as a pair of shoes, a bed in the hospital or a job as a teacher in the public school.

During this phase, voting fraud was frequent. Brazilians did not vote by free will, but rather at the behest of the local colonel, since they were completely dependent on his fate. Due to these circumstances, the expression *voto de cabresto* (which might be translated as "horse-collar votes" or "halter votes") came into being, which Leal has described as those cases in which voters – illiterate or nearly so and without access to healthcare or newspapers and information – looked to their patron (the colonel) as their sole benefactor and ignored the fact that they (at least formally) had the right to truly exercise the franchise.[16]

Consequently, voting was merely understood as an expression of loyalty to the colonel or as a bargaining chip to be exchanged for favors. The term *coronelismo* also references the complex system of negotiation existing between the local chiefs and their respective state governors and between the latter and the President of the Republic. In this way, in the early twentieth century, the Brazilian Republic achieved stability but only as the result of intense bargaining, favoritism, and negotiations.[17] Unfortunately, as Costa has expressed, the transition from Empire to Republic made little difference to the Brazilian population, since, once in power, the politicians of that era promoted only those institutional changes that were necessary to satisfy their own needs.[18] Moreover, as Valença[19] has noted, the institution of *coronelismo* or patronage is perhaps as strong today in Brazil as it used to be during the colonial, imperial and early republican periods, but with a different make-up: the system that was initiated at the local level climbed the ladder of power and established itself at the heart of the country's political center, branching out to all levels of government and policy-making agencies.

---

[16] LEAL, Victor Nunes, *Coronelismo, Enxada e Voto: Município e o Regime Representativo No Brasil*, São Paulo, Alfa-Omega, 1978.
[17] SCHWARCZ, Lilia M. and STARLING, Heloisa M., *Brasil Uma Biografia*, São Paulo, Companhia das Letras, 2015, pp. 319–322.
[18] Historian Emilia Viotti da Costa wrote: "The main difference [between Empire and Republic] was that the traditional rural oligarchy had been supplanted by a new one: the coffee planters of the [Paulista] West and their allies, who, once in power, promoted only those institutional changes that were necessary to satisfy their own needs". See: COSTA, Emilia Viotti da, *The Brazilian Empire: Myths and Histories*, Chicago and London, University of Chicago Press, 1985, p. 233.
[19] VALENÇA, Márcio M., "Patron-Client Relations and Politics in Brazil – An Historical Overview", *Research Papers in Environmental and Spatial Analysis*, vol. 58/1999.

Also, during the 1889–1930 period, control of the federal government alternated between the political parties representing the states of São Paulo (whose members were generally made up of landowners producing coffee for export) and Minas Gerais (whose members defended the interests of cattle producers and dairymen). This rotation in and out of power generated the so-called *Política do Café com Leite* (the Politics of Coffee with Milk). However, the *pax republicana* engendered by the "Coffee with Milk" status quo was broken in 1929, when President Washington Luiz, a member of the São Paulo oligarchy, offered his patronage to another *paulista* (named Julio Prestes) instead of supporting a representative of Minas Gerais state to run in the presidential election of 1930.

Washington Luiz's choice upset regional oligarchs who expected the President to nominate a candidate from the state of Minas Gerais. According to Fausto,[20] this dispute over presidential succession – in conjunction with the severe crisis in the export economy caused by the 1929 Stock Market Crash, the menace of a growing urban working class, the rise of a new industrial elite, and the expansion of certain segments of the urban middle class, imbued with nationalist ideas – led the "Republic of Colonels" to a crossroads.

Reluctant to support Julio Prestes as Washington Luiz's successor, elites from the states of Minas Gerais, Rio Grande do Sul, and Paraíba were more enthusiastic about the figure of Getúlio Vargas, Governor of Rio Grande do Sul state. Subsequently, Vargas was launched as an opposition candidate with the support of a new political party, the *Aliança Liberal* (Liberal Alliance) and a heterogeneous coalition of military officers, urban liberals and industrialists. However, the popularity of the *Aliança Liberal* was not enough to defeat the political powers of Julio Prestes and the old-line Republican Party establishment, and Vargas was defeated in the March 1930 election.

Later on, in July 1930, João Pessoa, the vice-presidential candidate in the defeated *Aliança Liberal* party, was shot and killed by a rival from his home state of Paraíba. Although the motive for the shooting was clearly local, Pessoa's allies blamed the federal government and, consequently, Vargas's supporters in the Armed Forces quickly made plans to overthrow the elected government. The Armed Forces' insurrection began on October 3, 1930 in the states of Rio Grande do Sul and Minas Gerais and quickly spread to the Northeast region. Once it became clear that Washington Luiz would be unable to maintain support among the loyalist troops, a military junta deposed the President and Washington Luiz's fall opened up the opportunity for Vargas to become the chief of the Provisional Government. In fact, as Williams has observed,[21] when Vargas entered the

---

[20] FAUSTO, Boris, *História Concisa do Brasil*, São Paulo, EDUSP, 2015.
[21] WILLIAMS, Daryle, *Cultural Wars in Brazil – The First Vargas Regime (1930–1945)*, Durham NC and London, Duke University Press, 2001, pp. 1–5.

Presidential Palace in the capital, Rio de Janeiro, as the new Head of State, he set a precedent that was to repeat itself on numerous occasions throughout the twentieth century: extraconstitutional measures, including threats of civil war, became legitimate tools for resolving political crises among competing elites.

By bringing Getúlio Vargas to power, the so-called "1930 Revolution" enshrined him as the country's leader for the next 15 years, first as provisional chief (1930–1934), then as the elected President (1934–1937), and finally as a dictator (1937–1945). Furthermore, as Bak has remarked,[22] under the Vargas regime, the State became the benefactor of an expanding urban working class, giving Vargas the contemporary nickname of *o pai dos pobres* (the father of the poor), a populist title. To be precise, this expression refers to the fact that the State started to trade social benefits and labor rights for political access and support, at the same time as the government was dedicated to aggressively intervening in the economy to promote Brazilian development.

Soon after, during the period 1945–1964, Brazil saw a deepening struggle between "populist" politicians,[23] whose opportunities were enlarged by rapidly expanding political participation, and military officers, who feared that popular mobilization might come under the control of revolutionary leaders. Skidmore has even pointed out that special emphasis should be given to the radicalization of the views of certain "middle sectors" who, in the early 1960s, grew increasingly fearful of the revolutionary potential of the urban lower classes.[24] Consequently, the political scenario from 1945–1964 was permeated by turmoil,[25] including the suicide of Getúlio Vargas in 1954 (interrupting another term as President beginning in 1951), the strong presence of the military in political affairs, and a President (Jânio Quadras) who resigned after only seven months in office, in 1961.

Concerning the presence of the Armed Forces in the political arena, a notable incident was the so-called "preventive" coup carried out by Marshall Henrique

---

[22] BAK, Joan L., "Cartels, Cooperatives, and Corporatism: Getúlio Vargas in Rio Grande do Sul on the Eve of Brazil's 1930 Revolution", *Hispanic American Historical Review*, vol. 63/1983, pp. 255–275.

[23] The term "populist" politician is used here as a "form of political conduct, adopted by a person or a group of people, that may be identified by the use of economic tools and other means designed to produce favorable results quickly, regardless of how short-lived they may be, in so much as these actions are instrumental to acquire and maintain authoritarian power". See: CASTRO, Paulo Rabello de Castro and RONCI, Marcio, "Sixty Years of Populism in Brazil", in DORNBUSCH, Rudiger and EDWARDS, Sebastian (eds.), *The Macroeconomics of Populism in Latin America*, Chicago IL, University of Chicago Press, 1991, pp. 151–173.

[24] SKIDMORE, Thomas E., "The Historiography of Brazil, 1889–1964 – Part 1", *Hispanic American Historical Review*, vol. 55/1975, pp. 716–748.

[25] FERREIRA, Marcos Alan S.V., "Peace and Conflict in Brazil", in RICHMOND O. and VISOKA, G. (eds.), *The Palgrave Encyclopedia of Peace and Conflict Studies*, Cham, Palgrave Macmillan, 2020.

Teixeira Lott in 1955, allegedly to prevent an actual military coup. In fact, the 1955 Preventive Coup or *Movement of November 11th* is the name given to the events that resulted in the countercoup organized by Marshall Lott, in order to guarantee that the elected President, Juscelino Kubitschek (known as "JK"), would be able to assume his post on January 31, 1956.[26]

A few days after the inauguration of JK's administration, on February 10, 1956, dissatisfied Air Force officers, led by Major Haroldo Veloso and Captain José Chaves Lameirão, arrived at the Jacareacanga air base, in the south of Pará state, where they set up the headquarters of another coup attempt. Those officers did not agree with the continuation in the JK government of the Aeronautics Minister, Vasco Alves Seco. With the support of the local population, the rebels took over the locations of Cachimbo, Belterra, Itaituba, and Aragarças, in addition to the city of Santarém. Although it was considered a minor rebellion, the government found it difficult to suppress it due to the reaction of other officers, especially from the Air Force, who refused to participate in the repression of the rebels. After 19 days, the rebellion was finally brought under control by loyalist troops, with the arrest of its main leader, Major Haroldo Veloso, but all the rebels eventually benefited from an amnesty which Congress was quick to grant, at the request of President Kubitschek himself.[27]

Despite the amnesty granted by JK to those involved in the Jacareacanga Rebellion in February 1956, the climate of conspiracy against the government continued, especially in the Air Force. The *Aragarças Uprising*, which broke out on December 2, 1959, was organized by the former leader of the *Jacareacanga Rebellion*, Haroldo Veloso, and dozens of other soldiers and civilians, among them lieutenant-colonel João Paulo Moreira Burnier, who was its main leader. The aim of their uprising was to start a "revolutionary movement" to remove the group that controlled the country, whose members, according to the conspiracy leaders, were corrupt and committed to international Communism. The rebels headed for Aragarças, in Goiás state, and intended to bomb the Laranjeiras and Catete palaces, located in the City of Rio de Janeiro, as well as to occupy the air bases of Santarém and Jacareacanga in Pará state. In reality, neither the bombing of the palaces nor the occupation of the bases took place, and the rebellion was restricted to Aragarças. The revolt lasted only 36 hours and its leaders fled by plane to Paraguay, Bolivia, and Argentina, only returning to Brazil during the Jânio Quadros administration in 1961.[28]

---

[26] FAUSTO, Boris, *História Concisa do Brasil*, São Paulo, EDUSP, 2015, pp. 232–233.
[27] *Centro de Pesquisa e Documentação de História Contemporânea do Brasil*, Faculdade Getúlio Vargas (CPDOC/FGV), "Revolta de Jacareacanga", https://cpdoc.fgv.br/producao/dossies/JK/artigos/Politica/Jacareacanga.
[28] *Centro de Pesquisa e Documentação de História Contemporânea do Brasil*, Faculdade Getúlio Vargas (CPDOC/FGV), "A Revolta de Aragarças", https://cpdoc.fgv.br/producao/dossies/JK/artigos/Politica/Aragarcas.

On the economic front, the governments of Jânio Quadros and João Goulart (1961–1964) were both marked by crumbling finances, as well as political impasses and the growing participation of social movements in the public sphere. As Skidmore has observed,[29] the large external debt left by the Kubitschek administration (1956–1961),[30] rising inflation, and the deterioration of the nation's commercial trade balance all obstructed Brazil's chances of gaining new international loans that might have alleviated some of the resulting economic pressure.

In addition, the political field was also unstable due to the resignation of President Jânio Quadros only seven months after his inauguration. This decision provoked a profound crisis when part of the military ministers (ministers of Army, Aeronautics and Navy) tried to prevent Vice President João Goulart from taking power,[31] on the pretext of his alleged leftist inclinations. Consequently, Goulart's inauguration was only made possible following a compromise under which the country changed from a presidential to a parliamentary form of government, a move which proved short-term when it was reversed by referendum in January 1963. Goulart promised a series of structural transformations, including land, education, tax, and electoral reform, but in March 1964, the military removed him, claiming that those reforms were Communist influenced. The military then proceeded to rule Brazil until 1985.

We have described all these back-and-forth oscillations in the Brazilian political scenario in the first half of the twentieth century because, in fact, when the military took power in the 1964 coup, they were terminating a democratic experience marked by several instances of interruptions or breakdowns in orderly presidential succession. The 1954 suicide of Getúlio Vargas, the opposition to JK's and later to João Goulart's taking office, and the aborted presidency of Jânio Quadros all created significant political instability[32] in the country that should not be neglected in any understanding of the subsequent actions during the '60s, '70s and '80s. Indeed, these facts demonstrate that military interventions during the Republican period are hardly a new idea.

During the 1964–1985 period, even though Brazilians could not directly elect their President,[33] congressional elections were held every four years[34]

---

[29] SKIDMORE, Thomas, *Brasil: de Getúlio a Castelo*, Rio de Janeiro, Paz e Terra, 1988, p. 240.
[30] In 1955, Juscelino Kubitschek was elected President, promising "50 years of progress in 5" with a new intense phase of import-substitution-industrialization and the construction of the inland capital Brasilia. Consequently, his projects led to a deep financial debt for the coming administrations. See: *Folha de São Paulo*, "Inflação Duplicou em 1965", January 12, 1997, https://www1.folha.uol.com.br/fsp/1997/1/12/brasil/31.html.
[31] SKIDMORE, Thomas, *Brasil: de Getúlio a Castelo*, Rio de Janeiro, Paz e Terra, 1988, p. 253.
[32] POWER, Timothy J., "The Brazilian Military Regime of 1964–1985: Legacies for Contemporary Democracy", *Iberoamericana*, vol. 62/2016, pp. 13–26.
[33] From the period 1964–1985 six indirect elections were held for President of the Republic, three by the National Congress and three by the Electoral College, the last of which was won by a civilian President, Deputy Tancredo Neves, who, having not assumed office because of

and political parties were allowed to operate, though with severe restrictions.[35] At a certain point, the military dictatorship hardened: rights were suspended, censorship was introduced, and Congress was temporarily closed on three occasions.[36] Those measures raised persistent doubts about the legitimacy of the regime,[37] in which a hybrid politics of domination endured by blending an engrained authoritarianism with vestiges of democratic legality.

Regarding legitimacy, dictatorships are marked by a contradiction in relation to democratic regimes, since they concentrate power and exercise it rigidly from the top down. It is natural that a dictatorship tends to present itself as a legitimate expression of the interests of the people, so dictators use every device to prove that they have the consent of the people, such as mass meetings and the like, in which the chief comes into direct contact with those he claims to represent.

---

his death, was replaced by the Vice President, José Sarney. The so-called Electoral College was a meeting of members of the National Congress and nominated delegates coming from each of the States' Legislative Assemblies. See: *Superior Electoral Court*, https://www.tse.jus.br/eleitor/glossario/termos/eleicao-indireta.

[34] The dictatorship prevented the more legitimate manifestation of citizenship by prohibiting direct voting for President of the Republic and representatives of other major positions, such as governor, mayor and senator. Only federal, state and city councilmen were chosen by direct elections. See: *Agência Câmara de Notícias*, https://www.camara.leg.br/noticias/143270-anos-60-e-70-ditadura-e-bipartidarismo/.

[35] From 1966 to 1979, there were only two parties: *Aliança Renovadora Nacional* – Arena (National Renovating Alliance) and the *Movimento Democrático Brasileiro* – MDB (Brazilian Democratic Movement). The Arena brought together the forces that supported the military regime, while the MDB was the opposition party to the government. During the military regime, members of parties prohibited by law, such as the Brazilian Communist Party (PCB) and the Communist Party of Brazil (PCdoB), among others, also used the MDB as a form of institutional protest against the regime. When the members of the dictatorship realized that the existence of only two parties ended up giving a plebiscitary character to the elections, because voting for one or another party meant to approve the government or not, the military agents again modified the party system in 1979, allowing the creation of other parties and extinguishing Arena and MDB. See: *Agência Câmara de Notícias*, https://www.camara.leg.br/noticias/90158-apenas-dois-partidos-no-regime-militar/.

[36] During the period of 1964–1985, Congress was closed three times. Beginning with the Institutional Act no. 2 (AI-2), which gave the President of the Republic the power to decree the Congressional recess, so, on October 20, 1966, Marshal Castelo Branco decreed the first closing of Congress for a month, under the pretext of containing an "assembling of counter-revolutionary elements" that had been formed in the Legislature "with the purpose of disrupting public peace". On December 13, 1968, Marshal Costa e Silva introduced the Institutional Act no. 5 (AI-5) and decreed the closing of Congress for the alleged purpose of combating subversion and "ideologies contrary to the traditions of our people". The last to decree the closure of the Congress was General Ernesto Geisel, in 1977, through the "April package", after Congress rejected a constitutional amendment. Geisel claimed that the opposition party (MDB) had established a "minority dictatorship" within Congress. See: *Agência Câmara de Notícias*, https://www.camara.leg.br/noticias/545319-parlamento-brasileiro-foi-fechado-ou-dissolvido-18-vezes/.

[37] VIDAL, Nicolás Alfredo and CASALECCHI, Gabriel Avila, "Legitimidade Democrática no Brasil e na Argentina em Perspectiva Comparada: Diferentes Transições Democráticas e Suas Consequências", *Teoria & Pesquisa – Revista de Ciência Política*, vol. 27/2018, pp. 54–74.

Hence, dictatorship represents a kind of subverted democracy,[38] in which the people are forced to manifest their full adherence to the dictator's political orientation and the dictator can claim that his actions are based on the popular will. However, all these tactics do not give a dictatorship democratic legitimacy, because they cannot eliminate the fact that political power passes from the top down, and not vice versa as in a democratic space.

Also, it is always valid to remember the statements made by Michels concerning organization and oligarchy,[39] when he remarked that a system where leaders possess the means and the disposition to ignore their followers' will is an undemocratic system. In this sense, while studying Michels' theory, May observed that he persistently associated democracy with equality,[40] with conditions suggesting the notion of popular sovereignty, and with the system in which delegates represent the mass and carry out its will – all aspects that are usually lacking in a dictatorial regime.

To understand the Brazilian political scene in the 1960s, before the military came to power, it is important to remember that the victory of the Cuban guerrilla movement in 1959 added new direction to nationalist movements in Latin America. In Brazil, for instance, leaders of peasant leagues in the Northeast region, sectors of the student movement, union leaders, and leftist intellectuals all found inspiration in the new Cuban regime and its revolution's radical discourse. Indeed, the period from 1961 to 1964 was marked by an increase in peasant organizing, labor strikes, and student agitation. Although the radical nationalist wing of President João Goulart's party (the *Partido Trabalhista Brasileiro*) favored measures to limit foreign capitalist investment and supported a program of land reforms, Green has argued that Goulart,[41] himself a large landowner, was far from interested in leading a socialist revolution in Brazil.

Actually, the transformative character of the structural reforms that the social movements at the time hoped to enact was never assimilated by Brazilian society as a whole, which had links with the landowner elite; nor were the reforms taken up by the modern representatives of an industrialized and internationalized capitalist model.[42] Thus, the increasingly polarized political situation provided the necessary conditions for the Armed Forces to stage a *coup d'état* on

---

[38] STOPPINO, Mário, "Ditadura", in BOBBIO, Norberto; MATTEUCCI, Nicola and PASQUINO, Gianfranco (orgs.), *Dicionário de Política*, Brasília, UnB, 1991.
[39] MICHELS, Robert, *Political Parties: A Sociological Study of the Oligarchical Tendencies of Modern Democracy*, New York, Heart's International Library Co., 1915.
[40] MAY, John D., "Democracy, Organization, Michels", *The American Political Science Review*, vol. 59/1965, pp. 417–429.
[41] GREEN, James N., "Clerics, Exiles, and Academics: Opposition to the Brazilian Military Dictatorship in the United States, 1969-1974", *Latin American Politics and Society*, vol. 45/2003, pp. 87–117.
[42] ALMEIDA, Lucilia Neves Delgado de, "O Governo João Goulart e o Golpe de 1964: Memória, História e Historiografia", *Tempo*, vol. 14/2010, pp. 125–145.

March 31, 1964. Also, in 1964, Brazil was a politically divided country paralyzed by economic crisis, and political radicalization was exacerbated by adversaries of democracy on the left and the right. As observed by Villa,[43] fearful of the new and societal transformations, the right sought to resort to an old technique that was initiated in 1889 with the creation of the Republic: bringing the Armed Forces to the center of the political struggle. And, unfortunately, President João Goulart was not successful in negotiating within this radicalized environment. Finally, another factor in the collapse of democracy in the early '60s was the effect of anti-Communist propaganda and the role of United States in the *coup d'état* in the light of US domestic politics and the anti-Communism in South America, as well as the history of US foreign policy tactics in the same region during that period.[44]

It is also important to remember the justification for this appropriation of power after the 1964 *coup* and what the prevailing military doctrine was at that time. According to Barros,[45] after the end of World War II, military doctrine envisioned three forms of conflict for which three types of military mission were prescribed. First, there was the possibility of confrontation between the great powers (i.e. USA and the USSR), in which case there would be very little for the Brazilian armed forces to do, should there be a nuclear conflict. Even if the confrontation was kept to conventional weapons within Europe, for example, the Brazilian military would still have little to do, even though it was allied with the United States.

The second type of conflict was related to regional conflicts in South America. In this type of mission, the Brazilian military would have a more specific task: to protect the national territory and its borders against threats to its integrity. However, even if this mission existed in theory, the Brazilian military would still have a limited role due to the hegemonic position of the United States and the quasi-monopoly it had on providing weapons, doctrine, and training.[46]

Therefore, the third type of mission was the most prevalent on the continent and in Brazil during the '60s, '70s, and '80s: threats to internal security. In such a scenario, the hypothesis was that the country's enemies were within its own territory, acting as nationals in the service of a foreign power or as foreigners in the service of the country's enemies. According to this doctrine, it was up to the military to combat these internal opponents. From 1964–1985 this thesis had a series of negative implications for the protection of human rights and citizenship,

---

[43] VILLA, Marco Antonio, "Coup Brazilian Style", The Brazilian Economy, vol. 6/2014.
[44] PEREIRA, Anthony W., "The US Role in the 1964 Coup in Brazil: A Reassessment", *Bulletin of Latin American Research*, vol. 37/2018, pp. 5–17.
[45] BARROS, Alexandre, "Problemas de Transição Democrática na Frente Militar: a Definição do Papel dos Militares, a Mudança da Doutrina e a Modernização do País", *Política e Estratégia*, vol. VI/1988, pp. 206–214.
[46] ROUQUIÉ, Alain, *O Estado Militar na América Latina*, São Paulo, Alfa-Omega, 1984.

causing not only the rise of a dictatorial regime but also the continuation of this extra-legal situation.[47]

The extra-legal nature of the Brazilian dictatorship became even clearer in the events of 1968. That year began with students' protests against the military dictatorship and ended with a harsh governmental decree – Institutional Act no. 5 ("AI-5") issued on December 13, 1968 – that included the temporary closure of Congress, the suspension of constitutionally guaranteed rights, and the revocation of the mandates of many elected officials. Thus, AI-5 heralded the darkest period of the military regime, in which the dynamics of the dictatorship were relentlessly imposed.[48] In response, members of several Brazilian leftist organizations started guerrilla activities, while the hardline government stepped up its campaign to wipe out all opposition to the regime. As a consequence, torture was routinely used as a means to extract information from detainees in order to dismantle the revolutionary resistance. It was also used to discourage non-violent opposition to the regime, as the military did not only resort to the use of electric shocks, beatings, and other measures against those who had taken up arms against it. In fact, people involved in a wide array of activities that were critical of the government – from organizing discussion groups to participating in community development projects – were also subjected to violence by the military and police.[49] And, later on, such systematic use of torture was confirmed by the National Truth Commission Report, which gathered evidence that arbitrary and illegal arrests, torture, executions, and enforced disappearances practiced in Brazil during the dictatorship constituted a State policy aimed at perpetuating the power of the military and the political forces that supported the regime, characterized by serious violations human rights and crimes against humanity.[50]

While sanctioning extreme levels of violence against its opponents, during the period from 1969–1974, the regime benefited from a booming economy that achieved growth rates of over 10% a year.[51] Moreover, the construction of the Trans-Amazonian Highway and of the world's largest hydroelectric dam on the Rio Paraná, at Itaipu, were lauded by the administration of that time as opportunities to lift the hinterland out of poverty and consolidate mastery over

---

[47] AGAMBEN, Giorgio, *Estado de Exceção*, São Paulo, Boitempo, 2004, pp. 11–13.
[48] DEL VECCHIO, Angelo, "A Lei e a Força no Regime Militar Brasileiro: da Proscrição da Frente Ampla à Edição do Ato Institucional n. 5", *Revista Espaço de Diálogo e Desconexão*, vol. 6/2013.
[49] GREEN, James N., "Clerics, Exiles, and Academics: Opposition to the Brazilian Military Dictatorship in the United States, 1969–1974", *Latin American Politics and Society*, vol. 45/2003, pp. 87–117.
[50] About the National Truth Commission Report, see Chapter 5 of this book.
[51] BOHOSLAVSKY, Juan Pablo and TORELLY, Marcelo D., "Financial Complicity: The Brazilian Dictatorship Under the Macroscope", in SHARP, D.N. (ed.), *Justice and Economic Violence in Transition* (Springer Series in Transitional Justice vol. 5), New York, Springer, 2014, pp. 233–262.

the rainforest.[52] Consequently, those modernizing projects and the economic success the country experienced pacified many sectors of Brazilian society and tapped into dormant hopes that Brazil would finally emerge as the "country of the future". As Pillay has noted,[53] those facts helped give rise to the idea of an "unfulfilled promise" that had long permeated the Brazilian collective psyche and political discourse. The idea was basically that, in spite of the country's massive size, huge population, rich culture, and incredible array of natural resources, it had remained a "sleeping giant", unable to mobilize its strength to emerge as a world power.

The process of *distensão* or "decompression" of the political system began to be orchestrated in 1974[54] by generals who were convinced that the dictatorship should make its choices and set the most convenient time to revoke its exceptional powers.[55] According to the understanding of several Armed Forces commanders and opinion leaders, the generals needed to relinquish control of the Presidency. First, this was because political life and the task of ensuring internal security were affecting the rank-and-file soldiers and those tasks were proving to be a risk to the military's own institutional interests. Second, the dictatorship had poisoned the internal structure of the Armed Forces, as numerous officers had been removed from the hierarchical command structures of their units, causing the training routines and the professional mission of the military to be replaced by alien policing and punitive functions, leading to a bureaucracy of violence that had been installed within the military and had become a source of power and conflict within the very same hierarchy.

Thirdly, there was a growing opposition to the government, with denunciations of violations of human rights not only from within but from outside the country and, as observed by Sales and Martins Filho,[56] outside the country, from late

---

[52] *New Internationalist*, "From Nothing to Nowhere – The Transamazonian Highway", October 2, 1980, https://newint.org/features/1980/10/01/brazil. *The New York Times*, "Brazil's Hydroelectric Project", November 14, 1983, https://www.nytimes.com/1983/11/14/business/brazil-s-hydroelectric-project.html.

[53] PILLAY, Navi, "Brazil's Indigenous and Afro-Brazilian Populations face Serious Discrimination", *The Huffington Post*, November 18, 2009, https://www.huffingtonpost.com/navi-pillay/brazils-indigenous-and-af_b_362183.html.

[54] The "political distension process" sponsored by the military regime dates back to the period in which General Ernesto Geisel held the Presidency of the Republic, during the years 1974 to 1979. Although, the succession of President Emílio Garrastazu Médici in 1973 had already revealed the preponderance of officers committed to the slowdown of the regime. See: SALOMÃO, Ivan, "Da Distensão Política à Nova República: Apontamentos sobre a Vitória Oposicionista no Colégio Eleitoral", *Textos e Debates*, vol. 32/2019, pp. 53–74. Also, other historians define the year of 1975 as the beginning of the decompression period, see: SCHWARCZ, Lilia M. and STARLING, Heloisa M, *Brasil: Uma Biografia*, São Paulo, Companhia das Letras, 2015, p. 467.

[55] GASPARI, Elio, *A Ditadura Envergonhada*, São Paulo, Companhia das Letras, 2002.

[56] SALES, Camila Maria Risso and MARTINS FILHO, João Roberto, "The Economist and Human Rights Violations in Brazil During the Military Dictatorship", *Contexto Internacional*, vol. 40/2018, pp. 203–227.

1968 to the mid-1970s, the situation in Brazil was portrayed in terms of two contrasting metaphors: "economic miracle" and "years of lead" (*anos de chumbo*). That means that Brazil's economic achievement led the international media to praise Brazil as a model of free market economics but at the same time, economic growth occurred in a context of rampant political repression, and neglect of human rights and individual freedom. In the early 1980s, Amnesty International even stated that, for at least six years, sectors of the Armed Forces and the police in Brazil had been free to treat members of the left with whatever degree of cruelty they deemed necessary.[57] In fact, the Médici Administration, also called the "years of lead" (1969–1974), was marked by denunciations of repressive violence in Brazil, and was considered as a paradigmatic case of government that violated human rights.[58] And, certainly, between the administrations of Costa e Silva (1967–1969) and Médici (1969–1974) there was the beginning of a debate, especially among politicians and businessmen, on a necessary transition.

So, against this background, the idea was that a kind of controlled policy of openness to democracy should be crafted to ensure that a change of power could be carried out in a safe manner and be restricted to allied civil circles without any institutional risks. Indeed, when the commanders of the Armed Forces considered relinquishing direct control of the Executive Branch, they also sought to preserve their specific interests and demanded the assurance that those involved in political repression would remain untouchable – that there would be no "revanchism", as was often said in the barracks.[59] Hence, as part of the final stage of transition from the military regime, a general amnesty for military personnel and for the regime's civilian opponents was granted.

As Codato observed,[60] the political transition initiated in 1974–1975 corresponded to the need for the military themselves to solve problems within their ranks, not a sudden democratic conversion on the part of the commanders. Therefore, through the progressive restoration of some minimum civil liberties, the ultimate goal was not exactly to revoke authoritarianism and institute "democracy", but rather to make the military dictatorship less conservative.

And many times, the process of political opening would suffer the periodic impact of many social and political forces. As an example of these ups and downs,

---

[57] POWER, Jonathan, *Amnesty International: The Human Rights Story*, Oxford, Pergamon Press, 1981.

[58] The increasing brutality and violations of human rights under Médici's Administration may be observed according to the files of the Report *Brasil: Nunca Mais*, in which was noted that the military itself registered 488 allegations of torture in 1964–1968, then 1027 cases in 1969, and 3479 cases of torture during the period 1970–1973. See: *Brasil: Nunca Mais*, http://bnmdigital.mpf.mp.br/pt-br/historia.html.

[59] SCHWARCZ, Lilia M. and STARLING, Heloisa M, *Brasil: Uma Biografia*, São Paulo, Companhia das Letras, 2015, pp. 467–470.

[60] CODATO, Adriano Nervo, "Uma História Política da Transição Brasileira: Da Ditadura Militar à Democracia", *Revista de Sociologia Política*, vol. 25/2005, pp. 165–175.

it's worth mentioning the fact that, in 1974, the results of the legislative elections went beyond the expectations of the government, as the opposition party (the MDB) considerably expanded its representation in the Senate by electing 16 senators out of 22 disputed vacancies. Consequently, the government reacted with the so-called *Falcão Law*, which imposed severe restrictions on the use of the media by candidates for elective office for the 1976 municipal elections. In addition, in 1977, President Geisel decreed the closure of Congress in the first half of April, promulgated a set of constitutional changes, known as the *Pacote de Abril* (April Package), and even maintained the indirect election of Governors for the year 1978. Therefore, as commented by Diniz,[61] this transitional process begun in 1974 was not linear and was marked by advances and setbacks, contradictory movements and oscillations that were not always predictable.

In summary, until 1974, the government sought to maintain in power either through the "fight" against subversion, supported by anti-Communist ideology, or through the success of its "economic miracle". Once the focus of radical opposition was eradicated and the conditions that allowed the economic growth were exhausted, the government had to seek a new source of "legitimacy". This would be labeled as the goal of returning to constitutional "normality" with the gradual restoration of the democratic scene.

In addition, from the economic perspective, what gave this transition its prolonged duration was the fact that it involved much more than a simple regime transition or the financial exhaustion of the State. According to Sallum,[62] what we saw in Brazil during the beginning of the '80s was the crisis of the "form" assumed by the Brazilian State since the Getúlio Vargas Era (1930–1945). In fact, the reproduction of this format, even if remodeled over the '50s, '60s, and '70s, proved to be unfeasible, since the Developmental State model – that is, the modality of State interventionism oriented not to avoid depressive phases of the capitalist economic cycle, but rather to boost industrialization in late developing countries – no longer had a place.

Then, after a prolonged 10-year period of "political transition", democracy finally returned to Brazil in January of 1985, when the Electoral College chose the candidate of the Brazilian Democratic Movement Party (PMDB), Tancredo Neves, as President of the Republic. However, Neves died before taking office and Vice-President José Sarney, who was a former politician of the military supporting party (ARENA), completed the five-year mandate. During this period, a new Constitution was approved in 1988, but rampant inflation inhibited development.[63]

---

[61] DINIZ, Eli, "A Transição Política no Brasil: Uma Reavaliação da Dinâminca da Abertura", *Dados*, vol. 28/1985, pp. 329–346.
[62] SALLUM, Brasílio Jr., *Labirintos. Dos Generais à Nova República*, São Paulo, Hucitec, 1996.
[63] RIDING, Alan, "Inflation War Makes Brazil Banks Act Like Banks", *The New York Times*, April 14, 1986, https://www.nytimes.com/1986/04/14/business/inflation-war-makes-brazil-banks-act-like-banks.html. HUNTER, Wendy and POWER, Timothy, "Rewarding Lula: Executive Power,

While there was ongoing pressure from the family members of disappeared people and of former political prisoners, who were seeking justice – as in the case of the so-called *Bagulhão*, which was a letter of complaint written by 35 political prisoners in 1975, addressed to the President of the Brazilian Bar Association (*Ordem dos Advogados do Brasil* – OAB)[64] and containing a denunciation of torture and a list of 233 people (soldiers, delegates, military police sergeants and lieutenants), who were involved into the practices of torture by the State – as Schneider has observed,[65] in the 1985–1990 period the government embodied an elite unwilling to make a clear break with the authoritarian past and completely ignored the human rights crimes committed under the military regime. Consequently, the first post-authoritarian period failed to acknowledge the authoritarian legacy, and that attitude and inaction may have shaped Brazil's way of addressing its past in the subsequent years of its democracy.

Moreover, another partial explanation for such failure is the fact that, after the 1988 Federal Constitution, efforts of the human rights movement in Brazil were centered on agrarian reform, gender rights, non-discrimination, the rights of children and young people, and environmental concerns, among others. Consequently, as observed by Friedman and Hochstetler,[66] for Brazilian civil society organizations, the mobilizing framework of Brazilian civil society, since 1985, was citizenship, featuring most of the topics on social equality and inclusion. And, as Abrão and Torelly concluded,[67] since the majority of Brazilians – as potential voters – have shown little concern in addressing the violations of human rights committed in the past, politicians have been able to simply draw back from confrontations with defenders of the dictatorial regime for a long time.

Indeed, it should be noted that the continuity of political personnel was one of the most notable characteristics of the post-1985 Brazilian democracy. For instance, according to Power,[68] in the National Constituent Assembly, which

---

Social Power, and the Brazilian Elections of 2006", *Latin American Politics and Society*, vol. 49/2007, pp. 1–30.

[64] At that time, it is said that the President of OAB, Caio Mário da Silva Pereira, commented that there were no arbitrary imprisonments in Brazil. See: *Truth Commission of the State of São Paulo, Final Report*, Volume I, Part I, "O Bagulhão, a Voz dos Presos Políticos contra a Ditadura", p. 1.

[65] SCHNEIDER, Nina, "Waiting for a Meaningful State Apology: Has Brazil Apologized for Authoritarian Repression?", *Journal of Human Rights*, vol. 13/2014, pp. 1–16.

[66] FRIEDMAN, Elisabeth Jay and HOCHSTETLER, Kathryn, "Assessing the Third Transition in Latin American Democratization: Representational Regimes and Civil Society in Argentina and Brazil", *Comparative Politics*, vol. 35/2002, pp. 21–42.

[67] ABRÃO, Paulo and Torelly, Marcelo D., "The Reparations Program as the Lynchpin of Transitional Justice in Brazil", in REÁTEGUI, Félix (ed.), *Transitional Justice: Handbook for Latin America*, New York, Ministry of Justice and International Center for Transitional Justice, 2011, pp. 443–485.

[68] POWER, Timothy J., "The Brazilian Military Regime of 1964–1985: Legacies for Contemporary Democracy", *Iberoamericana*, vol. 62/2016, pp. 13–26.

was responsible for drafting the 1988 Constitution, approximately 40% of the participants had been members of ARENA/PDS, which was the political party that supported the dictatorial regime. Also, the first President under democratic rule, José Sarney (1985–1990), was loyal to the military after 1964, and his successor, Fernando Collor de Mello (1990–1992), had a similar trajectory, since both were members of traditional Northeastern oligarchies supported by the generals. That's the reason why Fernandes and Martins Filho criticized the political transition that had been promoted as "slow, gradual and secure" in order to camouflage and strengthen within the "New Republic",[69] the conservative forces of the previous regime.

Against this background, when we ask how Transitional Justice measures have fared in Brazil – serving as historic landmarks or unfulfilled promises – we will be able to point to several steps. These include: the creation of a Reparations Program, which was based on both the Law of the Disappeared (enacted in 1995) and the Law on Political Amnesty (enacted in 2002); the 2010 decision of the Federal Supreme Court (*Supremo Tribunal Federal* – STF) regarding *SPFD no. 153*, which was focused on the interpretation of the 1979 Amnesty Law and the possibility of extending the benefit of amnesty to crimes committed by agents of the State during the dictatorship; the finding against Brazil by the Inter-American Court of Human Rights (IACtHR) in the *Araguaia Case* (in 2010) and the *Herzog Case* (in 2018); and the creation of the National Truth Commission (2012) and presentation of its Final Report (2014).

Looking at the outline laid out above, as well as the participation of civil society during the last three decades, this book aims to make an assessment of how Brazil has dealt with its past human rights violations by pointing out not only its weaknesses, but also its strengths, as well as giving some practical insights into the theoretical framework for Transitional Justice.

Indeed, it is never too late to examine a transition mechanism that started during the '80s to determine the grounds on which it was constructed, mainly because, as Pinheiro observed (echoing William Faulkner), in Brazil "the past is not dead, neither is it considered a past yet".[70] This quote rings true, as at the end of 2018, Mr. Bolsonaro's victory for President marked the first time a far-right candidate has won Brazil's elections since the military dictatorship and at the end of 2022, after a divisive presidential campaign, Brazil took a turn to the left as former president Luiz Inácio Lula da Silva was once again elected,[71]

---

[69] FERNANDES, Florestan and MARTINS FILHO, J.R. (eds.), *Florestan Fernandes: a Força do Argumento*, São Carlos, EDUFSCar, 1997.
[70] PINHEIRO, Paulo Sérgio, "Passado não está morto: nem passado é … ainda … [Prefácio]", in DIMENSTEIN, Gilberto (ed.), *Democracia em Pedaços: Direitos Humanos no Brasil*, São Paulo, Companhia das Letras, 1996. The original line was coined by William Faulkner in 1951 in his novel *Requiem for a Nun*: "The past is never dead. It's not even past".
[71] More than 30 years after the re-establishment of democratic rule, the Brazilian people elected a President who is an enthusiast of military rule: the right-wing nationalist Jair Bolsonaro,

and only in the years to come will it be possible to analyze whether or not this shift to the right posed a threat to the democratic buffer, using the theoretical analysis of Levitsky and Ziblatt to make this assessment.[72]

Much of Brazil's very recent political history, as mentioned at the beginning of this chapter, confirms the theory that once the past has been undervalued, it tends to repeat itself. And all those insights demonstrate the continued existence of the conservatism associated with the military dictatorship, even after 30 years of democratic rule. This fact raises doubts about the achievements of Transitional Justice measures implemented in the Brazilian scenario, aimed at non-repetition. Adding to the mix is the turmoil created by the giant corruption scandals like the *Mensalão* Judgment of 2012 (literally, "big monthly payment") – in which 25 officials, including high-level politicians, public administrators and businessmen, received prison sentences and fines for a money-laundering-cum-legislative-vote-buying operation[73] – the Operation Car Wash[74] and a bribery

---

a retired army captain and former member of the lower house of the Brazilian National Congress. During the 2018 election, he campaigned as an alternative for voters tired of the country's corrupt traditional parties and the endemic corruption scandals that had engulfed Brazil. Only one or two years ago, Bolsonaro was regarded as unelectable due to his radical views, his record as an apologist for the military dictatorship, his offensive comments about Afro-Brazilians, gay people, and other minorities, and his lack of a major party affiliation. Despite all these facts, this populist outsider candidate with his anti-establishment rhetoric was boosted to victory in 2018. See: *The Guardian*, "Dilma Roussef: Brazilian Congress votes to Impeach President", April 18, 2016, https://www.theguardian.com/world/2016/apr/18/dilma-rousseff-congress-impeach-brazilian-president. CARAZZA, Bruno, "Will Brazil's Next President Be a Far-Right Nationalist?", *Foreign Affairs*, July 12, 2018, https://www.foreignaffairs.com/articles/brazil/2018-07-12/will-brazils-next-president-be-far-right-nationalist. UCHOA, Pablo, "Jair Bolsonaro: Why Brazilian Women are Saying #NotHim", *BBC News*, September 21, 2018, https://www.bbc.com/news/world-latin-america-45579635. Recently, Luiz Inácio "Lula" da Silva has been elected the next president of Brazil, following a tight run-off race on October 2022. His victory heralds a new phase after four years of Jair Bolsonaro's far-right administration. See: *CNN*, "Lula da Silva will return to Brazil's presidency in stunning comeback", October 31, 2022, https://edition.cnn.com/2022/10/30/americas/brazil-election-lula-da-silva-wins-intl/index.html.

[72] LEVITSKY, Steven and ZIBLATT, Daniel, *How Democracies Die*, New York, Crown Publishing, 2018.
[73] MICHENER, Gregory and PEREIRA, Carlos, "A Great Leap Forward for Democracy and the Rule of Law? Brazil's *Mensalão* Trial", *Journal of Latin American Studies*, vol. 48/2016, pp. 477–507.
[74] For anyone watching the news recently, Brazil appears to be in a hazardous phase, since an enormous corruption scandal (named "Operation Car Wash") seems to involve every third person in the government. After five years of convictions and confessions, plus billions of dollars in recovered bribes, there is no doubt that the probe has made a lasting impact. Its findings spurred a wave of other investigations around Brazil and Latin America, taking down Presidents and rattling global firms. From 2014 to July of 2019, Operation Car Wash had brought 101 indictments against 445 people on charges from bribery and money laundering to obstruction of justice, winning 158 convictions in 50 trials so far. The investigation has recovered BRL 14 billion (US$3.4 billion) of public money, including BRL 3 billion returned to Petrobras (Brazil's State-owned petroleum corporation) from kickbacks skimmed off overpriced contracts. More recently, however, Car Wash, Brazil's biggest-ever corruption

scheme known as *Rachadinha*[75] of recent years. Those scandals are related to Brazil's persistent problems with governance caused by its coalition-based presidential system in which the maintenance of every administration's support base in Congress requires significant and shameful bargaining.[76]

Consequently, any positive assessment of Transitional Justice in Brazil is also limited by the fact that the Brazilian government waited until 2012 to establish a truth commission and never charged anyone with a crime in connection with the dictatorship; nor did it encourage a national dialogue about the country's authoritarian past. This then has developed into an unsubstantial politics of memory. Perhaps all these facts taken together may facilitate an understanding of the current Brazilian political scene.[77]

1.2. A GENERAL OVERVIEW OF TRANSITIONAL JUSTICE MECHANISMS IMPLEMENTED IN BRAZIL

While trying to map the Brazilian scenario following the authoritarian regime and in the midst of the reconstruction of democracy, this book will use a working definition of Transitional Justice as "the full range of processes and mechanisms associated with a society's attempt to come to terms with a legacy of large-scale past abuses, so as to ensure accountability, serve justice and achieve

---

investigation which jailed dozens – including a former President – has been threatened after leaked messages appeared to show a judge collaborating with prosecutors on their cases against several defendants. See: LONG, Ciara, "Brazil's Car Wash Investigations Faces New Pressures", *Foreign Policy*, June 17, 2019, https://foreignpolicy.com/2019/06/17/brazils-car-wash-investigation-faces-new-pressures/. BRITO, Ricardo, "Brazil Car Wash Corruption Probe Facing Worst Moment as Establishments Fights Back", *Reuters*, September 4, 2019, https://www.reuters.com/article/us-brazil-corruption-analysis/brazil-car-wash-corruption-probe-facing-worst-moment-as-establishment-fights-back-idUSKCN1VP2SR. ANDERSON, Jon Lee, "Jair Bolsonaro's Southern Strategy – In Brazil, a budding authoritarian borrows from the Trump playbook", *The New Yorker*, March 25, 2019, https://www.newyorker.com/magazine/2019/04/01/jair-bolsonaros-southern-strategy.

[75] The scheme known as *Rachadinha* is common in the lower rungs of politics in Brazil. It involves siphoning off taxpayer money by keeping ghost employees on payroll or hiring people who agree to kick back a share of their salary to the boss. In this case, the investigation began shortly after Mr. Bolsonaro's electoral victory in October 2018. He beat a leftist party whose enormous popularity crumbled as its leaders were charged in kickback schemes involving large government contracts and transnational business deals. See: *The New York Times*, "A Family Business: Graft Investigation Threatens Brazil's Bolsonaro", August 28, 2020, https://www.nytimes.com/2020/08/28/world/americas/brazil-bosonaro-corruption.html.

[76] CARVALHO, Maria Paula Schmidt, "Brazil's Future in the Shadow of the Mensalão", *Americas Quarterly*, August 22, 2013, https://www.americasquarterly.org/blog/brazils-future-in-the-shadow-of-the-mensalao/.

[77] SERBIN, Kenneth P., "The Ghosts of Brazil's Military Dictatorship. How a Politics of Forgetting Led to Bolsonaro's Rise", *Foreign Affairs*, January 1, 2019, https://www.foreignaffairs.com/articles/brazil/2019-01-01/ghosts-brazils-military-dictatorship.

reconciliation." It also sees the main goals of such measures as the recognition of the dignity of individuals; the redress and acknowledgement of violations; and preventing them from happening again.[78] Based on accountability and redress for victims of past human rights abuses, this book proposes to assess the mechanisms most commonly associated with Transitional Justice, such as criminal prosecutions, non-judicial truth-seeking processes to expose human rights violations, and reparations to victims of human rights abuses.[79] It shall examine how all these pillars have (or have not) been implemented throughout the last three decades in Brazil.

In fact, the field of Transitional Justice began to emerge in the late 1980s, as a consequence of new practical circumstances that human rights activists faced in countries where authoritarian regimes had been replaced by more democratic ones.[80] At that time, the turn away from "naming and shaming" and towards accountability for past abuses was taken up at the international level.[81] There the focus on political change representing a "transition to democracy" helped to legitimate those claims to justice that prioritized legal-institutional reforms and responses – such as punishing leaders, vetting abusive security forces, and replacing State secrecy with truth and transparency – over other claims to justice that were oriented toward social justice and redistribution. Although the Transitional Justice measures in the early days of the concept were framed in terms of how a successor regime ought to respond to abuses perpetrated by the State, as Teitel remarked,[82] the challenge of contemporary times is that transition also engages non-State actors and entails changing social norms within civil society. Consequently, the dichotomous framework that in previous years was centered on a set of binaries items like punishment in opposition of impunity, truth versus justice and justice versus peace is gradually being adapted to transformative justice.

This transition to democracy, as Weschler commented,[83] brought several questions that need to be answered, such as "who was there?", "who was

---

[78] United Nations, "Guidance Note of the Secretary-General – United Nations Approach to Transitional Justice", March 2010, https://www.un.org/ruleoflaw/thematic-areas/international-law-courts-tribunals/transitional-justice/.

[79] PAYNE, Leigh A.; PEREIRA, Gabriel; COSTA, Josefina Doz and BERNAL-BERMÚDEZ, Laura, "Can a Treaty on Business and Human Rights Help Achieve Transitional Justice Goals?", *Homa Publica International Journal on Human Rights and Business*, vol. 1/2017, pp. 3–33.

[80] ELSTER, Jon, *Closing the Books: Transitional Justice in Historical Perspective*, Cambridge, Cambridge University Press, 2004. TEITEL, Ruti G., "Transitional Justice Genealogy", *Harvard Human Rights Journal*, vol. 16/2003, pp. 69–94.

[81] BASTOS, Lucia Elena Arantes Ferreira, *Anistia: As Leis Internacionais e o Caso Brasileiro*, Curitiba, Juruá, 2009.

[82] TEITEL, Ruti G., *Globalizing Transitional Justice – Contemporary Essays*, New York, Oxford University Press, 2014.

[83] WESCHLER, Lawrence, *A Miracle, a Universe: Settling Accounts with Torturers*, Chicago, The University of Chicago Press, 1998.

screaming?", "who will be held accountable?", and "who will hold them accountable?". At the same time, in the foreground of the debate, there has always been the threat to the stability of the democratic regime that such questions might pose. And the questions raised were not only ones of justice, but also about prudence: how to balance competing moral imperatives, reconcile legitimate claims for justice with equally legitimate claims for stability and social peace, and foster the relationship between justice for crimes of the past and a more just political order in the present?

These so-called transitional "dilemmas" (prosecutions, truth-telling, reparations, political stability, and so on) were identified in the late-1980s to mid-1990s, a period when the field of Transitional Justice first began to emerge.[84] This was the same period of time when Brazil was starting to face its democratic reconstruction as well. Consequently, at the very beginning of its transition, Brazilian governments had no experience with or sensitivity to this set of practices, such as commissions of inquiry, prosecutions, explanations, or purges, nor with restitution or reparations programs. Despite the fact that mechanisms of accountability have been implemented since ancient Greece, as noted by Elster,[85] and they were remarkably developed in the post-World War II period, as pointed by Garapon[86] and Wilke,[87] the immediate response to past abuses in Brazil was amnesia, as will be described in Chapter 2 of this book which is dedicated to scrutinizing the 1979 Amnesty Law.

Thus, it was only in the mid-1990s and the beginning of the 2000s that a movement towards establishing a reparations program attempted to strike a balance between redressing the abuses of former governments and integrating victims and perpetrators in a post-conflict society, the subject of Chapter 3 of this book, along with an analysis of the work developed by the Special Commission on Political Deaths and Disappearances and the Amnesty Commission, whose efforts were not only in the field of pecuniary but also symbolic reparations.

In addition, Chapter 4 will present the consequences and impact of the lack of judicial accountability arising from the 1979 Amnesty Law, examining the roles of the local judiciary, the Federal Public Prosecutor's Office, and the Inter-American Court of Human Rights in the Brazilian context of Transitional Justice. It will juxtapose, for instance, the opposing judgments of different courts on these matters. To analyze these episodes, one must note that the National Congress approved the 1979 Amnesty Law, the content of which remains in

---

[84] ARTHUR, Paige, "How Transitions Reshaped Human Rights: A Conceptual History of Transitional Justice", *Human Rights Quarterly*, vol. 31/2009, pp. 321–367.
[85] ELSTER, Jon, *Closing the Books: Transitional Justice in Historical Perspective*, Cambridge, Cambridge University Press, 2004.
[86] GARAPON, Antoine, *Des Crimes Qu'on Ne Peut Ni Punir Ni Pardoner. Pour Une Justice Internationale*, Paris, Odile Jacob, 2002.
[87] WILKE, Christine, "Remembering Complexity? Memorials for Nazi Victims in Berlin", *The International Journal of Transitional Justice*, vol. 7/2013, pp. 136–156.

dispute, but which so far has precluded trials for military personnel involved in torture, persecution, and killing of opponents of the regime. And, although there was mobilization from family members of the victims of the dictatorship and political prisoners beginning in the '70s, since mid-2009, there has been a resurgence of the movement to modify the interpretation of the Amnesty Law in order to allow for the prosecution of those accused of perpetrating torture during the military era.

Following this trend, Chapter 5 will offer an overview of the truth-telling process that was implemented between 2012 and 2014, with the creation of the National Truth Commission. The chapter traces its relevant steps, its critical assessments, the consequences of the authoritarian legacy and the culture of impunity that has permeated the last three decades of Brazilian history.

Looking beyond the governmental measures seeking reconciliation and accountability, Chapter 6 is devoted to the role of civil society and non-governmental organizations in the search for truth, justice, and memory. Efforts such as the publication of the "Brazil: Never Again" Report, the opening of a clandestine gravesite in Perus, São Paulo, the strategies of family members of the forcibly disappeared people, and the activism derived from the *escrachos* will also be examined. Later, Chapter 7 proposes a discussion about the violations of the human rights of indigenous people during the dictatorship and the challenge for a broad and collective form of reparations.

Next, Chapter 8 investigates the role of gender in Brazilian Transitional Justice measures, successful initiatives towards visibility, recognition, transformation, and their respective struggles. Chapter 9 is dedicated to the role played by complicit corporations and private actors during the authoritarian regime, and the possibilities of reconciling with such approaches and patterns. Though each chapter individually ends with some conclusions about each specific subject, Chapter 10 will offer final remarks based on the concrete limits that a culture of democracy and the Rule of Law has been facing in the Brazilian political landscape during the last three decades.

With respect to the problems confronted by Brazil throughout its transition process and what to expect from this book, it is worth remembering that processes of democratization after periods of political violence and military dictatorships are never smooth. In the case of Brazil, the main challenge has become the very long and extended transition period, which has given rise to different politics of memory in a context that includes persistent social and economic inequalities and continuing instances of police brutality. In addition, more than three decades after the transition to democracy, many issues regarding the recent past are still ongoing.

For instance, there are still efforts to elucidate human rights violations and to implement trials for their perpetrators. At the same time, that there is a challenge to the 1979 Amnesty Law, a discussion about the reparation programs implemented in 1995 and 2002, and the hope that the recommendations of the

2014 National Truth Commission will finally be implemented, including the search for clandestine graves and the identification of remains. Finally, there is a debate about the construction of memorials. These initiatives have engendered disputes and controversies in a scenario where both the State and private social actors participate and disagree at some stage.[88]

So, rather than searching for best practice mechanisms, this book aims to elucidate the social dynamics operating in the specific historical context of post-authoritarian Brazil, and attempts to make the timeline of Transitional Justice in the Brazilian case useful, comprehensible, and ripe for dissemination abroad.

---

[88] JELIN, Elizabeth, "Public Memorialization in Perspective: Truth, Justice and Memory of Past Repression in the Southern Cone of South America", *The International Journal of Transitional Justice*, vol. 1/2007, pp. 138–156.

PART I

THE INTERSECTION BETWEEN AMNESTY, THE RULE OF LAW, AND AUTHORITARIAN LEGACIES

CHAPTER 2

OPTIONS FOR IMPUNITY AND AMNESTY

Forgetting the Past

> *"Amnesty, I am beginning to not understand what you mean.*
> *You come with an olive branch in your right hand,*
> *But, hidden in the other, something like a scourge.*
> *You forgive those who do not need forgiveness ...*
> *Do you think you are wise if you limit the scope of your wisdom?*
> *Do you consider yourself generous placing conditions on your generosity?"*[89]

Two months before the passage of the Amnesty Law, in June of 1979, commenting on the controversy surrounding the issue, the Brazilian poet Carlos Drummond de Andrade published a text in his column for the newspaper *Jornal do Brasil* – an excerpt of which is reproduced as the epigraph above – that would come to mark the course of the law in question from its inception until today: a lack of understanding of its real objectives and the resulting distortion of its essential function. Thus, 40 years after its passage, the amnesty which marked the gradual end of the dictatorial regime in Brazil continues to hold many unknowns, given that, rather than being an act of compassion or repentance and followed by public recognition of the errors committed, it ended up including even those injustices raised by the Inter-American Court of Human Rights.[90]

The fact is that, as Drummond so presciently foresaw, the acclaim for amnesty was the result of political convenience, as it was considered the best that could be achieved at the time.[91] Nevertheless, given the crooked course which the pardon

---

[89] ANDRADE, Carlos Drummond de, *Jornal do Brasil*, June 28, 1979.
[90] On international jurisdiction and amnesty laws, see Chapter 4 of this book.
[91] The jurist Dalmo Dallari, who participated in the debate on the Amnesty Law, once said that people knew that it was inevitable that limitations would have to be accepted, and admitted that, as an effect of the Amnesty Law, criminals protected by the government escaped the punishment they deserved, but at the time such a consequence was considered convenient, since besides such distortion brought by the Amnesty Law it would bring back from exile many politically persecuted people. See: DALLARI, Dalmo, "Anistia: Esquecimento Legal, Memória de Fato", *Fundação Perseu Abramo*, April 23, 2006, https://fpabramo.org.br/2006/04/23/dalmo-dallari-anistia-esquecimento-legal-memoria-de-fato/.

took in its creation, as will be seen below, it was not possible to achieve a model for amnesty that met the parameters of Transitional Justice and international law. As a result, those same past expectations remain unfulfilled, as the poet Drummond described in 1979:

> I want to see you high and perfect, and not a lowly amnesty ... scurrying about knock-kneed. I want to see you soar. Winged I imagine you above the rows and pettiness of those poor interpreters of your luminous grandeur.

Today, however, those hopes have been pinned on a future resignifying of that law as a task for Brazilian Supreme Court.[92] Below we will analyze the implementation of amnesty in the case of Brazil as one of the steps towards Transitional Justice.

In fact, when the military dictatorship ended, the transition to democratic rule posed one crucial question: whether the new government had a duty to investigate and to punish the crimes of its predecessors. The Amnesty Law was enacted still during the military regime, which means it was voted on by a Congress still controlled by the dictatorship, as a result of a devious process. The procedure was considered tortuous because in the 1970s, committees led by civil society and relatives of the victims of the regime began to introduce the amnesty issue in the public agenda.[93] The idea was related to the return of exiles and the annulment of penalties imposed by military courts. However, during the enactment process of the law, the government inserted some topics of its own interest, which subverted the initial proposition presented by civil society. With the revision of the text, it was understood at that time that crimes committed by agents of the State against opponents of the regime were also covered by the amnesty.[94] In this way, the history of the Amnesty Law may be explained as the regime's effort to appear democratic despite its reliance on dictatorial methods. It represents the so-called "democratic façade" or "legal façade",[95] since the regime provided legalistic arguments for its acts of repression and manipulated the democratic institutions to conceal its authoritarian rule.[96]

In the Brazilian case, impunity was the price charged by the military regime for giving up its means of government. And, based on a controversial interpretation of the text inserted in Law no. 6,683 (1979) which prevailed for

---

[92] About local jurisdiction and amnesty law, see Chapter 4 of the book.
[93] For a detailed description of the activities developed by the civil society and the campaign for the amnesty during the '70s, see Chapter 6 of the book.
[94] SCHWARCZ, Lilia M. and STARLING, Heloisa M., *Brasil: Uma Biografia*, São Paulo, Companhia das Letras, 2015, pp. 478–479.
[95] SCHNEIDER, Nina, "Impunity in Post-authoritarian Brazil: The Supreme Court's Recent Verdict on the Amnesty Law", *European Review of Latin American and Caribbean Studies*, vol. 90/2011, pp. 39–54.
[96] CHUEIRI, Vera Karam de and CAMARA, Heloisa Fernandes "(Des)ordem Constitucional: Engrenagens da Máquina Ditatorial no Brasil Pos-64", *Lua Nova*, vol. 95/2015, pp. 259–289.

decades, it was granted amnesty for political crimes and crimes with a political nexus committed by members of the Armed Forces, between September 2, 1961 and August 15, 1979. Since then, the Amnesty Law has continued to shield perpetrators from prosecution. Criminals are, therefore, safe for the moment; although their names are known,[97] and in the international scenario there are increasing doubts about whether their amnesties are valid or not.[98]

In addition, Transitional Justice has long favored the idea that States must prosecute perpetrators of mass violations of human rights in order to provide justice and redress for victims, since the concept of justice is apprehended also as a process of truth-finding, which is predictably attached to criminal prosecution.[99] Consequently, as commented by Uribe,[100] the international community is critical of States that choose not to pursue the path of criminal justice in the aftermath of a conflict. Even though it is undeniable that prosecution ought to play a crucial role in any country's peace process, it must also be understood that criminal adjudication is not the only option for achieving peace. In the Brazilian case, past experience has shown that the State for long time maintained a purely binary response to the transition, that was simply impunity *versus* justice, while alternatives like reparations programs and truth commissions were only implemented between 10 and 25 years after the end of the dictatorship. This, despite the fact that Transitional Justice mechanisms have demonstrated that the concept of justice cannot be solely understood as equivalent to prosecution and that the Rule of Law may be more long lasting if a holistic approach is adopted.[101]

2.1. THE AMNESTY LAW'S OVERVIEW: CONTEXT, SCOPE AND LEGITIMACY

2.1.1. THE SCENARIO IN WHICH THE AMNESTY LAW WAS ADOPTED

In Brazil, the amnesty granted in the final phase of the dictatorship, in 1979, was not the first initiative of this type in the twentieth century. In fact, this type

---

[97] See the 1995 report named *Brasil: Nunca Mais. Um Relato para a História* and the Final Report of the National Truth Commission of 2014.
[98] JOINET, Louis, *Report of the Special Rapporteur on the Study on Amnesty Laws and their Role in the Safeguard and Promotion of Human Rights*, U.N. Doc. E/CN.4/Sub.2/1985/16, June 21, 1985.
[99] BASTOS, Lucia Elena Arantes Ferreira, "Anistia e o Direito Internacional", *O Estado de São Paulo – Caderno Aliás*, November 9, 2008, p. 7.
[100] URIBE, Camila, "Do Amnesties Preclude Justice?", *International Law Revista Colombiana de Derecho Internacional*, vol. 21/2012, pp. 297–359.
[101] BORAINE, Alexander L., "Transitional Justice: A Holistic Interpretation", *Journal of International Affairs*, vol. 60/2006, pp. 17–27.

of measure had been provided for in law since the Penal Code of 1890, and consequently implemented during the President Vargas Era (1930–1945) and to contain rebellions during the '50s, as mentioned in Chapter 1 of this book. Furthermore, the provision has been maintained in the Penal Code in effect today which lists amnesty as one of the possible consequences of the extinction of a criminal prosecution or of the respective penalty.[102] Likewise, the constitutions in existence prior to the current Constitution of 1988 also provided for the power of pardon, with small modifications which did not alter the underlying meaning of amnesty.[103]

For example, soon after the Revolution of 1930,[104] an amnesty was granted which encompassed the political crimes committed both by civilians and soldiers during the period.[105] Later, in 1931 a new amnesty law excluded all ordinary crimes,[106] preserving amnesty only for political offences. In April of 1945, when it was announced that general elections would finally be held, the government granted amnesty to all those who had committed political crimes in the period from July 16, 1934 to April 18, 1945.[107] And, as noted by Rodeghero, in the campaign that preceded the amnesty of April 1945 there was already a strong association between the purposes of the amnesty and the objective of pacifying the "Brazilian family" (a metaphor for the divided Brazilian society), an argument also used in 1979.[108]

Additionally, in September of 1946, a new amnesty was offered for those accused of the crime of slander against the government and also for those responsible for crimes of any sort occurring during or soon after rallies, marches, or other political manifestations.[109] Subsequently, in 1951, a decree was issued to pardon workers who had lost their jobs due to their participation in strikes.[110]

---

[102] According to art. 107, para. II of the 1940 Brazilian Penal Code, the granting of amnesty, grace or pardon extinguishes the punishment of a crime.

[103] CARVALHO FILHO, Aloysio, *Comentários ao Código Penal*, vol. IV, Rio de Janeiro, Forense, 1958, pp. 103–161.

[104] To give some historical context, this was the revolutionary movement, which began in Minas Gerais and Rio Grande do Sul on October 3, 1930, and involved important sectors of the Army, under the command of Lieutenant Colonel Góis Monteiro. At that time, President Washington Luis offered little resistance against the revolutionaries and, consequently, the elected candidate (Julio Prestes) did not assume the presidency, and one of the leaders of the movement, Getúlio Vargas, took over provisional leadership of the government and remained in power until 1945. See: FAUSTO, Boris, "A revolução de 1930", in MOTA, Carlos Guilherme (ed.), *Brasil em Perspectiva*, São Paulo, Difel, 1981.

[105] According to Decree 19,395, of November 8, 1930.

[106] According to Decree-Law 20,558, of October 24, 1931 and Decree 10,119, of October 30, 1931.

[107] According to Decree-Law 7,474, of April 18, 1945.

[108] RODEGHERO, Carla Simone, "Pela Pacificação da Família Brasileira: Uma Breve Comparação entre as Anistias de 1945 e de 1979", *Revista Brasileria de História*, vol. 34/2014, pp. 67–88.

[109] According to Decree-Law 7,943, of September 10, 1945.

[110] CARVALHO FILHO, Aloysio, *Comentários ao Código Penal*, vol. IV, Rio de Janeiro, Forense, 1958, pp. 103–161.

Chapter 2. Options for Impunity and Amnesty

Also, in 1956, President Juscelino Kubitschek granted amnesty to the military involved in the *Jacareacanga Rebellion*.[111]

So, throughout the Brazilian history, as observed by Lemos,[112] amnesties have been granted both to persons accused of illegitimately violating the legality established – those that rose up against the dictatorships of the Estado Novo (1937–1945) and the military regime (1964–1985), for example – and to those that tried to subvert a legitimately established legality, such as those involved in the *Jacareacanga coup* of 1956.

With these previous instances in mind, it is worth noting that the amnesty for the crimes committed during the dictatorial regime of 1964–1985 by opponents of the regime and for those then in exile arose from a demand from civil society.[113] Though the majority of the population did not actively participate in the movements opposing the regime – in fact, the intrinsically revolutionary nature of the armed groups restricted the tenuous support that those organizations had from the regime's civilian opponents[114] – a considerable part of the middle class seemed to no longer understand the very regime it had aided in its ascent to power. In addition, in the opinion of both Gaspari[115] and of Mezarobba,[116] this lack of comprehension was related to the nature of the control that the dictatorship had been applying, one which used the power of terror.

Thus, at the same time that the government continued denying, in response to criticism, that torture was a State policy in Brazil, unconcerned with international pressure,[117] locally civil society began to mobilize so that support for amnesty acquired a wider social base. Imprisonment under a military regime represented much more than a deprivation of liberty; it symbolized a threat to physical integrity, a risk of imminent death which, little by little, became clear to society at large. This was so much so during the Brazilian dictatorship that the drive in favor of amnesty was always associated with the fight for the return

---

[111] Centro de Pesquisa e Documentação de História Contemporânea do Brasil, Faculdade Getúlio Vargas (CPDOC/FGV), "Revolta de Jacareacanga", https://cpdoc.fgv.br/producao/dossies/JK/artigos/Politica/Jacareacanga.

[112] LEMOS, Renato, "Anistia e Crise Política no Brasil pós-1964", *Topoi*, vol. 3/2002, pp. 287–313.

[113] For a detailed description of social movements and civil society, see Chapter 6 of this book.

[114] The journalist Elio Gaspari even mentions that oppositionist civil leaders to the dictatorial regime, such as Tancredo Neves and Ulysses Guimarães, used to see the armed guerrilla as an obstruction to the re-democratization they sought. See: GASPARI, Elio, *A Ditadura Escancarada*, São Paulo, Companhia das Letras, 2002, p. 194.

[115] GASPARI, Elio, *A Ditadura Envergonhada*, São Paulo, Companhia das Letras, 2002, p. 233.

[116] MEZAROBBA, Glenda, *Um Acerto de Contas com o Futuro – a Anistia e suas Conseqüências – um Estudo do Caso Brasileiro*. Dissertação (Mestrado). Faculdade de Filosofia, Letras e Ciências Humanas, Universidade de São Paulo (USP). São Paulo, 2003, p. 14.

[117] SAYURI, Juliana, "EUA Sabiam Já Nos Anos 1960 de Tortura no Regime Militar, Mostram Documentos", *Folha de São Paulo*, August 26, 2018, https://www1.folha.uol.com.br/ilustrissima/2018/08/eua-sabiam-ja-nos-anos-1960-de-tortura-no-regime-militar-mostram-documentos.shtml.

of democracy, for a return to the Rule of Law, and a recognition and respect for human rights, as defended by the jurist Goffredo Telles Júnior in his "Letter to Brazilians"[118] of August 1977.

The occurrence of student protests against the imprisonment and torture of political prisoners reinforced the cry for amnesty when, for example, approximately 10,000 students gathered on May 5, 1977, for a march in front of the University of São Paulo Law School in Largo de São Francisco,[119] carrying banners and distributing 30,000 copies of an open letter to the population in which the key demands were for amnesty, the release of political prisoners, democratic freedoms, and an end to economic impoverishment.[120] In 1975, the demand for amnesty began more concretely with the creation in São Paulo of the *Movimento Feminino pela Anistia* (MFPA) or "Women for Amnesty Movement", initiated by Therezinha Zerbini,[121] an attorney whose husband had been forced to retire from his activities as a soldier due to his resistance to the 1964 Coup. The movement received support both from politicians as well as the Catholic Church, so that the campaign for amnesty was at the root of the process of building democracy in Brazil.[122] Also, in 1978, the *Comitê Brasileiro pela Anistia* (CBA, Brazilian Committee for Amnesty) was created in the city of Rio de Janeiro[123] to defend the granting of amnesty.

On October 31, 1975, eight thousand people gathered at the *Catedral da Sé*, in the center of São Paulo city, for an ecumenical service led by the then cardinal-archbishop of São Paulo, Dom Paulo Evaristo Arns, by the rabbi of the *Confederação Israelita Paulista*, Henry Sobel, and by the Reverend Jaime Nelson Wright, a Presbyterian preacher. The service was to remember and honor the journalist Vladimir Herzog (nicknamed Vlado), who had been killed in the army's "basements" seven days earlier, and the gathering symbolized a real challenge to the dictatorship.[124]

And there were also significant mobilizations in 1976 in protest for the death of the worker Manuel Fiel Filho, which occurred in circumstances similar to those of Herzog, since the authorities repeated the official version of events that

---

[118] The request for a return to the Rule of Law can be found in the statement made by jurist Goffredo Telles Júnior, in August 1977, in his "Letter to the Brazilians", which was officially read before the students of the Faculty of Law of University of São Paulo. See: http://www.goffredotellesjr.adv.br/site/pagina.php?id_pg=30#um.

[119] *O Estado de São Paulo*, "Passeata Reúne 10 Mil Estudantes em São Paulo", May 6, 1977, p. 13.

[120] *Folha de São Paulo*, "Carta Aberta à População", May 6, 1977, p. 21.

[121] DUARTE, Ana Rita Fonteles, "O Movimento Feminino pela Anistia na Luta contra a Ditadura no Brasil: Entrevista com Therezinha Zerbini", *Revista Estudos Feministas*, vol. 27/2019, pp. 1–7.

[122] SCHWARCZ, Lilia M. and STARLING, Heloisa M, *Brasil: Uma Biografia*, São Paulo, Companhia das Letras, 2015, pp. 478–479.

[123] See: *Memorial da Anistia*, http://memorialanistia.org.br/comite-brasileiro-pela-anistia/.

[124] See: *Documentos Revelados*, https://documentosrevelados.com.br/missa-de-setimo-dia-em-homenagem-a-vladimir-herzog/.

he committed suicide in prison, as well as in the case of the death of the worker Santo Dias da Silva, which occurred during a strike in 1979 while the police repressed the protesters.[125]

Despite the intense mobilization that occurred during the transition period, the process was neither revolutionary nor radical. On the contrary, it was a period of the mildest political change in Brazilian history.[126] That is, the process of democratization that began with the restoration of civil government in 1985 was not the product of a rupture with the old order.[127] This resulted in a so-called "slow, gradual, and safe opening" and the reconstruction of the political system through making accommodations and a merging of old and new practices.[128] Indeed, the process of political opening (*abertura política*) was initiated by the military government itself, and not due to pressure from civil society – though the latter influenced the course and rhythm of events.[129]

It was precisely during the transition period, in which there was no great break with the past, that the Brazilian Amnesty Law was adopted. On June 27, 1979, the then President, João Baptista Figueiredo, signed the Amnesty Bill and sent it to the National Congress with a message that the times were ripe for peace-making and that amnesty required a disarming of the spirits in order to satisfy its political function, so that democratic co-existence might be achieved.[130] Nevertheless, this "disarming of the spirits" included the fact that, over the course of the dictatorship period, approximately 10,000 people were forced to live in exile,[131] 4,862 had their political offices and rights revoked,[132] 245 students were expelled from university,[133] 800 people were taken as political prisoners,[134] approximately 434 people had been identified as dead or

---

[125] SANTOS, José Vicente Tavares dos, "As Lutas Sociais contra as Violências", *Política e Sociedade*, vol. 11/2007, pp. 71–100.
[126] BARROS, Alexandre, "Problemas de Transição Democrática na Frente Militar: a Definição do Papel dos Militares, a Mudança da Doutrina e a Modernização do País", *Política e Estratégia*, vol. VI/1988, pp. 206–214.
[127] PINHEIRO, Paulo Sérgio, "The Legacy of Authoritarianism in Democratic Brazil", in NAGEL, Stuart S. (ed.), *Latin American Development and Public Policy*, New York, St. Martin Press, 1994.
[128] KINZO, Maria D'Alva G., "A Democratização Brasileira: Um Balanço do Processo Político desde a Transição", *São Paulo em Perspectiva*, vol. 15/2001, pp. 1–12.
[129] CODATO, Adriano Nervo, "Uma História Política da Transição Brasileira: Da Ditadura Militar à Democracia", *Revista de Sociologia Política*, vol. 25/2005, pp. 165–175.
[130] WESTIN, Ricardo, "Há 40 anos, Lei da Anistia Preparou Caminho para Fim da Ditadura", *Arquivo do Senado*, August 5, 2019, https://www12.senado.leg.br/noticias/especiais/arquivo-s/ha-40-anos-lei-de-anistia-preparou-caminho-para-fim-da-ditadura.
[131] *Special Commission of Political Deaths and Disappearances*, "Direito à Memória e à Verdade", Brasília, Secretaria Especial dos Direitos Humanos, 2007, p. 30.
[132] Ibid.
[133] Ibid.
[134] SCHWARCZ, Lilia M. and STARLING, Heloisa M, *Brasil: Uma Biografia*, São Paulo, Companhia das Letras, 2015, p. 478.

disappeared for political motives,[135] and, among those, 191 people had been subject to summary and illegal execution or died as the result of torture carried out by agents of the State.[136]

This contrast was so jarring that years later, in 1995, the jurist Fábio Konder Comparato questioned this peace-making attitude of the government in relation to the objectives of the amnesty.[137] He noted that it was politically indefensible that those that governed above the law would seek to obtain legitimacy from a subordinate legislature for amnesty for the crimes they had committed in the exercise of their authority. He added that the claimed "pacification of the spirits" was always a gross farce, since, at the time of the amnesty, there was not the least indication of armed opposition to the regime. It was as if a dictator, seeking to abandon power but at no risk to himself, negotiated with his successor for a previously arranged amnesty for his misdeeds.

2.1.2. THE SCOPE AND LEGITIMACY OF THE AMNESTY LAW

Specifically, with regard to the legislative process in which the 1979 Amnesty Law was approved, it should be noted that the party representing opponents to the military regime, the *Movimento Democrático Brasileiro* (MDB) or "Brazilian Democratic Movement", won the legislative elections of November 1974 in the large urban areas, electing a large number of federal deputies and several senators. This result demonstrated the population's growing discontent with the military regime and, thus, in order to maintain the slow pace of the transition process and to forestall a possible opposition victory in the 1978 elections, in April of 1977 the so-called *Pacote de Abril*[138] or "April Package" was initiated. That accord put off elections for state governors until 1982 and altered the composition of the electoral college with respect to states in the North and Northeastern regions of the country, giving them greater representation. Needless to say, it was precisely those regions in which the political party backing the government, the *Aliança Renovadora Nacional* (ARENA) or "National Alliance for Renewal", exercised the strongest political influence. The pact also defined the rules for the 1978 election campaign (known as the *surda-muda* or "deaf and dumb" campaign), in which candidates were only allowed to show a small photograph of themselves

---

[135] *National Truth Commission*, Final Report, Volume I, Chapter 11, p. 438.
[136] *National Truth Commission*, Final Report, Volume III, p. 26.
[137] COMPARATO, Fábio Konder. "Questão de Decência", *Folha de São Paulo*, September 10, 1995, https://www1.folha.uol.com.br/fsp/1995/9/10/opiniao/10.html.
[138] VIZENTINI, Paulo Gilberto Fagundes, "A Experiência Histórica do Brasil e da Argentina Contemporâneos: Autoritarismo e Desenvolvimento (1964–1985)", in LLADÓS, José Maria and GUIMARÃES, Samuel Pinheiro (eds.), *Perspectivas: Brasil e Argentina*, Brasília, IPRI, 2000, pp. 435–485.

on TV along with a mini-curriculum vitae and without any other type of message. Finally, the pact invented a new type of *senador biônico*[139] or "bionic senator" to fill one-third of the seats in the Senate following the 1978 election; these representatives would be elected indirectly by the same electoral college which would choose state governors.

Consequently, in light of this political scenario and the fact that the Amnesty Bill was proposed by the military government – in which the President was indirectly elected and the National Congress included "bionic" senators – amnesty in Brazil was only poorly shrouded in national legitimacy (understood as a representation of the popular will in a government elected by the citizens themselves). In fact the government that passed the law did not effectively represent the popular will, as at the time it was not the result of free and fair elections.[140] It should also be added that the Amnesty Law was passed by only 50.61% of the votes; that is, 206 votes in favor versus 201 votes opposed. Hence, this razor-thin margin for its passage reflects the popular discontent with a law which guaranteed protection for those accused of crimes against humanity.[141]

The lack of legitimacy for the Bill proposing amnesty in Brazil, in the sense that it did not adequately represent the will of the people, could be seen from the moment that amendments to the proposal began to be presented. In total, 134 legislators (26 senators and 108 federal deputies) offered 305 amendments.[142] Among the various alternative proposals were: (i) exclusion from the benefits of amnesty for all acts of abuse and torture; (ii) the inclusion from the list of those amnestied of persons who had already been convicted of terrorism, assault, kidnapping or assassination;[143] (iii) the withdrawal of the benefit of amnesty from persons who had ordered or carried out acts of imprisonment without observing the legal formalities or who had done so in an abusive manner.

With respect to the scope of the Law, in the text proposed by the military government, there was a provision in article. 1 granting amnesty to all those: (i) who had committed political crimes or those connected to them and whose

---

[139] The term "bionic senator" was used to designate a senator indirectly elected by the same electoral college that would choose future governors. The nickname was coined the opposition and referred to an American TV series ("*The Six Million Dollar Man*" – 1974–1978), whose protagonist, a cyborg, had artificial powers thanks to technology and worked as a special agent of the government. See: SCHWARCZ, Lilia M. and STARLING, Heloisa M, *Brasil: Uma Biografia*, São Paulo, Companhia das Letras, 2015, p. 468.

[140] BASTOS, Lucia Elena Arantes Ferreira, *Anistia: As Leis Internacionais e o Caso Brasileiro*, Curitiba, Juruá, 2009.

[141] ZELIC, Marcelo, "Lei da Anistia É um Ataque aos Direitos Humanos", *Conjur*, February 13, 2010, https://www.conjur.com.br/2010-fev-13/manter-lei-anistia-ataque-aos-avancos-direitos-humanos.

[142] FICO, Carlos, "A Negociação Parlamentar da Anistia de 1979 e o Chamado Perdão aos Torturadores", *Revista Anistia Política e Justiça de Transição*, vol. 4/2010, pp. 318–333.

[143] The amnesty did not include 195 political prisoners convicted because of their armed actions, which were referred to by the military as "blood crimes". See: *Isto É*, "Quarenta Anos da Lei da Anistia", August 30, 2019, https://istoe.com.br/quarenta-anos-da-lei-da-anistia/.

political rights had been suspended, (ii) to directly or indirectly employed public servants or those employed by foundations linked to public entities, (iii) to employees of the legislative and judicial branches, and (iv) to military personnel, directors, and union representatives who had been penalized under the so-called *Atos Institucionais* (AI) or "Institutional Acts" and their supplemental articles. Nevertheless, under article 1, paragraph 2, of the Bill, those who had been convicted of the crimes of terrorism, assault, kidnapping, or assassination which constituted political crimes in opposition to the established regime (the so-called *crimes de sangue* or "blood crimes") were excluded from the benefits of the amnesty being offered.

At the time, the exclusion of those convicted of "blood crimes" from the list of amnesty beneficiaries was controversial when the Bill was up for discussion before the National Congress, so much so that the then Senator Teotônio Vilela, in analyzing the government's Bill, criticized this provision, noting that the proposed language benefited some to the exclusion of others. Thus, two persons who had been accused of the same act would be given diametrically opposed treatment: the one who had already been convicted would remain in prison; whereas the other who had not yet been convicted would have his rights restored and would not be held responsible for his actions.[144] The same question arose in the discussion among jurists, as Batista has pointed out, namely, that it would be substantially unjust to allow co-defendants involved in the same act to find themselves in situations so disparate: one amnestied; the other definitively convicted.[145]

Also, with regard to the question of the proposed amnesty, it was clear that it involved the broadest possible scope, since it would be possible to encompass an innumerable list of human rights violations within the concept of a "connected crime" (that is, one connected to a political crime). To fix this situation, several legislators offered amendments: (i) to include the payment of pensions to the dependents of persons who had disappeared after being detained by State security agents; (ii) to open investigations by the Ministry of Justice to look into the forced disappearances; (iii) to initiate an inquiry by the Federal Police to identify the circumstances behind the disappearances; and (iv) to equate disappearance with natural death for legal purposes.

At the end of the discussions which took place in Congress, the legislator in charge of shepherding the bill through the legislature (the so-called *relator* or "reporting member") rejected all of the proposed amendments. Nevertheless,

---

[144] MEZAROBBA, Glenda, *Um Acerto de Contas com o Futuro – a Anistia e suas Conseqüências – um Estudo do Caso Brasileiro*. Dissertação (Mestrado), São Paulo, Faculdade de Filosofia, Letras e Ciências Humanas, Universidade de São Paulo (USP), 2003, p. 32.

[145] BATISTA, Nilo, "Aspectos Jurídico-Penais da Anistia", *Revista Encontros com a Civilização Brasileira*, vol. 19/1980, pp. 195–206.

the reporting member presented a substitute text to the Bill proposed by the government which added an additional seven articles to the original: (i) an extension in relevant time period for the grant of amnesty up to August 15, 1979; (ii) inclusion in article 1 of the possibility of an amnesty for electoral crimes; (iii) the guarantee to the dependants of a deceased amnestied individual of the same benefits that the latter would have been entitled to; (iv) the right for family members of disappeared persons to request an official declaration of absence (the equivalent of a presumption of death declaration); (v) the grant of amnesty to employees of private companies who had been penalized for their participation in industrial action; and (vi) the restoration of political rights to persons receiving amnesty (the right to vote and to be elected).

2.2. DILEMMAS OF THE AMNESTY LAW: CONNECTED CRIMES AND THE TWO-SIDED LAW THEORY

2.2.1. THE THEORY OF CONNECTED CRIMES

The first dilemma related to Law no. 6,683 (1979) could be found right in article 1, when it stipulated that amnesty would be granted to all those who had committed political or connected crimes, during the period from September 2, 1961 to August 15, 1979. The question immediately arose as to what such connected crimes were. According to the theory of criminal law, it was said that connected crimes were dependent violations, such that a nexus could be established between the two crimes. In other words, it had to be shown that one of the violations had been committed in order to carry out or hide the other, or to ensure to the perpetrator the benefit of the crime or impunity in its perpetration.[146]

In the Brazilian case, long before 1979, there was already established jurisprudence for the feasibility of applying amnesty to connected crimes, provided that this possibility was expressly mentioned in the text of the law granting the amnesty.[147] But at the same time, taking into consideration the serious nature of some of the crimes, there were those who argued that some crimes,[148] despite their connection with a political crime, should not receive

---

[146] MAGGIORE, Giuseppe, *Derecho Penal*, vol. 2, Bogotá, Temis, 1972, pp. 184–187.
[147] According to the Federal Court of Justice, the amnesty granted for political offenses extends to a related common crime only when expressly provided for in the law granting it. See: HC 29.797. Osvaldo Ribeiro Teixeira e outros. Rel. Min. Lafayette de Andrada, dated September 10, 1947.
[148] CARVALHO FILHO, Aloysio, *Comentários ao Código Penal*, vol. IV, Rio de Janeiro, Forense, 1958, pp. 103–161.

the benefit of a pardon. This was even the understanding of the Supreme Court which was against the adoption of the concept of connection with respect to amnesty in the case of murder, theft, arson, and sexual assault,[149] because those violations could never be confused with political crimes as they in no way might have been motivated by patriotism.

Nevertheless, the series of amnesty laws enacted in Brazil shows the predominance of applying such norms in an unrestrictive manner, given that the amnesty laws enacted in 1930, 1934, and 1945 unequivocally extended the benefit to connected violations.[150] Despite the previous examples in which the concept of connection was applied broadly, Aloysio Carvalho had already stated in 1958 that, in the case of amnesty, it was not wise to determine the existence of a connection with a political crime in the abstract; rather he argued that the ideal procedure would be to examine each concrete case and the relation of dependency existing in each case between the two deeds, with particular attention being paid to the political objective linking them.

On the occasion of the drafting of the 1979 Amnesty Law, as political prisoners were impeded from direct participation in the debate, they submitted written statements to Senator Teotônio Vilela in which they were critical of the principal articles of the proposed law and classed the amnesty on offer as discriminatory.[151] They pointed out that the objective of the law was to guarantee a broad amnesty to the torturers who had acted under the regime by including the expression of a "crime connected to a political crime" in the text. Also, with respect to connected crimes, the jurist Hélio Bicudo subsequently stated the following:[152]

> A question I have always asked myself about the Amnesty Law concerns the understanding that the law, at the same time, includes the victims of power as well as their executioners. This understanding of the so-called Two-Sided Law ["*lei de duas vias*"] was established in the final years of the military regime and has nothing to do with what one might identify as valid legal interpretation. The law in question clearly specifies who is to benefit from its terms and at no point mentions those who tortured and killed on behalf of the military regime.

---

[149] To the former Supreme Court Minister, Américo Lôbo, "The amnesty law on revolutionary movements, however generic, does not include premeditated murders or attempted assassinations, coldly and cowardly … with disguise, betrayal, surprise and superiority of arms". See: CARVALHO FILHO, Aloysio, *Comentários ao Código Penal*, vol. IV, Rio de Janeiro, Forense, 1958, pp. 103–161.

[150] See: Decree 19,395, of November 8, 1930; Decree 24,297, of May 28, 1934; Decree-Law 7,474, of April 18, 1945 and Decree-Law 7,943, of September 10, 1945.

[151] MOTTA, Marly, "Teotônio das Alagoas: O Menestrel da Abertura", *Maracanan*, vol. 8/2012, pp. 259–282.

[152] BICUDO, Hélio. "Lei de Anistia e Crimes Conexos", *Folha de São Paulo*, December 6, 1995.

Hélio Bicudo's concern essentially involved the amnesty granted to the perpetrators of human rights violations, that is, the interpretation of article 1, paragraph 1, of Law no. 6,683 (1979). According to the prevailing understanding until the present time, the law extended amnesty to those who had committed crimes connected with political violations, with the former being understood as crimes of any type that were related to political crimes or carried out for political reasons. However, in his analysis, Bicudo reached the conclusion that one could not find any equivalence between the causes or motivations of the acts in violation of the political system (committed by the opponents of the regime) and those committed by the agents of repression (the torturers) as the first sought to bring about change while the second sought to maintain the *status quo*, each one thus acting in accordance with the interests he sought to preserve. Hence, they should be characterized as independent crimes because they constituted different paths and sought different objectives, which do not allow for any confusion between the two.

Likewise, Batista notes that crimes connected to political crimes should be understood as those in which there is a relationship between the means and the ends of the political crimes in question. For this reason, the benefit of amnesty should not be extended to agents of the State who acted in the pursuit of repression and engaged in torture, because the latter crimes were not the logical result of the political motivation that led armed opposition groups to urban and rural guerrilla tactics. Also, in the words of Batista: "[t]he torture and murder of a prisoner are not political crimes, nor crimes connected to political crimes, either objectively or subjectively. They are ordinary crimes ... that deserve trial and judgement".[153]

2.2.2. THE TWO-SIDED LAW THEORY

Despite the discussions that took place in 1979 on the occasion of the proposed amendments to the Amnesty Law, the image that became fixed in civil society was that, following amnesty and the return of political exiles, reconciliation and the pacification of the spirits were really possible. At the beginning of the '80s, even though amnesty was also granted to State agents, it was a seen as a "justifiable evil" in the name of political transition. Such understanding was corroborated by the fact that shortly after the '80s the prosecuting body (the Federal Public Prosecutor's Office) did not carry out investigations and prosecutions related to the crimes committed during the dictatorship.

---

[153] BATISTA, Nilo, "Aspectos Jurídico-Penais da Anistia", *Revista Encontros com a Civilização Brasileira*, vol. 19/1980, pp. 195–206, p. 197.

To illustrate this argument, in her research Rodeghero concluded,[154] based on the analysis of records and print media of that time, that the meanings given to amnesty during the early years of the campaign (1975–1976) were transformed to represent the ideals of pacification and conciliation, by using the metaphor of Brazil as a "family", and based on the existence of a "tradition" of amnesty since the Vargas Era (1930–1945), and all these arguments would had helped to build the appeal to forget the past. Consequently, the amnesty of 1979 was no longer seen as a break with the regime, or as an act of benevolence, but rather as a collective society demanding its rights as a "family".

In this same sense, Lemos[155] explained that the tradition of amnesty in Brazilian history would reflect broader traditions like "conciliation" as a form of protecting the fundamental interests of the dominant classes in its society and that of preventive counter-revolution as an anti-crisis strategy.[156] And, in this context, Lemos also reminded us that it would be the so-called "spirit of reconciliation" that allowed the peaceful coexistence in power between former exponents of the military dictatorship – such as politicians Antônio Carlos Magalhães, José Sarney, Marco Maciel – and "subversives" of the 1960s – among them the former presidents Fernando Henrique Cardoso and Dilma Rousseff. Furthermore, it has also been the mask of such "spirit of reconciliation" that Brazil perpetuates to hinder the investigation of crimes of torture and murder practiced by members of the security services and covered up by military governments.

Such a proposition – that an amnesty law could dispense with responsibility for crimes against humanity committed in the past and that it was preferable to a period of conflict and violent transition – largely resembles the so-called "theory of the lesser evil" – as, according to that moral justification, in the face of two evils one must always opt for the lesser of the two. If applied to the question of amnesty, the theory of the lesser evil would tend to mandate that, faced with either (i) forgetting the crimes that were committed or (ii) enduring a violent political transition, the best option would be for amnesty, the lesser evil. The use of such an argument, however, is questionable at best. Arendt notes that its weakness lies in the fact that even if one has chosen the lesser evil,[157] it continues to be evil. And, with the passage of time, the tendency is for the public to forget that fact. That is where the danger lies: the risk of forgetting that an evil was committed, even if on a lesser scale.

---

[154] RODEGHERO, Carla Simone, "Pela Pacificação da Família Brasileira: Uma Breve Comparação entre as Anistias de 1945 e de 1979", *Revista Brasileria de História*, vol. 34/2014, pp. 67–88.
[155] LEMOS, Renato, "Anistia e Crise Política no Brasil pós-1964", *Topoi*, vol. 3/2002, pp. 287–313.
[156] For such strategy, see in Chapter 1 of this book the history of the 1955 Preventive Coup, which was organized by Marshall Lott, in order to guarantee that the elected President, Juscelino Kubitschek (JK), would assume his post on 31 January 1956.
[157] ARENDT, Hannah, *Responsabilidade e Julgamento*, São Paulo, Companhia das Letras, 2004.

The 1979 amnesty – which enabled and empowered the forgetting of both the political crimes committed by citizens against the State and crimes against humanity perpetrated by State agents against citizens[158] – has been recognized as being a "two-way" or "two-sided"[159] Law as it conveniently pardoned "both sides":[160] opponents of the regime who were tortured, imprisoned, or exiled and their torturers. What it is important to note, however, is whether the grounds for such two-sided amnesty really lie in theoretical justifications concerning political crimes and violations of human rights.

A first point which must be emphasized is the distinction between: (i) amnesty laws offered by States to their opponents, normally for political crimes, and (ii) those which grant immunity to the State itself for acts committed by its agents. The understanding is that only the first case is among the powers that a State may exercise, as the victim of the aggression and the guarantor of criminal justice, and that power does not extend to situations in which the State itself, through its agents, is the perpetrator of the violations.[161]

During the dictatorship, the justification that was given for the practice of serious violations of human rights was that the acts were committed in situations in which the moral responsibility of the State, as the guardian of national security, was compromised due to the actions of citizens acting for political reasons,[162] thereby justifying the later application of amnesty in such circumstances. Nevertheless, with regard to this aspect, acceptance of a two-sided amnesty suffers from an erroneous view of the concept of human rights violations and political crimes, since it diverges from the universally-accepted political and legal concept that amnesty is only applicable to political crimes committed by citizens.[163] The proposition which compares (a) genuine human rights violations and/or crimes against humanity committed by agents of the State, with (b) criminal acts committed by armed groups of dissidents (political crimes), distorts and perverts the very specific nature of human rights. That

---

[158] APOLINÁRIO, Silvia Menicucci O.S. and BASTOS, Lucia Elena Arantes Ferreira, "Ensaio sobre a Impunidade: Os Crimes Contra a Humanidade Cometidos no Brasil", *Universitas Jus*, vol. 27/2016, pp. 33–47.

[159] BASTOS, Lucia Elena Arantes Ferreira, "A Lei de Anistia Brasileira: Os Crimes Conexos, a Dupla Via e Tratados de Direitos Humanos", *Revista da Faculdade de Direito da Universidade de São Paulo*, vol. 103/2008, pp. 593–628.

[160] AQUINO, Maria Aparecida de, "Brasil: 1964–2014 – Uma Comemoraçãp Possível", *Cadernos de História*, vol. 15/2014, pp. 190–207.

[161] GOLDMAN, Robert, "Amnesty Laws and International Law: A Specific Case", in International Commission of Jurists, *Seminar on Justice Not Impunity*, Geneva, ICJ, 1992, https://www.icj.org/no-a-la-impunidad-si-a-la-justicia-encuentro-internacional-sobre-la-impunidad-de-los-autores-de-violaciones-graves-a-los-derechos-humanos-2-a-5-de-noviembre-de-1992-palacio-de-naciones-unidas-gi/.

[162] MERA, Jorge, "Chile: Truth and Justice under the Democratic Government", in ARRIAZA, Naomi Roth (ed.), *Impunity and Human Rights in International Law and Practice*, New York, Oxford University Press, 1995, p. 171–184.

[163] BASTOS, Lucia Elena Arantes Ferreira, *Anistia: As Leis Internacionais e o Caso Brasileiro*, Curitiba, Juruá, 2009.

is, the idea that the set of International Human Rights historically arose as a demand to limit the power of the State and represents a restriction on State sovereignty, in the sense that there are certain values in human behavior which not only the State, but all citizens must respect.

As Mera has stated, acts of terrorism or other illegitimate actions committed for political reasons may not be used to justify human rights violations committed by the State and its agents as if they were something to give up in exchange for other concessions. Thus, the true grounds for a broad, general, and unrestricted interpretation of the Amnesty Law are to be found in political considerations; namely, amnesty was tied to the central objective of avoiding conflict with the Armed Forces, whose actions might "put the success of the transition at risk".[164]

By privileging political considerations above all others, the danger lies in giving the impression that, rather than being a regime dominated by State-sponsored terror, what occurred in Brazil was a fight between rival groups, as if it were an armed conflict in international humanitarian law terms, which, once the regime ended, justified the application of amnesty.[165] This view devalues the search for the truth not only in relation to human rights violations, but also with respect to the crimes that were committed by citizens against the State and members of the Armed Forces.[166] The groups that attacked the military never were organized enough or exerted sufficient resistance to be capable of creating a situation in which the rules of international humanitarian law were applied in the country; or, better stated, the State was never in danger, nor did the actions of the armed groups create a generalized sense of insecurity in the populace as a result of their actions.[167]

2.3. CONCLUSIONS

At first glance, an amnesty law seems to offer quick and efficient advantages during a transition period, as it facilitates the surrendering of power through non-violent means and thus avoids the recourse to armed intervention – and this seems to have been the principal argument employed in the Brazilian case of Law no. 6,683 (1979). Moreover, international law and the domestic practice of

---

[164] DALLARI, Dalmo, "Anistia: Esquecimento Legal, Memória de Fato", *Fundação Perseu Abramo*, April 23, 2006, https://fpabramo.org.br/2006/04/23/dalmo-dallari-anistia-esquecimento-legal-memoria-de-fato/.

[165] SLYE, Ronald C, "The Legitimacy of Amnesties under International Law and General Principles of Anglo-American Law: Is a Legitimate Amnesty Possible?", *Virginia Journal of International Law*, vol. 43/2002, pp. 173–247.

[166] On crimes committed by armed opposition groups, see: GASPARI, Elio, *A Ditadura Escancarada*, São Paulo, Companhia das Letras, 2002, p. 161–162.

[167] According to: GASPARI, Elio, *A Ditadura Escancarada*, São Paulo, Companhia das Letras, 2002, p. 18 and p. 406.

States, at certain moments, allow and sometimes even require the application of an amnesty. For example, international law promotes the use of amnesty at the end of an armed conflict and that encouragement is codified in one of the principal documents of international humanitarian law.[168]

However, such amnesty must be analyzed distinctly from amnesty related to violations of human rights and crimes against humanity. Indeed, on the question of amnesty, according to Slye,[169] the International Committee of the Red Cross has already taken a position with respect to the Geneva Conventions, confirming that the amnesty mentioned in Additional Protocol no. II, from 1977, was designed to be applied only to those who have participated in hostilities and not to those who have violated international law and engaged in crimes against humanity. In fact, the amnesty for serious violations of human rights has been vehemently condemned by the Inter-American Court[170] and the precepts of no statute of limitations and universal jurisdiction have expanded to cover such violations in recent decades.[171]

From the perspective of Transitional Justice, what makes the use of amnesty today so problematic is not only the failure to hold responsible those individuals who committed systematic human rights violations, but also its increasing use and acceptance by a world which has at the same time globally adopted the idea that there are some universal human rights[172] for the violation of which amnesty is no longer permitted, in particular the absolute right not to be subjected to torture, slavery, or genocide. It is not that amnesty is now being used in areas previously unknown or in a new and distinct manner, but rather that a consensus has arisen over the last 70 years[173] that certain acts committed

---

[168] See article 6(5) of the Additional Protocol to the Geneva Conventions of August 12, 1949, and Relating to the Protection of Victims of Non-International Armed Conflicts (Protocol II), adopted on June 8, 1977: "At the end of hostilities, the authorities in power shall endeavour to grant the broadest possible amnesty to persons who have participated in the armed conflict, or those deprived of their liberty for reasons related to the armed conflict, whether they are interned or detained".

[169] SLYE, Ronald C., "The Legitimacy of Amnesties under International Law and General Principles of Anglo-American Law: Is a Legitimate Amnesty Possible?", *Virginia Journal of International Law*, vol. 43/2002, pp. 173–247.

[170] For detailed description on the amnesty condemned by the Inter-American Court of Human Rights, see Chapter 4 of this book.

[171] See: Convention on the Non-applicability of Statutory Limitations to War Crimes and Crimes against Humanity of November 26, 1968, article 1(2) and Inter-American Convention on Forced Disappearance of Persons of September 6, 1994, article VII.

[172] CABRILLAC, Rémy; FRISON-ROCHE, Marie-Anne and REVET, Thierry (eds.), *Libertés et Droits Fondamentaux*, Paris, Dalloz, 2006, p. 33.

[173] This change of perspective came from the Nuremberg and Tokyo Trials, which were held to prosecute crimes committed during World War II. These trials symbolized the answer to the horror of the Nazi genocide in Europe and the crimes committed by the Japanese during the occupation of Southeast Asia. At that time, there was already a widespread conviction that tyranny could never again disregard human dignity and go unpunished. See: CASSESE, Antonio, *International Criminal Law*, New York, Oxford University Press, 2003, pp. 329–330.

by agents of the State are not exempt from demands for their perpetrators to be held to account.[174]

Most notably the trend towards individual responsibility under the auspices of international law has accelerated since the end of the last century with two great developments. The first was the creation of the International Criminal Court to investigate and try individuals accused of committing,[175] among other crimes, those perpetrated against humanity. The second was the increase in the motivation for States to invoke universal jurisdiction in holding violators to account for serious human rights violations, as expressly recognized in the *Pinochet Case*.[176] Nevertheless, even with the expansion of the international system of criminal justice, many States continue to see amnesty as a mechanism they may choose to facilitate their own political transitions following a period of dictatorship – as has occurred in the case of Brazil, where judicial bodies have issued decisions validating the 1979 Amnesty Law, justifying their rulings based on the existence of the political grounds for the law. Thus, there has not been recognition in the domestic sphere of the responsibility of the State for crimes against humanity,[177] or in regards to the theoretical underpinnings of transitional justice.[178]

---

[174] As per the proposition of universal jurisdiction made by Bassiouni: "As an *action popularis*, universal jurisdiction may be exercised by a state without any jurisdictional connection or link between the place of commission, the perpetrator's nationality the victim's nationality, and the enforcing state. The basis is, therefore, exclusively the nature of the crime and the purpose is exclusively to enhance world order by ensuring accountability for the perpetration of certain crimes". See: BASSIOUNI, M. Cherif, "Universal Jurisdiction for International Crimes: Historical Perspectives and Contemporary Practice", *Virginia Journal of International Law*, vol. 42/2001, pp. 81–162.

[175] Rome Statute of the International Criminal Court, July 17, 1998, in force since July 1, 2002.

[176] While analyzing the *Pinochet Case*, Bianchi commented: "In fact, the *Pinochet* case should be a cause for international lawyers to inquire afresh whether former heads of state and other state officials may be held responsible before the municipal courts of a foreign state for acts, qualified as criminal under international law, which have allegedly been committed when they were in post". See: BIANCHI, Andrea, "Immunity versus Human Rights: The *Pinochet Case*", *European Journal of International Law*, vol. 10/1999, pp. 237–277, pp. 237–238.

[177] On the local jurisdiction and the applicability of the Amnesty Law in Brazil, see Chapter 4 of the book.

[178] For instance, according to the ICTJ: "amnesty laws should be adopted only along with transitional justice measures that promote truth-seeking, criminal accountability, institutional reform, and reparations to promote peace and reconciliation effectively. International treaties and customary law require states to prosecute certain serious international crimes – such as genocide, war crimes, and crimes against humanity. Amnesties must therefore not extend to such crimes". See: *International Center for Transitional Justice*, "Amnesty Must Not Equal Impunity", Focus 2009 DRC Amnesty Law, https://www.ictj.org/sites/default/files/ICTJ-DRC-Amnesty-Facts-2009-English.pdf.

PART II
STEPS TOWARDS REPARATIONS, ACCOUNTABILITY, AND TRUTH

CHAPTER 3
VICTIMS' REPARATIONS PROGRAM

> *"For each beloved hour*
> *Sharp pittances of years,*
> *Bitter contested farthings*
> *And coffers heaped with tears".*[179]

In general, shortly after a violent regime and following a transitional period there is pressure to prosecute those responsible for the large-scale crimes of the abusive regime. However, in many cases, prosecutions do not occur within the time and in the manner expected, mainly because of the existence of amnesty laws or a new administration's lack of the material and legal means to carry out prosecutions after a period of chaos and conflict. Hence, in light of the prosecutorial gap that such obstacles produce, Transitional Justice frameworks commonly suggest hybrid practices like truth commissions, lustrations (purge of government officials) and reparations programs in order to meet reasonable expectations of justice. From the above list, in addition to truth commissions, the most common gap-filling mechanism has been reparations,[180] which are intended to provide not only compensation, but also accountability through recognition and perhaps redemption for perpetrators.[181]

In the Brazilian case, as a result of the 1979 Amnesty Law and the delayed implementation of an official truth commission (which only occurred in the 2012–2014 period), the main Transitional Justice initiatives from 1995–2014 consisted of two different reparations programs. Over the years, it has been said that such plans constituted the "structural axis" of Brazilian Transitional Justice.[182] Moreover, as will be observed in this chapter, the benefits distributed

---

[179] DICKINSON, Emily, "Compensation", *The Poems of Emily Dickinson: Series Two*, Boston, MA, Roberts Brothers, 1896.
[180] HAYNER. Priscilla, *Unspeakable Truths – Transitional Justice and the Challenge of Truth Commissions*, New York, Routledge, 2002.
[181] LAPLANTE, Lisa J. and THEIDON, Kimberly, "Truth with Consequences: Justice and Reparations in Post-Truth Commission Peru", *Human Rights Quarterly*, vol. 29/2007, pp. 228–250.
[182] ABRÃO, Paulo and TORELLY, Marcelo D., "Mutações do Conceito de Anistia na Justiça de Transição Brasileira – A Terceira Fase de Luta pela Anistia", *Revista de Direito Brasileiro*, vol. 3/2012, pp. 357–379.

by such programs were both material and symbolic, taking the form of cash payments, social welfare entitlements (such as government pensions), reinstatement to prior employment, career promotions, public apologies, outreach work, memorials, educational initiatives, book-length publications, and funding for documentary films.

The origins of such reparations programs are in the 1988 Constitution, which, in addition to recognizing the duty of the State to promote fundamental human rights in article 5, briefly references the legacy of violence during the dictatorship period in the obligation it imposes on the State to make reparations to victims of the previous regime, as mentioned in the *Ato das Disposições Constitucionais Transitórias* (ADCT) ("List of Transitional Constitutional Provisions"). Indeed, the ADCT functions as an Annex to the Constitution and provides guidelines for issues that are not entirely covered in the principal portion of the document. Thus, article 8 of the ADCT contains strategies for a future reparations program for those whose lives were disrupted by extraordinary decrees issued during the period between September 18, 1946 and October 5, 1988. However, considering that article 8 of the ADCT merely provided guiding principles, the implementation of the rights foreseen there required specific legislation, which came into effect only in 1995 and 2002.

So, how to explain this lapse of time, from the end of the dictatorial regime (1985) until the implementation of victims' rights in 1995 and 2002, when civilian governments started to be more proactive regarding the reparations program envisaged as a Transitional Justice mechanism? Analysing this interval, Ryan reminds us that administrators during the period ranging from 1995 to 2016 were closely connected to the violations committed during the regime,[183] albeit in different forms and roles, such as university professors forced into exile, union leaders imprisoned for promoting strikes or members of armed opposition groups who were tortured and killed. So, their own background and personal experiences would have contributed to the promotion of initiatives concerning the rights to truth and memory.[184]

But, Ryan also agrees that there is a more significant and intuitive argument to explain this domestic silence, first from 1985 to 1995 and later up to 2012 (the year of the creation of the National Truth Commission), one that comes from the realm of international relations: the international pressure put on and the high political costs of ignoring calls to confront the past for a country that during

---

[183] Specifically, it would be the administrations of former Presidents Fernando Henrique Cardoso (1995–2002), Luiz Inacio Lula da Silva (2003–2010), and Dilma Rousseff (2011–2016). See Ryan, H.E., "From Absent to Present Pasts: Civil Society, Democracy and the Shifting Place of Memory in Brazil", *Journal of Civil Society*, vol. 12/2016, pp. 158–177.

[184] During the presidential campaign of 1994, both candidates Fernando Henrique Cardoso and Luis Inácio Lula da Silva affirmed that they would recognize the victims of the dictatorial regime. See: Special Commission on Political Deaths and Disappearances, *Direito à Memória e à Verdade*, Brasília, Secretaria Especial dos Direitos Humanos, 2007, p. 32.

the 2010's was aspiring to be a global player. Specifically, since Brazil's return to the Rule of Law, the international community and scholars have gradually paid more attention to the contradictions of the country in terms of its policies dealing with past atrocities.

For instance, in 1996, the Human Rights Watch Report on Brazil stated that the continued failure to investigate the disappearances and extrajudicial executions which occurred during the dictatorship constituted ongoing violations of Brazil's duty under the American Convention on Human Rights and the International Covenant on Civil and Political Rights to ensure justice and effective remediation for the victims of human rights abuses.[185] In 2009, Navi Pillay, the former United Nations High Commissioner for Human Rights, claimed that the absence of a debate around torture reaffirmed a legacy of legitimacy for authoritarianism in Brazil.[186]

Also, in analyzing the type and degree of human rights compliance from the perspective of "statehood", Börzel and Risse indicated that Brazil was an "imperfect democracy" and should be classified as exercising "limited statehood",[187] meaning that, even during the democratic era, violations of human rights would continue to occur due to a lack of state capacity to act. Later, when Roht-Arriaza examined the status of Latin American States which adopted amnesty laws during the 1970s, 1980s and 1990s,[188] she mentioned that Brazil was an "outlier" when compared to Argentina, Chile and Peru, given all of the latter's successful post-conflict strategies and Transitional Justice measures.

With this in mind, the sections below will address not only how Brazil has implemented its reparations program as a gap-filling measure due to the lack of criminal justice for past atrocities, but also how the program itself has changed over the years after a stint of criticism based on accusations of "blood money" (when reparations payments are made without truth-telling) that usually accompany initiatives involving pecuniary compensation in post-conflict societies.[189] To demonstrate that such mechanism may be a two-edged sword

---

[185] *Human Rights Watch World Report 1996 – Brazil*, https://www.refworld.org/docid/3ae6a8bf0.html.

[186] PILLAY, Navi, "Brazil's Indigenous and Afro-Brazilian Populations face Serious Discrimination", *The Huffington Post*, November 18, 2009, https://www.huffingtonpost.com/navi-pillay/brazils-indigenous-and-af_b_362183.html.

[187] BÖRZEL, Tanja A. and RISSE, Thomas, "Human Rights in Areas of Limited Statehood: The New Agenda", in RISSE, Thomas, ROPP, Stephen C. and SIKKINK, Kathryn (eds.), *The Persistent Power of Human Rights – From Commitment to Compliance*, Cambridge, Cambridge University Press, 2013.

[188] ROHT-ARRIAZA, Naomi, "After Amnesties Are Gone: Latin American National Courts and the New Contours of the Fights Against Impunity", *Human Rights Quarterly*, vol. 37/2015, pp. 341–382.

[189] BERNSTEIN, Anita, "Pecuniary Reparations Following National Crisis: A Convergence of Tort Theory Microfinance, and Gender Equality", *University of Pennsylvania Journal of International Law*, vol. 31/2009, pp. 1–51.

and always subject to criticism and disapproval, this chapter will detail how an apparently new cycle of revisions to the reparations program may be made in the near future, again raising the question of whether victims and society value pecuniary or symbolic measures more.[190]

Thus, in studying the reparations program, it is worth constantly keeping in mind the poem by Emily Dickinson quoted at the beginning of this chapter. Its lines remind us that compensation will always be unsatisfying, mainly because the periods of joy and of pain we experience in life will never be equal; consequently, each "beloved" hour is paid for by "years" of pain,[191] and the substantial issue is how to make amends when the feeling of pain seems never come to an end.

3.1. THE SPECIAL COMMISSION FOR POLITICAL DEATHS AND DISAPPEARANCES

The assuming of accountability by the Brazilian state for human rights violations committed during the dictatorial period began to take shape with Law no. 9,140 (1995), enacted on December 4 of that year. It is commonly known as the "Political Deaths and Disappearances Law" because it introduced a list with 136 names of persons considered forcibly disappeared during the previous authoritarian regime. This law also created the Special Commission on Political Deaths and Disappearances (SCPDD), whose mission would be: (a) to pay reparations to the relatives of those murdered and/or disappeared for political reasons; (b) to locate missing persons and/or their remains; and (c) to promote initiatives encouraging truth and memory.

According to the Political Deaths and Disappearances Law, pecuniary reparations for those considered dead or disappeared for political reasons would cover incidents which occurred from September 2, 1961 to October 5, 1988, with requests for reparations to be filed within 120 days of the law's ratification. Requests could be made by spouses, children, parents and some other relatives of the dead and disappeared. By 2019, in addition to 136 cases automatically recognized by Law no. 9,140 (1995), the SCPDD had approved an additional 226 claims for reparations for the dead and forcibly disappeared for political reasons, leaving the current official number of Dead and Disappeared whose families received pecuniary reparations at 362,[192] with the average value of

---

[190] ROHT-ARRIAZA, Naomi, "Reparations Decisions and Dilemmas", *Hastings International and Comparative Law Review*, vol. 27/2004, pp. 157–219.
[191] For a deep reflection on Dickinson's poem "Compensation", see: http://academic.brooklyn.cuny.edu/english/melani/cs6/instant.html.
[192] *Special Commission on Political Deaths and Disappearances*, https://cemdp.sdh.gov.br/modules/wfchannel/index.php?pagenum=11.

each compensation being BRL 120,000 (approximately US$30,000 at time of writing).[193]

Even though Law no. 9,140 (1995) represented an important step forward regarding reparations measures (both pecuniary and symbolic), it was also criticized in several aspects,[194] including the fact that it was considered a half-measure by most of the victims' relatives[195] since it exempted the State from having to identify the public agents involved in the crimes committed during the dictatorship and it did not impose any obligation on the Brazilian State to locate the bodies of the missing (although over the years the SCPDD has committed itself to complying with this task). The very procedure for obtaining pecuniary compensation was also criticized because family members had to prove that their relatives had been killed or had gone missing as a result of persecution by the State. Thus, the burden of proof imposed on family members was seen as a restrictive and costly factor since, in practice, the adoption of the so-called "partial presumption of truth standard" required a robust body of evidence for a person to be included on the list of political dead and disappeared.[196] Finally, there was criticism that the law precluded other interested parties from applying for recognition of deaths and/or disappearances, as the restriction to family applicants reinforced the view that the victims' relatives were the only interested parties. Such a view denied the collective and public nature of the issue.[197]

Protests and demands for the revision of Law no. 9,140 (1995) were partly answered in 2002 and 2004,[198] with an amendment introduced by Law no. 10,536 (2002) extending the time period covered for claims (article 1). While the initial period covered was from September 2, 1961 to August 15, 1979 (the date on which the Amnesty Law came into force), the subsequent amendment extended the outer limit to October 5, 1988 (the date of the promulgation of the Federal Constitution). In addition, the period for submitting claims for reparations was reopened in 2002 for an additional 120 days, beginning in

---

[193] MEZAROBBA, Glenda, "Entre Reparações, Meias Verdades e Impunidade: O Difícil Rompimento Com o Legado da Ditadura no Brasil", *SUR – Revista Internacional de Direitos Humanos*, vol. 7/2010, pp. 7–25.

[194] For a detailed description of the critiques of Law no. 9,140 (1995), see: SANTOS, Cecília MacDowell; TELES, Edson and TELES, Janaína de Almeida (eds.), *Desarquivando a Ditadura: Memória e Justiça no Brasil*, vol. 1, São Paulo, Hucitec, 2009, pp. 33–34.

[195] *Special Commission on Political Deaths and Disappearances*, "Direito à Memória e à Verdade", Brasília, Secretaria Especial dos Direitos Humanis, 2007, p. 34–35.

[196] TORELLY, Marcelo D., "Das Comissões de Reparação à Comissão da Verdade: Contribuições da Comissão sobre Mortos e Desaparecidos Políticos (1995) e da Comissão de Anistia (2001) para a Comissão Nacional da Verdade", in TOSI, Giuseppe; FERREIRA, Lúcia de Fátima Guerra; TORELLY, Marcelo D. and ABRÃO, Paulo (eds.), *Justiça de Transição: Direito à Justiça, à Memória e à Verdade*, João Pessoa, Editora da UFPB, 2014, pp. 215–232.

[197] GALLO, Carlos Artur, "Do Luto à Luta: Um Estudo sobre a Comissão de Familiares de Mortos e Desaparecidos Políticos no Brasil", *Anos 90*, vol. 19/2012, pp. 323–355.

[198] *Special Commission on Political Deaths and Disappearances*, "Direito à Memória e à Verdade", Brasília, Secretaria Especial dos Direitos Humanos, 2007, p. 44.

August of that year. Later, in 2004, another amendment – Law no. 10,875 (2004) – clarified a misconception in the original text and made it possible to request pecuniary reparations for cases where victims (i) were killed on the street while marching or otherwise taking action against the regime;[199] (ii) committed suicide immediately before being arrested[200] or even after arrest, while being subjected to torture while in prison;[201] or (iii) committed suicide due to mental disorders resulting from the State's repressive actions (article 4). Moreover, for these more inclusive cases, the claims period was once again reopened for an additional 120 days starting in June 2004.

The SCPDD has a broad mandate: in addition to its efforts regarding pecuniary reparations, the Commission also has a project dedicated to the preservation of the history of those involved in opposition to the dictatorship regime, and to this end it has produced several publications over the years. The most famous of these,[202] from 2007, is the book *Direito à Memória e à Verdade: Comissão Especial de Mortos e Desaparecidos Políticos* (The Right to Memory and Truth: The Special Commission on Political Deaths and Disappearances), which not only reported on the activities of the Special Commission but also served to strengthen the process of reparations as a truth-telling and symbolic initiative.[203]

Later on, in 2009, the SCPDD released another two publications. The first one was named *Direito à Memória e à Verdade: Aos Descendentes de Homens e Mulheres que Cruzaram o Oceano à Bordo de Navios Negreiros e Foram Mortos na Luta contra o Regime Militar* (The Right to Memory and Truth: To Descendants of the Men and Women Who Crossed the Ocean aboard Slavery Ships and Were Killed in the Fight Against Military Rule). Written in the form of an obituary, it briefly reported on 40 cases of the killing and/or forced disappearance of Brazilians of African descent who were persecuted by the dictatorial regime in the context of armed urban guerilla groups and the *Araguaia Guerrilla* fighters.

Although it functioned as a tribute to those men and women of African descent, it did not go further than an individual honor or memorial; that is, it did not describe the problems faced by other side-lined stakeholders such

---

[199] As in the emblematic case of Carlos Marighella. See: *Special Commission on Political Deaths and Disappearances*, https://cemdp.sdh.gov.br/modules/desaparecidos/acervo/ficha/cid/191.

[200] As in the illustrative case of Iara Iavelberg. See: *Special Commission on Political Deaths and Disappearances*, https://cemdp.sdh.gov.br/modules/desaparecidos/acervo/ficha/cid/230.

[201] As in the representative case of Vladmir Herzog. See: *Special Commission on Political Deaths and Disappearances*, https://cemdp.sdh.gov.br/modules/desaparecidos/acervo/ficha/cid/330.

[202] BACOCCINA, Denize, "Livro Conta História Oficial de Vítimas do Regime Militar", *BBC Brasil*, August 29, 2007, https://www.bbc.com/portuguese/reporterbbc/story/2007/08/070829_vannuchi_db_ac.shtml.

[203] *Special Commission on Political Deaths and Disappearances*, "Direito à Memória e à Verdade", Brasília, Secretaria Especial dos Direitos Humanos, 2007, https://www.mdh.gov.br/biblioteca/memoria-e-verdade/direito-a-memoria-e-a-verdade-2013-comissao-especial-sobre-mortos-e-desaparecidos-politicos/view.

as the wider population of Afro-Brazilians, nor did it discuss the root causes of racism. Rather, it stated that the dictatorial regime did not initiate the persecution against the black movement in Brazil,[204] since the root causes of racism are linked to (i) slavery, (ii) colonialism, and (iii) the fallacious theory that Brazil is a racial democracy. That argument, the racial democracy thesis, asserts that the disproportionate impoverishment of Brazilians of African descent and their relative absence from elite groups is due to class rather than racial discrimination and the legacy of slavery, and argues that the absence of state-sponsored segregation in Brazil, including a history of miscegenation (interracial breeding) and social recognition of intermediate racial categories, has produced a "unique" racial order.[205] All together, the long history of slavery, colonialism and the racial democracy thesis help to explain why Brazil's racial inequalities have gone unchallenged for so long;[206] even though the dilemma of those citizens who are most affected is very well known and oft discussed,[207] racism – which is socially instilled and permeates all of Brazilian hierarchical society – has not disappeared and continues to be a problem, far from being solved.[208]

The structural racism which correlates with poverty, income distribution, education and inadequate housing, continues to be discussed[209] but it has not been fundamentally addressed in terms of Transitional Justice mechanisms. For instance, in a 2019 interview, a former commissioner of the NTC concluded that Brazil is still an authoritarian and racist country and argued that the triumph of democracy, beginning in 1985, has only been enjoyed by white citizens, since Brazilians of African descent do not yet enjoy the possible benefits of a

---

[204] *Truth Commission of the State of São Paulo*, Final Report, Volume I, Part II, "Perseguição à População e ao Movimento Negros", http://comissaodaverdade.al.sp.gov.br/relatorio/tomo-i/parte-ii-cap1.html, p. 11.

[205] FREYRE, Gilberto, *Casa-Grande e Senzala*, São Paulo, Global, 2006.

[206] HTUN, Mala, "From Racial Democracy to Affirmative Action: Changing State Policy on Race in Brazil", *Latin American Research Review*, vol. 39/2004, pp. 60–98.

[207] In 1994, scholar and former commissioner of the NTC, Professor Paulo Sérgio Pinheiro, mentioned that, in Brazil, it was never necessary to institutionalize legal *Apartheid* because, in addition to social and economic discrimination, petty authorities and the "do you know to whom you are speaking?" syndrome have always had a role in containing black and poor people in civil society. See: PINHEIRO, Paulo Sérgio, "The Legacy of Authoritarianism in Democratic Brazil", in NAGEL, Stuart S. (ed.), *Latin American Development and Public Policy*, New York, St. Martin Press, 1994.

[208] THEODORO, Mário (ed.), *Desigualdades Raciais, Racismo e Politicas Públicas: 120 Anos após a Abolição*, Brasília, Instituto de Pesquisa Econômica Aplicada (IPEA), 2008.

[209] It is recognized that there is an interconnection between racial inequalities and social inequalities or between problems of racism and poverty, and in fact, in Brazil, the majority of poor people are also citizens of African descent. See: THEODORO, Mário (ed.), *Desigualdades Raciais, Racismo e Politicas Públicas: 120 Anos após a Abolição*, Brasília, Instituto de Pesquisa Econômica Aplicada (IPEA), 2008, pp. 172–173.

return to the Rule of Law.[210] In addition, the São Paulo State Truth Commission mentioned that it would be very hard to measure the range of violations suffered by the Afro-Brazilian population during the dictatorship.[211] Clearly, torture of political prisoners is over, but the transition to a civilian government has not defeated racism, and democratic rights have not truly been incorporated into the lives of the majority of Afro-Brazilians.[212]

The second publication produced by the SCPDD in 2009 was a narrative compiling the cases of children and adolescents who were victims of the regime, mainly, because their parents were opponents of the dictatorship or they were protesting students. The book *Direito à Memória e à Verdade: História de Meninas e Meninos Marcados pela Ditadura* (The Right to Memory and Truth: Stories of Girls and Boys Marked by the Dictatorship)[213] sought to document cases in which children were illegally imprisoned together with their parents or situations in which babies were born in prison while their mothers were detained for political reasons. These narratives demonstrated that, beyond the physical repression (torture and ill-treatment), the opponents of the regime also had to deal with the intimidation and psychological torture brought on by the imprisonment and forced exile of their sons and daughters.

In fact, in 2009, when the book was published, there were no documented cases of the Brazilian authoritarian regime kidnapping children – although in Argentina and Uruguay this practice was widespread during their respective military dictatorships.[214] In the Brazilian case, stories of kidnapped children and babies started to be discussed and uncovered very recently, in 2019, with the report of 19 cases revealed through the efforts of a journalist.[215] This fact demonstrates that the above-mentioned publication of the SCPDD on children and young people merits a new edition and revision.

---

[210] CHADE, Jamil, "Interview with Paulo Sérgio Pinheiro: Conquista da Democracia Foi para Brancos", *UOL Notícias*, March 15, 2019, https://jamilchade.blogosfera.uol.com.br/2019/03/15/conquista-da-democracia-foi-para-os-brancos/.

[211] *Truth Commission of the State of São Paulo*, Final Report, Volume I, Part II, "Perseguição à População e ao Movimento Negros", http://comissaodaverdade.al.sp.gov.br/relatorio/tomo-i/parte-ii-cap1.html, pp. 1–2.

[212] THEODORO, Mário (ed.), *Desigualdades Raciais, Racismo e Politicas Públicas: 120 Anos após a Abolição*, Brasília, Instituto de Pesquisa Econômica Aplicada (IPEA), 2008.

[213] *Special Commission on Political Deaths and Disappearances*, "Direito à Memória e à Verdade: Histórias de Meninas e Meninos Marcados pela Ditadura", Brasília, Secretaria Especial dos Direitos Humanos, 2009, https://www.mdh.gov.br/biblioteca/memoria-e-verdade/direito-a-memoria-e-a-verdade-2013-historias-de-meninas-e-meninos-marcados-pela-ditadura/view.

[214] GANDSMAN, Ari Edward, "Retributive Justice, Public Intimacies and the Micropolitics of the Restitution of Kidnapped Children of the Disappeared in Argentina", *The International Journal of Transitional Justice*, vol. 6/2012, pp. 423–443.

[215] The case of 19 kidnappings of children carried out by agents of State during the dictatorship was only recently reported. See: REINA, Eduardo, *Cativeiro Sem Fim – As Histórias dos Bebês, Crianças e Adolescentes Sequestrados pela Ditadura Militar no Brasil*, São Paulo, Alameda, 2019.

Chapter 3. Victims' Reparations Program

With the goal of not only reporting the heroic attitudes of some individuals, but also to describe the strategies of resistance and survival of peasants who confronted the dictatorship, in 2010 the SCPDD published the book *Retrato da Repressão Política no Campo (1962–1985): Camponeses Torturados, Mortos e Desaparecidos* (Portrait of Political Repression in the Countryside (1962–1985): Tortured, Dead and Missing Peasants)[216] which detailed the almost unknown daily routine of repressive practices carried out against peasants and rural labor organizers in the countryside. One of the merits of the book is the recognition that long before 1964 and the *coup d'état*, the countryside of Brazil was already marked by violence, which presumably started in colonial times. Moreover, when compared with the previous initiatives, this narrative had the added benefit of not only an individual but also a collective dimension.[217]

Following this project of truth-telling and narratives, in 2010 the SCPDD supported the release of a book entitled *Luta, Substantivo Feminino* (Fight, a Feminine Noun),[218] which comprised the stories of the life and death of 45 Brazilian women who fought against the dictatorship, along with those of 27 women who survived that brutal cycle. Of course, the book did not include the stories of all of the women who died or were victims of torture in that period of political persecution, since it was restricted to the work of the SCPDD, but the aim of the publication was to at least clarify some of the cases and to avoid helping to perpetuate a culture of oblivion, especially with respect to the cases of rape and sexual violence committed against women. Indeed, the book highlights the fact that sexual subordination was a key aspect of their oppression. Nonetheless, if we think about Transitional Justice as a transformative initiative, we may find some fault with the book for disregarding violations of the victims' social and economic rights, as well as not mentioning the historical patterns of structural violence which women experienced on an everyday basis long before the *coup d'état* of 1964.[219]

In September 2006, the SCPDD started collecting blood samples from relatives of over 100 of those listed as victims in order to constitute a database of genetic profiles, which could facilitate the scientific identification of bones that had already been located (i.e. those found in the clandestine mass grave in the Perus Cemetery, São Paulo[220]), as well as other items that might eventually

---

[216] CARNEIRO, Ana and CIOCCARI, Marta, *Retrato da Repressão Política no Campo (1962–1985) – Camponeses Torturados, Mortos e Desaparecidos*, Brasília, MDA, 2010.
[217] CIOCCARI, Marta, "Narrativas da Repressão: Trabalhadores do Campo e das Minas durante o Regime Militar no Brasil", *Teoria e Cultura*, vol. 6/2011, pp. 25–44.
[218] *Memórias Reveladas*, Book "Luta Substantivo Feminino", 2010, www.memoriasreveladas.gov.br/administrator/components/com_simplefilemanager/uploads/5851a57ad9db10.32446106/livro_mulheres.pdf.
[219] For a more detailed description about "Luta Substantivo Feminino", see Chapter 8 of this book.
[220] The description of the secret mass grave of Perus in São Paulo is in Chapter 6 of this book.

be identified in the future.[221] In fact, the SCPDD also continues to collect information on the possible locations of other clandestine gravesites in large cities[222] and in the countryside, such as in the Araguaia region.[223] Recently, the SCPDD began a joint project with the International Commission on Missing Persons (ICMP), headquartered in Bosnia, where 350 samples of bones have already been sent, since the laboratory there specializes in DNA analysis and the identification of victims who disappeared in cases of armed conflict and in the context of human rights violations. In 2018, as a result of this joint work, two more disappeared victims of the dictatorial regime were identified.[224]

3.2. THE AMNESTY COMMISSION AND AMNESTY CARAVANS: COMPENSATION, REHABILITATION, ACKNOWLEDGMENT

As the measures implemented by the Law of Political Deaths and Disappearances, institutionalized in 1995, had only covered those victims directly affected by death and forced disappearance, in 2001,[225] a second state-sponsored reparations program was established: one whose goals were applicable to a larger group, including victims who survived torture sessions and illegal imprisonment and also those who suffered purges because of their political opposition to the regime.

Thus, the reparation measures implemented by the SCPDD are not the only ones that merit study in the Brazilian case: a few years later, a second commission was created with a different scope and approach to the commission initially

---

[221] *Special Commission on Political Deaths and Disappearances*, "Direito à Memória e à Verdade", Brasília, Secretaria Especial dos Direitos Humanos, 2007, pp. 46–47.
[222] Body remains were found in the cemetery Dom Bosco, in Perus, in the northern zone of São Paulo City, Brazil. In 1990, 1049 boxes of bones were found in a clandestine grave. Enemies of the military regime were buried there as indigents. Since then, laboratory tests have been performed by two Brazilian universities, as well as by the Forensic Medicine Institute (IML). A group of forensic anthropologists from the Federal University of São Paulo (Unifesp) and international experts analyzed 112 of the 1049 boxes of bones and concluded that the bones correspond to 139 people – 27, however, are not identifiable. See: GUIMARAES, Maria, "Uma Luta Contra o Desaparecimento", *Pesquisa Fapesp*, vol. 250/2016, pp. 76–81, http://revistapesquisa.fapesp.br/wp-content/uploads/2016/12/076-081_Perus_250.pdf?486959.
[223] In the early 1970s, the Brazilian Army arrested, tortured, and killed members of a guerrilla group located in the Araguaia River region. The fate of many of the guerrilla members still remains unknown.
[224] PAES, Caio de Freitas, "Como é Feito o Trabalho de Identificar Restos Mortais de Desaparecidos na Ditadura", *BBC Brasil*, December 3, 2018, https://www.bbc.com/portuguese/brasil-46429950.
[225] The Amnesty Commission was created on 28 August 2001, according to the Provisional Measure no. 2,151, under the administration of President Fernando Henrique Cardoso. Later, on 13 November 2002, the provisional measure was voted and approved by the National Congress and enacted as Law no. 10,559.

formed in 1995. This demonstrates that the Brazilian State has initially clearly chosen to offer Transitional Justice remedies only by means of administrative procedures. According to Torelly,[226] this administrative decision is justified primarily due to the difficulty of obtaining substantial evidence of past incidents, making it virtually impossible to obtain legal redress. In fact, as the standard of proof imposed by the Judiciary before providing redress is greater in the criminal system, that heightened degree of complexity might have made it even harder for victims to succeed had administrative procedures not been offered. In contrast to that heightened judicial standard, the Amnesty Commission apparently works with a presumption of the truthfulness of the allegations made by victims and/or their family members, and it considers that the information provided and the documents forwarded are true, except when there is enough evidence to prove otherwise.

To exemplify such interpretation, according to the administrative procedures of the Amnesty Commission, the request made by victims and/or their families shall be guided by the principles of informality, speed and reasonable duration (article 15 of the Amnesty Commission Internal Regulations – Ordinance No. 376, of March 27, 2019); also, although the application must contain the narrative of the facts and means of proof (article 17 of the same Regulations) such documents may be simple copies, without the need for authentication (article 16, third paragraph of the Regulations).

Secondly, the administrative process has a broader purpose than mere pecuniary reparations, and that is the goal of restoring a sense of belonging to the political community to victims and their families and of restoring their confidence in their own country. This would probably not be possible in the context of legal proceedings since a court case has characteristics that instinctively put the parties in opposition to each other, as if they were adversaries. In contrast, in the context of an administrative commission which has the goal of making reparations, the expectation is that victims are not in opposition to the State, but rather they are exercising their rights to reconciliation with the State and vice versa.

Thirdly, due to the fact that the Amnesty Law is still in force in Brazil, over the years the Judiciary has often been recalcitrant in relation to the discussion and acceptance of issues associated with the reparatory process for violations that occurred during the dictatorial period, notably the recognition that crimes against humanity were committed during that era and that crimes of forced disappearance should be considered as ongoing crimes until the whereabouts

---

[226] TORELLY, Marcelo D., "Das Comissões de Reparação à Comissão da Verdade: Contribuições da Comissão sobre Mortos e Desaparecidos Políticos (1995) e da Comissão de Anistia (2001) para a Comissão Nacional da Verdade", in TOSI, Giuseppe; FERREIRA, Lúcia de Fátima Guerra; TORELLY, Marcelo D.; and ABRÃO, Paulo (eds.), *Justiça de Transição: Direito à Justiça, à Memória e à Verdade*, João Pessoa, Editora da UFPB, 2014, pp. 215–232.

of the victims are known.[227] Thus, at least in the current judicial climate, an administrative process is better able to deal with the issue than the Judiciary itself.

Briefly, the difference between the two commissions is that the SCPDD aims to recognize people who were killed as a result of the State's repressive activities or who suffered forced disappearance as a consequence of their political actions in opposition to the dictatorship, as well as to locate their remains and to pay reparations (symbolic and pecuniary) to their families. In contrast, the Amnesty Commission seeks to extend pecuniary and symbolic reparations to people who were affected by other acts of the dictatorial regime, for example, the political purges in the public and private sector, forced exile and expulsion from educational institutions, among others. Thus, the focus of the SCPDD is more limited, while the objectives of the Amnesty Commission are broader.[228]

The creation of the Amnesty Commission was linked to the proposition in the 1988 Constitution of granting reparations to those who had been persecuted for their political activities during the authoritarian regime,[229] but this provision was not self-executing and required specific legislation detailing its conditions. As a result, it took around 14 years to achieve first the issuing of Provisional Measure no. 2,151 (2001), on August 28th of that year, and later the passage of Law no. 10,559 (2002), enacted on November 12th of the following year, which defined the stipulations of the program and granted the Amnesty Commission the power to operate as the agency responsible for remedying the persecutory acts committed between 1946 and 1988.

According to Law no. 10,559 (2002) and its accompanying regulations (Ordinance no. 376, issued on March 27, 2009), the Amnesty Commission is supposed to function as a council made up of at least nine commissioners (including at least two members representing organizations and associations of surviving victims and the relatives of the dead and disappeared and at least two more members from the Ministry of Defense),[230] and all of the members of the Commission are nominated by the Minister of Women, Family and Human Rights.[231] The commissioners have the power to conduct investigations, to

---

[227] For a relevant discussion about the position of the Judicial Power and the violation of human rights that occurred during the dictatorial period see Chapter 4 of this book.

[228] TORELLY, Marcelo D., "Das Comissões de Reparação à Comissão da Verdade: Contribuições da Comissão sobre Mortos e Desaparecidos Políticos (1995) e da Comissão de Anistia (2001) para a Comissão Nacional da Verdade", in TOSI, Giuseppe; Ferreira, Lúcia de Fátima Guerra; TORELLY, Marcelo D.; and ABRÃO, Paulo (eds.), *Justiça de Transição: Direito à Justiça, à Memória e à Verdade*, João Pessoa, Editora da UFPB, 2014, pp. 215–232.

[229] According to article 8 of the *Ato das Disposições Constitucionais Transitórias* (Transitional Constitutional Disposition Act), which is an Annex to the 1988 Federal Constitution.

[230] The number of commissioners has been recently modified to at least 9, according to Ordinance no. 376 of 27 March 2009. Before that, the number of commissioners was at least 20, divided into different working groups (Ordinance no. 29, of 15 January 2018).

[231] According to the Amnesty Commission's Regulations (Ordinance no. 376 of 27 March 2019).

Chapter 3. Victims' Reparations Program

request information and documents[232] and, consequently, to recommend the granting of pecuniary reparations, with the final decision will be taken by the Minister of Women, Family and Human Rights.[233]

It is worth mentioning that, as the Amnesty Commission has operated for almost 20 years, over this period there have been many changes of members, according to the different governments, ministries and political orientations that prevailed at various times in the Brazilian history[234] and such nominations have been even disputed in the courts.[235] And, in October 2019, a team (Task Force) of lawyers from the Federal Attorney General's Office was set up to provide legal advice and consultancy in relation to the administrative proceedings that are still awaiting decision.[236]

As has been mentioned previously, a person is authorized to receive pecuniary benefits only after his or her application has been totally verified and approved by the Amnesty Commission and the Minister of Women, Family and Human Rights. Thus, reparations claims are subject to the completion of a prior investigation into the surviving victim or his or her successors and heirs. Moreover, under the pecuniary reparations program there are two types of compensation (the granting of one automatically excludes the other). The first form is calculated based on how many years of discrimination, persecution or intimidation the person suffered, specifically in those cases in which the victim has no proof of his or her employment relationship during the period of political persecution. This form of compensation is limited to BRL 100,000 (around US$30,000 at time of writing).[237] The second form provides monthly payments for cases in which the victim has proved the existence of an employment relationship when the political persecution occurred that resulted in his or her dismissal. This is typical in the case of university professors, labor union activists and journalists.[238]

In this second case (where there is proof of a previous employment relationship), the victim receives a monthly wage as if he or she were exercising

---

[232] According to article 12, para. 3, of Law no. 10,559 (2002) (and its amendment made by Law no. 13,844 (2019)).
[233] According to article 10 of Law no. 10,559 (2002) and article 28 of Ordinance no. 376 of 27 March 2019.
[234] See: *Editorial J*, "Mudanças na Comissão de Anistia geram controvérsias – Governo Temer decide trocar integrantes da Comissão de Anistia e decisão gera críticas e questionamentos em relação aos novos membros membros do conselho", September 8, 2016, http://www.editorialj.eusoufamecos.net/site/noticias/acontece/controversia-comissao-anistia/.
[235] See: *Orzil*, "Justiça mantém nomeação de integrantes da Comissão de Anistia", November 18, 2020, https://www.orzil.org/noticias/justica-mantem-nomeacao-de-integrantes-da-comissao-de-anistia/.
[236] See: Joint Ordinance no. 01 of the Minister of Women, Family and Human Rights and of the Federal Attorney General's Office, dated November 3, 2019, https://www.in.gov.br/web/dou/-/portaria-conjunta-n-1-de-3-de-outubro-de-2019-219919395.
[237] According to article 4 of Law no. 10,559 (2002).
[238] According to articles 5, 6 and 7 of Law no. 10,559 (2002).

the relevant professional activity. In addition, this type of reparations scheme may result in the reinstatement of the professional in question in the case of government employees, evaluated on a case-by-case basis. Examples of this include diplomats and professors at public institutions who were dismissed because of their political involvement during the authoritarian regime. In these cases, those reinstated are also granted the promotions they would have otherwise received, and finally, such reinstated professionals also have the time during which they were forcibly excluded from employment recognized for retirement purposes (according to the rules of the public system of social security and retirement). Students who were forced out of institutions of higher learning due to their political activities and/or the repression they suffered during the authoritarian rule may also be readmitted to those courses.

Observing this specific set of reparations granted by the Amnesty Commission, Bohoslavsky and Torelly have remarked that the vast majority of payouts were to workers who had to abandon their jobs due to political persecution at work,[239] especially after the 1979 Amnesty Law, when labor unions joined the struggle against the dictatorship, provoking many strikes at the beginning of the 1980s. What most caught their attention was that Brazil adopted the so-called abstract responsibility model; that is, pecuniary reparations are paid with public funds. This means that, from a civil liability perspective, the State assumes full liability for the human rights abuses perpetrated by individuals (State agents) and, consequently, the individuals who carried out such acts (such as purges, retaliation, and persecution) are discharged of any personal liability.

In fact, it is undeniable that the pecuniary reparations made by the Amnesty Commission introduced a significant mechanism for State accountability. Nevertheless, the calculation formula that the program employs has been the target both of public criticism of the expenditure involved and of victim's groups on the other side. It has also been described as a "reduced private procedure" rather than constituting a collective and public setting for a mechanism of Transitional Justice. As a result, Mezarobba has even suggested that the victims' movement has lost the power to mobilize that it had when it first appeared during the pro-amnesty campaign of 1979.[240] The reparation program's calculation formula has provoked civil society complaints because it is based on the victim's professional status, resulting in huge amounts being paid to well-trained professionals and very little being offered to unskilled laborers, although they both experienced

---

[239] BOHOSLAVSKY, Juan Pablo and TORELLY, Marcelo D., "Financial Complicity: The Brazilian Dictatorship Under the Macroscope", in SHARP, D.N. (ed.), *Justice and Economic Violence in Transition* (Springer Series in Transitional Justice vol. 5), New York, Springer, 2014, pp. 233–262.

[240] MEZAROBBA, Glenda, *O Preço do Esquecimento: as Reparações Pagas às Vítimas do Regime Militar – uma Comparação entre Brasil, Argentina e Chile*, Ph.D. Thesis, Faculdade de Filosofia, Letras e Ciências Humanas, Universidade de São Paulo (USP), São Paulo, 2007.

the same sort of human rights violations. By way of example, a university professor who was tortured during the dictatorship would receive a much higher sum than a student who suffered the same level of persecution. Thus, as noted by Schneider,[241] this systemic imbalance has accentuated disparities between citizens in a society already suffering from historically high levels of inequality.

Exactly because of the way Law no. 10,559 (2002) was written and envisaged – that is, with a focus on labor relations and the workers who were harmed by the acts of the dictatorial regime – or because its major concerns were of an economic and legalistic nature, it ended up provoking tension between petitioners (victims and the related social movements), the government (the Amnesty Commission) and even other State agencies. Family members of victims and victims' rights movements have questioned the main economic emphasis of the program, which has acted to the detriment of broader issues such as the clarification of the deaths and forced disappearances and accountability for torturers. On the other hand, both the Federal Public Prosecutor's Office and the *Tribunal de Contas da União* (Federal Auditing Board) have regarded the pecuniary amounts being paid as too high relative to Brazilian living standards.[242]

Faced with this general strain of criticism that post-atrocities reparations in Brazil were a mere financial process,[243] around the year 2007 the Amnesty Commission entered a new phase in which it sought to demonstrate that the program had broader goals than merely granting monetary reparations, and would henceforth adopt moral and symbolic measures. These included victims receiving an official apology from the State for the human rights violations committed during the dictatorship, at a ceremony in which representatives of the Amnesty Commission publicly thanked survivors for their resistance and issued the apology.[244] This new approach of the Amnesty Commission follows the guidance adopted in the 2005 United Nations Resolution on "Basic Principles and Guidelines on the Right to a Remedy and Reparations for Victims of Gross Violations of International Human Rights Law and Serious Violations of International Humanitarian Law", which determined that victims of such crimes should be provided with full and effective reparation, including restitution, compensation, rehabilitation, satisfaction and guarantees of non-repetition.[245]

---

[241] SCHNEIDER, Nina, "Waiting for a Meaningful State Apology: Has Brazil Apologized for Authoritarian Repression?", *Journal of Human Rights*, vol. 13/2014, pp. 1–16.

[242] ROSITO, João Baptista Alvares and DAMO, Arlei Sander, "A Reparação por Perseguição Política e os Relatos de Violência nas Caravanas da Anistia", *Horizontes Antropológicos*, vol. 42/2014, pp. 181–212.

[243] MEZAROBBA, Glenda, *Um Acerto de Contas com o Futuro: a Anistia e suas Conseqüências: um Estudo do Caso Brasileiro*, São Paulo, Humanitas Fapesp, 2006.

[244] ABRÃO, Paulo and TORELLY, Marcelo D., "The Reparations Program as the Lynchpin of Transitional Justice in Brazil", in REÁTEGUI, Félix (ed.), *Transitional Justice: Handbook for Latin America*, New York, Ministry of Justice and International Center for Transitional Justice, 2011, pp. 443–485.

[245] United Nations General Assembly Resolution no. 60/147, December 16, 2005.

Therefore, the formal act of the State's apology, starting in 2007, attempted to correct a purely financial interpretation of the law. The Amnesty Commission's members at the time claimed that the Law did not represent the imposition of oblivion through the payment of a pecuniary compensation,[246] but rather the acknowledge of the errors committed by the State. As a result, they argued, the judgment of claims by the Amnesty Commission – and the symbolic granting of a certificate at public hearings (the so-called *declaração de anistiado político* or declaration of political amnesty) – should be seen as the legal materialization of that recognition by State authorities.

However, this form of public apology which the Amnesty Commission engaged in was not exempt from criticism. For instance, Schneider observed that that gesture did not have the same meaning as a public State apology issued by the President of Brazil,[247] since the status of the speaker offering the apology was a key factor. It was argued that the representatives of the Amnesty Commission, who formally apologized in the name of the State with all good intentions, held a very different status than that of the highest State official.

In 2007, however, there was a shift in the structure of the Amnesty Commission, as the Ministry of Justice, which coordinated the Commission at the time, was concerned with reviewing the amounts of the pecuniary grants, speeding up trials and creating a broad project that would contribute to structuring the memory of the dictatorship, mainly through educational initiatives. It was against this background that the so-called *Caravanas da Anistia* (Amnesty Caravans) emerged. These gatherings were an educational project which included public hearings in the exact places (cities and regions) where persecution had occurred.

In addition to judgment of claims on location, which until then had only take place in the capital, Brasília (at the headquarters of the Ministry of Justice), these Amnesty Caravans also offered a tribute to the victims and enabled them to present their public testimonies, narrating their experiences throughout the years of the dictatorship. As consequence, testimonies rendered before an audience composed of different sectors of society (State agents and civil society members) established the conditions for a public report about the suffering inflicted and the resulting psychological wounds. Such initiatives sought to extend the reparations program beyond its purely economic aspects.[248] In fact, this educational and symbolic project came into being at the very time when the

---

[246] ABRÃO, Paulo and TORELLY, Marcelo D., "Mutações do Conceito de Anistia na Justiça de Transição Brasileira – A Terceira Fase de Luta pela Anistia", *Revista de Direito Brasileira*, vol. 3/2012, pp. 357–379.

[247] SCHNEIDER, Nina, "Waiting for a Meaningful State Apology: Has Brazil Apologized for Authoritarian Repression?", *Journal of Human Rights*, vol. 13/2014, pp. 1–16.

[248] ROSITO, João Baptista Alvares and DAMO, Arlei Sander, "A Reparação por Perseguição Política e os Relatos de Violência nas Caravanas da Anistia", *Horizontes Antropológicos*, vol. 42/2014, pp. 181–212.

work of the Amnesty Commission was being highly scrutinized starting from very critical premises.[249] However, those critiques only focused on the amounts that were being paid and on the type of beneficiaries receiving such reparations (such as renowned intellectuals, journalists and politicians).[250] As a result, the Amnesty Caravans aimed to recall and clarify historical facts while at the same time restoring dignity to the victims and giving them back a voice.[251]

Indeed, Ryan[252] has observed that, through initiatives such as the Amnesty Caravans,[253] the Brazilian State has provided new spaces for discussion, debate and listening, providing previously marginalized individuals with a place to speak and to have their memories amplified and legitimized. Moreover, allowing for public discussion of the memory of torture has prompted a re-examination of the present, specifically the persistence of high levels of violence and impunity throughout Brazil's criminal justice system.[254]

Additionally, it is important to mention the so-called "Stamps of Memory" Project, which was created in 2008 to rescue the memory of victims through the construction of a collection of oral and audiovisual resources. This project emerged as an alternative to the concentration of memory initiatives only at the governmental level, since it funds some activities that are directly developed and executed by non-governmental, civil society groups. Such initiatives funded by the State gather testimonies, systematize information and foster cultural events that allow the wider society to become familiar with the past and to extract lessons for the future.

Since 2019, however, the Amnesty Commission has ceased to be an organization attached to the Ministry of Justice and has been overseen by the newly created Ministry of Women, Family and Human Rights. In addition, it has been subject to investigation by the State itself in order to reassess the reparations it has granted (since there are allegations that many monetary claims

---

[249] In early 2008 reparations were called *Bolsa Ditadura* in an allusion to the federal government endowment policy called *Bolsa Família*. See: CONJUR, "Bolsa-Ditadura – Considerado anistiado, Ziraldo É Indenizado em R$1 Milhão", April 4, 2008, https://www.conjur.com.br/2008-abr-04/considerado_anistiado_ziraldo_recebe_milhao.

[250] SEQUEIRA, Cláudio Dantas and VALENTE, Rubens, "Comissão Aprovou R$2,9 bi de Indenização à Anistiados", *Folha de São Paulo*, April 12, 2008, https://www1.folha.uol.com.br/fsp/brasil/fc1204200802.htm. GUERREIRO, Gabriela, "Comissão de Anistia Aprova Indenização para Ex-Ministro Nilmário Miranda e mais 11", *Folha de São Paulo*, September 26, 2008, https://m.folha.uol.com.br/poder/2008/09/449441-comissao-de-anistia-aprova-indenizacao-para-ex-ministro-nilmario-miranda-e-mais-11.shtml.

[251] *Amnesty Commission*, http://www.justica.gov.br/seus-direitos/anistia/projetos/projetos-de-memoria-e-reparacao#caravana.

[252] See RYAN, H.E., "From Absent to Present Pasts: Civil Society, Democracy and the Shifting Place of Memory in Brazil", *Journal of Civil Society*, vol. 12/2016, pp. 158–177.

[253] From 2007 to 2010, 47 Amnesty Caravans were held. See: Amnesty Commission Report, http://memorialanistia.org.br/boletim-informativo-da-comissao-de-anistia-mj/.

[254] On authoritarianism's legacies and the culture of impunity, see Chapter 5 of this book.

that were granted involved purely labor-related issues rather than any political persecution).[255] There is also criticism that the aforementioned Commission has spent a great deal of money on publishing books, educational projects,[256] and funding for the construction of a memorial.[257] The government's current view of the work of the Commission is to restrict it to the field of only pecuniary reparations, and ultimately to dismantle the organization on the grounds that, after almost 35 years of democracy, there is no more reason for its existence.[258]

According to a recent amendment to the Regulations of the Amnesty Commission, enacted via Ordinance no. 376, of March 27, 2019, it can be inferred that in the near future the focus of the Commission will return to its initial status, that is, that of merely granting pecuniary reparations. Although the Ordinance includes a generic reference to the fact that the Amnesty Commission has the power to formulate and promote actions and projects on reparations and memory (article 1, paragraph III), there are no following articles detailing how such public policies (identified as symbolic redress to victims) will be effectively implemented. Just to illustrate by comparison, in the previous Regulations (that have now been supplanted by the 2019 Ordinance),[259] the Amnesty Commission used to have a sector specialized in proposing and coordinating public policies related to memory. The projects conceived by that sector included the so-called

---

[255] Among the controversial cases whose payments were questioned by the Brazilian State itself (by the Federal Attorney General) and are awaiting judgment by the Federal Supreme Court there are approximately 3,000 former military personnel of the Brazilian Air Force (FAB). These claimants requested reparations on the grounds that they were expelled from the organization for participating in a military association that was considered banned under the dictatorial regime, while the state claims that their dismissal occurred due to the mere excess number or personnel. This amount of reparations, in current values, is around BRL 16 billion. See: *Revista Isto É*, "Exclusivo: A Farra das Indenizações", February 7, 2019, https://istoe.com.br/a-farra-das-indenizacoes/.

[256] See: *UOL Notícias*, "A Escolhida", March 8, 2019, https://noticias.uol.com.br/reportagens-especiais/entrevista-com-damares-alves-ministra-da-familia-mulher-e-direitos-humanos/index.htm#a-escolhida.

[257] Moral reparation has also been made through the creation of the "Memorial of Political Amnesty of Brazil". This place, which is under construction in the city of Belo Horizonte, State of Minas Gerais, will preserve the legacy and archives of the Amnesty Commission, serving as a symbolic instrument of moral and collective reparations. The renovation of the building that will host the collection has already consumed BRL 19 million, and has not yet been completed. Moreover, since 2017, the project has been the subject of investigations by the Federal Police for misappropriation of approximately BRL 4 million of public money. See: SOUZA, Marcos de Moura, "Desvio em Memorial da Anistia é de Pelo Menos R$4 milhões, Informa PF", *Jornal Valor Econômico*, December 6, 2017, https://www.valor.com.br/politica/5219871/desvio-em-memorial-da-anistia-e-de-pelo-menos-r-4-milhoes-informa-pf.

[258] VALENTE, Rubens and URIBE, Gustavo, "À Espera de Mudanças, Comissão de Anistia Paralisa Reuniões", *Folha de São Paulo*, February 18, 2019, https://www1.folha.uol.com.br/poder/2019/02/a-espera-de-mudancas-comissao-de-anistia-paralisa-reunioes.shtml.

[259] For the previous Regulations of the Amnesty Commission and the public policies of symbolic reparations see Ordinance no. 29 of January 15, 2018, arts. 25 and 26 and Ordinance no. 1,797, of October 30, 2007, article 5, item V and article 11, item V.

"Amnesty Caravans", the construction of monuments, documentary films, publications, the "Stamps of Memory" project, and also the strategy related to the mental health of victims (known as the "Witnesses' Clinics").

However, it is possible that this resumption of the purely financial aspect of reparations policy in Brazil will also reawaken the view of money as a nuisance or distraction. One notable expression of this view was when Clara Charf, the wife of Carlos Marighella (founder of the National Liberation Action and killed by agents of the State in 1969), upon receiving the Amnesty Commission indemnity, declared that money would not be the most important factor, but rather the publicity and disclosure of the facts of his death, as that would more certainly promote the policy of non-repetition.[260]

There is also the example of Argentina, where the issue of pecuniary reparations was central in dividing the Mothers of the Plaza de Mayo, in Buenos Aires, into two different organizations in the 1990s. One of the groups argued that claiming reparations should be optional and decided individually, while the other opposed it for all concerned as matter of principle. This division led Sveaass and Sonneland to conclude that, in the Argentinean case, mere economic reparation was problematic and contradictory.[261]

This is because a reparations program included as a Transitional Justice mechanism should not be merely framed as putting the victim back where he or she would have been if the offenses had not occurred (which is the classical view of reparations established in the local law of civil responsibility). This means that, in order to deal with the past atrocities committed during the dictatorship, reparations should not be simply backward-looking, as Roht-Arriaza comments,[262] but should also be balanced with a forward-looking stance. Such forward-oriented reparations serve a dual function as they aim to compensate victims for past losses but also to reintegrate those who were marginalized and isolated into a society that is also being rebuilt.

The same pattern was noted by Laplante when stating that Transitional Justice challenges the more traditional notions of corrective justice associated with a court calculating the amount of damages that a specific defendant owes for harm caused to an individual plaintiff.[263] Consequently, this backward-looking form

---

[260] Andrade, Claudia, "Companheira de Carlos Marighella Recebe Indenização do Governo", *UOL Notícias*, March 7, 2008, https://noticias.uol.com.br/ultnot/2008/03/07/ult23u1413.jhtm.

[261] SVEAASS, Nora and SONNELAND, Anne Margrethe, "Dealing with the Past: Survivors' Perspectives on Economic Reparations in Argentina", *International Perspectives in Psychology: Research, Practice, Consultation*, vol. 4/2015, pp. 223–238.

[262] ROHT-ARRIAZA, Naomi, "Reparations Decisions and Dilemas", *Hastings International and Comparative Law Review*, vol. 27/2004, pp. 157–219.

[263] "The Plural Justice Aims of Reparations", in BUCKLEY-ZISTEL, Susanne; BECK, Teresa Koloma; BRAUN, Christian and MIETH, Friederike (eds.), *Transitional Justice Theories*, New York, Routledge, 2014, pp. 66–84.

of redress usually consists of purely monetary compensation, but, when seen as a Transitional Justice mechanism instead, a reparations program is expected to do much more than simply seeking corrective justice.

Briefly, the future of the Amnesty Commission lies in the very understanding that, in addition to pecuniary amounts (or so-called monetary compensation), scholars have insisted on the recognition of a broad array of material reparations,[264] as well as more "symbolic" measures, including apologies and remembrance. In particular, the reparations program as a mechanism of Transitional Justice requires, as Gray has said,[265] adopting a Janus-like posture, simultaneously facing the past and the future, in order to correct and reshape the underlying causes of dictatorial abuses and their continuum within a democratic period.

According to data from 2019,[266] nearly 75,400 amnesty requests had been submitted, and nearly 62,800 cases had been decided, meaning that the Commission still has around 12,600 claims to verify. Of the cases already judged, the Commission has accepted 39,300 claims and denied 23,500. Also, it is important to remember that, in that universe of 39,300 accepted cases, nearly 25,000 persons were awarded pecuniary reparations (in the total amount of BRL 6.7 billion, from 2002 until December 2018) and the remaining claims refer to the expanded types of reparation offered by Law no. 10,559 (2002), such as reinstatement of the victim in their previous employment and inclusion of the excluded employment period in the pension calculation for retirement purposes.[267]

As the work of the Amnesty Commission is ongoing, there are not yet any systematic and consolidated records with details of the violations that have been identified, and, unfortunately, the poor data that has been published on the Commission's website cannot be further broken down year-by-year to determine the concentration of violations for certain periods of time.[268] However,

---

[264] VERDEJA, Ernesto, "A Normative Theory of Reparations in Transitional Democracies", *Metaphilosophy*, vol. 37/2006, pp. 449–468. RUBIO-MARÍN, Ruth and DE GREIFF, Pablo, "Women and Reparations", *The International Journal of Transitional Justice*, vol. 1/2007, pp. 318–337. LAPLANTE, Lisa J. and THEIDON, Kimberly, "Truth with Consequences: Justice and Reparations in Post-Truth Commission Peru", *Human Rights Quarterly*, vol. 29/2007, pp. 228–250.

[265] GRAY, David C., "A No-Excuse Approach to Transitional Justice: Reparations as Tools of Extraordinary Justice", *Washington University Law Review*, vol. 87/2010, pp. 1043–1103.

[266] *Revista Veja*, "Damares Critica Antecessores e Quer Agilizar Comissão de Anistia", May 22, 2019, https://veja.abril.com.br/politica/damares-critica-antecessores-e-quer-agilizar-comissao-de-anistia/.

[267] VALENTE, Rubens and URIBE, Gustavo, "À Espera de Mudanças, Comissão de Anistia Paralisa Reuniões", *Folha de São Paulo*, February 18, 2019, https://www1.folha.uol.com.br/poder/2019/02/a-espera-de-mudancas-comissao-de-anistia-paralisa-reunioes.shtml.

[268] *Amnesty Commission*, https://www.mdh.gov.br/navegue-por-temas/comissao-de-anistia-1/transparencia.

the empirical data on the age of applicants, together with the conclusions of preliminary studies already carried out,[269] may confirm that the vast majority of violations were concentrated in two periods of time: (i) while Institutional Act no. 5 (known by the acronym "AI-5" in Portuguese) was in force; and (ii) during the general strikes of the 1980s. The Act suspended civil rights and political freedoms from 1968 to 1979 when it was in effect and the latter coincided with the economic miracle, when several union leaders were persecuted.

There are expectations that the integration of the SCPDD data together with that of the Amnesty Commission may begin to provide a sense of the large scale of human rights violations perpetrated during the Brazilian dictatorship. As no data has been able to be cross-checked, the superficial reading that the Brazilian dictatorship was milder than those of neighboring countries persists. What remains to be observed and studied, as Bohoslavky and Torelly have mentioned,[270] is the fact that the Brazilian dictatorship just used other methods. Even if these did not necessarily come with the severity associated with killings and disappearances, they were nonetheless highly detrimental to human rights, especially the systematic and widespread practice of torture. From this perspective, recent discoveries related to the violations committed against rural peasants and indigenous populations may dramatically increase the total number of documented deaths and incidents of torture,[271] and may bring about a new analysis of the Brazilian case that is not centered only on the persecution of armed guerrillas and the official political opponents of the regime.

3.3. MONUMENTS, MEMORIALS AND COMMEMORATIVE PRACTICE

Another aspect of reparations is commemorative expressions, that is, the renaming of streets, roads, squares and public buildings; the construction of new museums and documentation centers; the identification and marking of sites remembering historical events; and the installation of memorials and monuments.

---

[269] Abrão, Paulo Abrão and Torelly, Marcelo, "The Reparations Program as the Lynchpin of Transitional Justice in Brazil", in Reátegui, Felix (ed.), *Transitional Justice – Handbook for Latin America*, Brasília/New York, Ministry of Justice and ICTJ, 2011, p. 443–485.

[270] Bohoslavsky, Juan Pablo and Torelly, Marcelo D., "Financial Complicity: The Brazilian Dictatorship Under the Macroscope", in Sharp, D.N. (ed.), *Justice and Economic Violence in Transition*, Springer Series in Transitional Justice vol. 5, New York, Springer, 2014, pp. 233–262.

[271] See "SDH identifica cerca de 1,2 mil camponeses mortos e desaparecidos entre 1961 e 1988", *Agência Brasil*, September 27, 2012, http://memoria.ebc.com.br/agenciabrasil/noticia/2012-09-27/sdh-identifica-cerca-de-12-mil-camponeses-mortos-e-desaparecidos-entre-1961-e-1988.

As Marschall has said,[272] monuments and statues are necessary to tell the other side of the story; to expose suppressed histories and preserve narratives of the past; to contradict biased interpretations, to praise the achievements of groups previously sidelined; and, lastly, to acknowledge suffering and pay tribute to individuals or groups who lost their lives through acts of resistance.

In the Brazilian case of Transitional Justice measures regarding these objectives we may cite, for instance, the SCPDD project known as *Lugares de Memória* (Sites of Memory),[273] in which that body seeks to locate and identify the spots where direct or indirect violations of human rights were perpetrated during the authoritarian regime, since many of these locations were secret and were not recognized as official buildings pertaining to the State. Such research has sought to relate the places of historical memory mostly to cases of dead or missing people, so that the same spot may be related to different people victimized by repression at different times from 1964–1985. In this case, the SCPDD initiative refers to a question of perception – similar to the initiatives which began at the end of World War II, when a new order of relations between History and Memory was revealed through the opening up of former concentration camps to visitation.[274] Those journeys of pilgrimage have constituted a further degree of empathetic travel or, as Miles put it,[275] a "darker tourism". Since then, understanding memory in the twentieth century has become an exercise in many fields of knowledge, as it involves the multiple facets of man and society when faced with technological change, the consequences of world wars and, later, the nuclear threat. Ultimately historians have become interested in everything that could allow man to acquire a more varied perception of himself and the legacy imposed on him by the past,[276] in both a collective and individual way.

It is not by chance that a deep interest in the issues of trauma and resentment emerged in this context, justified by the notion that feelings could also indicate a way of seeing and positioning ourselves in the world. Thus, History came to announce that the physical place itself – that is, the site where an incident took place – plays a role, and that it was imperative to think how the individual and collective experience located in those sites of memory would reveal itself to the citizen of the twentieth and the twenty-first century. What does make us what

---

[272] MARSCHALL, Sabine, *Landscape of Memory: Commemorative Monuments, Memorials and Public Statuary in Post-Apartheid South Africa*, Leiden, Brill, 2009.
[273] *Special Commission on Political Deaths and Disappearances*, http://cemdp.sdh.gov.br/modules/wfchannel/index.php?pagenum=14.
[274] TEKLIK, Joanna and MESNARD, Phillipe. "El Viaje a Auschwitz: Turismo de la Memoria o Turismo Cultural?", in FLEURY, Beatrice and JACQUES, Walter, *Memorias de la Piedra: Ensayos em Torno a Lugares de Detención y Massacre*, Buenos Aires, Ejercitar la Memoria, 2011.
[275] MILES, William F.S., "Auschwitz: Museum Interpretation and Darker Tourism", *Annals of Tourism Research*, vol. 29/2002, pp. 1175–1178.
[276] DURAN, Maria Renata da Cruz and BENTIVOGLIO, Julio, "Paul Ricoeur e o Lugar da Memória na Historiografia Contemporânea", *Dimensões*, vol. 30/2013, pp. 213–244.

we really are today and how might we comprehend those who lived and narrated life long before us? These are central questions when it comes to the analysis of sites of memory.

In the Brazilian case of recent times (the memories and experiences lived during the military dictatorship), the duty of Memory emerges as a task that compels the State and civil society to recognize the suffering imposed on particular population groups, especially in those episodes where the State was responsible for that suffering. Thus, those individuals who endured human rights violations under the military regime – who were persecuted, tortured or killed – appear as an expression of truth, as protagonists of traumatic experiences. Regarding this observation, Nora has commented that *Lieux de Memoire* (sites of memory) originated with the sense that there is no spontaneous memory; that we must deliberately create archives,[277] observe important dates, organize celebrations, pronounce tributes, and endorse statements because such activities no longer occur naturally. In this way, the truth of *Lieux de Memoire* is that without commemorative vigilance, History would soon sweep certain minorities away.

Even an apparently purely material site, like a street or a house, becomes a site of memory only if the imagination invests it with a symbolic aura or if it is subjected to ritual. In this regard, the SCPDD has been implementing a taskforce in order to recover, rethink and transmit certain traumatic past facts or processes to civil society by officially identifying and naming those sites related to the violations of human rights during the authoritarian regime. Up to the present date, the SCPDD has cataloged and recorded 222 sites of memory related to the Brazilian dictatorship in its database, including three outside of Brazil. Indeed, in going through the database it is possible to perceive how technology may assist the ritualistic and symbolic aspects of some locations, since the SCPDD has used a database of historical memory locations on its website and users are granted access to an App integrated with the Google Maps platform, allowing them to look for such places based on their geographical location on the map.[278] This initiative merits praise, as Haskins has observed,[279] as even permanent memorials and museums built with an eye to stimulating public engagement and their capacity to share memory work with ordinary people fade away in comparison with digital memorials and archives.

With similar objectives in mind, between 2012 and 2016 the Amnesty Commission worked in partnership with a civil society organization called

---

[277] NORA, Pierre, "Between Memory and History: Les Lieux de Mémoire", *Representations*, vol. 26/1989, pp. 7–24.

[278] *Special Commission on Political Deaths and Disappearances*, https://cemdp.sdh.gov.br/modules/lugares_memoria/search.php.

[279] HASKINS, Ekaterina, "Between Archive and Participation: Public Memory in a Digital Age", *Rhetoric Society Quarterly*, vol. 37/2007, pp. 401–422.

Agência Livre para a Informação, Cidadania e Educação – ALICE (Free Agency for Information, Citizenship and Education)[280] and subsidized the project *Trilhas da Anistia – Marcas de Caravanas e Recontes de Histórias* (Amnesty Trails – Caravan Marks and Storytelling), whose purpose was the creation of totems/landmarks in busy public locations, in the same cities where the Amnesty Caravans were held. Such markers could symbolize popular struggles against the excesses that provoked violations of human rights during the dictatorship.[281] Hence, in the context of this project, totems were installed in cities such as Belo Horizonte, São Paulo, Rio de Janeiro, Curitiba, Florianópolis, Ipatinga, Porto Alegre and Recife.[282]

This totems project – aimed at the remembrance of places where the Amnesty Caravans where held – reinforces what Jelin has articulated about territorial markers when she explains that,[283] just as there are significant dates, there are also significant sites and physical markers of the past. In fact, memorializing the sites of horror and repression by monuments and memorials, museums, plaques and commemorative inscriptions in institutions are all ways in which official and unofficial agents try to convey and materialize their memories, and these initiatives may function as a method for the intergenerational transmission of memories of historical continuities and discontinuities.

In Brazil, memorialization initiatives have taken a variety of forms, such as the transformation of jails used during the dictatorship into museums. One such initiative was the conversion of a warehouse and office of the Sorocabana Railway – later used by the São Paulo State Department of Political and Social Order (Deops/SP) to detain and interrogate prisoners considered subversive by the dictatorial regime – into *The Memorial of the Resistance*, where since 2009, following an initiative of the state of São Paulo, there has been a memorial dedicated to the preservation of the memories of political repression.[284] The Brazilian project is not an isolated case and follows interventions employed in the *Escuela de Mecánica de la Armada* (ESMA) in Argentina and the Robben Island Museum in South Africa, where, by using the architecture of a prison a public site of mourning and reconciliation was created.

---

[280] *Agência Livre para a Informação, Cidadania e Educação*, http://www.alice.org.br/quem-somos/.
[281] *Amnesty Commission*, https://www.justica.gov.br/seus-direitos/anistia/projetos/marcas-da-memoria-iii-2012.
[282] All totems were created by the artist Cristina Pozzobon and the architect Tiago Balem. See: RIBEIRO, Marcelle, "RJ: Inaugurado Momumento a Militares Cassados pela Ditadura", *Terra Notícias*, April 1, 2014, http://noticias.terra.com.br/brasil/cidades/rj-inaugurado-monumento-a-militares-cassados-pela-ditadura,b74d5c2347e15410VgnVCM5000009ccceb0aRCRD.html.
[283] JELIN, Elizabeth, "Public Memorialization in Perspective: Truth, Justice and Memory of Past Repression in the Southern Cone of South America", *The International Journal of Transitional Justice*, vol. 1/2007, pp. 138–156.
[284] SOUSA, Priscila Paula de, "Memória, Objetos e Edifícios. Uma Análise Arqueológica sobre o Edifício que Sediou o DEOPS/SP", *Revista de Arqueologia Pública*, vol. 10/2014, pp. 196–211.

Chapter 3. Victims' Reparations Program

Just to mention a few other initiatives,[285] in what by no means comprises a complete list, we may cite the following:

- a plaque installed in 2017 at the Dom Bosco Cemetery (located in São Paulo) to honor those opponents who were buried in the clandestine grave in Perus;[286]
- the marker located in the city of Salvador (state of Bahia), dated 2015, which lists the names of 32 people from the state of Bahia who were victims of oppression;[287]
- the monument located at the Ibirapuera Park (in the City of São Paulo) containing the names of the 434 persons who were identified as victims of the dictatorial regime by the NTC, and which was inaugurated in 2014;[288]
- the headstone installed in 2011 at the University of São Paulo in honor of students, professors and employees who were killed or disappeared during the dictatorship;[289]
- the monument dedicated to the dead and disappeared, installed in 2004 in the city of Goiânia (state of Goiás);[290] and
- the monument located in the city of Recife (state of Pernambuco) representing a man hung from a "macaw's perch" (a torture method), inaugurated in 1993.[291]

In particular the monuments located in the clandestine mass grave of Perus, Ibirapuera Park, the University of São Paulo (all in Sao Paulo) and in Salvador evoke the pioneering initiative of the *Vietnam Veterans' Memorial* in Washington,

---

[285] As noted here, the present overview of monuments and memorials is not intended to be exhaustive, but instead seeks to illustrate the range and types of memorialization practices in the Brazilian scenario for Transitional Justice.
[286] Cruz, Elaine Patrícia, "Placa Instalada no Cemitério de Perus Lembra Mortos durante a Ditadura Militar", *Agência Brasil*, September 4, 2017, http://agenciabrasil.ebc.com.br/direitos-humanos/noticia/2017-09/placa-instalada-no-cemiterio-de-perus-lembra-mortos-durante.
[287] França, Patrícia, "Salvador Recebe Monumento a Mortos na Ditadura Militar", *A Tarde*, August 25, 2015, https://atarde.uol.com.br/politica/noticias/1707620-salvador-recebe-monumento-a-mortos-na-ditadura-militar.
[288] Prado, Carol, "Monumento com Nomes de Mortos na Ditadura é Inaugurado no Ibirapuera", *Folha de São Paulo*, December 8, 2014, https://www1.folha.uol.com.br/poder/2014/12/1559332-monumento-com-nomes-de-mortos-na-ditadura-e-inaugurado-no-ibirapuera.shtml.
[289] Cristina, Ane, "Memorial Relembra membros da USP Vítimas da Ditadura Militar", *Jornal da USP*, January 10, 2018, https://jornal.usp.br/cultura/memorial-da-ditadura-e-o-esquecimento-do-passado/.
[290] *Goiânia Municipality*, "Prefeitura Revitaliza Monumento aos Mortos e Desaparecidos na Luta contra a Ditadura Militar", February 18, 2016, http://www4.goiania.go.gov.br/portal/pagina/?pagina=noticias&s=1&tt=not&cd=9346&fn=true.
[291] Moura, Márcio Cabral de, "Monumento contra Tortura", *Memórias da Ditadura*, http://memoriasdaditadura.org.br/combate-a-tortura/5846575298_059d6d142e_b/.

D.C and later replicated in memorials sites such as the *Wall of Names* (in Srebrenica/Bosnia and Herzegovina) or the *Villa Grimaldi Memorial* (in Chile); that is, the strategy of naming names on a public marker and the statement that everyone deserves equal recognition. In contrast, the monuments in Recife and Goiânia recall the representation of a heroic stance or the heroic acts of fallen "soldiers" and the suffering of the families. The great challenge in all cases is how to create and use memorials not only to commemorate victims, but also to stimulate a dialogue about the past. Gravestones, sculptures, markers and any other form of artistic representation are intended to provoke a sensation of unease, instability and solitude in visitors, inducing introspection, but also to surprise and even disturb viewers.[292]

The so-called rituals of remembrance are also mentioned by Jelin as a part of the construction of the symbols of the nation whereby the collective past is brought to the present and whereby people are faced with the reality of disturbing feelings,[293] including asking themselves how deadly repression could have coexisted with normal and undisturbed everyday life. Other initiatives related to memory and markers may also be seen in the Brazilian case of Transitional Justice, in the educational project of the Amnesty Commission and in the abovementioned "Amnesty Caravans". Such projects may be categorized as "outreach programs", as defined by Ramírez-Barat,[294] since the caravans included a set of tools and strategies in order to build direct channels of communication with civil society and to promote an open dialogue.

Ultimately, the Amnesty Caravans project has not only raised awareness, but also contributed to the legitimacy of the Brazilian Transitional Justice initiative. In this case, the importance of the Amnesty Caravans as a ritual and a marker resides in what Hamber previously noticed;[295] that is, for any reparations program to be successful, ongoing space has to be provided for victims to express their feelings of sadness and rage as they struggle to come to terms with the psychological and emotional impact of their loss, because indisputable reparation does not occur simply through the delivery of an object (such as a pecuniary amount or a grave marker), but through the very process that takes place around such an object. In fact, it is how each individual processes the symbolic meaning of reparations

---

[292] BRETT, Sebastian; BICKFORD, Louis; SEVCENKO, Liz; and RIOS, Marcela, *Memorialization and Democracy: State Policy and Civic Action*, New York, International Center for Transitional Justice, 2007.

[293] JELIN, Elizabeth, "Public Memorialization in Perspective: Truth, Justice and Memory of Past Repression in the Southern Cone of South America", *The International Journal of Transitional Justice*, vol. 1/2007, pp. 138–156.

[294] RAMÍREZ-BARAT, Clara, "Transitional Justice and the Public Sphere", in RAMÍREZ-BARAT, Clara (ed.), *Transitional Justice, Culture, and Society Beyond Outreach*, New York, International Center for Transitional Justice and Social Science Research Council, 2014, pp. 27–45.

[295] HAMBER, Brandon, "Repairing the Irreparable: Dealing with the Double-Binds of Making Reparations for Crimes of the Past", *Ethnicity and Health*, vol. 5/2000, pp. 215–226.

that is significant. For this reason, rituals like those which the Amnesty Caravans engaged in, where there was a space for surviving victims to air their complaints, should be seen as a vital factor in the Brazilian reparations program.

Finally, another field of struggle in settling accounts with the past refers to archives and the preservation of documentation. In the Brazilian case, this should be the role of the *Memorial da Anistia Política do Brasil* (Memorial of Political Amnesty in Brazil), which was under construction as a joint venture of the Brazilian State (the Amnesty Commission), the *Universidade Federal de Minas Gerais* (Federal University of Minas Gerais) and the City of Belo Horizonte (in the state of Minas Gerais). However, it was suspended in 2019,[296] mainly due to an 2017 investigation conducted by the Federal Police, under the allegation of corruption and deviation of public funds in the memorial's construction,[297] and at the present time such suspension is still pending a judicial decision.[298] The expectation is that the proposed memorial should function as the archives of the work developed by the Amnesty Commission – and, as Jelin has said,[299] the whole of range of documents referring to the repressive activities of the dictatorial regime are highly significant, insofar as they are taken as unquestioned evidence of State-sponsored institutional practices – but there are still doubts about the conclusion of such project.

Considering that more than 30 years have passed since the beginning of democratic rule in Brazil and, until now, no national memorial, either sponsored by state governments or federal government, has been inaugurated demonstrates that governments over the years usually have had political priorities they consider more urgent and demanding than their debt to survivors of past atrocities. As has been described by Brett, Bickford, Sevcenko and Rios,[300] governments are often bent on creating political alliances that permit governability and avoid disruptive conflict that might weaken the consolidation of democracy.

---

[296] See: *Hoje em Dia*, "Damares cancela a construção de Memorial da Anistia e diz que prédio deve ter outra função", August 13, 2019, https://www.hojeemdia.com.br/primeiro-plano/damares-cancela-a-constru%C3%A7%C3%A3o-de-memorial-da-anistia-e-diz-que-pr%C3%A9dio-deve-ter-outra-fun%C3%A7%C3%A3o-1.735117.

[297] See: *Agência Brasil*, "PF investiga desvio de recursos para Memorial da Anistia Política", December 6, 2017, https://agenciabrasil.ebc.com.br/politica/noticia/2017-12/pf-investiga-desvio-de-recursos-para-memorial-da-anistia-politica.

[298] See: *Ministério Público Federal*, "MPF entra na Justiça para obrigar União a concluir construção do Memorial da Anistia Política", http://pfdc.pgr.mpf.mp.br/informativos/edicoes-2019/outubro/mpf-entra-na-justica-para-obrigar-uniao-a-concluir-construcao-do-memorial-da-anistia-politica/.

[299] JELIN, Elizabeth, "Public Memorialization in Perspective: Truth, Justice and Memory of Past Repression in the Southern Cone of South America", *The International Journal of Transitional Justice*, vol. 1/2007, pp. 138–156.

[300] BRETT, Sebastian; BICKFORD, Louis; SEVCENKO, Liz; and RIOS, Marcela, *Memorialization and Democracy: State Policy and Civic Action*, New York, International Center for Transitional Justice, 2007.

As matter of fact, there always is the great compulsion to accept the pressure to merely turn the page on the past. Or, as Marschall has commented,[301] a less hurried or longer-term approach to the transformation of the official memory landscape demonstrates that the psychological need for monuments and memorials has been taken into account. Memorialization is frequently seen as a part of the desire for healing and establishing the truth, because commemoration involves the development of a coherent narrative which helps people to understand what happened and to come to terms with the past. However, the risk of following this strategy is that from time to time memories will resurface and abruptly re-open old wounds, putting the past back on the front pages of the news, as has recently been occurring in Brazil.[302] This has set off a phase where public policies are clearly intended to erase, forget and once again drive underground the disturbing truth.[303]

Moreover, it is worth mentioning that sites of memory are vehicles for the transmission of the "Never More" or "Never Again" ideal and symbolize the importance of democratic values and unconditional respect for human rights under the Democratic Rule of Law.[304] Thus memorials, museums and other sites of memory must be understood not only as art objects, but also as democratic spaces which are foundational to a healthy democracy.[305] In this context, they are sites for democratic action and not static representations of national identity. Therefore, the elements that refer to everything that must not be repeated should be preserved in order to stimulate debate, rather than only encourage remembering the injustices endured by victims. As a result, they may also help people to think critically about how the abuses came about and what forces within their own society allowed oppression to grow.

In addition to the elapse of time since the first transitional years and the existence of fewer memorialization practices in Brazil, even the public reception of such sites of conscience and memory remains a neglected aspect of

---

[301] MARSCHALL, Sabine, *Landscape of Memory: Commemorative Monuments, Memorials and Public Statuary in Post-Apartheid South Africa*, Leiden, Brill, 2009.

[302] MARGOLIS, Mac, "Bolsonaro Celebrates a Coup Brazilians Want to Forget", *Bloomberg*, March 31, 2019, https://www.bloomberg.com/opinion/articles/2019-03-31/bolsonaro-celebrates-a-1964-coup-brazilians-want-to-forget. STARGARDTER, Gabriel, 'Brazil Prosecutor Opposes President on Commemoration of Coup", *Reuters*, March 27 2019, https://www.reuters.com/article/us-brazil-politics-military/brazil-prosecutor-opposes-president-on-commemoration-of-coup-idUSKCN1R8001.

[303] MURAKAWA, Fabio and ARAÚJO, Carla, "Vélez Quer Alterar Livros Didáticos para Resgatar Visão sobre o Golpe", *Valor Econômico*, April 3, 2019, https://www.valor.com.br/politica/6195975/velez-quer-alterar-livros-didaticos-para-resgatar-visao-sobre-golpe.

[304] SOARES, Inês Virgínia Prado and QUINALHA, Renan Honório, "A Memória e Seus Abrigos: Considerações sobre os Lugares de Memória e seus Valores de Referência", *Revista Anistia Política e Justiça de Transição*, vol. 4/2010, pp. 250–279.

[305] BRETT, Sebastian; BICKFORD, Louis; SEVCENKO, Liz; and RIOS, Marcela, *Memorialization and Democracy: State Policy and Civic Action*, New York, International Center for Transitional Justice, 2007.

Transitional Justice initiatives. Namely, one thing that is important but has been overlooked in the country is the role of tourism in this entire process. As Light and Young[306] have commented, memorial museums are intended to be visited (and as such they function as visitor attractions, even if their subject matter is far from attractive or even dark[307]). Indeed, some of the visitors for the future to the *Memorial da Anistia Política do Brasil* will be children and young people, studying the dictatorial period as part of their educational curriculum, or people visiting the place during their leisure time and vacation. Therefore, it is expected that such sites may be used as a way of telling visitors the story of what Brazilians lived through and the events that shaped them as a society, while at the same time it will also be a way of affirming a commitment to the democratic agenda.

What remains to be further explored in the Brazilian Transitional Justice experience with regard to memorialization practices and sites of memory is how curators might ask visitors to think about how knowledge is constructed by the very audience in a public arena. As established by Crane,[308] a memorial must challenge visitor expectations, and therefore the memories associated with the lives which others lived in the past. The future exhibitions of the *Memorial da Anistia Política do Brasil* should offer visitors the opportunity to create new meanings for themselves, since at stake will be the trustworthiness of the museum as a memory institution and a site of conscience. At the end of the tour, visitors should be able to deeply interrogate themselves and ask themselves: did this museum mess with my mind?

As a consequence, museum experiences instruct us in social codes of behavior, condition a sense of cultural literacy, and instill appreciation for art, the past and science. Even more, according to Catela,[309] in these situations what is at stake is the exact role that sites of memory play as producers of political meaning, symbols and signifiers in the public space. But since initiatives in memorialization practices related to the dictatorship in the Brazilian context are still fresh (i.e. The Memorial of the Resistance in São Paulo (*Memorial da Resistência de São Paulo*) was inaugurated in 2009 and the plaque in Ibirapuera Park was installed in 2014) or not even open yet (i.e. *The Memorial da Anistia Política do Brasil* in Belo Horizonte) no direct inferences are possible, even from the use of guestbooks for feedback and documentation and studies of museum attendance and educational projects.

---

[306] LIGHT, Duncan and YOUNG, Craig, "Public Memory, Commemoration and Transitional Justice: Reconfiguring the Past in Public Space", in STAN, Lavinia and NEDELSKY, Nadya (eds.), *Post-Communist Transitional Justice: Lessons from 25 Years of Experience*, Cambridge, Cambridge University Press, 2015, pp. 233–251.

[307] MILES, William F.S., "Auschwitz: Museum Interpretation and Darker Tourism", *Annals of Tourism Research*, vol. 29/2002, pp. 1175–1178.

[308] CRANE, Susan, "Memory, Distortion and History in the Museum", *History and Theory*, vol. 36/1997, pp. 44–63.

[309] CATELA, Ludmila da Silva, "Staged Memories: Conflicts and Tensions in Argentine Public Memory Sites", *Memory Studies*, vol. 8/2014, pp. 9–21.

3.4. CONCLUSIONS

While analyzing the reparations program in South Africa, Hamber commented that no matter how well-meaning,[310] all reparations strategies face the same, albeit obvious, intractable problem: acknowledgement, apology, recognition and even substantial material assistance can never bring back the dead or be guaranteed to address and ameliorate all the levels of psychological pain suffered by survivors. Indeed, this standpoint immediately reminds us of Emily Dickson's poem "Compensation" that introduced this chapter. Thus, in the case of the Brazilian reparations program as well, the truth is that reparations are a double-edged sword: symbolic acknowledgement and pecuniary compensation can be valuable, but they can never wholly meet all the psychological needs of victims and survivors of a repressive regime. The result is that Brazil has lived with reparations policies for a long time, and they still remain a site of social and personal struggles.

From the early stages of both the SCPDD and the Amnesty Commission, their members and collaborators realized that pecuniary reparations would leave the effects of human rights violations committed during the dictatorial regime simply unrepaired. As Bernstein has said,[311] merely pecuniary reparations do not take recipients back to an idyllic past where they were safe from large-scale horrific wrongdoing. They provide no truth-telling or guarantees of non-recurrence; nor do they ensure the kind of government and civil society that could defend themselves against any wrongdoing before it even occurs. Consequently, the initiatives based on symbolical reparations later implemented by the SCPDD and the Amnesty Commission listed above merit genuine praise as a transitional moment for both institutions.

Since reparations programs themselves are not a natural fact, both commissions have faced dissent and criticism, not only from the families and relatives of the dead and disappeared, but also from wider civil society and from within the different political administrations over these years. Moreover, commissioners of both reparations programs have consistently acknowledged that the effective exercise of reparations and memorialization is not just about paying pecuniary amounts, including a celebration day in the official calendar, publishing reports and books, creating documentary films, building memorials and archives or even assembling a monument to the victims; rather, as Soares

---

[310] HAMBAER, Brandon, "Repairing the Irreparable: Dealing with the Double-Binds of Making Reparations for Crimes of the Past", *Ethnicity and Health*, vol. 5/2000, pp. 215–226.

[311] BERNSTEIN, Anita, "Pecuniary Reparations Following National Crisis: A Convergence of Tort Theory Microfinance, and Gender Equality", *University of Pennsylvannia Journal of International Law*, vol. 31/2009, pp. 1–51.

and Quinalha have stated,[312] it is the *combination* of these diverse initiatives, collections and places that enhances the unique action of each one of them, constituting a map or a landscape of memory capable of enriching attitudes in the current democratic context and providing a mirror for a future intergenerational perspective.

Despite the efforts that have been made – to overcome societal skepticism, to deal with a lack of funds to maintain educational projects and to identify missing persons and body remains, to carry on through corruption scandals related to the unfinished construction of a national memorial, as well as any number of additional adversities – there is always the question of what can be considered "success" in the area of reparations and memorialization and the State's role in providing public funds and resources for the expression and exteriorization of private grief and suffering. Any analysis couched in terms of accomplishments, as previously perceived by Hite and Collins in commenting on the Chilean case,[313] must not be simplistic and must always note the desire of the State to take a more active role.

In fact, the results of reparations programs and memorialization efforts in Brazil that this chapter has examined in the context of Transitional Justice measures have so far been rather encouraging. Nevertheless, all these initiatives do not leave the observer free from mixed emotions, since the past they seek to refer to and the meaning they seek to establish are not without controversy and commonly give rise to efforts to promote a supposedly unique interpretation of the past. These ambiguous feelings are further stoked by the 2019, 2020 and 2021 proposals to celebrate the *coup d'état* of 1964 as a "democratic revolution" that saved Brazil from communism, rather than an event that gave rise to a regime that restricted fundamental rights, systematically repressed political dissidence and, under the Cold War rhetoric of anti-communism, eliminated democracy for 21 years in Brazil.[314] It was only some days later – due to local[315]

---

[312] SOARES, Inês Virgínia Prado and QUINALHA, Renan Honório, "A Memória e Seus Abrigos: Considerações sobre os Lugares de Memória e seus Valores de Referência", *Revista da Anistia Política e Justiça de Transição*, vol. 4/2010, pp. 250–279.

[313] HITE, Katherine and COLLINS, Cath, "Memorials Fragments, Monumental Silences and Reawakenings in 21st-Century Chile", *Millennium Journal of International Studies*, vol. 38/2009, pp. 379–400.

[314] PHILLIPS, Dom, "Fury as Bolsonaro Orders Brazil Army to Mark the 55th Anniversary of Military Coup", *The Guardian*, March 27, 2019, https://www.theguardian.com/world/2019/mar/27/brazil-bolsonaro-military-coup-1964. AUGUSTO, Otávio, "Bolsonaro comemora golpe militar de 1964: Dia da Liberdade", *Metropolis*, March 31, 2020, https://www.metropoles.com/brasil/politica-brasil/bolsonaro-comemora-golpe-militar-de-1964-dia-da-liberdade. MAGENTA, Matheus, "Golpe de 1964: novo ministro da Defesa fala em celebrar aniversário 'no contexto histórico' – mas qual é este contexto?", *BBC News*, March 31, 2021, https://www.bbc.com/portuguese/brasil-56591969.

[315] *France 24*, "Bolsonaro's Call to Celebrate Coup Anniversary Triggers Brazil Protests", https://www.france24.com/en/20190401-bolsonaro-coup-anniversary-brazil-protest-dictator.

and international[316] pressure – that that suggestion was reframed by stating that the event should be "remembered" rather than "celebrated".[317]

Moreover, the description of initiatives concerning memorialization practices under the coordination of the SCPDD and the Amnesty Commission confirmed the use of symbolic acts in order to establish and assert democratic values within society, but also as policies to come to terms with previously denied and shameful aspects of the country's past. However, it should be taken into consideration that the negotiated transition of power which occurred in Brazil[318] kept the country in persistent continuity with the old order, which is more striking than the efforts towards Transitional Justice measures that have been implemented so far. Perhaps because of this spirit of negotiated transition, post-dictatorial governments have largely refrained from radical measures such as changing the names of streets, roads, public buildings and squares which still serve as representations of the old order,[319] thus confirming that the tendency to sanitize history and suppress unwanted memories is still common in Brazil. But, as Marschall reminds us,[320] memorialization practices always empower some and simultaneously disempower others.

Another point of significant praise is the initiative of the Amnesty Commission to fund and promote activities led by civil society organizations and individuals interested in coordinating projects implementing the truth-telling and remembering pillar of Transitional Justice (the Stamps of Memory Project), mainly, because it avoids the repetition of merely top-down initiatives, and also because, in Brazil, the government tends to assume a strong paternalistic role.[321] Here government officials see themselves as public representatives who must develop strategies on behalf of the people who elected them, in a context where the majority of the population strongly relies on the government to provide development and services and where individuals often lack the capacity and experience to actively participate in the decision-making processes and especially to take the initiative and follow through with the implementation of projects.

---

[316] United Nations Human Rights Office of the High Commissioner, "Brazil Must Reconsider Plan to Celebrate Military Coup Anniversary, says UN Expert", https://www.ohchr.org/EN/NewsEvents/Pages/DisplayNews.aspx?NewsID=24431&LangID=E.

[317] Deustche Welle, "Bolsonaro diz que Ordenou Rememorar Golpe de 1964, Não Comemorar", https://www.dw.com/pt-br/bolsonaro-diz-que-ordenou-rememorar-golpe-de-1964-n%C3%A3o-comemorar/a-48107395.

[318] For details concerning the negotiated transition to democracy see Chapters 1 and 2 of this book.

[319] Mello, Daniel, "Mesmo Após Debates, SP Mantém Nomes de Ruas que Lembram Agentes da Ditadura", Agência Brasil, September 9, 2017, http://agenciabrasil.ebc.com.br/direitos-humanos/noticia/2017-09/mesmo-apos-debates-sp-mantem-nomes-de-ruas-que-lembram-agentes-da.

[320] Marschall, Sabine, Landscape of Memory: Commemorative Monuments, Memorials and Public Statuary in Post-Apartheid South Africa, Leiden, Brill, 2009.

[321] Andrade, Regis de Castro, "Política e Pobreza no Brasil", Lua Nova, vol. 19/1989, pp. 107–121.

Thus, the Stamps of Memory Project must constantly struggle against the paternalistic role of the State as it encourages the exercise of authority arising from civil society itself. Nevertheless, the proliferation of such initiatives and the desirable growing contribution of civil society and corporations[322] are contingent on economic growth and more widespread prosperity among the Brazilian population, as well as on capacity-building, a strengthening of civil society and a firm entrenchment of the democratic order within the country. It is also dependent on a truly shared identification with the very concepts of Transitional Justice measures as lasting, solid proposals towards a consolidated democracy with more widespread social identification with the factual narrative of what actually occurred during the dictatorial regime. This book argues that, at the moment, such a democracy and social identification are not yet prevalent in Brazilian society.[323] Thus, in a context where the vision of a democratic nation still clashes with the reality of continuity with an authoritarian past and where denials and revisionism with respect to human rights violations during the dictatorship persist, how successful this strategy is likely to be remains to be seen.

---

[322] For initiatives of private actors and corporations, see the case of *Volkswagen do Brasil* in Chapter 9 of this book.

[323] For a detailed description of the role of civil society in the Brazilian transition to democracy, see Chapter 6 of this book.

CHAPTER 4
CRIMINAL JUSTICE AND JUDICIAL ACCOUNTABILITY

Except for the reparations programs which assisted some of the victims, after 1985 the transition scenario in Brazil remained unchanged for more the 20 years. In fact, although victims and family members of the disappeared never ceased to discuss the topic,[324] it was only at the beginning of 2010 that the societal debate regarding the right to truth and memory made a return, reinforcing the theory that reluctance pervades the local experience with Transitional Justice. The proof of this uncertain process is in the decisions in two cases, filed in different judicial levels, had opposite outcomes. These cases were (i) *Gomes Lund et al. (Guerrilha do Araguaia) v. Brazil* (the *Araguaia Case*), under the jurisdiction of the Inter-American Court on Human Rights (IACtHR), decided on November 24, 2010, and (ii) *Allegation of Disobedience of a Fundamental Precept (Argüição de Descumprimento de Preceito Fundamental* – ADFP*) no. 153*, filed by the Federal Council of the Brazilian Bar Association of Brazil (*Ordem dos Advogados do Brasil* – OAB) in the Brazilian Federal Supreme Court (*Supremo Tribunal Federal* – STF), decided on April 28, 2010. The following analysis of both cases is useful to forming a broad view of the judicial pillar of Transitional Justice in the Brazilian experience.

4.1. NATIONAL TRIALS

4.1.1. THE STF'S JUDGMENT ON THE LEGALITY OF THE 1979 AMNESTY LAW: CONTINUITY WITH THE PAST

Under Brazilian law,[325] the STF has the power to rule on the constitutionality of any statutes. In light of this authority, the Federal Council of the OAB challenged the legitimacy of the Brazilian Amnesty Law, Law no. 6,683 (1979),[326] in a case known as *ADFP no. 153*. In that case, the initial petition requested that the

---

[324] For further explanations, see Chapter 6 of this book.
[325] Art. 102, para. 1, of the 1988 Federal Constitution and Law no. 9,882 (1999).
[326] For information about the scope of the Brazilian Amnesty Law, see Chapter 2 of this book.

STF declare that amnesty granted under the law should not extend to crimes committed by agents of the State against political opponents. In the Brazilian legal system, a reporting judge (or justice in the higher courts) drafts an opinion which the other members of the court either follow or reject. In *ADFP no. 153*, the reporting justice ruled that the Amnesty Law was in compliance with the Constitution and rejected the plaintiff's claims, a ruling which the majority endorsed by a vote of 7 to 2. The STF, the highest constitutional court in Brazil, thus reaffirmed the validity of the Amnesty Law and once again prevented convictions for forced disappearances, torture and other crimes committed by agents of State[327] during the dictatorship.

ADFP no. 153 did not seek the total annulment of the Amnesty Law. In fact, what it demanded was a new interpretation of said law. The allegation of the OAB was that amnesty should not extend to crimes committed by public agents against political opponents, based on the understanding that torture and murder of persons being held prisoner illegally are not political crimes per se, but rather common crimes requiring regular prosecution and trial.[328]

During the course of the *ADFP no. 153* hearing, some members of the STF justified their decisions based on the existence of political reasons to support a broad amnesty.[329] The reporting judge in *ADFP no. 153*, Justice Eros Grau, rejected the possibility of punishing agents of the State because, according to him, the amnesty encompassed in the law was the result of a crucial moment in Brazilian democratization. Justice Grau believed that our transition was rooted in the concept of reconciliation; that is, a non-violent political transition. According to the final judgment of the STF, any analysis of the Amnesty Law could not be separated from the historical moment in which it was enacted, or from the foundations of its origins. Therefore, little consideration was given to the State's duty to prosecute crimes against humanity, and the debate questioning the connection between political crimes committed by opponents of the regime and repression crimes committed by public agents was forgotten and put aside. Thus, the decision not only rejected the recognition of the violations committed during the dictatorship as crimes against humanity, but also supported the absence of any international obligations on the part of Brazil to prosecute those crimes. In addition, the court ruled that any potential criminal defendants could no longer be prosecuted because the statute of limitations for their crimes had already expired.

---

[327] *Brazilian Federal Supreme Court,* http://redir.stf.jus.br/paginadorpub/paginador.jsp?docTP=AC&docID=612960.

[328] ROBERTSON, Geoffrey, *Crimes Against Humanity – the Struggle for Global Justice*, New York, The New Press, 2000.

[329] For the debate surrounding the political scenario and the 1979 amnesty, see Chapter 2 of this book.

For Streck, the judgment of *ADPF no. 153* represented a simplistic interpretation of the 1979 Amnesty Law or "*tabula rasa*" decision, which served to spread even further the idea that, in Brazil, criminal law has more emphasis when applied to those who are deprived of economic and/or political protection, bearing in mind, by contrast, the still very restrained application of penalties for crimes of corruption and money laundering.[330]

Shortly after the decision in *ADFP no. 153* was handed down, in August of 2010, the plaintiff filed a Clarification Appeal (*Embargos de Declaração*),[331] seeking to have the court better explain its prior ruling in the case. A decision on that appeal is still pending at the time of writing, mainly because, in May of 2014, a new claim was filed and also because, as Arguelhes and Hartmann argued, there is no mechanism to force the court to comply with deadlines.[332] As of the date of that filing, the two cases, the appeal in *ADFP no. 153* and the new claim known as *ADFP no. 320*,[333] were unified into a single action. *ADFP no. 320* alleges that the previous decision in *ADFP no. 153* failed to evaluate: (a) the impossibility of granting amnesty for crimes against humanity, in accordance with the jurisprudence of the IACHR, and (b) the fact that the crime of forced disappearance is not subject to any statute of limitations. At time of writing, there has not yet been any resolution of *ADFP no. 320*[334] and such analysis may require the acceptance of the hierarchy of international human rights treaties in Brazilian law considering that, since 2008,[335] the STF has changed its previous

---

[330] To illustrate this perception, Streck reproduces the phrase of a Salvadoran peasant to characterize the Brazilian punitive system: "*la ley es como la serpiente, solo pica los descalzos*" ("The law is like a snake: it only bites those who are barefooted"). See: STRECK, Lênio Luiz, "A lei de anistia e os limites interpretativos da decisão judicial: o problema da extensão dos efeitos à luz do paradigma do Estado Democrático de Direito", *Revista do Instituto de Hermenêutica Jurídica*, vol. 8/2010, pp. 171–181.

[331] Brazilian Federal Supreme Court, http://www.stf.jus.br/portal/processo/verProcessoAndamento.asp?incidente=2644116.

[332] Concerning the STF agenda, Arguelhes and Hartmann explained the following: "The Brazilian Supreme Court's experience shows that, when there are no mechanisms to force the Court to comply with deadlines, the importance of formal mechanisms of docket control is overrated, and the absence of discretionary case selection mechanisms might actually mean very little. Coupled with the justices' freedom to indefinitely postpone the insertion of cases in the agenda, the Court's mandatory jurisdiction means only that, over the years, the justices will have a wide-ranging pool of cases from which to pick one, at the convenient time, and decide an underlying constitutional question". See: ARGUELHES, Diego Werneck and HARTMANN, Ivar A., "Timing Control without Docket Control: How Individual Justices Shape the Brazilian Supreme Court's Agenda", *Journal of Law and Courts*, vol. 5/2017, pp. 105–140.

[333] Brazilian Federal Supreme Court, http://portal.stf.jus.br/processos/detalhe.asp?incidente=4574695.

[334] Ibid.

[335] In December of 2008 by the judgment in Extraordinary Appeal no. 466.343, the STF modified its understanding of the hierarchy of international human rights treaties inside the Brazilian

position and has accepted that international human rights treaties have supra legality and should serve as a parameter of constitutional interpretation in order to permit the harmonization of constitutional and international provisions.

In fact, *ADFP no. 320* makes reference to the binding decision of the IACHR in the second case we will analyze, the *Araguaia Case*, which was issued after the decision in *ADFP no. 153*. Although both *ADFP no. 153* and *ADFP no. 320* concern the question of holding public agents criminally responsible for the crimes they committed during the dictatorship, the substantive question in each of them is different. *ADFP no. 320* does not seek to reinterpret the Amnesty Law, nor does it question its validity (which was the core object of *ADFP no. 153*), but rather it aims to establish a bridge between the international jurisdiction of the IACHR and local jurisdiction.[336]

Thus, *ADFP no. 320* opens a new chapter in the history of Brazilian Transitional Justice regarding the interpretation of the enforceability of international precedents by local courts. This is a subject that Cavallaro has already mentioned as being the greatest challenge facing human rights lawyers in Brazil,[337] which is the inherent weakness of the mechanism established to oversee compliance with treaty norms and assure implementation of decisions by international bodies within the country. This non-compliance or failure to implement the rulings of the Inter-American Court of Human Rights (IACtHR) will be analyzed below in the discussion of the *Araguaia Case*.

4.1.2. CRIMINAL TRIALS AND THE WORK OF THE FEDERAL PUBLIC PROSECUTOR'S OFFICE

Although the position of the national courts is still seen as being non-compliant with the rulings of international judicial bodies, on the other hand, one of the great changes that has taken place in the politics of memory in Brazil is the role played by Federal Public Prosecutor's Office (*Ministério Público Federal – MPF*). As is described below, it is possible to see how the decision of the IACHR in the *Araguaia Case* impacted the work of that Office by influencing

---

system of law. Before that, the STF used to argue that such treaties were equal in rank to ordinary laws, and since the analysis involving the civil imprison of dishonest trustees, according the 1988 Constitution and the American Convention on Human Rights, the STF ruled that international human rights treaties acquired supra-legal status, remaining lower in rank than the Constitution, but higher than other laws. See: MAUÉS, Antonio Moreira, "Supra-legality of International Human Rights Treaties and Constitutional Interpretation", *SUR – International Journal on Human Rights*, vol. 10(18)/2013, pp. 205–223.

[336] See the Declaration of the Federal Public Prosecutor's Office in ADFP no. 320, pp. 29–30, http://portal.stf.jus.br/processos/detalhe.asp?incidente=4574695.

[337] CAVALLARO, James L, "Toward Fair Play: A Decade of Transformation and Resistance in International Human Rights Advocacy in Brazil", *Chicago Journal of International Law*, vol. 3/2002, pp. 481–492.

prosecutors' strategies and arguments. Those prosecutors have not only applied the recommendations of the IACHR but have even done so in defiance of the STF's decision in *ADFP no. 153*.

According to the MPF,[338] organs that are part of the judicial system cannot refuse to enforce an IACtHR ruling under a claim of the prevalence of domestic constitutional law, since it is precisely that same Constitution that subjects the State's authority to the decisions of the international court. In other words, so long as the American Convention on Human Rights is in effect in Brazil, the MPF must comply with the IACtHR's ruling on the *Araguaia Guerrilla*.

As discussed above, claims for truth and justice used to be interpreted by the local courts according to the Amnesty Law, and they have been constantly denied. However, the work of the MPF may suggest an improvement in the Brazilian case related to the application of Transitional Justice.[339] In fact, the systematic and coordinated bringing of criminal charges by the MPF for violations committed during the military period only started after 2010, when the IACtHR ruled on the *Araguaia Case* and the Second Criminal Chamber of MPF changed its understanding about such cases.[340] Before that, the MPF had engaged in administrative actions – such as filing requests for injunctions seeking access to classified documents, investigations on the concealment of corpses, location and identification of bones in several cases in the clandestine grave of Perus Cemetery in São Paulo, with the identifications of Flavio Carvalho Molina, Luiz José da Cunha and Miguel Nuet, searches at the Vila Formosa Cemetery (São Paulo), and searches for the dead and missing persons of the *Araguaia Guerrilla* – and had also established working groups to provide advisory opinions in civil lawsuits. For instance, between 2008 and 2009, the MPF began eight criminal investigations (six in São Paulo, one in Rio de Janeiro and one in Uruguaiana – a city located in the south of the country). These investigations were related to

---

[338] Federal Public Prosecutor's Office, "Memorandum of the Federal Prosecution Office Concerning the Effects of Araguaia Case" – Document no. 1/2011 of March 21 2011, http://www.mpf.mp.br/atuacao-tematica/ccr2/coordenacao/comissoes-e-grupos-de-trabalho/justica-transicao/documentos/decisoes-e-atos-administrativos-internos/2a%20Camara%20-%20Doc.%201%20-%20Caso%20Gomes%20Lund%20versus%20Brasil.pdf.

[339] The Federal Public Prosecutor's Office acts on matters regulated by the Constitution and federal laws whenever the public interest is implicated. The MPF is also responsible for ensuring compliance with the laws including international agreements. Furthermore, it acts as the "guardian" of democracy, ensuring respect for principles and rules that guarantee popular participation. The MPF is entitled to begin criminal actions and protect Brazilian society. Its functions are listed in the Brazilian Constitution and, as described in this article, the MPF has begun many initiatives against human rights violations during the Brazilian military regime. See: Brazilian *Federal Public Prosecutor's Office*, http://www.mpf.mp.br/o-mpf/sobre-o-mpf.

[340] *Federal Public Prosecutor's Office*, "2017 Report of the Transitional Justice Working Group of the Federal Public Prosecutor's Office", pp. 17–18, http://www.mpf.mp.br/atuacao-tematica/ccr2/publicacoes/roteiro-atuacoes/005_17_crimes_da_ditadura_militar_digital_paginas_unicas.pdf.

cases of kidnapping, disappearance, murder and execution, and according to a report published in 2014 by the MPF's Transitional Justice Working Group, these were isolated initiatives of criminal prosecution and were not systematized or standardized within the institution.[341]

The failure to regulate such initiatives as an internal policy gave rise to an emblematic example of the gap in the MPF's response to the crimes committed during the dictatorship, namely a particular episode in which human remains were discovered at a clandestine gravesite.[342] In 1999, a non-governmental organization (The Commission for Families of the Dead and Disappeared) asked the MPF to investigate why there had been such a long delay in the identification of the remains that had been discovered nine years before in the Perus Cemetery (located in the City of São Paulo). As a consequence, in 2009, the MPF filed a civil class action to force the Federal Government and the state of São Paulo to take the necessary measures to exhume the remains and begin the process of identifying the dead.

The fact is that, except for the Perus Cemetery case, before 2010 there was no consensus among MPF prosecutors themselves as to the appropriate actions to take. At that time, as Favero notes,[343] it was common for prosecutors to file actions relating to human rights violations based on their individual beliefs. Thus, as prosecutors held differing opinions, it was not uncommon for a case to be begun by one prosecutor but ended by another, before completion, who was assigned the case during a subsequent phase of the litigation. In 2010, the Office of the Prosecutor General (*Procuradoria Geral da República* – PGR), the highest organ of the MPF, even defended the validity of the Amnesty Law with respect to the immunity granted to agents of the State in the Legal Opinion it proffered in the case of *ADFP no. 153*.[344] According to the PGR's Legal Opinion the Amnesty Law should remain in effect since it had been the result of a long national debate as part of the transition to a democratic regime. In light of that historical context, it represented a commitment that could not subsequently be broken. In fact, an analysis of the Legal Opinion itself reveals a great lack of ideas within the institution.

However, with the appointment of a new head of the PGR, there was a change in direction towards a more unified comprehension of the elements

---

[341] *Federal Public Prosecutor's Office*, "2014 Report of the Transitional Justice Working Group of the Federal Public Prosecutor's Office", http://www.mpf.mp.br/atuacao-tematica/ccr2/publicacoes/roteiro-atuacoes/docs-cartilhas/Relatorio%20Justica%20de%20Transicao%20-%20Novo.pdf.

[342] For more information about the clandestine mass grave in Perus, see Chapter 6 of this book.

[343] Favero, Eugenia Augusta Gonzaga, "Crimes da Ditadura: Iniciativas do Ministério Público Federal em São Paulo", in Soares, Inês Virgínia Prado and Shimada, Sandra Akemi, (orgs), *Memória e Verdade – A Justiça de Transição no Estado Democrático de Direito Brasileiro*, Belo Horizonte, Forum, 2009, pp. 213–232.

[344] Legal Opinion of the Prosecutor General Roberto Monteiro Gurgel Santos, http://www.sbdp.org.br/arquivos/material/615_ADPF%20153%20PGR.PDF.

of Transitional Justice within the MPF as a whole. Thus, on August 28, 2014 – the 35th anniversary of the Amnesty Law – the then head of the PGR gave his support for adopting the decision of the IACtHR in the *Araguaia Case* as a binding precedent to be followed, as well as defending the impossibility of extending amnesty to crimes against humanity or applying the statute of limitations bar to them.[345]

That 2014 Legal Opinion of the Prosecutor General consolidates the understanding that has been adopted by prosecutors since 2012, when four criminal actions were proposed following a specific approach formulated by the MPF, in 2011, which aimed to unify and regulate such types of action.[346] Also, despite many controversial actions in the past, it is worth mentioning that there has been much improvement in the application of standards of Transitional Justice, resulting in a positive balance within the MPF despite its heterogeneity and independence.[347] One example of the agenda that fostered the changing landscape was the initiative by prosecutors to organize "South American Debate on Truth and Responsibility in Crimes Against Human Rights", in partnership with the International Center for Transitional Justice (ICTJ), the Center for Justice and International Law (CEJIL) and the Special Secretariat for Human Rights attached to the Office of the President. This event which took place in São Paulo, in 2007, resulted in a declaration known as the Charter of São Paulo (*Carta de São Paulo*), which contained propositions to end the framework of impunity relating to the dictatorship.[348]

In addition, a special MPF task force was created in 2010 known as the Working Group for the Right to Memory and Truth, aimed at both academic research and at establishing Transitional Justice objectives for MPF prosecutors.[349] Likewise, on March 21, 2011, the MPF published a document regarding the effects in Brazil of the IACtHR decision in the *Araguaia Case*, including the role of the MPF in that case in particular. According to this document, the ruling of the Court amounted to a new fact in relation to the

---

[345] Legal Opinion of the Prosecutor General, Rodrigo Janot Monteiro de Barros, http://www.mpf.mp.br/pgr/copy_of_pdfs/ADPF%20000320.pdf/view.

[346] *Federal Public Prosecutor's Office*, "Memorandum of the Federal Public Prosecutor's Office Concerning the Effects of the Araguaia Case" – Document no. 1 (2011), March 21, 2011, http://www.mpf.mp.br/atuacao-tematica/ccr2/coordenacao/comissoes-e-grupos-de-trabalho/justica-transicao/documentos/decisoes-e-atos-administrativos-internos/2a%20Camara%20-%20Doc.%201%20-%20Caso%20Gomes%20Lund%20versus%20Brasil.pdf.

[347] SOARES, Inês Virgínia Prado, "Um Pouco da Vasta Atuação do Ministério Público Federal no Tema da Ditadura", in GONÇALVES, Oksandro; HACHEM, Daniel Wunder and SANTANO, Ana Claudia (eds.), *Desenvolvimento e Sustentabilidade*, Curitiba, Íthala, 2015, pp. 59–83.

[348] *Federal Public Prosecutor's Office*, "Charter of São Paulo", http://www.justicadetransicao.mpf.mp.br/eventos/posicionamento.

[349] *Federal Public Prosecutor's Office*, "Working Group for the Right to Memory and Truth", http://pfdc.pgr.mpf.mp.br/institucional/grupos-de-trabalho/direito-a-memoria-e-a-verdade/apresentacao.

judgment of *ADFP no. 153*, and, as a result, prosecutors should continue their investigations of crimes involving forced disappearances and extrajudicial executions, as they had a constitutional duty to satisfy Brazil's treaty obligations with respect to the IACtHR decision.[350]

In 2011, the MPF also organized a working group to study the theory of Transitional Justice with the objective of adopting institutional positions and forming guidelines for prosecutors' legal opinions in that area.[351] Later on, in 2012, this Working Group presented a report listing all its activities and defining arguments that the prosecutors should adopt.[352] In summary, according to that report, crimes committed by agents of repression should not receive the benefits of amnesty for three reasons: (i) because they were committed in the context of a systematic attack on the Brazilian civilian population; (ii) because Brazil was found liable by the IACtHR in the *Araguaia Case*; and (iii) because international criminal law determines that crimes against humanity are not subject to amnesty or statutes of limitations bars.[353] Subsequent to the first report, the MPF issued a second one in 2014 which outlined its activities in the field of Transitional Justice from 2011 to 2013 and,[354] in April 2017, it issued a third report on its activities. That third report stated that, despite many difficulties, the MPF was currently the only public institution in Brazil that was committed to complying with the IACtHR's ruling in the *Araguaia Case*, and it would be the only institution seeking to investigate and promote criminal accountability relating to dictatorship's violations.[355]

The difficulties mentioned by the MPF in its report released in 2017 were related to the fact that, as of the date of drafting of that third report (December

---

[350] *Federal Public Prosecutor's Office*, "Memorandum of the Federal Public Prosecutor's Office Concerning the Effects of the Araguaia Case" – Document no. 1 (2011), March 21, 2011, http://www.mpf.mp.br/atuacao-tematica/ccr2/coordenacao/comissoes-e-grupos-de-trabalho/justica-transicao/documentos/decisoes-e-atos-administrativos-internos/2a%20Camara%20-%20Doc.%201%20-%20Caso%20Gomes%20Lund%20versus%20Brasil.pdf.

[351] *Federal Public Prosecutor's Office*, http://www.justicadetransicao.mpf.mp.br/eventos/mpf-articulado.

[352] SOARES, Inês Virgínia Prado, "Um Pouco da Vasta Atuação do Ministério Público Federal no Tema da Ditadura", in GONÇALVES, Oksandro; HACHEM, Daniel Wunder and SANTANO, Ana Claudia (eds.), *Desenvolvimento e Sustentabilidade*, Curitiba, Íthala, 2015, pp. 76–78.

[353] *Federal Public Prosecutor's Office*, http://www.mpf.mp.br/sp/sala-de-imprensa/noticias-sp/ex-legistas-sao-denunciados-por-fraudarem-laudo-de-preso-politico-morto-em-virtude-de-torturas.

[354] *Federal Public Prosecutor's Office*, "2014 Report of the Transitional Justice Working Group of the Federal Public Prosecutor's Office", http://www.mpf.mp.br/atuacao-tematica/ccr2/publicacoes/roteiro-atuacoes/docs-cartilhas/Relatorio%20Justica%20de%20Transicao%20-%20Novo.pdf.

[355] *Federal Public Prosecutor's Office*, "2017 Report of the Transitional Justice Working Group of the Federal Public Prosecutor's Office", http://www.mpf.mp.br/atuacao-tematica/ccr2/publicacoes/roteiro-atuacoes/005_17_crimes_da_ditadura_militar_digital_paginas_unicas.pdf.

2016), almost all of the lawsuits filed by MPF were in limbo,[356] that is, they were awaiting judgment on appeal. Moreover, even though none of the lower-court decisions identified any lack of evidence of the crimes alleged, in 100% of cases the unfavorable decisions were based on the impossibility of there being any resulting punishment, due to the application of the Amnesty Law, as well as the statute of limitations bar. Thus, all of the decisions disregarded the continuing nature of crimes of forced disappearance.

It is also worth noting that, in 2013, the MPF created a special working group to analyze how indigenous people were treated during the military regime.[357] The main objectives of this group are: (1) to qualify and quantify the violations against indigenous people; (2) to propose Transitional Justice measures that match the particular nature of indigenous cases; (3) to support the work of prosecutors in cases involving violations of indigenous rights during the military dictatorship; and, (4) to join with civil society in the quest for memory and truth regarding indigenous issues.

The MPF is especially concerned with reparations in the following cases: (1) the cases of the *Tenharim* and *Jiahui* tribes, for the damage caused during the construction of the Trans-Amazonian Highway (*Rodovia Transamazônica*), which resulted in forced displacements; (2) the case of the *Krenak* tribe, involving the creation of a reformatory school for indigenous children, as well as, their forced displacement to Guarani Farm, in the state of Minas Gerais (including situations of forced labor, torture, and compulsory displacement); and (3) the case of the *Waimiri-Atroari* tribe, for damage caused during the construction of Highway BR-174, in the Amazon rainforest, between the state of Roraima and the Venezuelan border.[358]

Following publication of the Final Report of the National Truth Commission (NTC) (*Comissão Nacional da Verdade*), prosecutors held a joint meeting in February of 2015 in order to increase the level of coherence among the existing working groups. At that meeting it was recognized that, given the amount of time that had elapsed, much evidence had been lost and many offenders and witnesses had died, greatly increasing the difficulty of both investigating and punishing the

---

[356] In summary, up until December 2016, MPF had initiated 27 criminal actions against 47 agents of the State, that were involved in 43 crimes (the list includes 11 homicides, 7 kidnappings, 6 concealment of corpses, 1 rape, etc.) committed against 37 victims. See: Federal Public Prosecutor's Office, "2017 Report of the Transitional Justice Working Group of the Federal Public Prosecutor's Office", http://www.mpf.mp.br/atuacao-tematica/ccr2/publicacoes/roteiro-atuacoes/005_17_crimes_da_ditadura_militar_digital_paginas_unicas.pdf.

[357] For more details about indigenous people and the crimes committed against them during the dictatorship, see Chapter 7 of this book.

[358] *Federal Public Prosecutor's Office*, "Report of the Working Group on Indigenous Tribes and Military Regime", http://www.mpf.mp.br/atuacao-tematica/ccr6/dados-da-atuacao/grupos-de-trabalho/violacao-dos-direitos-dos-povos-indigenas-e-registro-militar/docs-1/docs_relatorios_atividades/relatorio-2014_gt-violacao.pdf.

relevant crimes. However, prosecutors also praised the importance of the wide exposure given to the dictatorship's repressive structures, as well as publicity regarding and acknowledgement of the 434 cases of forced disappearance identified by the NTC (the so-called strategy of "naming names").[359]

The MPF has stated, in light of the current scenario, that it is clear that not all the investigations underway will reach a positive conclusion and that several crimes will remain unpunished. Still, the MPF is certain of the historical and legal significance of its attempts to clarify the facts. It has stated:

> Some people ask why we insist. We insist because the role of the MPF is to promote justice and republican values, including the State's duty to act in accordance with the law and to protect the physical integrity of all its citizens … We must know what happened to the dead and disappeared, who were the executioners and who gave the orders and, then, we must hold them accountable. Following this track, we will comply with the decision in the *Gomes Lund* case. By clarifying the past, we will better understand the present and, if we are lucky, we will not repeat the errors of such an outlaw regime in the future.[360]

4.2. INTERNATIONAL TRIALS

As previously commented on in this book, the debate over criminal justice and amnesty must take place with an understanding of existing obligations under international law.[361] As Olson clearly explained,[362] international law requires the prosecution and punishment of certain criminal conduct at the same time as it reduces the State's legal options, including barring the passage of amnesty laws for specific violations. The proper understanding is that if States are required to prosecute offenders, amnesty laws for those crimes are thus forbidden; and only in those cases where it is possible to identify a lesser duty of non-criminal accountability may the perpetrators be held responsible through civil suits or being named by a truth commission (the "naming names strategy"), clarification of the facts, and other symbolic mechanisms.

---

[359] *Federal Public Prosecutor's Office*, Public Note of February 3, 2015, http://pfdc.pgr.mpf.mp.br/temas-de-atuacao/direito-a-memoria-e-a-verdade/atuacao-do-mpf/temas-de-atuacao/direito-a-memoria-e-a-verdade/atuacao-do-mpf/nota-publica-sobre-relatorio-da-cnv-mpf.

[360] *Federal Public Prosecutor's Office*, "2017 Report of the Transitional Justice Working Group of the Federal Public Prosecutor's Office", p. 16, http://www.mpf.mp.br/atuacao-tematica/ccr2/publicacoes/roteiro-atuacoes/005_17_crimes_da_ditadura_militar_digital_paginas_unicas.pdf.

[361] For the analysis of the amnesty law vis à vis international law principles, see Chapter 2 of this book.

[362] OLSON, Laura M., "Provoking the Dragon on the Patio. Matters of Transitional Justice: Penal Repression vs. Amnesties", *International Review of the Red Cross*, vol. 88/2006, pp. 275–294.

Besides this theoretical approach regarding international law, there is also a sensitive and controversial question concerning the relationship between an international court and national reconciliation measures such as amnesty and truth commissions.[363] Specifically, in the case of Latin America, the IAtCHR has played a vital role in the international effort to eliminate the climate of impunity that has sheltered many examples of crimes against humanity in the region,[364] and it is well recognized that the IACtHR has been an active defender of human rights in Latin America by developing an innovative jurisprudence with respect to forced disappearances, extrajudicial killings, and in many other fields of human rights violations.[365]

The proactive role played by the IACtHR has achieved an even greater impact with respect to a crucial Latin American legacy: the passing of amnesty laws to avoid prosecutions of serious human rights violations, given that in such cases the IACtHR has ruled for the nullity of such domestic legislation and also obliged domestic courts to engage in a form of decentralized control of the relevant countries' treaty obligations.[366] Under those measures, domestic courts are prohibited from applying national laws which violate the American Convention on Human Rights.

However, as noted by Binder,[367] the challenge is that, besides the role of IACtHR as a guardian of human rights in critical areas, there is still much progress to be made, as the IACtHR needs domestic courts and institutions (like the Federal Public Prosecutor's Office) to effectively enforce its decisions. Hence, the future of the IACtHR's important role depends not only on its well-reasoned judgments, but also on support from the public prosecutors and local

---

[363] ROBINSON, Darryl, "Serving the Interests of Justice: Amnesties, Truth Commissions and the International Criminal Court", *European Journal of International Law*, vol. 14/2003, pp. 481–505.

[364] The IACtHR's interpretations of amnesty laws were locally accepted in Peru and in Chile, mainly because of its jurisprudence in cases like Barrios Altos, La Cantuta and Almonacid Arellano. And also the domestic courts in Argentina praised the IACtHR's amnesty jurisprudence, which caused a spill-over effect. See: SOARES, Inês Virgínia Prado and BASTOS, Lucia Elena Arantes Ferreira, "Direito à Verdade na Corte Interamericana de Direitos Humanos: as Perspectivas no Julgamento do Brasil – Caso Araguaia", *Revista Anistia Política e Justiça de Transição*, vol. 3/2010, pp. 288–305.

[365] BURGORGUE-LARSEN, Laurence and TORRES, Amaya Ubeda de, *Les Grandes Décision de la Cour Interaméricaine des Droits de L'Homme*, Bruxelles, Bruylant, 2008.

[366] Reference is made to the landmark judgment of IACtHR in the *Barrios Altos v. Peru*, in 2001, and later with the *La Cantuta v. Peru*, in 2006, and *Almonacid Arrelano v. Chile*, in 2006. See: Inter-American. Court of Human Rights, Barrios Altos v. Peru, Merits, Judgment of March 14, 2001, Series C, No. 75. Inter-American. Court of Human Rights, La Cantuta v. Peru, Merits, Reparations and Costs, Judgment of November 29, 2006, Series C, No. 162. *Inter-American Court of Human Rights, Almonacid Arellano y otros v. Chile*, Preliminary Objections, Merits, Reparations and Costs, Judgment of September 26, 2006, Series C, No. 154.

[367] BINDER, Christina, "The Prohibition of Amnesties by the Inter-American Court of Human Rights", *German Law Journal*, vol. 12/2011, pp. 1203–1230.

Part II. Steps Towards Reparations, Accountability, and Truth

judiciaries in accepting its jurisprudence in the affected States. In the following sections, this sensitive issue will be addressed in light of the Brazilian case, proving that, as Cavallaro and Brewer have already noted,[368] an evaluation of the domestic impact of supranational decisions may reveal a vast gap between what regional courts order and what actually happens in a country, unfortunately demonstrating that a greater institutionalization of human rights protection at the supranational level does not necessarily increase respect for human rights on the ground locally.[369]

4.2.1. THE *ARAGUAIA CASE* AND THE INTER-AMERICAN CONVENTIONALITY CONTROL DOCTRINE: CLASH OF JURISDICTIONS

In contrast to the Supreme Court of Argentina, which applies the IACtHR's jurisprudence as a paradigm in its judgments,[370] in the Brazilian case of *ADFP no. 153*, the STF did not rely on international treaties such as that of the Organization of American States (OAS), or the jurisprudence of the IACtHR. Quite to the contrary, in his opinion, Justice Celso de Mello expressly stated that the jurisprudence of the IACtHR could not be used in the Brazilian case because Brazil would constitute a unique position in Latin America.[371] According to his reasoning, unlike other countries (like Peru and Chile) in which a "white amnesty" or a self-amnesty was set up (meaning that it was enacted only in favor of the State) – Brazil had adopted a "double-handed amnesty",[372] implying that it extended to both opponents of the regime and agents of repression. Thus, the amnesty granted in Brazil fell outside of the scope of the IACtHR's jurisprudence.

---

[368] CAVALLARO, James L. and BREWER, Stephanie Erin, "Reevaluating Regional Human Rights Litigation in the Twenty-First Century: The Case of the Inter-American Court", *The American Journal of International Law*, vol. 102/2008, pp. 768–827.

[369] To illustrate such point, the Inter-American System of Human Rights has been under pressure from conservative lobby groups since 2013, see: *Open Democracy*, "Attack the OAS: Inside the ultra-conservative war on the Inter-American human rights system", December 5, 2019, https://www.opendemocracy.net/en/5050/attack-oas-inside-ultra-conservative-war-inter-american-human-rights-system/.

[370] For the example of the *Argentinian Supreme Court* and the application of the IACtHR's jurisprudence see: Sentence no. 1767. XXXVIII. Case Simón, Julio Héctor y otros s/ privación ilegítima de la libertad, etc; Case no. 17,768, http://www.asser.nl/upload/documents/20121101T045118-Simon_Corte_Suprema_Fallo_amnestia_14-6-2005.pdf, pp. 28–35.

[371] See: Vote of Justice Celso de Mello in ADFP no. 153, http://www.stf.jus.br/arquivo/cms/noticiaNoticiaStf/anexo/ADPF153CM.pdf, pp. 25–27.

[372] For a description of the Brazilian amnesty and the double-handed argument, see Chapter 2 of this book.

Chapter 4. Criminal Justice and Judicial Accountability

However, the argument that the Brazilian Amnesty Law was bilateral, as Justice Celso de Mello argued, has been highly criticized,[373] mainly because, at the time it was passed, in 1979, the regime was not characterized by the kind of political freedom which was capable of endowing such a law with domestic legitimacy.[374] In addition, by refusing the jurisprudence of the IACtHR, Brazil wasted the chance to apply what has been considered a very rich, unique and daring approach to the understanding of amnesty laws applicable in post-conflict periods.[375] That understanding derives from the fact that the IACtHR has already examined several cases similar to the Brazilian one, and in all of them the respective measure of pardoning serious violations of human rights was ruled to be invalid and unenforceable. Currently, those cases offer the only systematic analysis of various examples of amnesty which have been reviewed by an international court.[376]

The Brazilian Amnesty Law was examined by the IACtHR based on the violations of human rights committed in the Araguaia region (located in the states of Pará, Maranhão and Goiás), between 1972 and 1974.[377] According to the summary made by the IACtHR,[378] the *Araguaia Guerrilla Movement* was a resistance movement of the Communist Party of Brazil against the military regime, and its objective was to fight against the regime via the creation of a popular liberation army. Beginning in 1972, the movement was made up of almost 70 persons, and between April 1972 and January 1975, approximately

---

[373] SCHNEIDER, Nina, "Impunity in Post-authoritarian Brazil: The Supreme Court's Recent Verdict on the Amnesty Law", *European Review of Latin American and Caribbean Studies*, vol. 90/2011, pp. 39–54. ABRÃO, Paulo and TORELLY, Marcelo D., "Resistance to Change. Brazil's Persistent Amnesty and its Alternatives for Truth and Justice", in LESSA, Francesca and PAYNE, Leigh A. (eds.), *Amnesty in the Age of Human Rights Accountability: Comparative and International Perspectives*, New York, Cambridge University Press, 2012, p. 167. BASTOS, Lucia Elena Arantes Ferreira, "A Lei de Anistia Brasileira: Os Crimes Conexos, a Dupla Via e Tratados de Direitos Humanos", *Revista da Faculdade de Direito da Universidade de São Paulo*, vol. 103/2008, pp. 593–628.

[374] For a detailed description of the legitimacy of the Amnesty Law in Brazil, see Chapter 2 of this book.

[375] MARTIN-CHENUT, Kathia, "Introduction", in MARTIN-CHENUT, Kathia and ABDELGAWAD, Elisabeth Lambert (eds.), *Reparer les Violations Graves et Massives des Droits de L'Homme: La Cour Interaméricaine, Pionnière et Modèle?*, Paris, Société de Législation Comparée, 2010, p. 26.

[376] In many trials the IACtHR already declared the impossibility of granting the effects of self-amnesty laws: *Barrios Altos v. Peru* (2001), *Almonacid Arellano v Chile* (2006), *La Cantuta v. Peru* (2006), and *Gelman v. Uruguay* (2011).

[377] For the background of the efforts of the family members of the disappeared persons in the *Araguaia Guerrilla* to reach the proposition of the Case before the IACtHR, see Chapter 6 of this book, and also: SANTOS, Cecília MacDowell, "Memória na Justiça: A Mobilização dos Direitos Humanos e a Construção da Memória da Ditadura no Brasil", *Revista Crítica de Ciências Sociais*, vol. 88/2010, pp. 127–154.

[378] *Inter-American Court of Human Rights*, http://www.corteidh.or.cr/docs/casos/articulos/seriec_219_ing.pdf, pp. 33–34.

3,000 to 10,000 men from the Army, Marines, Air Force, Federal Police, and Military Police carried out a campaign of repression against the group. The Army received the order to capture, kill, and bury the dead guerilla fighters in the jungle, and by the end of 1974, the movement had no more members. It is likely that their bodies were subsequently exhumed and incinerated or thrown in the rivers of the region to conceal these crimes. However, the government imposed absolute silence regarding the events in Araguaia and, for a long time, it even denied the existence of the resistance movement.

In light of all of these facts, the IACtHR decided that the application of amnesty to perpetrators of serious human rights violations, such as those of the forced disappearances in the *Araguaia Guerrilla* campaign was incompatible with the obligations of the American Convention on Human Rights[379] and of its own jurisprudence.[380] Indeed, the IACtHR remarked that forced disappearances constitute a permanent offense, so their effects do not stop until the fate of victims is revealed.[381]

In fact, judgments like that in *ADFP no. 153* and the *Araguaia Case* arose from a clash of understandings between local and international jurisdictions. In recent years, this conflict has not only had an impact among scholars, who have enthusiastically discussed the subject,[382] but it has also encouraged the Federal Public Prosecutor's Office to file legal claims using many of the same arguments

---

[379] According to articles 8 and 25 of the American Convention on Human Rights.

[380] In this sense, the IACtHR unanimously declared that: "The provisions of the Brazilian Amnesty Law that prevent the investigation and punishment of serious human rights violations are not compatible with the American Convention, lack legal effect, and cannot continue as obstacles for the investigation of the facts of the present case, neither for the identification and punishment of those responsible, nor can they have equal or similar impact regarding other serious violations of human rights enshrined in the American Convention which occurred in Brazil". See: *Inter-American Court of Human Rights*, p. 113, http://www.corteidh.or.cr/docs/casos/articulos/seriec_219_ing.pdf.

[381] *Inter-American Court of Human Rights*, pp. 38–41, http://www.corteidh.or.cr/docs/casos/articulos/seriec_219_ing.pdf.

[382] CHOUKR, Fauzi Hassan, "Diálogos Possíveis entre o Supremo Tribunal Federal e a Corte Interamericana de Direitos Humanos no Caso Araguaia: uma Defesa Ampla, Geral e Irrestrita dos Direitos Humanos?", *Revista Brasileira de Direito Processual Penal*, vol. 2/2016, pp. 269–299. TORELLY, Marcelo D., "Gomes Lund vs. Brasil Cinco Anos Depois: Histórico, Impacto, Evolução Jurisprudencial e Críticas", in PIOVESAN, Flavia and SOARES, Inês Virgínia Prado (eds.), *Impacto das Decisões da Corte Interamericana de Direitos Humanos na Jurisprudência do STF*, Salvador, Jus Podivm, 2016, pp. 525–560. TANG, Yi Shin, "International Justice Through Domestic Courts: Challenges in Brazil's Judicial Review of the Amnesty Law", *International Journal of Transitional Justice*, vol. 9/2015, pp. 259–277. GOMES, Luis Flavio and MAZZUOLI, Valerio de Oliveira, "Crimes da Ditadura Militar e o Caso Araguaia: Aplicação do Direito Internacional dos Direitos Humanos pelos Juízes e Tribunais Brasileiros", *Revista Brasileira de Direito da Comunicação Social e Liberdade de Expressão*, vol. 2/2011, pp. 199–234. VENTURA, Deisy, "A Interpretação Judicial da Lei de Anistia Brasileira e o Direito Internacional", *Revista Anistia Política e Justiça de Transição*, vol. 4/2010, pp. 196–227.

raised by the IACtHR (as identified above). However, the Brazilian courts have been very reluctant to adopt those ideas and have obstructed many of the initiatives of the Federal Public Prosecutor's Office, using the Amnesty Law as a shield against the argument, and leaning in favor of a national reconciliation effort.[383]

At first, it would seem that the beliefs and arguments of the STF and the IACtHR are irreconcilable, unless, that is, one allows for the hypothesis of a functional separation of their duties. In other words, if we understand that the STF exercises constitutional control and that the IACtHR is in charge of conventionality control, we may reach the conclusion that the Brazilian Amnesty Law might be in "constitutional" compliance (as previously decided by the STF in *ADFP no. 153*), but not in "treaty obligation" compliance (or not in accordance with the American Convention on Human Rights, as the IACtHR decided in the *Araguaia Case*).[384]

According to this hypothesis, there would be no conflict between the decision in *ADFP no. 153* and in the *Araguaia Case*, because those judgments would be the result of a system of double control: (1) one derived from the from the validity of a law under the domestic Constitution and (2) the other resulting from an analysis of the legality of the law with respect to the country's international treaty obligations (e.g., the American Convention on Human Rights). Theoretically, in order to be totally valid, the law would have to pass muster under *both* levels of control. In the present case, as the Amnesty Law was not endorsed by the IACtHR, it should not be applied anymore by domestic courts as well.[385]

This theory would explain why, in *ADFP no. 153*, the STF avoided making its own ruling on the validity of the Amnesty Law under the international treaties that Brazil has ratified. In fact, this demonstrates that the judgment in *ADFP no. 153* merely postponed one of the problems that Brazil has been facing since the beginning of its transition to democracy: how judges should deal with the legacy of the authoritarian regime and how magistrates should apply the jurisprudence of international courts in local decisions. Indeed, with the decision in *ADFP no. 153*, the STF sent a subliminal message to local judges that they might continue to act contrary to the IACtHR's jurisprudence with no adverse consequences. The problem is that this clash of understandings demonstrates a persistently repeated

---

[383] See *Federal Public Prosecutor's Office*, "2017 Report of the Transitional Justice Working Group of the Federal Public Prosecutor's Office", http://www.mpf.mp.br/atuacao-tematica/ccr2/publicacoes/roteiro-atuacoes/005_17_crimes_da_ditadura_militar_digital_paginas_unicas.pdf.

[384] RAMOS, André de Carvalho, "A ADPF 153 e a Corte Interamericana de Direitos Humanos", in GOMES, Luiz Flavio and MAZZUOLI, Valerio Oliveira (eds.), *Crimes da Ditadura Militar*, São Paulo, Revista dos Tribunais, 2011, p. 217.

[385] RAMOS, André de Carvalho, "Pluralidade das Ordens Jurídicas: Uma Nova Perspectiva na Relação entre o Direito Internacional e o Direito Constitucional", *Revista da Faculdade de Direito da Universidade de São Paulo*, vols. 106–107/2011–2012, pp. 497–524.

reality of Brazilian local courts: although Brazil has ratified international treaties and has recognized the jurisdiction of international courts, in their daily decisions, domestic judges refuse to apply such international jurisprudence.[386]

Therefore, the chief importance of the future decision in *ADFP no. 320* will be in the judgment it must make on the binding effect of international human rights treaties on local courts and on whether the IACtHR's decisions interpreting those treaties are binding on those same courts. In fact, to supersede the debate, the STF will have to return to the debate regarding dualism and monism in international law, even though, as Bogdandy has said,[387] both theories are currently unsatisfactory and too hermetic, and the general relationship between international law and domestic law should be placed on a new conceptual basis.[388]

Moreover, between the realism of international law, human rights activism, and the legalism of criminal law, the decision in *ADFP no. 320* might result in, as Delmas-Marty has called it,[389] the construction of a form of justice without hierarchy, one developed by a kind of porous and capillary diffusion between local and international courts that could lead to a truly global legal order. The expectation remains that so-called "cross-interpretation" may educate and guide a community of judges, which in the future will promote the avoidance of contradictory positions.

4.2.2. THE *HERZOG CASE*

Over the years, one photograph has marked the period of dictatorship in Brazil: the picture shows a hanged man in a cell in the so-called Department of Information Operations – Center for Internal Defense Operations (*Departamento*

---

[386] See the conclusions of the *Ministry of Justice*, "2014 Report on the Impact of International Treaties on the Prosecution System", p. 167–168, https://issuu.com/justicagovbr/docs/pesquisa_-_tratados_internacionais_.

[387] BOGDANDY, Armin von, "Pluralism, Direct Effect, and the Ultimate Say: on the Relationship Between International and Domestic Constitutional Law", *International Journal of Constitutional Law*, vol. 6/2008, pp. 397–413.

[388] Such debate shall include not only the Conventionality Control Theory but also the fact that, since 2008, International Treaties on Human Rights in Brazil have supra legality and not constitutional status, that is to say that they remain lower in rank than the Constitution, but higher than other laws. See: MAUÉS, Antonio Moreira, "Supra-legality of International Human Rights Treaties and Constitutional Interpretation", *SUR – Revista Internacional de Direitos Humanos*, vol. 18/2013, pp. 205–223, and RAMOS, André de Carvalho, "A ADPF 153 e a Corte Interamericana de Direitos Humanos", in GOMES, Luiz Flavio and MAZZUOLI, Valerio Oliveira (ed.), *Crimes da Ditadura Militar*, São Paulo, Revista dos Tribunais, 2011, p. 217.

[389] DELMAS-MARTY, Mireille, *Le Pluralisme Ordonne: Les Forces Imaginantes Du Droit*, Paris, Seuil, 2006.

de Operações de Informações – Centro de Operações de Defesa Interna – DOI/CODI), in the city of São Paulo, in 1975. The man in the picture was Vladimir Herzog, a journalist and editor in chief of the television station TV Cultura. According to the version of the police at the time, Mr. Herzog committed suicide by hanging himself with a belt in his prison cell after arriving at DOI/CODI headquarters to make a statement on October 25, 1975. However, besides the fact that the journalist was arbitrarily detained without a warrant from any judicial authority, there was a missing link to the scene, since prisoners routinely had their belts removed before interrogation. Also, from the photo released by public authorities to prove the "suicide" it was possible to observe that his legs were folded on the floor, which fostered doubt since at that height he would have been able to stand; hence he would not have been able to suffocate by himself.[390] So, these facts raised increasing doubts as to whether Mr. Herzog could have killed himself in the way described by DOI/CODI agents. Moreover, there were marks on his neck pointing to clear signs of strangulation, and not hanging.[391]

Following the journalist's death, a Military Police investigation was opened, but its final conclusion was that the cause of his death was suicide by hanging, and the investigation was closed on March 8, 1976. However, that same year, the victim's family (his widow and children) filed a civil action for declaratory judgment in which they sought to have the federal government found liable for his arbitrary detention, torture, and subsequent death, in addition to seeking appropriate compensation. The decision in the case, handed down on October 28, 1978, established that the victim had indeed been arbitrarily detained, tortured, and killed in DOI/CODI's São Paulo headquarters. Nevertheless, following that decision, on August 28, 1979, Law no. 6,683 (the Amnesty Law) was enacted, which granted a pardon for all individuals who had committed political or related crimes in the period from 1961 to 1979.[392]

Despite the Amnesty Law, in 1992 the São Paulo State Public Prosecutor's Office (*Ministério Público Estadual de São Paulo* – MPE/SP) asked the Civil Police to begin an investigation into Mr. Herzog's death. This came after an article was published in the magazine *Isto É, Senhor*, on March 25, 1992, in which a DOI/CODI official stated that he had interrogated the journalist and in which he admitted being personally involved in Mr. Herzog's death. Later on, in the course of that suit, the same official filed a *habeas corpus* appeal based on the Amnesty Law, which appeal was granted and resulted in the ending of the

---

[390] MARETTI, Eduardo, "Ditadura: Fotógrafo Reafirma Montagem da Cena de Suicídio de Herzog", *Rede Brasil Atual*, May 27, 2013, https://www.redebrasilatual.com.br/cidadania/2013/05/fotografo-reconstitui-cena-de-suicidio-de-vladimir-herzog-1709/.
[391] *Instituto Vladimir Herzog*, https://vladimirherzog.org/casoherzog/.
[392] *Inter-American Commission on Human Rights*, Report n. 80/12, Petition P-859-00, November 8, 2012.

police investigation. That decision was later upheld by the High Court of Justice (*Superior Tribunal de Justiça* – STJ) on August 18, 1993. On March 5, 2008, the Federal Public Prosecutor's Office began an investigation into the death of Mr. Herzog based on new facts contained in the conclusions of the 2007 report of the Commission on Political Deaths and Disappearances. However, on January 9, 2009, a federal judge hearing the case handed down a decision that the crime was no longer subject to punishment and refused to apply the concept of crimes against humanity in the context of Brazilian domestic law. Consequently, the case was once again closed.[393]

Subsequently, on July 10, 2009, the Inter-American Commission on Human Rights received a petition related to the death of Mr. Herzog[394] and, on April 22, 2016, the case was submitted to the jurisdiction of the IACtHR which delivered its decision on March 15, 2018.[395] That decision found the Brazilian State liable for the lack of investigation, as well as for failure to prosecute and punish those responsible for the torture and death of Mr. Herzog. The IACtHR decision went on to state that such impunity was caused, among other factors, by the application of the Amnesty Law.

Therefore, with this judgment, the IACtHR maintained its understanding that the Brazilian Amnesty Law is incompatible with the American Convention on Human Rights, and that the Law cannot continue to represent an obstacle to the investigation of the serious human rights violations committed during the dictatorship.[396] Moreover, the IACtHR recognized that the prohibition of amnesty for crimes against humanity is an imperative norm of international law (*jus cogens*), and that, even when certain behaviors considered crimes against humanity are not formally typified as such in the domestic legal system, this does not exempt the perpetrators from liability under international law. The IACtHR also affirmed that the imperative norm that prohibits amnesty for crimes against humanity pre-dated the Amnesty Law[397] and thus was binding on

---

[393] *Inter-American Commission of Human Rights*, Report n. 80/12, Petition P-859-00, November 8, 2012 (admissibility).

[394] *Inter-American Commission of Human Rights*, Report n. 71/15, Case 12.879, October 28, 2015 (merits), http://www.oas.org/en/iachr/decisions/court/2016/12879fondoen.pdf.

[395] *Inter-American Court of Human Rights*, Herzog and others vs. Brazil, Preliminary Objections, Merits, Reparations and Costs, Judgment of March 15, 2018, Series C, No. 353.

[396] *Inter-American Court of Human Rights*, Herzog and others vs. Brazil, Preliminary Objections, Merits, Reparations and Costs, Judgment of March 15, 2018, Series C, No. 353, item 138.

[397] It is not clear in which context the term "crimes against humanity" was first developed. For instance, Schabas points to the use of this term as early as late eighteenth and early nineteenth century, particularly in the context of slavery and the slave trade, and to describe atrocities associated with European colonialism in Africa. SCHABAS, William, *Unimaginable Atrocities – Justice, Politics, and Rights at the War Crimes Tribunals*, Oxford, Oxford University Press, 2012. On the other hand, Bassiouni mentions the declaration issued, in 1915, by the Allied governments (France, Great Britain, and Russia) condemning the mass killing of Armenians by the Ottoman Empire, to be the origin of the use of the term as the label for a category of international crimes. BASSIOUNI, M. Cherif, *Crimes Against Humanity in International*

the Brazilian State at the time of the events (i.e., when Mr. Herzog was tortured and killed).[398]

In its 2018 judgment, the IACtHR also ruled that the acts performed by agents of the State during the Brazilian dictatorship were part of a systematic and widespread plan of attack against the civilian population deemed "opposed" to the regime; thus, according to the IACtHR, the facts surrounding Mr. Herzog's death should be considered as crimes against humanity.[399] Finally, in the *Herzog Case*, the IACtHR invoked the importance of domestic judges exercising so-called "conventionality control" when, in the course of their duties, they come across an internal law which is in conflict with the American Convention on Human Rights. This is even more the case when the conduct in question meets the threshold of a crime against humanity.[400]

This comment of the IACtHR reinforces the ideal of pluralism that must permeate the analysis of any judge, or what Slaughter has defined as a "participating judge" who sees himself not only as servant and representative of a particular society,[401] but also as a fellow professional in a common endeavor that transcends national borders. A model judge of this type would face common substantive and institutional problems and learn from the experience and reasoning of other professionals like himself, as well as cooperating directly to resolve specific disputes. Over time, it should be expected that regardless of whether this type of professional sits on a national supreme or constitutional court or on an international court or tribunal, he would increasingly come to recognize each judge as participants in a common judicial enterprise.

4.3. CONCLUSIONS

Lastly – more than 35 years after Brazil's return to democracy, 10 years after the decision in *ADFP no. 153* and the *Araguaia Case* trials, and 6 years after the NTC

Criminal Law, The Hague, Kluwer Law International, 1999. See: https://www.un.org/en/genocideprevention/crimes-against-humanity.shtml. Nevertheless, on November 11, 1970, the United Nations Convention on the Non-Applicability of Statutory Limitations to War Crimes and Crimes Against Humanity was already into force. See: https://www.ohchr.org/EN/ProfessionalInterest/Pages/WarCrimes.aspx.

[398] *Inter-American Court of Human Rights*, Herzog and others vs. Brazil, Preliminary Objections, Merits, Reparations and Costs, Judgment of March 15, 2018, Series C, No. 353, items 259 and 269.

[399] *Inter-American Court of Human Rights*, Herzog and others vs. Brazil, Preliminary Objections, Merits, Reparations and Costs, Judgment of March 15, 2018, Series C, No. 353, items 241 and 242.

[400] *Inter-American Court of Human Rights*, Herzog and others vs. Brazil, Preliminary Objections, Merits, Reparations and Costs, Judgment of March 15, 2018, Series C, No. 353, item 292.

[401] SLAUGHTER, Anne-Marie, "Global Community of Courts", *Harvard International Law Journal*, vol. 44/2003, pp. 191–219.

recommendations were made – both the IACtHR decision in the *Herzog Case* and the still pending STF decision in *ADFP no. 320*, confirm that the transition process in the Brazil still requires profound reflections on the part of the local courts. Based on the analysis made here, it seems that the Brazilian Judiciary has been recalcitrant in recognizing the binding nature of the IACtHR's decisions, as judges continue to interpret the Amnesty Law in a manner that prolongs the existing culture of impunity.[402]

Considering the previous overview and specially the criminal actions, which are still in progress within different levels at the Brazilian courts and with several contradictory decisions,[403] there is no prediction on what the next steps will be. But what can be easily discerned is that within the Judiciary there is a movement seeking forgetfulness and silence, rather than investigation and access to justice. Consequently, there is a possibility that most of cases proposed by the Federal Public Prosecutor's Office (MPF) will not succeed. Such trend may cause a considerable gap in the approaches of rival proponents of Transitional Justice in Brazil.

In fact, in the Brazilian landscape of Transitional Justice, one of the biggest challenges for the coming years is whether or not it will be feasible to find a balance between (a) access to justice for the victims of the dictatorship and/or their relatives, and (b) the use of the legal principles and defense mechanisms such as *habeas corpus*, principles of due process of law and the proper defense to be granted to the agents of the State, who allegedly committed those crimes. This is because, in order to be exempted, such alleged offenders are usually seeking protection under the shield of the very questionable Amnesty Law of 1979[404] and the statutory time limits for criminal charges.

Certainly, under the Brazilian Rule of Law, everyone has the fundamental right to defend themselves against accusations of crimes, even the most harmful ones, even those considered crimes against humanity, which are so serious and heinous that the international community labeled them as not subject to the

---

[402] ABRÃO, Paulo and TORELLY, Marcelo D., "Resistance to Change. Brazil's Persistent Amnesty and its Alternatives for Truth and Justice", in LESSA, Francesca and PAYNE, Leigh A. (eds.), *Amnesty in the Age of Human Rights Accountability: Comparative and International Perspectives*, New York, Cambridge University Press, 2012, pp. 152–181.

[403] For more information, see the Repository of Criminal Actions organized by the Center of Studies on Transitional Justice of the Federal University of Minas Gerais (*Centro de Estudos sobre Justiça de Transição da UFMG*), which is available at https://cjt.ufmg.br/acoes-criminais/. See also: GONÇALVES, Raquel Cristina Possolo and MEYER, Emilio Peluso Neder, "Responsabilização Individual de Perpetradores de Crimes Contra a Humanidade em Regimes Autoritários: Importância de sua Implementação no Contexto Brasileiro", in MEYER, Emilio Peluso Neder (ed.), *Justiça de Transição em Perpsectiva Transnacional*, Belo Horizonte, Initia Via, 2017, pp. 273–297.

[404] For more details about the 1979 Amnesty Law see Chapter 2 of this Book.

status of limitation.[405] Nevertheless, as stated by Soares,[406] the Judiciary's reply, while safeguarding fundamental rights and the stability of the legal system, should not merely serve to reaffirm impunity or to encourage forgetting about crimes committed during an exceptional regime. Indeed, the Judiciary should not forget the timeless reflection of Ost in the sense that,[407] even though, at first glance, the judge decides a case by looking at a past fact, his or her decision is equally capable of influencing future events.

Years ago, authors like Baggio and Miranda stated that the Brazilian legal framework has a conservative, pragmatic and conciliatory character.[408] Probably, those are determinant ingredients for the option not to confront human rights abuses from the dictatorial regime. Under the argument of resignation and social pacification in the aftermath of the 1964–1985 period, the choice not to scrutinize those cases may affect the re-democratization process by not changing the old structures or even fostering the continuity of violent practices by Brazilian security forces in general.[409] And, certainly, the use of violent practices like torture is a weakness that our democracy still has, as has been constantly reported through the years.[410] As Schwinn and Schmidt pointed out,[411] the perception that still remains is that an assessment of the negative consequences of the Brazilian transition (such as the continuation of the practice of torture and the perpetuation of the cycle of violence) was not even considered by the Federal Supreme Court at the time of the judgment in *ADPF no. 153*.

---

[405] See the Convention on the Non-Applicability of Statutory Limitations to War Crimes and Crimes Against Humanity, adopted by United Nations General Assembly Resolution 2391 (XXIII) of November 26, 1968 and into force since November 11, 1970.

[406] Soares, Inês Virgínia Prado, "Uma é pouco, duas … bom, sete nem é demais: as ações do MPF pelos crimes da ditadura militar", *Correio Cidadania*, December 20, 2013, available at: https://www.correiocidadania.com.br/colunistas/dicionario-da-cidadania/9205-20-12-2013-uma-e-pouco-duasbom-sete-nem-e-demais-as-acoes-do-mpf-pelos-crimes-da-ditadura-militar?.

[407] Ost, François, *O tempo do Direito*, Lisboa, Piaget, 1999.

[408] Baggio, Roberta Camineiro and Miranda, Lara Caroline, "Poder Judiciário e estado de exceção no Brasil: as marcas ideológicas de uma cultura jurídica autoritária", *Revista do Instituto de Hermenêutica Jurídica*, vol. 8/2010, pp. 149–179.

[409] Adorno, Sérgio, "Insegurança versus Direitos Humanos: entre a Lei e a Ordem", *Tempo Social*, vol. 11/1999.

[410] Ziemkiewicz, Nathalia and Daudén, Laura, "O Brasil que tortura", *Revista Isto É*, July 24, 2013, https://istoe.com.br/315063_O+BRASIL+QUE+TORTURA/. Bortoni, Larissa and De Santi, Maurício Riveiro, "Lei de Tortura completa 20 anos, mas ainda há relatos do crime no país", *Senado Notícias*, April 12, 2017, https://www12.senado.leg.br/noticias/especiais/especial-cidadania/lei-da-tortura-completa-20-anos-mas-ainda-ha-relatos-do-crime. Pires, Breiller, "Entre a Vida e a Morte sob Tortura, Violência Policial se Estende por todo o Brasil, Blindada pela Impunidade", *El País*, June 30, 2020, https://brasil.elpais.com/brasil/2020-06-30/entre-a-vida-e-a-morte-sob-tortura-violencia-policial-se-estende-por-todo-o-brasil-blindada-pela-impunidade.html.

[411] Schwinn, Simone Andrea and Schmidt, João Pedro, "Da Ditadura à Democracia: a Inacabada Transição Brasileira", *Reflexão e Ação*, vol. 23/2015, pp. 25–53.

In addition, Almeida and Torreão mentioned that what still needs to be taken into account by the Brazilian courts is that mechanisms of Transitional Justice represent such a valuable piece in the consolidation of democracy that they are incompatible with the simplicity of an orthodox reasoning or an inflexible judicial decision.[412] So far, the Judiciary's failure to acknowledge Transitional Justice's exceptional trajectory and its innovations is clear. Moreover, what seems to be missing from the Brazilian Judiciary's point of view – by successively insisting on closing down the relevant criminal suits – is the recognition that, through judicial proceedings stories are retold, feelings are made explicit and sensations of sharing are consolidated.

In this sense, Osiel remarked that Judicial Power is based on rituals of respect,[413] which are enshrined in traditions. The rules stipulated in a process are valuable in creating trust, which is one of the ancient purposes of judicial institutions. The verdict alone has no value in itself; what is important is the process,[414] as this is what allows rival stories to be told in the same space and time. With this in mind, Nino had already said that the charges against the Military Junta, in Argentina,[415] was necessary to instill in the collective conscience the idea that no sector of the population was above the Rule of Law. In other words, prosecution would not only be necessary for reparations or to inflict a penalty, but mainly to foster deterrence within a society.

In fact, one of the challenges of Transitional Justice is to find standards of accountability that emphasize factors beyond punishment and the desire for revenge. From this perspective, trials should be conducted with a pedagogical purpose, since those crimes have affected the collective memory, and judgments themselves may serve as reparations for gross violations of human rights. Such trials may be of great relevance in periods of democratic consolidation. As Osiel has argued,[416] by discussing violence and official complicity, a trial promotes a revision of the fundamental beliefs about those political events. These pedagogical aspects were quoted in the judgment of the IACtHR, but were denied in *ADFP no. 153*.

From this point of view, judicial activity should not be identified as an open field for revenge, but as a space for social action.[417] The Brazilian Judiciary has

---

[412] ALMEIDA, Eneá de Stutz e and TORREÃO, Marcelo Pires, "O Papel Institucional do Poder Judiciário nas Quatro Dimensões do Sistema de Justiça de Transição", *Revista de Movimentos Sociais e Conflitos*, vol. 3/2017, pp. 20–41.
[413] OSIEL, Mark, *Juger les Crimes de Masse – La Mémoire Collective et le Droit*, Paris, Seuil, 2006.
[414] BOHLEN, Celestine, "Italy Opens Trial in Wartime Massacre in Rome", *New York Times*, December 8, 1995, p. A4.
[415] NINO, Carlos S., "Transition to Democracy, Corporatism and Constitutional Reform in Latin America", *University of Miami Inter-American Law Review*, vol. 44/1989, pp. 129–136.
[416] OSIEL, Mark, *Juger les Crimes de Masse – La Mémoire Collective et le Droit*, Paris, Seuil, 2006.
[417] FABRIZ, Daury Cesar, "Cidadania, democracia e acesso à justiça", in ALMEIDA, Eneá de Stutz e (ed.), *Direitos e Garantias Fundamentais*, Florianópolis, Fundação Boiteux, 2006.

been non-compliant and resistant to understanding the Transitional process itself and such has been observed by Brazilian scholars in the sense that the Judicial Power should be more inclined to perceive that as an institution the Judiciary is also a part of a transitional process within the course of Brazilian history.[418]

Unfortunately, as consequence of this lack of critical assessment on the part of the Judiciary the number of judicial decisions tending to demonstrate lack of knowledge or refusal to implement Transitional Justice mechanisms in Brazil is still very high.[419] While dealing with reparations derived from the dictatorial regime, or topics related to memory, institutional reforms or prosecution of perpetrators, the Judiciary should be more aware that such matters represent the achievement of Transitional Justice at the national and international level. In her reflections on the challenges to be faced by the Judiciary, Schinke[420]

---

[418] Several scholars have expressed their opinion about the need for the Judiciary to carry out a self-criticism regarding the process of Transitional Justice: SOUSA JÚNIOR, José Geraldo de, "Ideias para a Cidadania e para a Justiça", Porto Alegre, Sergio Antônio Fabris Editor, 2008. PRZEWORSKI, Adam, ALVAREZ, Michael, CHEIBUB, José Antonio, and LIMONGI, Fernando, "O que mantém as democracias?", *Lua Nova*, vols. 40–41/1997. ABRÃO, Paulo, RAMPIN, Talita Tatiana Dias and FONSECA, Lívia Gimenes Dias da, "Direito à Justiça e Reforma das Instituições", in SOUSA, José Geraldo de Jr., SILVA FILHO, José Carlos Moreira da, PAIXÃO, Cristiano, FONSECA, Lívia Gimenes Dias da, and RAMPIN, Talita Tatiana Dias (eds.), *O direito achado na rua: introdução crítica à justiça de transição na América Latina*, Brasília, UnB, vol. 7, 2015. SCHINKE, Vanessa Dorneles, *Judiciário e autoritarismo: regime autoritário (1964-1985), democracia e permanências*, Rio de Janeiro, Lumen Juris, 2016.

[419] See: *Federal Public Prosecutor's Office*, "2017 Report of the Transition Justice Working Group of the Federal Public Prosecutor's Office", http://www.mpf.mp.br/atuacao-tematica/ccr2/publicacoes/roteiro-atuacoes/005_17_crimes_da_ditadura_militar_digital_paginas_unicas.pdf. Also, we mention the 2017 ruling issued by the Federal Court of Petrópolis (Rio de Janeiro) in the criminal action related to the torture and rape of Inês Etienne, which closed the investigation. Symbolically, such a ruling represents an outrage to the rights of all women who were victims of violence, since Inês Etienne was treated as a dangerous terrorist, and her testimony as a victim was not valued as evidence of crime. See: NITHAHARA, Akemi, "O Terceiro Estupro de Inês Etienne Romeu: Justiça Rejeita a Denúncia de Presa Política", *HuffPost Brasil*, March 9, 2017, http://www.huffpostbrasil.com/2017/03/09/o-terceiro-estupro-de-ines-etienne-romeu-justica-rejeita-denu_a_21878754/. Another example is the decision handed down in 2021 by the Regional Court of the 3rd Region (*Tribunal Regional da 3ª Região*), which overturned a first instance decision that granted moral compensation to the widow and children of a Volkswagen employee, the toolmaker Antonio Torini, a victim of atrocities during the military regime. In the rapporteur's opinion, accompanied by unanimity of the other judges, it is stated that "In this way, it is not possible to indemnify the supposed 'moral pain' of those who submitted to the rigors of the laws in force at the time by their own free will, knowing that it violated the criminal legislation of that time, where, the investigation, the process and the trial were the legal consequences, not to mention the consequences of the criminal conviction" (free translation). Process no. 5000493-21.2020.4.03.6126, *APELAÇÃO CÍVEL Órgão julgador colegiado: 6ª Turma Órgão Relator Desembargador Federal JOHONSOM DI SALVO*, March 5, 2021, https://www.conjur.com.br/dl/quem-combateu-ditadura-assumiu-risco.pdf.

[420] SCHINKE, Vanessa Dorneles, *Judiciário e autoritarismo: regime autoritário (1964-1985), democracia e permanências*, Rio de Janeiro, Lumen Juris, 2016.

recalls that Transitional Justice, *par excellence*, confronts the limits of the Judiciary's discursive-bureaucratic action, insofar as it incites the displacement of pragmatic arguments to implement principles of protection of human rights.

Within the scope of Transitional Justice and in order to advance the pillar of access to justice, the Brazilian Judiciary is still lagging behind with the formulation of a collective strategy, as the Federal Public Prosecutor's Office did, starting in 2010.[421] Such an urge for a turning point was also observed in Chile, when Collins concluded that the complexity of the investigations led to the involvement of a large cast of auxiliary actors during the Chilean trials of dictatorial crimes: officials, police, lawyers and technicians.[422] These individuals, often younger than the judges they served, were more likely opened to research and innovations, and this enhanced the effects of the cases, whether (a) with the dissemination of practical knowledge of international law, or (b) with technical knowledge in relation to the needs of the victims and their relatives. In fact, several Supreme Court judges in Chile recognized that they were forced to accelerate their learning curve of international law in view of the dictatorship cases. Many magistrates who were responsible for these special investigations have adopted forms of collegiate work; they were surrounded by multidisciplinary teams with younger employees, who invested time and effort in understanding the facts; and they counted on the close collaboration of police officers, forensic specialists and associations of the victims' relatives, all of them aiming to ensure dignified treatment for victims of crimes against humanity.

In addition, the need for a strategy to deal with the judicial processes of cases involving dictatorial crimes was also pointed out by De Greiff,[423] as the former UN Special Rapporteur on the promotion of truth, justice, reparation and guarantees of non-recurrence,[424] when he recognized the importance of dialogue between national prosecutors, since prosecutors whose work is related

---

[421] For details, see section 4.1.1 of this chapter.

[422] COLLINS, Cath, "Human rights defense in and through the courts in (post) Pinochet Chile", *Radical History Review*, vol. 124/2016, pp. 129–140.

[423] DE GREIFF, Pablo, "On Making the Invisible Visible: The Role of Cultural Interventions in Transitional Justice Processes", in RAMÍREZ-BARAT, Clara (ed.), *Transitional Justice, Culture, and Society Beyond Outreach*, New York, International Center for Transitional Justice and Social Science Research Council, 2014, pp. 11–24.

[424] *2017 UN Report of the Special Rapporteur on the promotion of truth, justice, reparation and guarantees of non-recurrence on his global study on transitional justice*, August 7, 2017: "2.43. Transitional justice has contributed to the realization of the right to justice through the articulation of prosecutorial strategies, something that prosecutors confronting common crimes in ordinary jurisdictions never develop, as they typically stand under the obligation to consider cases as they come. By contrast, in the typical transitional situation the number and types of violations vastly outstrip the State's capacity to take in all cases that might be presented at any one time and even over time. A strategy is then necessary in order to rationalize the deployment of scarce resources and to maximize the impact of those efforts", available at https://undocs.org/A/HRC/36/50/Add.1.

to common crimes are not trained to face typical Transitional Justice situations, where the number and magnitude of violations exceeds the usual capacity of the Judicial Power. Therefore, a strategy would be necessary in order to rationalize the already scarce human resources and to maximize the impact of these efforts on the judicial level, as well.

In conclusion, the revision of the Amnesty Law seems to be very shameful for political reasons, and the position of the STF and most of the levels of the Judiciary in Brazil has shown that judges apply international law only superficially, practically disregard international jurisprudence, and barely make use of comparative law.[425] The consequences of this failure to prosecute crimes against humanity committed during the dictatorship are not confined to the victims and their families. Rather, impunity in Brazil still contaminates State institutions and the Rule of Law and continues to undermine the credibility of the State itself.[426]

---

[425] VENTURA, Deisy, "A Interpretação Judicial da Lei de Anistia Brasileira e o Direito Internacional", *Revista Anistia Política e Justiça de Transição*, vol. 4/2010, pp. 196–227.

[426] We hope that such status may undergo new changes by virtue of the new Resolution 364 of the National Council of Justice (CNJ), of January 12, 2021, which created the Unit for Monitoring and Enforcement of the decisions and deliberations of the Inter-American Court of Human Rights involving the Brazilian State, under the Department for Monitoring and Enforcement of the Prison System and the System for the Execution of Socio-Educational Measures (DMF).

According to the approved Resolution, it will be up to the Monitoring and Inspection Unit, *inter alia*, to maintain a database with the decisions of the IACtHR involving Brazil, to provide for the monitoring and inspection of compliance with the judgments, provisional measures and advisory opinions of the Court, to suggest proposals, to better attend to the fulfilment of its deliberations, to verify the processes and procedures related to the material and non-material reparation of the victims of violations of human rights determined by the IACtHR, to report annually on the measures adopted by Brazil to comply with such decisions, as well as monitor the implementation of human rights parameters established by the Court or other international instruments that establish international obligations on Brazil within the field of human rights.

CHAPTER 5
THE TRUTH-TELLING PROCESS

"Effective democratization is always measured by this essential criterion: participation and access to the files, to their formation and interpretation".[427]

It took 26 years from the end of the dictatorship for Brazil to finally see the creation of an official truth commission. For a long time it seemed that Transitional Justice measures in the country would not go beyond the reparation programs of 1995 and 2002, in the quest for reconciliation and reconstruction. On the other hand, despite the efforts of the 1985 "Brazil: Never Again" Report,[428] the truth-telling indirectly produced by the Commission on Political Deaths and Disappearances, and the work of the Amnesty Commission, there was still the impression that what had been done up until then was not enough. This puzzling sense of an unfinished task may be explained, as Hamber has commented in the context of the South African Truth and Reconciliation Commission,[429] because it is highly unlikely that conflict survivors will react in an overly forgiving way, at least in the short term, towards the perpetrators of the violence against them. However, what can we say if this "short-term" reticence lasts for more than 30 years?

In this sense, though the work of the Special Commission on Political Deaths and Disappearances and the Amnesty Commission have been very important for the reconciliation process, in most cases, victims will not be ready to simply put the past behind them at the very moment when reparations are granted. This is because victims might feel that pecuniary reparations are being used to buy their silence in the absence of the truth. Thus, in the Brazilian case, the creation of an official mechanism of truth-telling like the National Truth Commission (NTC) (*Comissão da Verdade*) in 2012 was a great initiative to combat the belief that pecuniary reparations isolated from truth recovery would be a governmental strategy to close the past prematurely and leave many facts unknown.

---

[427] Personal translation of: DERRIDA, J., *Mal de Arquivo. Uma Impressão Freudiana*, Rio de Janeiro, Relume Dumará, 2005, p.16.
[428] For detailed information about the 1985 "Brazil Never: Again" Report, see section 6.1 in Chapter 6 of this book.
[429] HAMBER, Brandon, "Repairing the Irreparable: Dealing with the Double-Binds of Making Reparations for Crimes of the Past", *Ethnicity and Health*, vol. 5/2000, pp. 215–226.

This chapter will observe how the NTC was formed and identify its main goals and achievements, but will also comment on gaps in its assessments. This retrospective is important due to the repercussions of its work which still echo in society, several years after the Commission's end. A recent incident well illustrates the point. On February 16, 2018, the federal government issued a decree authorizing the intervention of the Armed Forces to perform police work in the state of Rio de Janeiro. Soon after, the commander of the Brazilian Army declared that, to agree to intervene to maintain domestic order and public safety, the Armed Forces would need a guarantee that they could avoid the risk of a "new truth commission".[430] This comment made by a representative of the Brazilian Army illustrates that the truth-telling process and the related access to the archives of this chapter of Brazilian history still evoke distinct interpretations of that history and that process.

5.1. THE LONG ROAD TO A NATIONAL TRUTH COMMISSION

To understand the late creation of the NTC in Brazil we must comprehend the role of new neoliberal economic policies in the period after re-democratization and how these might have eclipsed calls for measures of accountability and truth. Indeed, shortly after 1985, the demands for historical, political, moral, and pecuniary reparations were not in evidence, while the political leaders of that time favored other directives that merely reproduced the discourse of "national reconciliation" based on the 1979 Amnesty Law.

In fact, such law even created a type of division between, on the one hand, those who have been tortured and family members of the dead and disappeared and, on the other hand, those who underwent other modalities of repression such as job loss, exile or mandatory termination of political mandate. The latter had their objectives fulfilled by the 2002 reparations program, while the former did not obtain the right to truth and memory for more than three decades. This scenario became more acute in the 1990s when so-called "market-oriented" reforms were initiated, including the privatization of State-owned enterprises, attempts to control inflation and public debt, reductions in social spending in the areas of education, health and welfare, and the opening of the internal market commercially and financially.

As Amann and Baer have asserted, during the 1990s, Brazil's policy increasingly conformed to the so-called Washington Consensus,[431] and

---

[430] BENITES, Afonso, "Intervenção Federal no Rio Desperta Fantasmas sobre o Papel do Exército", *El País*, February 21, 2018.
[431] The so-called Washington Consensus policy orientation consisted of the combination of measures like (i) an effective attack on inflation through fiscal adjustment; (ii) privatization

consequently, at the political level, democracy became the policy preference of neoliberalism in Brazil. Thus, Saad Filho has concluded that,[432] in the Brazilian case, the neoliberal transition and the democratic transition were mutually reinforcing and, eventually, merged into the same phenomenon. In fact, economic reforms during the 1990s sidelined real political reform, and the neoliberal governments in power had as preconditions the maintenance of some of the authoritarian arrangements, leading to a symbiotic relationship between the liberal ideological discourse and post-authoritarian political practices.

Nevertheless, at the same time, the 1988 Constitution became the first Brazilian Constitution to include international rights in the list of constitutionally guaranteed rights, and, concerning the indivisibility of human rights, it must be emphasized that the 1988 Charter is the first Constitution that includes a list of fundamental social and economic rights, which in the previous Charters were scattered among the relevant chapters on the economic and social order. And, as observed by Piovesan and Vieira,[433] even though since 1934 successive Brazilian Constitutions have provided protection to social and economic rights, it was the 1988 Federal Constitution that, for the first time, treated them as fundamental rights and gave them immediate applicability.

Therefore, as observed by Codato,[434] such symbiosis between the liberal discourse, the post-authoritarian political practices and the social democratic content of the 1988 Constitution was an inheritance of the so-called Brazilian model of transition; that is to say, it was controlled by the Army in partnership with the political and economic elite of the country. This type of "transition from the top to the bottom" – slow, secure, and gradual – imprinted its marks not only on democracy, but also on future Commissions designed to investigate the truth and restore the country's historical and political memory. Schneider recalls that even the electoral success of the left-wing Workers' Party in 2002 – a political party that had its origins in the labor union movements against the dictatorship – has not led to a clear break with the authoritarian past either.[435,436]

---

of State-owned enterprises; (iii) trade liberalization with declines in tariff and non-tariff protection; (iv) the prevalence of market interest rates; and (v) opening of most economic sectors to foreign investments. See: AMANN, Edmund and BAER, Werner, "Neoliberalism and its Consequences in Brazil", *Journal of Latin American Studies*, vol. 34/2002, pp. 945–959.

[432] SAAD FILHO, Alfredo, "Neoliberalism, Democracy, and Development Policy in Brazil", *Development and Society*, vol. 39/2010, pp. 1–28.

[433] PIOVESAN, Flavia and VIEIRA, Renato Stanziola, "Justiciabilidade dos Direitos Sociais e Econômicos no Brasil: Desafios e Perspectivas", *Araucaria Revista Iberoamericana de Filosofia, Política y Humanidades*, vol. 15/2006, pp. 128–146.

[434] CODATO, Adriano Nervo, "Uma História Política da Transição Brasileira: Da Ditadura Militar à Democracia", *Revista de Sociologia Política*, vol. 25/2005, pp. 165–175.

[435] SCHNEIDER, Nina, "Waiting for a Meaningful State Apology: Has Brazil Apologized for Authoritarian Repression?", *Journal of Human Rights*, vol. 13/2014, pp. 1–16.

[436] VALENTE, Rubens, "Em Vídeo, Jobim Detalha como Atuou para Impedir Revisão da Lei da Anistia", *Folha de São Paulo*, August 27, 2019, https://www1.folha.uol.com.br/poder/2019/08/em-video-jobim-detalha-como-atuou-para-impedir-revisao-da-lei-da-anistia.shtml.

Despite Brazil's alignment with the standards of international human rights law, which started in 1989 and gradually increased during the 1990s,[437] the mere formulation of ideas and standards preparatory to the formation of a truth commission caused enormous stress in the relationship between the Executive Branch and the Army in 2009, when the initiative was included in the National Human Rights Program. In fact, the creation of the NTC was on the Executive Branch's political agenda for that year, but the approval of the project provoked an internal crisis in the government (setting the Ministry of Defense against the Ministry of Foreign Affairs). It also provoked protests from sectors of the Armed Forces and gave rise to criticism from some sectors of the civil society against alleged "revanchism",[438] in addition getting attention from the press, right-wing parties, intellectuals, and corporate sectors.[439]

To illustrate the tension of those times, Schneider notes that the government of the period favored compromise over a definitive rupture during the crisis surrounding the National Truth Commission,[440] when the then Defense Minister and three leading military generals successfully extracted amendments to the text of the proposed law from the President by threatening to resign, thereby getting key phrases changed. Most significantly, the term "political repression" was downgraded to "political conflict", while any precise reference to those who had committed human rights violations – military personnel or the militant opposition – was erased. Also, the number of commissioners remained small (seven members), the activities of the NTC had no jurisdictional or prosecutory character and consequently some people summonsed to testify at the NTC filed a request for *habeas corpus* to guarantee their right to remain silent[441] (article 4 of Law no. 12,528 (2011)).[442]

---

[437] In 1989, Brazil ratified the Convention against Torture and Other Cruel, Inhuman or Degrading Treatment and the Inter-American Convention to Prevent and Punish Torture; In 1990 Brazil ratified the Convention on the Rights of the Child; then in 1992, the country ratified the International Covenant on Civil and Political Rights, the International Covenant on Economic, Social and Cultural Rights and the American Convention on Human Rights; and in 1995, Brazil ratified the Inter-American Convention to Prevent, Punish, and Eradicate Violence against Women.

[438] ADORNO, Sergio, "História e Desventura: O 3° Programa Nacional de Direitos Humanos", *Novos Estudos CEBRAP*, vol. 86/2010, pp. 5–20.

[439] QUERO, Caio, "Entenda a Polêmica sobre a Comissão Nacional da Verdade", *BBC Brasil*, January 13, 2010, https://www.bbc.com/portuguese/noticias/2010/01/100112_comissao_qanda_cq.

[440] SCHNEIDER, Nina, "Waiting for a Meaningful State Apology: Has Brazil Apologized for Authoritarian Repression?", *Journal of Human Rights*, vol. 13/2014, pp. 1–16.

[441] See: *Associação do Ministério Público de Minas Gerais*, "Ustra com Habeas Corpus para se Calar", https://amp-mg.jusbrasil.com.br/noticias/100506253/ustra-com-habeas-corpus-para-se-calar.

[442] This is a free translation of article 4 of the Law no. 12,528 (2011): "Art. 4 For the execution of the objectives foreseen in art. 3, the National Truth Commission may:

I– receive testimonies, information, data and documents that are sent to it voluntarily, ensuring the non-identification of the holder or deponent, when requested;

Furthermore, although the creation of the NTC had been discussed since 2009, much of its implementation was a response to the ruling against Brazil in 2010 in the *Araguaia Case*, when the Inter-American Court of Human Rights (IACtHR) found that the establishment of a Truth Commission would be an important compliance measure to restore the right to truth and memory and to ascertain the institutional, social, and political responsibility for what transpired during the dictatorship. Hence, the framework of the NTC may be understood as an intermediary way of responding to, on the one hand, the pressure brought to bear by the IACtHR and, on the other, the counter-demands of the most conservative sectors of Brazilian society who feared the possibility of any judgment against those responsible for serious human rights violations.

5.2. THE RELEVANT STEPS TAKEN BY THE NATIONAL TRUTH COMMISSION

Certainly, the great merit of a truth commission is to officially reveal the events of the past and to assist society in order to better understand the facts so revealed, letting society learn how to deal with its past. In the Brazilian case, due to the delay in forming the Commission, expectations for this Transitional Justice mechanism were more related to the non-repetition ("Never Again") effects that it could provide to society than to any healing effects. This is because, unlike other countries that have adopted this type of commission soon after authoritarian periods, Brazil began its NTC operations almost 30 years after the end of the dictatorship. Indeed, this postponement caused some peculiarities in the historical and institutional context. First, great effort was needed to access files and documents due to the long period that had passed.[443] Second, any

---

II– request information, data and documents from government agencies and entities, even if classified in any degree of confidentiality;
III– summon, for interviews or testimony, people who can keep any relationship with the facts and circumstances examined;
IV– determine the performance of expertise and diligence to collect or recover information, documents and data;
V– promote public hearings;
VI– request protection from public bodies for anyone who is in a situation of threat due to their collaboration with the National Truth Commission;
VII– promote partnerships with bodies and entities, public or private, national or international, for the exchange of information, data and documents; and
VIII– request assistance from public entities and bodies ...
§4 The activities of the National Truth Commission will not have jurisdictional or persecutory character.

[443] QUINALHA, Renan Honório, "Com Quantos Lados se Faz uma Verdade? Notas sobre a Comissão Nacional da Verdade e a Teoria dos Dois Demônios", *Revista Jurídica da Presidência*, vol. 15/2013, pp. 181–204.

possible reconciliation benefits for the victims and their families were severely curtailed, since many of them were already very old or had died by the time the NTC's Final Report was issued.

However, there is a positive factor associated with this deferred action: the NTC was able to investigate the facts at a distance from the ideological disputes which are inherent in periods shortly after the end of an authoritarian regime. In this sense, by 2014, there was no fear that the revelation of the truth would pose a risk to democracy or jeopardize the rule of law.[444]

Also, the NTC profited from many background factors that had been developed and implemented during the preceding 30 years. These included: the searches for evidence conducted by the Church, human rights activists, and victims and their families in the research for and publication of the "Brazil: Never Again" Report; the task forces created by the Special Commission on Political Deaths and Disappearances; and the contributions made by the Amnesty Commission. Thus, the NTC promised smaller impacts in terms of innovation, mainly because previous truth-seeking initiatives had produced a reasonable amount of information about the past. But some key issues, such as the fate of the forcibly disappeared, have yet to be fully explored and answered.

In fact, it is worth highlighting the main conclusion reached by the NTC: the confirmation that the Brazilian State had committed serious human rights violations that amount to crimes against humanity.[445] This recognition alone of the State's complicity in fact has both a healing effect for the nation and acts as a form of symbolic reparation.

In general overview, the NTC mission comprised the following tasks, according to article 3 of Law no. 12,528 (2011): (a) to clarify the facts and circumstances related to gross violations of human rights; (b) to produce a detailed description of cases of torture, enforced disappearances, and concealment of corpses; (c) to identify structures, places, institutions and practices related to those violations; (d) to submit to government agencies any information that could assist in locating bodies of the disappeared persons; (e) to collaborate with all levels of government in order to determine the existence of human rights violations; (f) to recommend the adoption of measures to prevent future human rights violations, to ensure their non-repetition and to promote national reconciliation; and (g) to encourage the historical reconstruction of cases, and to contribute to the assistance of the victims.

In its day-to-day work, the NTC used working groups to carry out its activities.[446] This task-force-based organization allowed for the de-centralization

---

[444] WEICHERT, Marlon Alberto, "O Relatório da Comissão Nacional da Verdade: Conquistas e Desafios", *Projeto História*, vol. 50/2014, pp. 86–137.

[445] *NTC Report*, Volume I, Chapter 18, pp. 963–964, cnv.memoriasreveladas.gov.br/images/pdf/relatorio/Capitulo%2018.pdf.

[446] *National Truth Commission*, http://cnv.memoriasreveladas.gov.br/institucional-acesso-informacao/grupos-de-trabalho.html.

of field research focused around the following themes: (i) dictatorship and gender; (ii) the *Araguaia Guerrilla* movement; (iii) contextualization, grounds and reasons for the 1964 *coup d'état*; (iv) dictatorship and the judicial system; (v) dictatorship and the repression of workers and the labor movement; (vi) the repression structure; (vii) the dead and disappeared; (viii) gross violations of human rights committed in rural areas or against indigenous people; (ix) Operation Condor;[447] (x) the role of churches during the dictatorship; (xi) oppression within the military; (xii) human rights violations of Brazilians living abroad and foreigners living in Brazil; and (xiii) military rule. Based on this division of work, the NTC promoted public hearings to obtain the testimony of victims and witnesses, as well hearing from agents of repression. It also organized 80 "events", either in the form of hearings (or collections of statements) or public sessions (to present the results of its research). In total, these events collected 565 witness statements which constituted extremely important source material for the interpretation of cases and for the historical reconstruction of the practices and structures of repression.[448]

The NTC's Final Report confirmed the deaths and disappearances of 434 victims during the military regime, which were divided as follows: 191 deaths, 210 disappearances where the bodies were never located, and 33 disappearances where the bodies were located.[449] However, it is important to remember that, due to the legally defined powers of the NTC, the Commission had no authority to initiate prosecutions. Thus, the naming of names exercised in Chapter 16 of the Final Report did not directly result in any criminal, civil or administrative procedures begun by the Commissioners, even though many of the conclusions reached by the NTC are being used to support the claims and class actions initiated by the Public Prosecutor's Office in recent years.

Certainly, these numbers presented by the NTC's Final Report do not correspond to the total of the dead and disappeared persons during the Brazilian dictatorship, but only to those cases of which evidence emerged from the work done by the NTC from 2011–2014. This evidence was obtained despite obstacles faced during the investigations, in particular the lack of access to documents produced by the Armed Forces, which in many cases were "formally" and "officially" considered as destroyed.[450]

---

[447] Operation Condor was a campaign of political repression and State terror involving intelligence operations and assassination of opponents. It was implemented by the dictatorships of the Southern Cone of South America (Argentina, Chile, Uruguay, Paraguay, Bolivia and Brazil). See: MCSHERRY, J. Patrice, "Tracking the Origins of a State Terror Network: Operation Condor", *Latin American Perspectives*, vol. 29/2002, pp. 38–60.

[448] *National Truth Commission*, http://cnv.memoriasreveladas.gov.br/audi%C3%AAncias-p%C3%BAblicas.html.

[449] *NTC Report*, Volume III, cnv.memoriasreveladas.gov.br/images/pdf/relatorio/volume_3_digital.pdf.

[450] JOFFILY, Mariana, "Direito à Informação e Direito à Vida Privada: Os Impasses em Torno do Acesso aos Arquivos da Ditadura Militar Brasileira", *Estudos Históricos*, vol 25/2012, pp. 129–148.

5.2.1. HIGHLIGHTS AND RECOMMENDATIONS

Still, to have a full sense of the work developed by the NTC, other positive facts presented by the Final Report are worth highlighting:

(a) *The extraterritorial projection of the dictatorship.* The Final Report contains chapters detailing the Brazilian State's participation in violations committed abroad, including the repressive alliance (Operation Condor) implemented in the Southern Cone region. This revelation was due to research in the archives of the Ministry of Foreign Affairs, which had been little examined before.[451]

(b) *The role of the judiciary during the dictatorship.* The NTC showed that until 1968, the Brazilian Supreme Court maintained a minimum standard of protection for politically persecuted citizens, but after December 1968, during the cruelest years of political repression, the same Supreme Court silently ignored witnesses denouncing the practice of torture.[452]

(c) *Detailed information on locations associated with the practice of human rights violations.* The Final Report identified such locations, such as military units, ships, and clandestine prisons (physically located outside official facilities, but maintained by military or police officers).[453]

In addition to the truth-telling program and in order to ensure non-repetition and to promote the democratic Rule of Law, the NTC recommended the adoption of a set of 17 institutional measures, eight legal reforms, and four follow-up measures to its own recommendations. Of these, the following recommendations merit highlighting:

(a) the recognition by the Armed Forces of their responsibility for the gross violations of human rights committed during the dictatorship;

(b) the holding accountable (in criminal and civil proceedings) of public agents that committed violations of human rights during the dictatorship, thus precluding application of the Amnesty Law to such cases;

(c) as a form of symbolic reparation, the rectification of the medical records stating the cause of death for victims of torture whose deaths occurred inside military units, since many of these documents often listed "suicide" instead of "physical torture" as the cause of death;

(d) the prohibition of official events to celebrate the *coup d'état* of 1964;

(e) public identification of urban and rural properties where serious violations of human rights occurred;

---

[451] *NTC Report*, Volume I, Chapter 6, pp. 219–273.
[452] *NTC Report*, Volume I, Chapter 17, pp. 935–947.
[453] *NTC Report*, Volume I, Chapter 15, pp. 728–839.

(f) creation of a Museum of Memory; and
(g) modification of the names of public places, roads, buildings, and institutions that honor State agents or individuals who are known to have been perpetrators.

Though those recommendations are to be applauded, one must still avoid the misconception that the primary task of a truth commission is to produce a Final Report. This is because, in the Brazilian case, many tasks related to Transitional Justice measures had already been implemented long before the NTC's creation. Thus, its findings should not be appreciated in an isolated manner but rather as one piece of a puzzle. The truth-telling process itself definitely warrants praise, including the public hearings, the efforts to combine the information previously collected by civil society and other governmental agencies like the Special Commission on Political Deaths and Disappearances and the Amnesty Commission, and the symbolic role the Commissioners played in representing the process to the nation as a whole.

Hence, despite the gaps that will be pointed out below, this author endorses the idea that the process of searching for truth and memory that the NTC engaged in served as a form of moral redress and symbolic reparation for the violations committed in the past. As Engstrom has noted,[454] any official Transitional Justice initiative is better than none, so the simple creation of a truth commission in Brazil already constituted a major advance and should be welcomed as such. However, though the Final Report offered an authoritative contribution to the understanding of the country's recent past and history, it nevertheless received some unfavorable appraisals, as will be discussed below.

5.2.2. THE CREATION OF AN EXTENSIVE NETWORK OF LOCAL TRUTH COMMISSIONS AS A POSITIVE EFFECT OF THE NTC

Another topic that should be addressed as a positive step is the fact that although in countries where dictatorships were installed and the transition to democracy included Transitional Justice methods, usually there was only one Truth Commission, Brazil innovated in this respect In the Brazilian case, despite the fact that a truth commission was organized decades after the end of the dictatorship, it is necessary to consider that Brazil created an extensive network

---

[454] ENGSTROM, Par, "Brazilian Post-Transitional Justice and the Inter-American Human Rights System", *Conference on Post-Transitional Justice in Brazil*, Brazil Institute, King's College London, 2013.

of truth commissions within states, municipalities, and in sectoral areas and academic spaces.[455]

It is worth mentioning that this network of commissions was important for the implementation of Transitional Justice measures in Brazil, as the NTC alone did not have the number of people and the capillarity necessary to undertake the broad investigation in a country with continental dimensions.

Therefore, the NTC encourages and coordinated local and regional initiatives with the proliferation of similar commissions at the state and municipal levels, as well as at universities, unions, and associations. In those cases, the NTC took a coordinating role with other commissions and avoided duplication of work. With this aim, NTC Resolution no. 4, dated September 17, 2012,[456] established that the NTC would promote cooperation and the exchange of information with any other similar structure or agency seeking to investigate the past so that the NTC would not reopen procedures that were already under analysis by local commissions.

---

[455] This is the list of the truth commissions that have entered into a technical cooperation agreement with the NTC: Comissão Anísio Teixeira de Memória e Verdade da UnB; Comissão da Memória e da Verdade Eduardo Collier Filho da Faculdade de Direito da UFBA; Comissão da Memória e Verdade da UFPR; Comissão da Memória, Verdade e Justiça de Natal "Luiz Ignácio Maranhão Filho"; Comissão da Verdade da Câmara Municipal de Araras; Comissão da Verdade da OAB/PR; Comissão da Verdade da Pontifícia Universidade Católica de São Paulo – Reitora Nadir Gouveia Kfouri; Comissão da Verdade do Estado de São Paulo Rubens Paiva"; Comissão da Verdade do Município de São Paulo "Vladimir Herzog"; Comissão da Verdade dos Jornalistas Brasileiros (Federação Nacional dos Jornalistas); Comissão da Verdade e da Memória Advogado Luiz Maranhão (OAB/RN); Comissão da Verdade e do Memorial da Anistia Política da OAB/MG; Comissão da Verdade e Memória: pela construção do Nunca Mais! (Escola de Sociologia e Política de São Paulo); Comissão da Verdade "Marcos Lindenberg" da Universidade Federal de São Paulo; Comissão da Verdade "Professor Michal Gartenkraut" da Câmara Municipal de São José dos Campos; Comissão Especial da Memória, Verdade e Justiça da OAB (Conselho Federal da OAB); Comissão Especial da Verdade da Assembleia Legislativa do Espírito Santo; Comissão Estadual da Memória e Verdade Dom Helder Câmara (PE); Comissão Estadual da Memória, Verdade e Justiça Deputado Estadual José Porfírio de Souza (GO); Comissão Estadual da Verdade da Bahia; Comissão Estadual da Verdade do Rio de Janeiro; Comissão Estadual da Verdade do Rio Grande do Sul; Comissão Estadual da Verdade e da Preservação da Memória do Estado da Paraíba; Comissão Estadual da Verdade Francisco das Chagas Bezerra "Chaguinha" (AP); Comissão Estadual da Verdade Paulo Stuart Wright (SC); Comissão Memória, Verdade e Justiça do Sindicato dos Trabalhadores nas Empresas Próprias e Contratadas na Indústria e no Transporte de Petróleo, Gás, Matérias-Primas, Derivados e Afins, Energia de Biomassas e Outras Renováveis e Combustíveis Alternativos no Estado do Rio de Janeiro; Comissão Municipal da Verdade no Âmbito do Município de Juiz de Fora (MG); Comissão Parlamentar Especial da Verdade da Assembleia Legislativa do Estado do Maranhão; Subcomissão Parlamentar Memória, Verdade e Justiça da Comissão de Direitos Humanos da Câmara dos Deputados. See: SEIXAS, Ivan Akselrud de and SOUZA, Silvana Aparecida de, "Comissão Nacional da Verdade e a Rede de Comissões Estaduais, Municipais e Setoriais: A Trajetória do Brasil", Revista Estudos de Sociologia, vol. 20/2015, pp. 347–367.

[456] National Truth Commission, http://cnv.memoriasreveladas.gov.br/institucional-acesso-informacao/resolucoes.html.

By its final report, the NTC even observed that, although the dissemination of truth commissions throughout the country was not foreseen by the Brazilian law which created the NTC, such initiative was fruitful and assisted the NTC to multiply its efforts.[457] Considering this background, Hollanda and Israel[458] even observed that the subsequent creation of a large number of non-national truth commissions originated a new phenomenon, which they named "*commissionism*" in order to explain not only the process of multiplying truth commissions in the country, but also the fact that, although the NTC occupied a pioneering role during a significant part of this process, with some effort in inducing similar structures in the states and municipalities, the NTC did not come to assume a leading role in a robust way or to exercise a directive function in this landscape.

Such phenomenon included different institutional designs of the various commissions – which corresponded with different mandates, budget availability, and actions. Just to present an overview, 28 of these commissions were created by state or municipal laws or decrees; that is to say, some were linked to the Executive Power (in 14 states and in 14 municipalities), and another 17 commissions were created by the initiative of Legislative Power (state assemblies or city councils), and in this case 14 of them were connected to city councils, mainly concentrated in the states of São Paulo and Rio de Janeiro, and other four commissions were linked to state assemblies.[459]

Although such commissions had various designs, according to the research carried out by Seixas and Souza,[460] in the same way as the NTC, all of these commissions held public hearings, presented results, published reports and books, and carried out political acts on set dates to remember important episodes in Brazil's history or honor victims of the dictatorship.

Nevertheless, as recalled by Schneider and Almeida,[461] on some occasions, the work of the NTC was contested by local commissions, which demonstrated a sort of clash over how the official history ought to be told, such as the dispute between the NTC and the truth commission of São Paulo concerning the circumstances of former President Juscelino Kubitschek's death. For many years,

---

[457] *NTC Report*, Volume I Chapter 2, p. 69.
[458] HOLLANDA, Cristina Buarque de and ISRAEL, Vinícius Pinheiro, "Panorama das Comissões da Verdade no Brasil: uma reflexão sobre novos sentidos de legitimidade e representação democrática", *Revista de Sociologia e Política*, vol. 27/2019, pp. 2–21.
[459] Ibid.
[460] SEIXAS, Ivan Akselrud de and SOUZA, Silvana Aparecida de, "Comissão Nacional da Verdade e a Rede de Comissões Estaduais, Municipais e Setoriais: A Trajetória do Brasil", *Revista Estudos de Sociologia*, vol. 20/2015, pp. 347–367.
[461] SCHNEIDER, Nina and ALMEIDA, Gisele Iecker de, "The Brazilian National Truth Commission (2012–2014) as a State-Commissioned History Project", in BEVERNAGE, B. and WOUTERS, N. (eds.), *The Palgrave Handbook of State-Sponsored History After 1945*, Palgrave Macmillan, London, 2018, pp. 637–652.

JK's death was believed to have been caused by a car accident; however, following a number of hearings and an analysis of evidence, the São Paulo local commission reached the conclusion that Kubitschek was murdered in a politically motivated crime.[462] On the other side, the NTC Final Report countered the perspective of the local commission and claimed that the homicide thesis lacked satisfactory proof.[463]

But while harshly criticized at the beginning[464] and during episodes like JK's circumstances of death, the network of truth commissions created in Brazil proved to be positive and productive and even served to mitigate the fact that Brazil set up a National Truth Commission without having created a permanent structure to continue, after its end, the movement of respecting and preserving the right to memory and justice.

5.3. THE NTC'S WORK ON THE EFFECT OF THE BRAZILIAN DICTATORSHIP ON THE LGBTI POPULATION

Concerning the findings of NTC regarding particular groups affected by the regime, specific chapters in this book are devoted to analyzing victims in which gender played a role and the repression of indigenous people, as well as cases of financial complicity, all of which should be integral to any complete analysis of the NTC's work. As a result, the following sections will discuss the major conclusions of the NTC for which there are no specific chapters, such as the treatment of the LGBTI (lesbian, gay, bisexual, transgender, and intersex) community. They will also examine additional positive results from the NTC Final Report.

With respect to how the LGBTI population was affected by the Brazilian dictatorship, recent experience in other Latin American cases may provide some guidance. Over the last several decades, the search for truth-telling shortly after an authoritarian regime ends has focused much attention on gender difference,[465] but only more recently, as Green and Quinalha have observed,[466]

---

[462] *São Paulo State Truth Commission*, Relatório sobre a Morte do Presidente Juscelino Kubitschek de Oliveira, http://comissaodaverdade.al.sp.gov.br/relatorio/tomo-iv/.

[463] *NTC Report*, Volume I, Chapter 2, pp. 72–75.

[464] HOLLANDA, Cristina Buarque de and ISRAEL, Vinícius Pinheiro, "Panorama das Comissões da Verdade no Brasil: uma reflexão sobre novos sentidos de legitimidade e representação democrática", *Revista de Sociologia e Política*, vol. 27/2019, pp. 2–21.

[465] NESIAH, Vasuki, "Discussion Lines on Gender and Transitional Justice: An Introductory Essay Reflecting on the ICTJ Bellagio Workshop on Gender and Transitional Justice", *Columbia Journal of Gender and Law*, vol. 15(3)/2006.

[466] GREEN, James N. and QUINALHA, Renan, *Ditadura e Homossexualidades: Repressão, Resistência e a Busca da Verdade*, São Carlos, Edufscar, 2014.

have Latin American truth commissions expanded their purview to include cases of violence against sexual minorities as human rights violations. Hence, the still developing visibility of LGBTI rights poses an obstacle to Transitional Justice mechanisms which seek to develop a theoretical approach to addressing cases of violence against sexual minorities. As a matter of fact, attention to violence against sexual minorities has remained largely absent from Transitional Justice methods, mainly because of a background construction of gender-based violence strictly limited to a normative and binary male–female view and its corresponding assumption of heterosexuality.

In the Brazilian case, among the NTC's innovations in this field, was a public hearing on the dictatorship and homosexuality, aiming to provide an interdisciplinary analysis of both the politics of repression and social control and the LGBTI population's ongoing resistance.[467] Moreover, the Final Report included a chapter focusing on the impact of the repression of the LGBTI population.[468] According to that chapter, discrimination against the LGBTI population did not begin during the dictatorship, but dates back to much earlier periods of Brazilian history. However, the elimination of democratic rights and public freedoms triggered by the authoritarian regime no doubt delayed the possibility of greater acceptance of differences in the field of sexuality. Consequently, because of repression and censorship, the monitoring and the study of homophobic aggression in Brazil only began in the 1980s, when data began to be collected on the violent deaths of gays and lesbians. In Brazil, the relationship between the repression caused by the dictatorship and its more general effects on political culture and social institutions has only been very recently scrutinized, since most of the efforts previously were related to research concerning the apparatus of political repression that was created to repress the "communist threat".

According to the NTC analysis, there was not a formalized State policy to exterminate homosexuals during the dictatorship, just as there was not a clear campaign to eliminate armed struggle and other sectors of the opposition over those same years. Thus, in the Brazilian case, homosexuality was not the main reason for the detention, repression, and torture of opponents of the regime, since repression was implemented much more to suppress the "communism treat". However, the ideology that justified the authoritarian regime contained a homophobic perspective, accentuating a social belief that homosexuals were harmful, dangerous, and contrary to the security of the family and the moral principles of the time. Finally, at the end of the Final Report's chapter on the LGBTI population, there are seven recommendations regarding the issue, among which are: (a) the criminalization of homophobia, lesbophobia, and

---

[467] BUENO-HANSEN, Pascha, "The Emerging LGBTI Rights Challenge to Transitional Justice in Latin America", *International Journal of Transitional Justice*, vol. 12/2018, pp. 126–145.
[468] *NTC Report*, "Ditadura e Homossexualidades", Volume 2, Text 7, pp. 300–311, cnv. memoriasreveladas.gov.br/images/pdf/relatorio/Volume%202%20-%20Texto%207.pdf.

transphobia;[469] (b) the enactment of a law guaranteeing free gender identity; and (c) an official apology from the State and the construction of memory sites for LGBT sectors linked to repression and resistance. None of these proposals, however, were included in the specific chapter containing the conclusions and formal recommendations of the NTC.

Indeed, specifically regarding the cases of sexual violence, Rubio-Marín has already emphasized the need to link reparations initiatives to broader conversations about the necessary structural, institutional, and legal reforms that would allow the construction of more inclusive and sex-egalitarian democracies.[470] In addition, Bueno-Hansen has stated that any holistic reparations for LGBTI victims must not be limited to restoring their standard of living prior to the conflict-related violence,[471] since usually the living conditions of LGBTI populations were already deeply impacted by marginalization and heteronormative structural violence well before the authoritarian period. Therefore, reparations must include the restitution of rights and rectification of oppressive living conditions so that victims do not return to the same situation of vulnerability. Consequently, as countries in transition begin to include LGBTI rights on the broader human rights agenda, there are expanding possibilities for full citizenship of that population.

However, in the Brazilian case, despite the impressive initiative to address the situation of violations committed against the LGBTI population during the dictatorship, the NTC Final Report did not address how to tackle these structural issues in favor of a more egalitarian democracy in any depth.[472] Considering the growing backlash opposing gender equality, abortion, same-sex marriage, comprehensive sex education, and transgender rights that Brazil is currently facing,[473] those in-depth suggestions and evaluations would have been very welcome.

---

[469] In 2019, the Brazilian Federal Supreme Court decided that until there is no specific law criminalizing homophobia and transphobia; such cases will be prosecuted based on the legislation regarding racism, according to Law no. 7,716 (1989). See: *Supremo Tribunal Federal*, "STF Enquadra Homofobia e Transfobia como Crimes de Racismo ao Reconhecer Omissão Legislativa", June 13, 2019, http://www.stf.jus.br/portal/cms/verNoticiaDetalhe.asp?idConteudo=414010.

[470] RUBIO-MARÍN, Ruth and DE GREIFF, Pablo, "Women and Reparations", *The International Journal of Transitional Justice*, vol. 1/2007, pp. 318–337.

[471] BUENO-HANSEN, Pascha, "The Emerging LGBTI Rights Challenge to Transitional Justice in Latin America", *International Journal of Transitional Justice*, vol. 12/2018, pp. 126–145.

[472] It should be mention that the material produced by the NTC concerning homosexuality was under the coordination of Commissioner Paulo Sérgio Pinheiro, although, the elaboration of the text was conducted by external researchers like James N. Green, Carlos Manuel de Céspedes and Renan Quinalha. See: *NTC Report*, "Ditadura e Homossexualidades", Volume 2, Text 7, pp. 300–311, cnv.memoriasreveladas.gov.br/images/pdf/relatorio/Volume%20 2%20-%20Texto%207.pdf.

[473] KALIL, Isabela Oliveira, "Gender Ideology Incursions in Education", *Sur International Journal on Human Rights*, vol. 29/2019. Assis, Mariana Prandini and OGANDO, Ana Carolina, "Gender Ideology and the Brazilian Elections", http://www.publicseminar.org/2018/11/gender-ideology-and-the-brazilian-elections/.

5.4. THE NTC'S FAILURE TO ADDRESS ACCOUNTABILITY FOR VIOLATIONS OF ECONOMIC AND SOCIAL RIGHTS

As Pinheiro has observed, the end of the dictatorship in Brazil did not necessarily mark the beginning of democracy.[474] This is because democracy is more than writing a constitution and introducing a new participatory electoral system.[475] Rather, it is the whole set of mechanisms – such as popular sovereignty through free and competitive elections, alternating turns in political power, the separation of powers, the independence of the judiciary, and civilian control of the Armed Forces – that may, at a certain moment, begin to produce real democracy. Moreover, at any stage, democracy also requires the economic development of the population in order to reach fruition. On this matter, O'Donnell has already stated that the combination of extreme inequality and very authoritarian patterns of social relations poses great difficulties in creating a more solid democracy.[476]

Indeed, it is hardly a new finding that Brazil faces dramatic levels of inequality between the rich and the poor. This historical gap continues to divide society, while it reinforces a social hierarchy where, for the most excluded sectors, many rights and the rule of law continue to be purely illusory. As a consequence, only a few sectors of society have access to adequate economic and social conditions in daily life.[477] Also, in this scenario, the exclusion of important segments of the population from economic progress and political participation very often offers them little hope of a better quality of life. The Brazilian case thus confirms the perception that countries facing transitions in such circumstances will only be able to achieve imperfect or restricted forms of democracy.[478]

Despite these structural imbalances being so deeply rooted in Brazilian social relations, the NTC gave much of its emphasis to political freedoms and civil rights and little priority to mapping the facts of the distribution of economic growth as an important factor for consolidating democracy in the country.

---

[474] PINHEIRO, Paulo Sérgio, "Democracy without Citizenship: Democratization and Human Rights", *International Conference on Democratic Transitions in Latin America and in Eastern Europe: Rupture and Continuity*, Paris, 1996.

[475] BOLLEN, K.A., "Issues in the Comparative Measurement of Political Democracy", *American Sociological Review*, vol. 45/1980, pp. 370–390.

[476] O'DONNELL, Guillermo, "On the State, Democratization and Some Conceptual Problems – La Latin American View with Glances at Some Post-Communist Countries", Working Paper 192, *The Helen Kellogg Institute for International Studies*, April, 1993.

[477] According to the *2018 Statistical Update on the Human Development Index* (HDI), Brazil ranked the 79th position in a range of 189 countries. See: *United Nations Development Programme*, Human Development Reports, http://hdr.undp.org/en/2018-update.

[478] STAVENHAGEN, Rodolfo, "América Latina: Derechos Humanos y Desarrollo", *International Foundation for Development Alternatives – IFDA Dossier*, vol. 79/1990, pp. 41–52.

The experience of countries in transition demonstrates a difficulty in separating the damage caused by violations of civil and political rights from those caused by violations of economic, social and cultural rights (ESCR).[479] Accordingly, what the NTC apparently neglected is that violations of a first category of human rights – such as extrajudicial executions, disappearances and arbitrary arrests – also occur in a context of violations of a second category of rights, that is, the failure to meet the basic needs of a majority of the population with respect to health, education, employment, etc. In the end, what was missing in the NTC Final Report was the recognition that disrespect for civil and political rights only exacerbates the lack of ESCRs within the same country.

For instance, as contemporary human rights scholars[480] have tended to comment, what was deficient in the broad analysis of the Final Report of the NTC was the acknowledgement that practices like the dictatorship's extensive grip on cultural life through methods of censorship (cutting and editing of song lyrics, books, and movies), the closure of educational institutions to prevent the growth of the intelligentsia, and the starvation of indigenous communities might also be seen as ESCR violations.

Indeed, such practices suggest that a certain number of international crimes (such as crimes against humanity) can sometimes simultaneously be ESCR violations. Unfortunately, other atrocities attract much more attention than the deliberate starving and sickening of indigenous people within the rainforest or in other remote areas of the country, as such practices are often noted only marginally or when they intersect with other forms of oppression. As Carranza has argued,[481] abuses of both civil and political rights and ESCRs are committed against overlapping sets of victims, by an invariably coinciding set of perpetrators. This creates an impunity gap when Transitional Justice mechanisms deal with only one kind of abuse while ignoring accountability for ESCR violations.

Just to illustrate this fact using the scenario previously described by Schmid,[482] adapted to the Brazilian scenario, the NTC might have addressed the case of indigenous women who suffered severe patterns of rape and deliberate aggression,[483] but little attention was paid to the fact that those same perpetrators

---

[479] SOARES, Inês Virgínia Prado and BASTOS, Lucia Elena Arantes Ferreira, "A Verdade Ilumina o Direito ao Desenvolvimento? Uma Análise da Potencialidade dos Trabalhos da Comissão Nacional da Verdade no Cenário Brasileiro", *Revista Anistia Política e Justiça de Transição*, vol. 6/2011, pp. 44–69.

[480] SCHMID, Evelyne, *Taking Economic, Social and Cultural Rights Seriously in International Criminal Law*, Cambridge, Cambridge University Press, 2015, pp. 2–4.

[481] CARRANZA, Ruben, "Plunder and Pain: Should Transitional Justice Engage with Corruption and Economic Crimes?", *International Journal of Transitional Justice*, vol. 2/2008, pp. 310–330.

[482] SCHMID, Evelyne, *Taking Economic, Social and Cultural Rights Seriously in International Criminal Law*, Cambridge, Cambridge University Press, 2015, pp. 2–4.

[483] *NTC Report*, Volume II, Text 5, p. 228, http://cnv.memoriasreveladas.gov.br/.

might have stolen their household items or livestock in the same attack. In such a case, it would not have been clear that the perpetrators had violated the women's ECSRs, in particular by interfering with their access to food and water, and the first and immediate reaction would merely have been to classify them as victims of sexual violence. In this hypothesis, the destruction of their communal property is likely to be downgraded or given marginal importance, or be considered only in the context of the rape. The question that was not raised by the NTC Final Report was the "what if" one: what if those indigenous women urgently needed their household utensils to carry drinking water from the river? What if the stealing of their livestock had deprived them and their families of their only sources of protein and income? What if their forced displacement from their lands had caused the destruction of their cultural identity and communal life?

In summary, the exclusion of specific considerations related to the rights to food, health, and education poses significant ethical and political questions that the NTC was not able to deal with in an appropriate manner. The transformation of savannah forest into pasture land, the exploitation of itinerant workers engaged in clearing operations on huge tracts of land without respect for their social rights, the destruction of homes, the cutting off of water sources, the exclusion of certain groups from their cultural life, and the forcing of people to work in inhumane conditions have been commonplace throughout Brazilian history. Rarely, however, have such violations been addressed through legal processes relying on the international human rights framework, and the NTC missed a great opportunity to do so.

Indeed, Brazil is not an isolated case. As Laplante has already found,[484] truth commissions, in particular, demonstrate a tendency to simplistically assume that international crimes and ESCR violations do not overlap, and they fail to see that if the underlying socioeconomic structures that lead to violence are not addressed, sustainable democracy will usually remain beyond reach.

That structural socioeconomic violence existed in Brazil is well known, since it has not been forgotten that, during the period of the dictatorship, there was a great concentration of wealth[485] at the same time that both rural[486] and urban[487] workers faced severe repression. The São Paulo State Truth Commission, for

---

[484] LAPLANTE, Lisa, "Transitional Justice and Peace Building: Diagnosing and Addressing the Socioeconomic Roots of Violence through a Human Rights Framework", *International Journal of Transitional Justice*, vol. 2/2008, pp. 331–355.

[485] BOHOSLAVSKY, Juan Pablo and TORELLY, Marcelo D., "Financial Complicity: The Brazilian Dictatorship Under the Macroscope", in SHARP, D.N. (ed.), *Justice and Economic Violence in Transition*, Springer Series in Transitional Justice vol. 5, New York, Springer, 2014, pp. 233–262.

[486] CARNEIRO, Ana and CIOCCARI, Marta, *Retrato da Repressão Política no Campo (1962–1985) – Camponeses Torturados, Mortos e Desaparecidos*, Brasília, MDA, 2010.

[487] KOPPER, Christopher, *VW do Brasil in the Brazilian Military Dictatorship 1964–1985: A Historical Study*, https://www.volkswagenag.com/en/group/history.html.

example, emphasized this violence as expressed in the military's alliance with the major economic groups[488] in the country. The Minas Gerais State Truth Commission dealt with social rights by creating a subcommittee to investigate the serious violations of the fundamental rights of rural workers, urban workers, and trade unionists.[489] The NTC itself highlighted the link between large economic groups and repression and authoritarian rule.[490]

But the wider challenge these facts pose from an ESCR perspective was not met in the NTC's conclusions – findings which, if they had been so oriented, might have substantially contributed to the future of Brazilian democracy. For instance, by deciding not to address the regime's violations from an ESCR standpoint, or the impact of the ongoing and historic structural socioeconomic violence, the list of 377 perpetrators of serious human rights violations that the NTC came up with failed to include the businessmen who collaborated with the regime.[491] Albeit and Fernandes have noted that the NTC's working group no. 13, formally assigned to research "Dictatorship and Repression of Workers and Trade Union Movements", did in fact propose holding accountable companies that collaborated with repression.[492] This idea was not accepted by the drafters of the Commission's Final Report, however, and that decision ultimately softened the Transitional Justice demands regarding the socioeconomic violence that occurred during the authoritarian regime.

It is consequently not a coincidence that there is a general view prevalent in Brazil that excludes peasants and indigenous peoples from the official accounting of the victims of the dictatorship and from reparation programs. This omission ultimately deepens the invisibility of the conflicts and political resistance that took place in the countryside and in border regions. Such invisibility originates in certain misunderstandings and detrimental beliefs such as: (i) the passive acceptance that conflicts over land and rural violence preceded the dictatorship period and did not cease with its end; (ii) the erroneous assumption that peasants and indigenous people were not actors in the political struggles against authoritarianism or that they were not genuine victims of State repression,

---

[488] *Truth Commission of the State of São Paulo*, Report, Vol. 1, Part 1, "O Financiamento da Repressão".

[489] Truth Commission of the State of Minas Gerais, "As Graves Violações de Direitos Humanos no Campo (1961–1988)", Chapter 5, Vol. 2, http://www.comissaodaverdade.mg.gov.br/handle/123456789/1169.

[490] *National Truth Commission*, "2014 Final Report", Vol. 2, Chapter 8, "Civis que Colaboraram com a Ditadura".

[491] *National Truth Commission*, "2014 Final Report", Vol. 1, Part IV, Chapter 16, "A Autoria das Graves Violações de Direitos Humanos", pp. 842–931.

[492] FERNANDES, Pádua, "Justiça de Transição e o Fundamento nos Direitos Humanos: Perplexidades do Relatório da Comissão Nacional da Verdade Brasileira", in KASHIURA, Celso Naoto Jr., AKAMINE, Oswaldo Jr., and MELO Tarso de (eds.), *Para a Crítica do Direito: Reflexões sobre Teorias e Práticas Jurídicas*, São Paulo, Editorial Dobra, 2015, pp. 717–745.

since they did not participate in armed resistance to the regime in the same way that politically organized segments did in urban areas; and (iii) the allegation that violence and social exclusion in rural areas were already so entrenched in the country that they did not suffer any substantial further impacts related to the dictatorship.[493] In fact, these are all negative narratives that promote an institutionalized forgetting of violations. These false narratives could have been better dissected and contradicted by the efforts of the NTC if it had adopted an ESCR perspective in its analysis.

It seems that in the Brazilian experience with the NTC, Transitional Justice and its mechanisms of truth-seeking, prosecution, reparations, and institutional reform were designed solely to hold accountable the perpetrators of massive violations of human rights (like forced disappearances and torture), while providing their victims with *some* measure of truth and justice. The prevailing assumption, as theoretically defined by Carranza,[494] seems to be that truth commissions and reparations programs are meant to engage mainly, if not exclusively, with violations of civil and political rights that involve either physical integrity or personal freedom, and not with violations of economic and social rights.

Consequently, this focus on civil and political rights violations and the corresponding hesitation to address violations of socioeconomic rights may be an extension of the larger dichotomy in human rights discourses. Civil and political rights violations are seen not only as justiciable but also as susceptible to being redressed through Transitional Justice mechanisms. Socioeconomic rights violations, meanwhile, are usually considered non-justiciable and, therefore, better addressed by a catch-all reference to development programs. Consequently, Carranza concludes, post-transition developing countries that are chronically poor and conflict-ridden in terms of socioeconomic structural violence are likely to remain so.

Notwithstanding the introduction of Transitional Justice measures, allowing these structural inequalities to persist through the avoidance of certain hard facts and with limited acknowledgement, Transitional Justice mechanisms can rightly be accused of creating and then frustrating expectations of meaningful change.

Or, quoting Arthur,[495] Transitional Justice requires more than legal-institutional reforms and the transformation of an abusive State security apparatus; rather, it also requires a redistribution of wealth that was unjustly

---

[493] Ibid.
[494] CARRANZA, Ruben, "Plunder and Pain: Should Transitional Justice Engage with Corruption and Economic Crimes?", *International Journal of Transitional Justice*, vol. 2/2008, pp. 310–330.
[495] ARTHUR, Paige, "How Transitions Reshaped Human Rights: A Conceptual History of Transitional Justice", *Human Rights Quarterly*, vol. 31/2009, pp. 321–367.

accumulated through an inhuman political and economic system. This author agrees with her arguments:

> Where, as in Brazil, Guatemala, El Salvador, and Haiti or the Philippines, land-owning is concentrated in large *latifundia*, with a dependent and impoverished peasantry, the overthrow of the Marcoses or the Duvaliers may mean little without a reform of the socio-economic system.[496]

5.5. THE NTC'S FAILURE TO CATALYZE CHANGES IN THE COUNTRY

While analyzing Transitional Justice and the public sphere, Ramírez-Barat has said that,[497] along with other factors, such as performance and credibility, the impact of Transitional Justice measures is significantly related to the relationship they establish with the societies in which they operate. Thus, for members of affected communities to be able to participate in and contribute to this process, they need to be properly informed and to understand the work of Transitional Justice measures, along with knowing their options and especially their right to participate. Hence, those responsible for the implementation of Transitional Justice measures have to take proactive steps to build direct communication with different stakeholders, while making complex information accessible to the general population and to specific groups.

Furthermore, in examining the NTC's work, it is possible to say that the Commissioners did not follow much of the advice offered by Ramírez-Barat, and this gap resulted in a weak level of trust on the part of society in the NTC's work.[498] Hence, its activities were severely criticized as not being transparent, inclusive or participatory, as they were originally supposed to be.[499] For instance, Westhrop, Peluzio and Simi[500] have stated that the work of the NTC was

---

[496] Ibid.
[497] RAMÍREZ-BARAT, Clara, "Transitional Justice and the Public Sphere", in RAMÍREZ-BARAT, Clara (ed.), *Transitional Justice, Culture, and Society Beyond Outreach*, New York, International Center for Transitional Justice and Social Science Research Council, 2014, pp. 27–45.
[498] CABRAL, Paulo, "Comissão da Verdade Enfrenta Críticas e Iniciativa Paralela de Militares", *BBC Brasil*, May 16, 2012, https://www.bbc.com/portuguese/noticias/2012/05/120515_comissao_verdade_pc.
[499] DUAILIBI, Julia, "A Verdade da Comissão", *Revista Piauí*, vol. 91/2014, https://piaui.folha.uol.com.br/materia/a-verdade-da-comissao/.
[500] WESTHROP, Amy Jo, PELUZIO, Luciana and SIMI, Gustavo, *Comissão Nacional da Verdade: Balanços e Perspectivas da Finalização de seu Processo Político-Institucional*, Rio de Janeiro, ISER, 2015.

characterized by very little openness to civil society participation, with low levels of dialogue even with former political prisoners and the family members of the dead and disappeared. Civil society organizations cited this lack of transparency as a fundamental problem for the NTC. As a result, it is not surprisingly that the majority of the population demonstrated a indifferent attitude towards the NTC that has never gone away. Engstrom too has identified that the NTC had unfortunately low visibility and its products and efforts remained disconnected from wider society.[501]

Perhaps, to the general public, the NTC's working methodology appeared not to be sufficiently well defined, and there were also fissures between the Commissioners with regard to what the objectives and purposes of a truth commission should be.[502] For instance, the Commissioners disagreed about what was the most appropriate public relations strategy to pursue: while some Commissioners advocated publicly discussing their work as it proceeded, others preferred to work behind closed doors and only present their findings after the investigations had been completed.[503]

Thus, the NTC was internally the victim of some of the same obstacles seen in the broader process of negotiation that led to its creation. These internal disputes left it isolated within the government and unable to advance with the necessary reconstruction of truth and memory in Brazil. Also, as Teles and Quinalha have found,[504] without being able to confront the military due to the lack of effective support from the Brazilian President, the Commission spent much of the time immobilized, consumed in internal conflicts, and condemned, as in the myth of Sisyphus, to push a boulder up a mountain only to have it roll back down again. This scenario within which the NTC did its work proves, as Jelin previously observed,[505] that the struggle is often not between memory on the one hand and oblivion and silence on the other, but rather between opposing memories

---

[501] ENGSTROM, Par, "Brazilian Post-Transitional Justice and the Inter-American Human Rights System", *Conference on Post-Transitional Justice in Brazil*, Brazil Institute, King's College London, 2013.

[502] JERONIMO, Josie, "Luta pela Memória da Ditadura Está em Perigo. Conspiração, Sabotagem e Estrelismo Atrapalham as Apurações da Comissão da Verdde", *Isto É*, July 26, 2013, https://istoe.com.br/316230_LUTA+PELA+MEMORIA+DA+DITADURA+ESTA+EM+PERIGO/.

[503] SCHNEIDER, Nina, "Too Little too Late or Premature? The Brazilian Truth Commission and the Question of Best Timing", *Journal of Iberian and Latin American Research*, vol. 19/2013, pp. 149–162.

[504] TELES, Edson and QUINALHA, Renan, "Lógica da Governabilidade como Escolha da Democracia – O Trabalho de Sísifo da Comissão Nacional da Verdade", *Le Monde Diplomatique Brasil*, September 2, 2013, https://diplomatique.org.br/o-trabalho-de-sisifo-da-comissao-nacional-da-verdade/.

[505] JELIN, Elizabeth, "Public Memorialization in Perspective: Truth, Justice and Memory of Past Repression in the Southern Cone of South America", *The International Journal of Transitional Justice*, vol. 1/2007, pp. 138–156.

and points of view within the very same government, political institutions, and society, whose discourses have their own silences and voids.

Moreover, while analyzing the media perspective and the 2014 release of the NTC Final Report, Mello and Baccega[506] concluded that the conflicting nature of collective memory and historical narratives in Brazil was on display when the mass media[507] accused the NTC of having listened only to one side of the story (the perspective of those who were persecuted), ignoring those allegedly harmed by left-wing activists during the dictatorship. Consequently, instead of helping with national reconstruction and overcoming disagreements, it turns out that the NTC very often exacerbated old wounds within the society.

Another critical assessment that remains to be explored is the fact that while tending to restrict its investigations on the deliberate State policies of genocide against indigenous communities, the NTC has not only failed to translate its revelations into a rethinking of State-indigenous relations, but it has in some way served as an excuse for inaction. For instance, some have said that an Indigenous National Truth Commission should be established, exclusively for the study of serious human rights violations against indigenous peoples, in order to obtain a deeper view of the cases not detailed in the current report.[508] As Corntassel and Holder explained,[509] it is possible to conclude that, although truth commissions succeeded in uncovering the need for indigenous restitution, the adoption of reparation measures is still a pending issue and has yet to be prioritized, just as has happened in the Brazilian case, since the overall focus of the NTC's was on crimes and individual citizenship rights rather than recognizing communal grievances and restoring communal independence.

In addition, after more than six years since the release of the NTC Final Report, the Commission's findings seem to have achieved few changes in local prosecutions, and they have not opened the door to prosecution of politicians and members of the Armed Forces, as the Amnesty Law is still in force. So, what explains this failure to realize the promise of the Commission's final report? It is generally recognized that truth commissions involve a trade-off between justice for victims and national healing; however, in the Brazilian case, the tiny impacts of the Final Report raise doubts whether this trade-off ever existed in that country's experience. The fact that almost six years later very

---

[506] MELLO, Felipe Correa and BACCEGA, Maria Aparecida, "Imprensa e Discurso Histórico: A Comissão Nacional da Verdade na Folha de São Paulo e no Estado de São Paulo", *Comunicação e Educação*, vol. 20(1)/2015, pp. 105–116.

[507] *Folha de São Paulo*, "Comissão da Verdade É Feita de Cínicos", December 14, 2014, p. A18. BUCCI, Eugênio, "Duas Notas para o Dia Seguinte", *O Estado de São Paulo*, December 11, 2014, p. A2.

[508] National Truth Commission, "2014 Final Report", Volume II, Text 5, p. 253.

[509] CORNTASSEL, Jeff and HOLDER, Cindy, "Who's Sorry Now? Government Apologies, Truth Commissions, and Indigenous Self-Determination in Australia, Canada, Guatemala and Peru", *Human Rights Review*, vol. 9/2008, pp. 465–489.

few of its recommendations have been fully adopted demonstrates this lack of support for the Commission's findings. In fact, according to a survey conducted in March of 2019,[510] over 80% of the NTC's proposals were either not fulfilled or only partially accepted. This means that of the 29 recommendations, 18 were not implemented, six were partially implemented, and only five were effectively implemented.

The five recommendations that have been more promptly to be implemented are: (a) the rectification of the death certificates for victims of the dictatorship;[511] (b) the introduction of custody hearings in court; (c) the existence of an agency to ensure the maintenance of the NTC's work (the Special Commission on Political Deaths and Disappearances); (d) the pursuit of the search for bodies of victims of the military dictatorship (also carried out by the Special Commission on Political Deaths and Disappearances); and (e) the maintenance of the military dictatorship's archives.[512]

As Melo and Martins have mentioned, the NTC's decision to effectively name names and recommend the punishment of State perpetrators was received with apprehension by the government, in 2014, so that, in the days immediately following the issuing of the NTC Final Report, it soon became clear that the government was not only unwilling to implement the accountability measures recommended by the NTC, but also feared an outburst of judicial claims questioning the report's conclusions and recommendations. Indeed, the day after the report was released the press recorded the government's first reaction in off-the-record statements from some government sources, already signaling the difficult assimilation of the Commission's recommendations by the government at that time.[513]

Although some areas of the Executive Branch considered the possibility of implementing the set of recommendations in the NTC Final Report, including the proposal to create a permanent follow-up body or agency, the prevailing and majority understanding was that there was a lack of urgency behind the

---

[510] POTTER, Hyury, "Quatro Anos Depois, Brasil Ignora Maioria das Recomendações da Comissão da Verdade", *Aos Fatos*, March 29, 2019, https://aosfatos.org/noticias/quatro-anos-depois-brasil-ignora-maioria-das-recomendacoes-da-comissao-da-verdade/.

[511] The rectification of death certificates still requires the reinforcement of judicial decisions. See: MARQUES, José, "Após decisão da Justiça, cartórios corrigem certidões de óbito de torturados pela ditadura", *Folha de São Paulo*, December 18, 2019, https://www1.folha.uol.com.br/poder/2019/12/apos-decisao-da-justica-cartorios-corrigem-certidoes-de-obito-de-torturados-pela-ditadura.html.

[512] See: POTTER, Hyury, "Quatro Anos Depois, Brasil Ignora Maioria das Recomendações da Comissão da Verdade", *Aos Fatos*, March 29, 2019, https://aosfatos.org/noticias/quatro-anos-depois-brasil-ignora-maioria-das-recomendacoes-da-comissao-da-verdade/.

[513] MAGALHÃES, João Carlos and NERY, Natuza, "Para Planalto, Recomendações do Relatório da Comissão São Genéricas", *Folha de São Paulo*, 11 December 2014. See also: *Agência Estado*, "Governo Não Retaliará General que Criticou Relatório da CNV", December 11, 2014.

application of the rules suggested by the Commissioners.[514] Following this uneasy situation expressed by sources within the government, Bucci[515] even observed that the dimensions of the NTC's work were so impressive that it was not surprising that government did not readily assimilate it. The federal government's support – which had been resounding at the beginning of the NTC's work but was elusive at its conclusion – shows that the material that was produced was actually more problematic than had been anticipated.

Setting aside the intensity of the revelations brought out in the NTC's work, as previously stated in this chapter another important part of the explanation for the low impact of the Final Report is the Commission's own treatment of such issues, in particular, the lack of dialogue with major groups of civil society. So, the question that should be posed is: how to make the information elaborated by the NTC Final Report more attractive? For instance, the Office of the United Nations High Commissioner of Human Rights (OHCHR) has suggested that the key sections of the report should be serialized in a daily national newspaper.[516] Another example concerning the distribution of truth commissions' reports comes from Argentina, where they turned the memory of the dead and missing into cartoons and comics, mostly satirical, in order to criticize the years of dictatorship.[517]

In addition, the report should be shortened and turned into a more accessible version, and the report should be translated into the different languages not only pertaining to the country – for instance in indigenous dialects – but also into English or Spanish. This is because, as Langler previously observed,[518] for most victims the report does not mean much, due to high levels of illiteracy and the time required and other challenges involved in reading a document of thousands of pages.

Because, as Ramírez-Barat has explained,[519] the message of acknowledging past abuses and recognizing victims needs to be delivered to the wider society, making it essential to explain and broadly publicize the aims and results of the truth-telling process. Thus, beyond what happens inside a testimony-gathering

---

[514] FERNANDES, Maria Cristina, "Justiça de Transição Sem Ativismo", *Valor Econômico*, July 29, 2016, https://valor.globo.com/eu-e/coluna/justica-de-transicao-sem-ativismo.ghtml.

[515] BUCCI, Eugênio, "A Letra da Verdade", *Revista de Estudos Avançados da USP*, vol. 30/2016, pp. 297–302.

[516] *Office of the United Nations High Commissioner of Human Rights* (OHCHR), "Rule of Law Tools for Post-Conflict States – Truth Commissions", New York and Geneva, 2006, p. 31.

[517] CARRASCO, Jorge Catala; DRINOT, Paulo Drinot and SCORER, James, *Comics and Memory in Latin America*, Pittsburgh PA, University of Pittsburgh Press, 2017.

[518] LANGLER, Johannes, "Are Truth Commissions Just Hot-Air Balloons? A Reality Check of the Impact of Truth Commission Recommendations", *Desafíos*, vol. 29/2017.

[519] RAMÍREZ-BARAT, Clara, "Transitional Justice and the Public Sphere", in RAMÍREZ-BARAT, Clara (ed.), *Transitional Justice, Culture, and Society Beyond Outreach*, New York, International Center for Transitional Justice and Social Science Research Council, 2014, 27–45.

exercise, commissioners should consider the way in which these actions and public hearings resonate or are acknowledged at the societal level. Put this way, for the work of the NTC to have a lasting legacy, the Commissioners should have striven to promote public engagement, as society has the responsibility to keep pushing for the reforms and changes that that work could only begin to advance. Moreover, the success of initiatives like the NTC depends on their capacity to catalyze change in a country's political culture. Otherwise, there is often the risk that the report will be seen as a monumental work unable to generate discussion for more than a week or two.[520]

With respect to the feasibility of catalyzing of public opinion, some of the representatives of the victims' families regarded the NTC as a weak and compromised version of a truth commission and have accused the Brazilian State of cynically installing the NTC solely to divert attention from the more controversial issue of punishment, something barred by the Amnesty Law. These critics suspected that the NTC was a strategic game designed by the State which would serve as a mere diplomatic project, with the goal of reconciliation with the international human rights community (mainly the expectations of the Inter-American Court of Human Rights) rather than clarification of crimes or rehabilitating victims.[521]

This point of view of the representatives of the victims' families demonstrates that the dynamics of truth commissions differ from those of judicial proceedings, and the fact that the offenders are not punished gives rise to a variety of reactions in the victims. Their individual responses ranged from a profound feeling of injustice that some victims feel, at the pardon seemingly being granted to the perpetrators, to a return to some measure of serenity felt by others. In analyzing the framework of truth commissions and their impacts, Hazan has stated that some victims do actually derive satisfaction from publicly stating their version of the truth,[522] and they may also find it satisfying to see society punish their tormentors at least symbolically. But, for other victims, however, public disclosure of their suffering and the process of recalling that past brings very little relief. On the contrary, it causes serious psychological problems.

To sum up, as Gready and Robins noted,[523] Transitional Justice sponsors often make broad assumptions that its components will always provide

---

[520] DUAILIBI, Julia, "A Verdade da Comissão", *Revista Piauí*, vol. 91/2014, https://piaui.folha.uol.com.br/materia/a-verdade-da-comissao/.

[521] SCHNEIDER, Nina, "Too Little too Late or Premature? The Brazilian Truth Commission and the Question of Best Timing", *Journal of Iberian and Latin American Research*, vol. 19/2013, pp. 149–162.

[522] HAZAN, Pierre, "Measuring the Impact of Punishment and Forgiveness: A Framework for Evaluating Transitional Justice", *International Review of the Red Cross*, vol. 88/2006, pp. 19–47.

[523] GREADY, Paul and ROBINS, Simon, "Transitional Justice and Theories of Change: Towards Evaluation as Understanding", *International Journal of Transitional Justice*, vol. 14/2020, pp. 280–299.

significant changes in a country – meaning that truth-telling contributes to reconciliation, that prosecutions act as a deterrent, that institutional reform can aid non-repetition of violations, and so on. The problem is that from a theoretical perspective those initiatives are taken for granted, as if the use of said framework will definitely lead to change, or as if the mere conclusion of the 2014 NTC Final Report would promote Brazil to a new level in terms of democracy. In this sense, as Gready and Robins stated, notwithstanding a significant growth in evaluation and theory-based work in the last decade, many theories of change in Transitional Justice remain purely normative rather than empirically rooted, resulting in a tendency to present interventions as a self-evident good. The Brazilian case of the NTC Final Report demonstrates that still there is a long way to go for truth commissions to achieve particular outcomes and greater coherence as a mechanism of Transitional Justice.

5.6. GENERAL ASSESSMENTS OF THE NATIONAL TRUTH COMMISSION: THE HIDDEN CASES

The Final Report definitely made enormous contributions to the process of truth-telling about the dictatorship in Brazil; however, it is also clear that the NTC could not exhaustively examine the whole subject to be investigated due to the relatively short period in which it functioned, its limited budget, and the fairly small number of personnel that it was able to hire.[524] Thus, there are at least three major aspects of the NTC Final Report that may require further comprehension and should receive a more in-depth approach in the near future.

First, one must mention the need for a detailed identification of victims who, although they were illegally detained and tortured, after a period of imprisonment were released. That means that they did not disappear, nor were they killed, but nevertheless suffered the consequences of the violations of human rights practiced by the regime. In this sense, Schneider and Almeida raised the question of whether the NTC has used a narrow concept of victimhood by reinforcing the notion that the victims of the dictatorship consisted only of those 434 individuals.[525] As Weichert has stated,[526] this seems to be the biggest failing in the Commission's work, since it represents an essential data point to measure

---

[524] DUAILIBI, Julia, "A Verdade da Comissão", *Revista Piauí*, vol. 91/2014, https://piaui.folha.uol.com.br/materia/a-verdade-da-comissao/.
[525] SCHNEIDER, Nina and ALMEIDA, Gisele Iecker de, "The Brazilian National Truth Commission (2012–2014) as a State-Commissioned History Project", in BEVERNAGE, B. and WOUTERS, N. (eds.), *The Palgrave Handbook of State-Sponsored History After 1945*, Palgrave Macmillan, London, 2018, pp. 637–652.
[526] WEICHERT, Marlon Alberto, "O Relatório da Comissão Nacional da Verdade: Conquistas e Desafios", *Projeto História*, vol. 50/2014, pp. 86–137.

the patterns of repression in the country. Due to this lack of information, Brazil has not yet achieved the level of accuracy which would allow for the different types of analysis of Transitional Justice which are frequently available for quantitative or survey-based studies and for qualitative methodologies.[527] For further analysis of the subject of databases, the reader is directed to Chapter 3 of this book discussing the reparations programs that have been implemented, especially by the Amnesty Commission.

Second, there is an ongoing need for a framework of proposals in cases that were obscured or hidden in the set of 29 official recommendations listed in the NTC Final Report. These are "hidden cases" because, although they were discussed in Volume II of the Final Report as thematic texts, they did not receive formal suggestions in the conclusions offered in Chapter 18, Volume I. Such "hidden cases" are, for example, the violence in rural areas, the repression inside the Armed Forces, the collaboration of the Catholic Church with the repressive State, and the participation of corporations and civil actors inside the authoritarian regime.

Particular attention should be drawn to the legacy of violations related to indigenous peoples and peasants, because, although in most cases they were not involved in political movements or ideological disputes, they still suffered the consequences of authoritarianism[528] when their lands were considered to be a barrier to certain national development plans, such as the opening of roads, the construction of hydroelectric dams, and the implementation of agricultural projects.[529]

Likewise, the support of corporations for the *coup d'état* and their subsequent collaboration with the regime's repressive policies – that is, private sector participation in the authoritarian model – also requires particular consideration. After 1968, businessmen financed the repressive structure, and various companies harassed workers who participated in trade unions or movements protesting for better working conditions or other social and economic rights.

---

[527] For an analysis of the significance of datasets as truth-telling and memorialization measures of Transitional Justice, see: RAUSCHENBACH, Mina; SCAGLIOLA, Stef; PARMENTIER, Stephan; and DE JONG, Franciska, "The Perfect Data-Marriage: Transitional Justice Research and Oral History Life Stories", *Transitional Justice Review*, vol. 1/2016, pp. 7–58.

[528] For this type of assessment, see Chapter 7 of this book relating to Transitional Justice and indigenous communities.

[529] The reference is to the "*Figueiredo Report*", which was an investigation carried out in 1967 by the Public Prosecutor Jader de Figueiredo Correia. That report described the killing of entire communities, along with torture and cruel treatment against indigenous people in Brazil. This report was believed to have been destroyed by a fire at the Agriculture Ministry soon after it came out, prompting suspicions of a cover-up by the dictatorship and its allies among the big landowners. However, most of the document was recently discovered, in 2013, in an archive (located at the Indian Museum in Rio de Janeiro City). See: http://www.mpf.mp.br/atuacao-tematica/ccr6/dados-da-atuacao/grupos-de-trabalho/violacao-dos-direitos-dos-povos-indigenas-e-registro-militar/relatorio-figueiredo.

Companies not only organized blacklists – which prevented such workers from finding new employment – but reported their names to the Armed Forces.[530]

Third, there is the need for careful research concerning the consequences of a dictatorial government for everyday life, i.e., aspects related to economic and social rights and the educational system. As the Office of the United Nations High Commissioner for Human Rights states in its guidelines for Transitional Justice,[531] truth commissions can be suitable platforms for considering the root causes of repression and ESCR violations. However, in the Brazilian case, the NTC focused its work on violations of civil and political rights and gave little attention to how economic, social, and cultural rights were affected during that period.

5.7. AUTHORITARIANISM'S LEGACIES AND THE CULTURE OF IMPUNITY

In its list of conclusions, the NTC mentioned that practices such as illegal and arbitrary detention, torture, executions, forced disappearances, and concealment of corpses still persist in Brazil until today. It also stated that, despite the fact that those violations did not occur in the context of political repression anymore – as happened during the dictatorship – those practices are still part of contemporary reality. In addition, the NTC recognized that this background derives from the fact that the violations of human rights perpetrated during the dictatorship were not properly denounced, nor were the criminals held responsible for their acts; thus, this scenario creates and fosters the conditions for the perpetuation of the above-mentioned types of crime.[532]

But in fact, this "finding" of the NTC is not new, and a wide range of authors including Linz and Stepan, Zaverucha, Pinheiro and Mesquita Neto have remarked on the *continuísmo* (continuity) that characterized the Brazilian democratic transition, meaning that some of the same Brazilian political elites that were implicated in the abuses of the military regime remained in power after that regime ended.[533] Indeed, scholars like Adorno[534] and Pinheiro have

---

[530] For a broad discussion of this subject, see Chapter 9 of this book which is dedicated to the complicity of corporations and private actors.
[531] *The Office of the United Nations High Commissioner for Human Rights*, Transitional Justice and Social, Economic and Cultural Rights, http://www.ohchr.org/Documents/Publications/HR-PUB-13-05.pdf.
[532] *NTC Report*, Volume I, Part V, Chapter 18, "Conclusions and Recommendations", p. 964.
[533] LINZ, Juan J. and STEPAN, Alfred, *Problems of Democratic Transition and Consolidation. Southern Europe, South America and Post-Communist Europe*, Baltimore MD, Johns Hopkins University Press, 1996. ZAVERUCHA, Jorge, *Rumor de Sabres: Tutela Militar ou Controle Civil?*, São Paulo, Ática, 1994. PINHEIRO, Paulo Sérgio, "The Legacy of Authoritarianism in Democratic Brazil", in NAGEL, Stuart S. (ed.), *Latin American Development and Public Policy*,

commented on the ability of the State to carry out a type of "anti-human rights actions" or *continuism* as a factor linked to the past levels of impunity, whose source dates from before the dictatorship and is embodied in a range of social, political and cultural practices.

This sociological perception has been labelled as a "socially rooted authoritarianism",[535] and in this case, Adorno adds that the reconstruction of a democratic society in Brazil implies a discussion of the reasons why the State has not been rigorous enough to contain the arbitrary violence committed by its own representatives since the dictatorship. Similarly, it is argued by Pinheiro,[536] that the return to democratic constitutionalism has done little to eradicate authoritarian practices entrenched not only in the State but in society as well. And, even now, this conclusion based on the authoritarianism deeply engrained in the mindset of the citizenry may still be seen inside Brazilian society, according to the review undertaken by Schwarcz.[537]

In 2014, the NTC Final Report articulated that the consequences of the non-prosecution of crimes against humanity committed during the dictatorship were not limited to the effect on the victims and their families, since impunity in Brazil still contaminated State institutions and the rule of law, undermining the credibility of the State itself. Actually, the idea that only poor people and excluded persons are imprisoned still persists in the country[538] – punishment that does not seem to apply to politicians, businessmen and other members of the elite who only just very recently have begun to be prosecuted on a large scale for corruption[539]

New York, St. Martin Press, 1994. MESQUITA NETO, Paulo de, "Crime, Violence and Political Uncertainty in Brazil", *Crime and Policing in Transitional Societies Conference*, Johannesburg, 2000.

[534] ADORNO, Sérgio, "Criminal Violence in Modern Brazil: The Case of the State of São Paulo", in SHELLEY, Louise and VIGH, József (eds.), *Social Changes, Crime and Police: International Conference*, Amsterdam, Harwood, 1995.

[535] The concept of socially rooted authoritarianism, in Brazil, is seen as having its source before the dictatorship and is embodied in a range of social, political and cultural practices. It is regarded as preceding and surviving the authoritarian regimes and is independent of political periodization. See: PINHEIRO, Paulo Sérgio, "The Legacy of Authoritarianism in Democratic Brazil", in NAGEL, Stuart S. (ed.), *Latin American Development and Public Policy*, New York, St. Martin Press, 1994.

[536] PINHEIRO, Paulo Sérgio, "Democracy without Citizenship: Democratization and Human Rights", *International Conference on Democratic Transitions in Latin America and in Eastern Europe: Rupture and Continuity*, Paris, 1996.

[537] SCHWARCZ, Lilia M., *Sobre o Autoritarismo Brasileiro*, São Paulo, Companhia das Letras, 2019.

[538] KROETZ, Flávia Saldanha, "Reflexos da Impunidade dos Agentes Estatais por Graves Violações aos Direitos Humanos Cometidas Durante a Ditadura Militar no Brasil", *Revista Jurídica da Procuradoria-Geral do Distrito Federal*, vol. 39/2014, pp. 175–196.

[539] *Financial Times*, "What is the Petrobras Scandal that is Engulfing Brazil?", April 1, 2016, https://www.ft.com/content/6e8b0e28-f728-11e5-803c-d27c7117d132.

and bribery.[540] Observing these facts, Fleischer[541] has stated that Brazil's legal system permits literally hundreds of appeals and other legal maneuvers that competent and high-priced lawyers can use to string out proceedings for years.[542] Generally, citizens receive a fair and public hearing, but it is rarely timely. Although all defendants have the right to independent counsel, the poor must depend on public defenders, of which there is a shortage in almost all states. All these factors converge to give some truth to the old claim that only poor people go to jail in Brazil.

Also, as a consequence of the non-prosecution of the past crimes, there is a perception that it will always be possible to suppress the rule of law in Brazil. This tolerance spreads the idea that "some" Brazilians occupy a different status before the law because their behavior, although quite outrageous, remains without any criminal response.[543] Likewise, impunity regarding past atrocities gives rise to the idea that agents of repression today may also be immune to the law – as argued during the 2018 intervention of the Armed Forces in the state of Rio de Janeiro, when it was stated that to ensure the maintenance of public security the troops deployed would need the guarantee that there would be no "truth commission".[544] In short, the Brazilian case continues to be an illustration of the fact that authoritarianism and arbitrariness may persist despite democratic openness, elections, and constitutional reforms.[545]

This impunity lies at the heart of the popular belief that "sometimes" torture is justified. This conception may be one of the causes of the continuing use of violence in policing in the country – that is, the persistent use of torture as a procedure in investigations. This legacy of authoritarianism was even mentioned by the United Nations Special Rapporteur on Torture during his mission in Brazil in 2016. His report stated that torture and ill-treatment in the course of interrogation are frequent occurrences and that killings by police and by prison staff are not isolated incidents, such that impunity remains the rule rather than

---

[540] *Financial Times*, "A Brazilian Bribery Machine", December 28, 2016, https://www.ft.com/content/8edf5b2c-c868-11e6-9043-7e34c07b46ef.

[541] FLEISCHER, David, *Countries at the Crossroads 2012: Brazil*, https://freedomhouse.org/sites/default/files/Brazil%20-%20FINAL.pdf.

[542] For a detailed description of how claims based on the crimes committed during the dictatorship are being constantly blocked in the Brazilian judicial system, see Chapter 4 of this book about criminal justice and judicial accountability.

[543] FAVERO, Eugenia Augusta Gonzaga, "Crimes da Ditadura: Iniciativas do Ministério Público Federal em São Paulo", in SOARES, Inês Virgínia Prado and SHIMADA, Sandra Akemi (eds.), *Memória e Verdade – A Justiça de Transição no Estado Democrático de Direito Brasileiro*, Belo Horizonte, Forum, 2009, pp. 213–232.

[544] BENITES, Afonso, "Intervenção Federal no Rio Desperta Fantasmas sobre o Papel do Exército", *El País*, February 21, 2018.

[545] PINHEIRO, Paulo Sérgio, "Autoritarismo e Transição", *Revista da Universidade de São Paulo*, vol. 9/1991, pp. 45–56.

the exception.[546] As Vriezen has observed,[547] for victims of human rights crimes, the lack of accountability as a result of impunity is tough, but not only victims and their families suffer from impunity, since it affects the whole society and spreads cynicism and distrust of authority. This scenario of skepticism in Brazil has improved very little since 2016 when a survey conducted by the *Forum Brasileiro de Segurança Pública* and the *DataFolha* Institute indicated that 70% of Brazilian citizens have the perception that police officers commit acts of excessive violence in the exercise of their authority.[548]

Looking at the results of this survey, another fact that should be taken into account is that, as a result of impunity, it is not possible to separate the guilty from the innocent. As Aguirre has noted,[549] as soon as impunity takes root in a nation, all members of the Armed Forces and all members of the police who served during the past reign of terror, without any distinction, are potentially put into the ranks of the "guilty". An ominous consequence of such indiscriminate classifications is that all citizens will tend to suspect and see as guilty anyone who wore a uniform during these years.

All the factors described above, arising from *continuism* and rooted in authoritarianism, demonstrate that violence committed in the past by individuals and through institutions like the police should be viewed as linked to human rights violations committed in the present, even if the motives are significantly different. This is clearly seen in Brazil, where most incidents of death and torture are publicly attributed to the prisoner's resistance or efforts to escape, just as occasionally deaths of political prisoners under the military rule were. Moreover, until now Brazilian society has failed to recognize the link between past and present human rights violations. As Hamber has observed,[550] for the majority of society, where a level of socially rooted authoritarianism exists, people are not concerned by arbitrary violence against the poor – particularly if the person is a suspected criminal – just as the majority of Brazilians were not concerned about the violence against suspected political dissidents during the dictatorship.

---

[546] *Human Rights Council Report of the Special Rapporteur on Torture and Other Cruel, Inhuman or Degrading Treatment or Punishment on his Mission to Brazil*, A/HRC/31/57/Add.4, January 29, 2016, https://digitallibrary.un.org/record/831519.

[547] VRIEZEN, Vera, *Amnesty Justified? The Need for a Case by Case Approach in the Interests of Human Rights*, Cambridge, Intersentia, 2012.

[548] CRUZ, Fernanda, "Para 70% dos Brasileiros, Policiais Cometem Excessos de Violência", *Agência Brasil*, November 2, 2016, http://agenciabrasil.ebc.com.br/direitos-humanos/noticia/2016-11/para-70-dos-brasileiros-policiais-cometem-excessos-de-violencia.

[549] AGUIRRE, Luis Pérez, "The Consequences of Impunity in Society", International Commission of Jurists, *Justice Not Impunity, International Meeting*, November 2–5 1992, Geneve, International Commission of Jurists, 1993.

[550] HAMBER, Brandon, "Living with the Legacy of Impunity: Lessons for South Africa about Truth, Justice and Crime in Brazil", *Latin American Report*, vol. 13/1998, pp. 4–16.

5.8. CONCLUSIONS

In general, the NTC Final Report and the alignment of its recommendations with the agenda of a consistent democracy and respect for human rights have recognizable value. However, the principal merit of having encouraged these initiatives cannot be attributed to the NTC, since most of its recommendations represent a reinforcement of the claims previously articulated by civil society.[551] In addition, the criticism of how the NTC's work was conducted leads to the conclusion that the low level of dialog between the Commission and society has affected the transformative potential that its recommendations might have had not only on popular opinion, but also on the institutions, patterns, and cultural perspectives that need to be changed towards the reconstruction and stabilizing of democracy in the country.

The final moments of the NTC's existence and the period immediately after its conclusion are also considered decisive due to the resounding silence that currently surrounds the fulfilment of its recommendations. This fact may be associated with a culture that praises oblivion and the disappearance of collective memory, which has neglected many of the issues of Transitional Justice in the three decades since democracy was restored in Brazil. Thus, as Westhrop, Garrido et al.[552] have observed, the ephemeral nature of the NTC's work represents negligence that undermines ongoing resistance to current human rights violations not being as broad as it could be.

As Hazan has discussed,[553] the only value of a truth commission lies in its public impact and in its ability to educate a divided society on forgiveness and reconciliation. The key question here is the way in which the authorities and the NTC spread that message with respect to past abuses: as extensively as possible or using a minimalist approach? In fact, this type of choice is often dictated by the kind of message to be conveyed and by the balance of power between the human rights activists and those who embody the past repression.

In fact, the very forum for the presentation of the NTC Final Report reveals the underlying political project of which the NTC was merely the messenger. In the Brazilian case, the views popularized by the media the very next day after the launching of the Final Report – stating that the recommendations were no more

---

[551] For an analysis of the role of civil society in fostering Transitional Justice measures, see Chapter 6 of this book on this subject.
[552] WESTHROP, Amy Jo; GARRIDO, Ayra Guedes; PARREIRA, Carolina Genovez; and SANTOS, Shana Marques Prado dos, *As Recomendações da Comissão Nacional da Verdade: Balanços sobre a Sua Implementação Dois Anos Depois*, Rio de Janeiro, ISER, 2016.
[553] HAZAN, Pierre, "Measuring the Impact of Punishment and Forgiveness: A Framework for Evaluating Transitional Justice", *International Review of the Red Cross*, vol. 88/2006, pp. 19–47.

than guidelines or general advice[554] – help us to better understand the reality in which the Commissioners did their work. Consequently, as has already been cited in news reports,[555] the NTC Final Report is a monumental work that was not able to generate discussion for more than a week or two.

Certainly, it has to be considered that the efforts of the NTC Final Report were also obscured due to the surrounding environment of 2015: Brazil's economy had lost more than one million jobs in the most severe recession in decades; the families of the victims of the Mariana dam disaster (Minas Gerais state) were still searching for people missing in the sludge released;[556] police officers were clashing with students on the streets of São Paulo over school closings;[557] and Brazil's leaders were facing major crises on multiple fronts and were consumed by a power struggle, culminating in the start of an impeachment proceedings of the then President.[558]

In addition, as most of the NTC recommendations have not been implemented,[559] nor has there been any substantive discussion of them by society, the question remains to what extent these recommendations may contribute to the democratic development of Brazilian society, despite not being put into practice.

There were those who said that the content of the NTC Final Report was not new,[560] as the biggest challenge for the Commissioners was to prevent the document from resulting in a long and repetitive record that would add little to the documentation related to the period, such as the "Brazil: Never Again" Report of 1985 and the book "Right to Memory and Truth", coordinated by

---

[554] MAGALHÃES, João Carlos and NERY, Natuza, "Para Planalto, Recomendações do Relatório da Comissão São Genéricas", *Folha de São Paulo*, December 11, 2014. See also: *Agência Estado*, "Governo Não Retaliará General que Criticou Relatório da CNV", December 11, 2014.

[555] DUAILIBI, Julia, "A Verdade da Comissão", *Revista Piauí*, vol. 91/2014, https://piaui.folha.uol.com.br/materia/a-verdade-da-comissao/.

[556] See: *Slate*, "A Disaster Prompted by Economic Activity", December 3, 2015, https://slate.com/news-and-politics/2015/12/brazil-mining-dam-disaster-toxic-sludge-and-irreversible-environmental-damage.html.

[557] See: *UOL*, "PM usa bombas de gás em protestos de estudantes em SP, 4 foram detidos", December 3, 2015, https://educacao.uol.com.br/noticias/2015/12/03/policia-militar-usa-bombas-de-gas-em-protestos-de-estudantes-em-sp.htm.

[558] See: *The New York Times*, "Faced with many crises, Brazil focused on Dilma Rousseff's Impeachment Case", December 3, 2015, https://www.nytimes.com/2015/12/04/world/americas/faced-with-many-crises-brazil-focuses-on-dilma-rousseffs-impeachment-case.html.

[559] POTTER, Hyury, "Quatro Anos Depois, Brasil Ignora Maioria das Recomendações da Comissão da Verdade", *Aos Fatos*, March 29, 2019, https://aosfatos.org/noticias/quatro-anos-depois-brasil-ignora-maioria-das-recomendacoes-da-comissao-da-verdade/.

[560] *Carta Capital*, "A Comissão da Verdade Fracassou, Reclamam Escritores", July 15, 2016, https://www.cartacapital.com.br/sociedade/comissao-da-verdade-fracassou-reclamam-escritores/.

the Secretariat of Human Rights and the Commission on Political Deaths and Disappearances of 2007. And, at first glance, the Commission's efforts did not even generate many findings. The number of the dead and missing it reported, for example, was not new. The report recognized that the possible number might be higher but, in the total included in the first volume, the NTC listed only cases that were individually and fully proven.

There were new findings to report, however, as could be found in the series of detailed demonstrations of procedures on disappearances, as well as in the vision of the whole landscape that emerges from the thousands of pages fully documented.[561] For those who had always said that the Brazilian dictatorship was fairly mild, since the death toll was lower than in the dictatorships in Argentina and Chile, the work of the NTC demonstrated that repression in Brazil was pursued as a well-planned industry, and this evidence was quite new. The pages of the report unveiled the State's command lines and the physical facilities of a meticulous and selective repressive apparatus – one that was accurate and cold in its murders. The relationship between these efficient and inhuman gears is clear as the Final Report unfolds.

Finally, thinking about the dissemination of contents of the Final Report, it should be remembered that, although the volumes offer priceless research material, the report is not easy to consult, and it is only available in Portuguese. It would be expected that, in the aftermath of all of the work performed, the NTC would publish a book in journalistic language that would condense and explain its main conclusions to the ordinary citizen, unfamiliar with the vocabulary of Transitional Justice. As observed by Schneider and Almeida,[562] the fact that the Final Report does not contain an Executive Summary may suggest that the report was not written with a mass audience in mind.

Also, the website from which the Commission's work may be downloaded contains various volumes. The search engine is not the most user-friendly and could be more agile and offer cross referencing. From a technological and database management perspective, it should be recalled that truth commission records are government property, and citizens have the right to demand that property be well-preserved and easily accessible. However, as Peterson has observed,[563] when a truth commission starts its operation, it is extremely focused on producing a report within the time allotted. To this end, the truth commission creates and

---

[561] BUCCI, Eugênio, "A Letra da Verdade", *Revista de Estudos Avançados da USP*, vol. 30/2016, pp. 297–302.
[562] SCHNEIDER, Nina and ALMEIDA, Gisele Iecker de, "The Brazilian National Truth Commission (2012–2014) as a State-Commissioned History Project", in BEVERNAGE, B. and WOUTERS, N. (eds.), *The Palgrave Handbook of State-Sponsored History After 1945*, Palgrave Macmillan, London, 2018, pp. 637–652.
[563] PETERSON, Trudy Huskamp, *Final Acts: A Guide to Preserving the Records of Truth Commissions*, Woodrow Wilson Center Press with The Johns Hopkins University Press, 2005.

receives a large quantity of information in a short period of time. The problem is that, although the commission recognizes that it must manage the flow of information of all kinds into its offices, until it faces the end of its existence it rarely gives a thought to what will happen to its records once it closes its doors. In the case of the NTC, it operated a website during its existence and, when it ceased its work, all of its databases, reports, maps, audiotapes, and videotapes were stored in the "Revealed Memories" Portal, as the National Archives were designated to be the successor organization to maintain and facilitate access to information on the NTC.[564]

Certainly, the initiatives mentioned above would help to spread the NTC's legacy to the general public, and this should be a priority task. By not sensitizing the general public, its work was far from transformative of society. Nevertheless, there is a growing sense that this information needs to be released in a friendly, creative, and interesting way for anyone who wishes to access it, especially for future generations. The information about what happened decades ago cannot simply exist as a collection of dusty folders in a PDF file. In 2006, the Office of the United Nations High Commissioner for Human Rights stated that the impact of a final report of a truth commission may ultimately depend less on its content than on a variety of surrounding factors, including when and in what circumstances the report is released and publicized, how widely it is distributed, how much coverage it receives in the media, and, perhaps most importantly, how the political authorities treat the report and whether they have any interest in publicizing and implementing its conclusions and recommendations.[565]

Following the above guidelines of the Office of the United Nations High Commissioner for Human Rights, in addition to the policy and institutional reforms that are suggested in the report, the NTC should also have aimed to affect the way that the public understood their own national history and the conflict and violence of recent years. Thus, it is important that the conclusions of the NTC Final Report now be made widely available throughout the country, which does not seem to be happening in the Brazilian case. If this does not occur, what will remain is the sense that no priority was given to the dissemination of the report's conclusions and to the fulfillment of its recommendations on human rights.[566]

---

[564] National Archives, *Revealed Memory*, "Final Report of the National Truth Commission", http://cnv.memoriasreveladas.gov.br/index.php/outros-destaques/574-conheca-e-acesse-o-relatorio-final-da-cnv#.

[565] Office of the United Nations High Commissioner for Human Rights, "Rule-of-Law Tools for Post-Conflict States: Truth Commissions", New York and Geneva, 2006, https://www.un.org/ruleoflaw/blog/document/rule-of-law-tools-for-post-conflict-states-truth-commissions/.

[566] MARTINS, André Saboia and ISHAQ, Vivien, "O Legado da Comissão Nacional da Verdade: Dois Anos Depois da Publicação do Relatório, o Reconhecimento Judicial do Direito à Verdade Desafia a Falta de Justiça Efetiva", in WESTHROP, Amy Jo; GARRIDO, Ayra Guedes; PARREIRA, Carolina Genovez; and SANTOS, Shana Marques Prado dos, *As Recomendações da Comissão Nacional da Verdade: Balanços sobre a Sua Implementação Dois Anos Depois*, Rio de Janeiro, ISER, 2016, pp. 42–65.

To conclude, the great challenge lies in transforming the theme of the right to truth and memory into a collective sensibility within society, especially in a country where, as late as 2018, the opinion of six out of 10 citizens was still that "human rights only benefit undeserving people, such as criminals and terrorists".[567] Such pressure on Brazilian civil society was noted by Schneider and Almeida when commenting on the work of the NTC they said that the "majority of Brazilians appear to have little interest in human rights violations and efforts to raise public awareness of this topic have been very limited".[568]

---

[567] Franco, Luiza, "Mais da Metade dos Brasileiros Acham que Direitos Humanos Beneficiam Quem Não Merece, Diz Pesquisa", *BBC News Brasil*, August 11, 2018, https://www.bbc.com/portuguese/brasil-45138048.

[568] Schneider, Nina and Almeida, Gisele Iecker de, "The Brazilian National Truth Commission (2012–2014) as a State-Commissioned History Project", in Bevernage, B. and Wouters, N. (eds.), *The Palgrave Handbook of State-Sponsored History After 1945*, Palgrave Macmillan, London, 2018, p. 647.

PART III
COMPLEX FORMS OF REPARATIONS, ACCOUNTABILITY, AND TRUTH-SEEKING
Actors Beyond Agents of the State

CHAPTER 6
THE ROLE OF CIVIL SOCIETY AND NGOs IN THE QUEST FOR TRUTH, JUSTICE, AND MEMORY

Victims' movements have driven democratization processes in different parts of the world and, as Gready and Robins have observed,[569] have received credit for the creation of the contemporary discourse regarding Transitional Justice. In the case of the Mothers of Plaza de Mayo (*Madres de Plaza de Mayo*) and the Grandmothers of Plaza de Mayo (*Abuelas de Plaza de Mayo*), both in Argentina, women searching for the whereabouts of their children and grandchildren used to come together in the center of power in Buenos Aires, wearing their white headscarves and carrying huge placards with the faces of their missing relatives, and demand their return. Indeed, these women became some of the most visible opponents of the Argentinian regime and gained international recognition with their marches and protest actions.[570] It has even been said that the Argentinian process of accountability has been mainly the result of civil society action and especially action by those grassroots women's organizations.[571] It is a good example of a case in which public pressure has acted as an important catalyst for Transitional Justice measures and in which victims' families and human rights organizations have progressively been able to mobilize politicians and judges to seek accountability for past atrocities.[572]

The efforts of the Khulumani Support Group, in South Africa, mark another leading case. That group was formed in 1995 by survivors and families of political

---

[569] GREADY, Paul and ROBINS, Simon, "Rethinking Civil Society and Transitional Justice: Lessons from Social Movements and "New" Civil Society", *The International Journal of Human Rights*, vol. 21/2017, pp. 956–975.
[570] HOWE, Sara Eleanor, "The Madres de la Plaza de Mayo: Asserting Motherhood; Rejecting Feminism?", *Journal of International Women's Studies*, vol. 7/2006, pp. 43–50.
[571] GUILLÉN, Ana Laura Zavala, "Argentinian Transitional Justice Process: Women Behind", *Journal of Peace, Conflict & Development*, vol. 20/2013, pp. 52–60.
[572] CATELA, Ludmila D.S., "Em Nome da Pacificação Nacional: Anistias, Pontos Finais e Indultos no Cone Sul", in CASTRO, Celso and D'ARAÚJO, Maria C. (eds.), *Democracia e Forças Armadas no Cone Sul*, Rio de Janeiro, Editora Fundação Getúlio Vargas, 2000, pp. 301–315.

violence under the Apartheid regime. The group was founded on the premise that encouraging people to "speak out" (the word *Khulumani* means "speak out" in Zulu) about the atrocities of the past was psychologically beneficial. Moreover, their strong focus on advocacy worked to keep the Truth and Reconciliation Commission (TRC) and the reconciliation process victim-oriented.[573] Subsequently, *Khulumani* has grown from just being a support group concerned with helping members to engage with the TRC to being a movement concerned with issues of social justice and Transitional Justice as broadly defined, and has declared that its goals are to end impunity, to ensure reconciliation, and to create agency in place of dependency.[574]

However, despite the emergence of Transitional Justice as a separate field of academic study and the growing interest in the role of civil society in those processes around the world, as Rangelov and Teitel have observed,[575] the literature on civil society and the academic field of research remain rather limited in their focus and scope. Indeed, as Gready and Robins have commented,[576] civil society remains on the margins of Transitional Justice discourse, and this continues to be the case in the Brazilian experience, as will be seen in this chapter.

In fact, after ratification of the Federal Constitution in 1988, the focus of the human rights movement in Brazil changed and began to center mainly on agrarian reform, gender rights, non-discrimination, the rights of children and young people, and environmental issues. As a matter of fact, in analyzing the role of civil societies in transitions and comparing the cases of Argentina and Brazil, Friedman and Hochstetler deduced that,[577] for Brazilian civil society organizations, the mobilizing framework since 1985 has been citizenship, with most of the emphasis on equitable participation and inclusion.

Somehow the struggle for Transitional Justice in Brazil has not been a part of the agenda of these social movements. In their absence, Transitional Justice

---

[573] HAMBER, Brandon; MOSIKARE, Ntombi; FRIEDMAN, Maggie; and MAEPA, Traggy, "Speaking Out. The Role of the Khulumani Victim Support Group in Dealing with the Past in South Africa", *Psychosocial Programmes after War and Dictatorship Conference*, Frankfurt, Germany, June 17–21, 2000, http://www.brandonhamber.com/publications/pap_khulumani.doc.

[574] MADLINGOZI, Tshepo, "On Transitional Justice Entrepreneurs and the Production of Victims", *Journal of Human Rights Practice*, vol. 2/2010, pp. 208–228.

[575] RANGELOV, Iavor and TEITEL, Ruti, "Global Civil Society and Transitional Justice", in ANHEIER, Helmut; GLASIUS, Marlies; KALDOR, Mary; PARK, Gil-Sun; and SENGUPTA, Chandan. (eds.), *Global Civil Society 2011: Global Civil Society Yearbook*, London, Palgrave Macmillan, 2011, pp. 162–177.

[576] GREADY, Paul and ROBINS, Simon, "Rethinking Civil Society and Transitional Justice: Lessons from Social Movements and "New" Civil Society", *The International Journal of Human Rights*, vol. 21/2017, pp. 956–975.

[577] FRIEDMAN, Elisabeth Jay and HOCHSTETLER, Kathryn, "Assessing the Third Transition in Latin American Democratization: Representational Regimes and Civil Society in Argentina and Brazil", *Comparative Politics*, vol. 35/2002, pp. 21–42.

Chapter 6. Civil Society and NGOs in the Quest for Truth, Justice, and Memory

efforts have come much more from the Commission of the Families of the Dead and Disappeared (*Comissão dos Familiares dos Mortos e Desaparecidos Politicos – CFMD*) – which has always been active and relevant – but those efforts are restricted to a small number of relatives aiming to clarify the circumstances of the disappearances and to the search for reparations for workers who were dismissed or prevented from working during the dictatorship. Abrão and Torelly even remarked that,[578] since the majority of Brazilians – and thus potential voters – appear to have taken little interest in such matters, politicians have been able to easily shy away from confrontations with nostalgic defenders of the regime. Due to the absence of pressure from both influential interest groups and the wider public, Schneider concluded that post-1985 governments apparently thought it would be unnecessary to meaningfully apologize for past atrocities.[579]

In Brazil, the CFMD never managed to make its own way into the majority of human rights organizations, political parties or the agenda of the mass media. Observing this fact, Torelly has commented that several factors contribute to this phenomenon: the number of fatal victims, the control of the authoritarian regime over the democratization process, and the priority given to other political agendas for human rights militancy.[580] Schneider has added that the Amnesty Law has neither been reviewed by the Legislative Branch nor resulted in substantial disapproval from civil society,[581] which would suggest that there is only minor social interest in Transitional Justice in the country.

This so-called minor social interest is attested to, for instance, by a poll conducted 25 years after the end of the dictatorship, in 2010, by the research institute *DataFolha*. In that survey, 45% of Brazilians were against holding the perpetrators of human rights abuses accountable for their actions, while 40% endorsed their punishment. Another 4% were indifferent and 11% had no opinion about the subject.[582] Later on, on March 31, 2014, on the fiftieth anniversary of the *coup d'état*, the same institute published another survey

---

[578] ABRÃO, Paulo and TORELLY, Marcelo D., "As dimensões da Justiça de Transição no Brasil, a Eficácia da Lei de Anistia e as Alternativas para a Verdade e a Justiça", in PAYNE, Leigh A.; ABRÃO, Paulo; and TORELLY, Marcelo D. (eds.), *A Anistia na Era da Responsabilização: o Brasil em Perspectiva Internacional e Comparada*, Oxford, Oxford University Press, 2011.

[579] SCHNEIDER, Nina, "Waiting for a Meaningful State Apology: Has Brazil Apologized for Authoritarian Repression?", *Journal of Human Rights*, vol. 13/2014, pp. 1–16.

[580] TORELLY, Marcelo, "Gomes Lund vs. Brasil Cinco Anos Depois: Histórico, Impacto, Evolução Jurisprudencial e Críticas", in PIOVESAN, Flavia and SOARES, Inês Virgínia Prado (eds.), *Impacto das Decisões da Corte Interamericana de Direitos Humanos na Jurisprudência do STF*, Salvador, Jus Podivm, 2016, pp. 525–560.

[581] SCHNEIDER, Nina, "Impunity in Post-authoritarian Brazil: The Supreme Court's Recent Verdict on the Amnesty Law", *European Review of Latin American and Caribbean Studies*, vol. 90/2011, pp. 39–54.

[582] FRANCO, Bernardo Melo, "Punição a Tortura na Ditadura Divide Opiniões no País", *Folha de São Paulo*, June 7, 2010, http://www1.folha.uol.com.br/fsp/poder/po0706201008.htm.

which found that 41% of Brazilians were against any criminal initiatives against torturers, while 46% of citizens were in favor of their punishment, with 13% expressing no opinion either way.[583] According to this 2014 survey, although it is feasible to affirm that a large portion of the population (46%) is against amnesty for agents of the State, this number is still too small to serve as an overwhelming instrument of social pressure, mainly because the margin of error in the poll was around 2%. Thus, the results of the 2014 survey continue to demonstrate a deep division in society with respect to Transitional Justice measures.

Meanwhile, in spite of this divergence within Brazilian society, this chapter intends to outline the efforts towards the implementation of Transitional Justice measures, not only through State or top-down initiatives – such as reparations laws, the Amnesty Commission, the CFMD, the National Truth Commission (NTC) (*Comissão Nacional da Verdade*) and the work of the Federal Public Prosecutor's Office (*Ministério Público Federal* – MFP) – but also through the work of civil society movements. To this end, this chapter will divide its observations of civil society efforts towards Transitional Justice into two different phases.

The first phase may be said to have begun at the end of the 1970s, when civil society mobilized the necessary forces to impose the concession of amnesty for political opponents on the military government (the so-called pro-amnesty campaign). At that time, society was concerned with repression and political liberalization. However, once censorship was abolished, political prisoners were released, amnesty was granted, *habeas corpus* was restored, and the ban on all but two official political parties was revoked, as Codato has commented,[584] it seemed that social mobilization started to face its limits.

Nevertheless, in this post-dictatorship phase, there was also the release of the "Brazil: Never Again" Report in 1985, which was a founding act in the movement for the right to truth and memory about the crimes of the dictatorship. This first phase may be said to have ended in 1990, through the investigative efforts of journalists and the relatives of the dead and disappeared which led to the discovery of a clandestine mass grave (the *Vala de Perus*) in the Dom Bosco Cemetery, in the Perus neighborhood of the City of São Paulo.

A second phase of civil society's commitment towards Transitional Justice initiatives began in the 2000s with the enactment of Law no. 10,559 (2002)[585]

---

[583] MENDONÇA, Ricardo, "Maior Parte da População Quer Anular Lei da Anistia, Aponta DataFolha", *Folha de São Paulo*, March 31, 2014, http://www1.folha.uol.com.br/poder/2014/03/1433374-maior-parte-da-populacao-quer-anular-lei-da-anistia-aponta-datafolha.shtml.

[584] CODATO, Adriano Nervo, "Uma História Política da Transição Brasileira: Da Ditadura Militar à Democracia", *Revista de Sociologia Política*, vol. 25/2005, pp. 165–175.

[585] Note that Law no. 10,559 (2002) must be understood as part of a process of long-term democratic transition, whose legal frameworks would also be Law no. 6,683 (1979) (the Amnesty Law), Law no. 9,140 (1995) (Law of the Disappeared) and Law no. 12,528 (2011) (the Law that created the National Truth Commission).

(the so-called reparations program or Law of the Missing). In this phase, new fronts of mobilization were encouraged following along broad guidelines for Transitional Justice[586] as a matter of symbolic and collective interest in democracy, and not as a private interest only on the part of the victims of the repressive regime.

As a result, there were new strategies, like the filing of civil claims against the torturers of the regime, which were brought by the relatives of the dead and disappeared. Later on, in 2009, the theme of Transitional Justice became more evident when it was mentioned in the government's National Human Rights Plan.[587] Furthermore, the legal discussion of the Amnesty Law before the Supreme Court, in 2010, was able to unite forces that had previously been scattered, as it brought together initiatives of the Brazilian Bar Association (*Ordem dos Advogados do Brasil* – OAB), the Federal Public Prosecutor's Office (MPF), the Association of Judges for Democracy (*Associação Juízes para a Democracia* – AJD), the Brazilian Association of Political Amnesty Recipients (*Associação Brasileira de Anistiados Políticos* – ABAP), the National Democratic Military Association (*Associação Democrática e Nacionalista de Militares* – ADNAM), and the Center for Justice and International Law (CEJIL).

And, more recently, after the creation of the NTC in 2012, there has also been the emergence of new social actors employing Transitional Justice mechanisms such as the political acts known as "*escrachos*" (public demonstrations designed to shame the military oppressors) and the work of artists reassessing the debate around measures of truth and memory. Hence, in the following sections, we will discuss these two major phases of the work of the civil society towards Transitional Justice mechanisms in more detail.

6.1. FROM THE AMNESTY MOVEMENT TO THE DRAFTING OF "BRAZIL: NEVER AGAIN" AND DISCOVERY OF THE MASS GRAVE IN PERUS

During the 1964–1985 military regime, social struggles were heavily suppressed, leaving thousands of opponents dead, imprisoned or in exile; nevertheless, Brazil has been far slower to address its past atrocities than neighboring states and, as a consequence, the country has been described as one of the outliers

---

[586] ROSITO, João Baptista Alvares and DAMO, Arlei Sander, "A Reparação por Perseguição Política e os Relatos de Violência nas Caravanas da Anistia", *Horizontes Antropológicos*, vol. 42/2014, pp. 181–212.

[587] The 3rd National Human Rights Program, launched in December 2009 by Decree no. 7,037 (2009), adopted the right to truth and memory as one of its guidelines, something previously unknown in human rights programs in Brazil.

of Latin America by Roht-Arriaza[588] and as a country with a pervasive culture of amnesia, by Schneider.[589] We will show that such labels cannot be properly understood when they are detached from an examination of the role of civil society throughout the years of democratization.

It is undeniable that the dictatorship persecuted, imprisoned, and tortured many individuals considered enemies of the State and that the consequences of their deaths and disappearances extended beyond the direct victims. The families and friends of the dead and disappeared were not allowed to fully mourn and had to live with uncertainty regarding the fate of their loved ones. Facing these circumstances, Gallo has found that,[590] in the Brazilian case, the struggle of the relatives of the dead and disappeared originated almost instinctively: at the exact moment when those families had no information about the whereabouts of their family members, when their detention was denied by the agents of the State, or when the official version of their death was permeated with obscure episodes.

Thus, in the 1970s, this drama, initially restricted to the private space of families, began to appear in the public sphere,[591] when for example, with the support of the Catholic Church, various public demonstrations repudiating repression were organized, as in the masses in memory of Luiz Eduardo Rocha Merlino (in 1971),[592] Alexandre Vannucchi Leme (in 1973),[593] Vladimir Herzog (in 1975)[594] and Manoel Fiel Filho (in 1976),[595] who were all victims of State repression.

With the passage of time, the mobilizations of family members of the dead and disappeared, who until then had produced scant results, found in the struggle for amnesty the opportunity to mature their strategies. Thus, between 1978 and 1979, those family members were integrated into the campaign for

---

[588] ROHT-ARRIAZA, Naomi, "After Amnesties Are Gone: Latin American National Courts and the New Contours of the Fights Against Impunity", *Human Rights Quarterly*, vol. 37/2015, pp. 341–382.

[589] SCHNEIDER, Nina, "Breaking the Silence of the Military Regime: New Politics of Memory in Brazil", *Bulletin of Latin American Research*, vol. 30/2010, pp. 198–212.

[590] GALLO, Carlos Artur, "Do Luto à Luta: Um Estudo sobre a Comissão de Familiares de Mortos e Desaparecidos Pol'ticos no Brasil", *Anos 90*, vol. 19/2012, pp. 323–355.

[591] TELES, Janaína de Almeida, "Entre o Luto e a Melancolia: a Luta dos Familiares de Mortos e Desaparecidos no Brasil", in SANTOS, Cecília MacDowell; TELES, Edson; and TELES, Janaína de Almeida (eds.), *Desarquivando a Ditadura: Memória e Justiça no Brasil*, vol.1, São Paulo, Hucitec, 2009, pp. 151–176.

[592] On Luiz Eduardo da Rocha Merlino, see: Truth Commission of the State of São Paulo, http://comissaodaverdade.al.sp.gov.br/mortos-desaparecidos/luiz-eduardo-da-rocha-merlino.

[593] On Alexandre Vannucchi Leme, see: SERBIN, Kenneth P., "The Anatomy of a Death: Repression, Human Rights, and the Case of Alexandre Vannucchi Leme in Authoritarian Brazil", *Working Paper no. 248, The Helen Kellogg Institute for International Studies*, 1998, https://kellogg.nd.edu/documents/1543.

[594] On Vladimir Herzog, see: *Instituto Vladimir Herzog*, "Biografia de um Jornalista", https://vladimirherzog.org/biografia/.

[595] On Manoel Fiel Filho see: *Truth Commission of the State of São Paulo*, http://comissaodaverdade.al.sp.gov.br/mortos-desaparecidos/manoel-fiel-filho.

amnesty for political opponents of the regime, but also calling for the elucidation of the deaths and disappearances as well as for the location and identification of bodies and the punishment of those involved in such crimes.[596]

Actually, the period known as the *Distensão* or "Decompression" years (1974–1979) – that sought a "slow, gradual, and safe" transition to democracy[597] – featured a range of carefully "calculated gestures" which regulated the collective memory of the nation, as has been pointed out by Ryan.[598] Among these actions were Law no. 6,683 (1979) (the Amnesty Law), which had come into being following a widespread campaign[599] by the Brazilian Amnesty Committees (*Comitês Brasileiros pela Anistia* – CBAs) and the Women for Amnesty Movement (*Movimento Feminino pela Anistia* – MFPA),[600] two main forces in the Amnesty Movement which gained momentum from 1975 onwards. During that period, victims and their families formed associations and received support from parts of the Catholic Church, human rights lawyers, and both local and global human rights activists.[601] Although that campaign succeeded, the final version of the law covered not only the opponents of the regime but also its own torturers,[602] since it was mainly based on a strategy of reconciliation with the previous regime.[603]

Indeed, to the exasperation of the relatives of the dead and disappeared, the work carried out in the 1970s by social movements like the CBAs and the MFPA was insufficient to meet their demands. After everything, the only benefit that the Amnesty Law offered to those families was the issuance of certificates

---

[596] GALLO, Carlos Artur, "Do Luto à Luta: Um Estudo sobre a Comissão de Familiares de Mortos e Desaparecidos Pol'ticos no Brasil", *Anos 90*, vol. 19/2012, pp. 323–355.

[597] For the analysis of the proposition of a slow, gradual and safe opening and the logic of decompression, see: RESENDE, Pâmela de Almeida, "Da Abertura Lenta, Gradual e Segura à Anistia Ampla, Geral e Irrestrita: A Lógica do Dissenso na Transição para a Democracia", *Revista Sul-Americana de Ciência Política*, vol. 2/2014, pp. 36–46.

[598] RYAN, Holly Eva, "From Absent to Present Pasts: Civil Society, Democracy and the Shifting Place of Memory in Brazil", *Journal of Civil Society*, vol. 12/2016, pp. 158–177.

[599] FICO, Carlos, "A Negociação Parlamentar da Anistia de 1979 e o Chamado Perdão aos Torturadores", *Revista Anistia Política e Justiça de Transição*, vol. 4/2010, pp. 318–333.

[600] Among the social efforts organized to confront the military regime was the Women for Amnesty Movement (MFPA), founded in São Paulo in 1975 under the leadership of the lawyer Therezinha Zerbine. It was a pioneering organization not only in the pro-amnesty campaign, but it was also the first such movement to oppose the government. In February 1978, in Rio de Janeiro, the first Brazilian Amnesty Committee (CBA) was founded with the participation of MFPA supporters and also students, lawyers, artists, and members of the Catholic Church. See: DEL PORTO, Fabíola Brigante, "A Luta pela Anistia no Regime Militar Brasileiro: A Constituição da Sociedade Civil e a Construção da Cidadania", *Revista Perseu: História, Memória e Política*, vol. 3/2009, pp. 43–72.

[601] SCHNEIDER, Nina, "Waiting for a Meaningful State Apology: Has Brazil Apologized for Authoritarian Repression?", *Journal of Human Rights*, vol. 13/2014, pp. 1–16.

[602] For a detailed discussion about the Amnesty Law see Chapter 2 of this book.

[603] SCHNEIDER, Nina, "Impunity in Post-authoritarian Brazil: The Supreme Court's Recent Verdict on the Amnesty Law", *European Review of Latin American and Caribbean Studies*, vol. 90/2011, pp. 39–54.

attesting to the unknown whereabouts or presumed death of the disappeared.[604] As a result, in the middle of the celebrations organized for the return of the exiles and the release of many political prisoners, the pain of the families left with their unburied dead (as in the case of the *Araguaia Guerrillas*)[605] and their unanswered questions continued without relief.

In fact, for many, the most representative image of this time is that of leftist militants landing at Galeão Airport, in Rio de Janeiro, having as their soundtrack the João Bosco and Aldir Blanc song "*O Bêbado e Equilibrista*", as sung by Elis Regina.[606] The scene of the return of intellectuals, politicians, labor union leaders, ex-guerrillas, journalists, and former students crystallized in the popular imagination as a kind of triumph for those who had been forced to leave the country years before.[607] The narratives transmitted by television at that time gave the idea of a reunion of friends, of reconstruction of lost ties, which then carried a strong symbolic and emotional charge as a moment of catharsis.[608]

Another key event in this first post-dictatorship phase was the release of the "Brazil: Never Again" (*Brasil: Nunca Mais* – BNM) Report, in 1985, which was a foundational moment in the quest to preserve the memory of the past atrocities committed during the dictatorship. The report was organized by the

---

[604] According to article 6 of Law no. 6,683 (1979), http://www.planalto.gov.br/ccivil_03/leis/L6683.htm.

[605] Concerning the background of the *Araguaia Guerrillas*, we mention the description made by Franco: "In the late 1960s, under the auspices of the Communist Party of Brazil (PC do B), Maurício Grabois, João Amazonas, and Ângelo Arroyo settled in a mostly rural area of Brazil called Bico do Papagaio, along the Araguaia River. All three were members of what became known as the Araguaia Guerrilla, a political movement that had as its principal goals the instigating of a communist revolution in the country and the undermining of the Brazilian military regime (1964–1985). By 1972, when Brazil was governed by then President General Emílio Garrastazu Médici, the Araguaia Guerrilla included hundreds of young university students from major cities, all of whom were instructed to relocate to the movement's hideouts in several municipalities within the Bico do Papagaio region. That same year, the armed forces discovered the movement's existence and mobilized soldiers to combat the guerrilla through several operations … After seven military operations, the movement was completely suppressed and came to an end in 1975". FRANCO, Shirley Carvalhêdo, "The Notion of Ramification of Archival Documents: The Example of the 'Fonds' Related to the Brazilian Political Movement Araguaia Guerrilla", *The American Archivist*, vol. 78/2015, pp. 133–153. For more information about the *Araguaia Guerrilla* see Chapter 4, section 4.2.1 of this book.

[606] SILVA, Fernando Lopes da, "O Poético e o Factual na Letra da Canção 'O Bêbado e a Equilibrista'", *Revista Alpha*, vol. 17(1)/2016, pp. 115–127.

[607] FEIJÓ, Sara Duarte, "Em Teu Nome e Batismo de Sangue: Formas Cinematográficas de Representar o Exílio na Ditadura Brasileira", *Projeto História*, vol. 43/2011, pp. 481–495.

[608] See images at *Projeto Memória Globo*, "Anistia e Volta dos Exilados", http://memoriaglobo.globo.com/programas/jornalismo/coberturas/anistia-e-volta-dos-exilados/anistia-e-volta-dos-exilados-a-historia.htm.

Metropolitan Archdiocese of São Paulo with the assistance of the Presbyterian Church and funding from the World Council of Churches,[609] and had many supporters.[610] The book was based on the military court records, which were secretly photocopied over six years by lawyers and Church activists.

The extraction and reproduction of the files from the Superior Military Court (*Superior Tribunal Militar* – STM), located in Brasília, was made possible thanks to the Amnesty Law, as lawyers needed to consult the case files from that court in order to know whether their clients were eligible for amnesty or not. Under this pretext, participants managed to copy 710 case files, gathering about 850,000 pages of documents and 543 rolls of microfilm. Based on this collected material, a document known as "Project A" was drafted, containing 6,891 pages divided into 12 volumes. In addition, a book summarizing all the material collected was also published (known as "Project B"). All these projects were finally organized and published in 1985, very shortly after the Brazilian opening to democracy. Schneider has even identified these 12 volumes and the smaller, abridged edition as "a private first truth commission for the Brazilian transition",[611] since the participants in the project collected evidence of torture based on the files of the military tribunals.

Indeed, from their analysis of "Project A", it was possible to identify, for instance, (a) how many prisoners were submitted to the military courts; (b) how many people had been formally charged; (c) how many were arrested; (d) how many people reported being tortured; (e) how many people were reported as disappeared; (f) which were the most widely practiced forms of torture; and (g) which were some of the detention centers where torture was practiced. In fact, much of this information was discovered because many of the regime's opponents submitted to the military courts formal statements containing denunciations of torture and the names of torturers. Thus, the 1985 report revealed some of the repressive strategies implemented by the regime.

The BNM Report influenced a series of initiatives to rescue this part of Brazilian history. The report in book form was a sales phenomenon and stayed on the bestseller list for non-fiction books for 91 consecutive weeks.[612] It also

---

[609] *Brasil: Nunca Mais*, http://bnmdigital.mpf.mp.br/pt-br/historia.html.
[610] The project was supported by lawyers Eny Raimundo Moreira, Luiz Eduardo Greenhalgh, Luís Carlos Sigmaringa Seixas, and Mário Simas; journalists Paulo Vannuchi and Ricardo Kotscho; Frei Betto (a Dominican friar); sociologist Vânya Santana; and historian Ana Maria de Almeida Camargo, among others. See: TELES, Janaína de Almeida, "A Constituição das Memórias sobre a Repressão da Ditadura: o Projeto Brasil Nunca Mais e a Abertura da Vala de Perus", *Anos 90*, vol. 19/2012, pp. 261–298.
[611] SCHNEIDER, Nina, "Waiting for a Meaningful State Apology: Has Brazil Apologized for Authoritarian Repression?", *Journal of Human Rights*, vol. 13/2014, pp. 1–16.
[612] WRIGHT, Jaime, "Dez Anos de Brasil: Nunca Mais", *Folha de São Paulo*, July 14, 1995, https://www1.folha.uol.com.br/fsp/1995/7/14/opiniao/10.html.

fostered a series of doctoral theses,[613] research reports,[614] and other books,[615] as well as encouraging the launch of counter-narrative books intended to respond to the BNM project.[616] Finally, the information contained in the 1985 report also supported the investigations conducted by the NTC in the period from 2012-2014. In the context of civil society mobilization, the BNM Report encouraged the creation of movements like the "Torture: Never Again" groups (*Tortura: Nunca Mais*), whose first manifestation was in 1985, in Rio de Janeiro State, and accelerated the ratification of the treaty against torture proposed by the United Nations.[617]

However, these grassroots mobilizations expressing oppositional protests and a generalized desire for democracy – which started with campaigns like those seeking amnesty (1975-1979) and in favor of direct election of a civilian President (in 1984), as well as initiatives like the BNM Report (1979-1985) – collapsed shortly after that, along with the rise of Brazil's emerging civilian regime. According to Hochstetler,[618] the story goes that after that point more traditional political actors regained control over the post-military agenda, while social movements faced new dilemmas and internal conflicts.

Also, referring to the 1985 publication of the BNM Report, Wilcken has stated that in any other context a book like *Brazil: Never Again* would have created ripple effects,[619] as cases, names, and methods were all detailed. In post-dictatorship Brazil, however, none of the torturers suffered any sanctions other than occasional harassment by campaign groups like Amnesty International. In fact, Ryan[620] has even commented that a large number of torturers continued to work in police centers across the country, and most have ended up retiring with

---

[613] Example: REIS FILHO, Daniel Aarão, "As Organiações Comunistas e a Luta de Classes – 1961–1968", Ph.D thesis, *Faculdade de Filosofia, Letras e Ciências Humanas da Universidade de São Paulo*, 1987, http://caph.fflch.usp.br/node/4265.

[614] Examples: TESSITORE, Viviane, "Projeto Brasil Nunca Mais: Reconstrução, História, Recuperação e Aplicação da Metodologia", *Revista Projeto História*, vol. 50/2014, pp. 275–288. TELES, Janaína de Almeida, "A Constituição das Memórias sobre a Repressão da Ditadura: o Projeto Brasil Nunca Mais e a Abertura da Vala de Perus", *Anos 90*, vol. 19/2012, pp. 261–298.

[615] Examples: OLIVEIRA, Luciano, *Do Nunca Mais ao Eterno Retorno – Uma Reflexão sobre a Tortura*, São Paulo, Brasiliense, 1994. WESCHLER, Lawrence, *Um Milagre, Um Universo: O Acerto de Contas com os Torturadores*, São Paulo, Companhia das Letras, 1990.

[616] Examples: GIORDANI, Marco Pollo, *Brasil Sempre*, Porto Alegre, Tchê, 1986. USTRA, Carlos Alberto Brilhante, *Rompendo o Silêncio*, São Paulo, Thesaurus, 1987. RODRIGUES, Oswaldo Lima, *Verdade e Realidade*, Cantagalo, Jornal da Região, 1987.

[617] SILVA, Amanda Romanelli, "Brasil: Nunca Mais – Imprensa, Memória da Ditadura e Transição Democrática", *Seminário História & Democracia: Precisamos Falar Sobre Isso*, UNIFESP – Campos Guarulhos, September 2018.

[618] HOCHSTETLER, Kathryn, "Democratizing Pressures from Below? Social Movements in New Brazilian Democracy", *XX International Congress of Latin American Studies Association*, Mexico, 1997.

[619] WILCKEN, Patrick, "The Reckoning", *New Left Review*, vol. 78/2012, pp. 63–78.

[620] RYAN, Holly Eva, "From Absent to Present Pasts: Civil Society, Democracy and the Shifting Place of Memory in Brazil", *Journal of Civil Society*, vol. 12/2016, pp. 158–177.

Chapter 6. Civil Society and NGOs in the Quest for Truth, Justice, and Memory

generous state pensions. All the while, domestic civil society support for truth and justice initiatives has faded away, though some organizations such as the Torture: Never Again groups, the OAB,[621] the Popular "Esculacho" Front (*Frente de Esculacho Popular*) and the Popular Youth Uprising (*Levante Popular da Juventude*)[622] have worked on behalf of victims and challenged the entrenched culture of silence and "unremembering" in Brazil.[623]

But the year 1990 marked another shift in the culture of "unremembering" that permeated most of the 1980s. That year, through the investigative efforts of journalists and relatives of the dead and disappeared, a clandestine mass grave was discovered in the Dom Bosco Cemetery, in the Perus neighborhood in the City of São Paulo (the *Vala de Perus*). Inside this grave there were 1049 boxes with bones, many of whom were thought to be destitute people who lived on the streets, but there were also the remains of political opponents of the military regime. Until now, between 20 to 40 political activists are believed to have been buried in this clandestine grave.[624]

It is said that in 1990, when the journalist Caco Barcellos was informed by the cemetery administrator about the existence of a secret mass grave where political prisoners were buried, some of their family members already knew of its existence,[625] but it was the journalist's report that created the public commotion necessary to open the grave.[626] However, it was only in 1990 that family members gained access to the files of the São Paulo Coroner's Office (*Instituto Médico Legal/SP*), a forensic center where they found requests for the examination of

---

[621] The *Ordem dos Advogados do Brasil* (OAB) brought the ADPF no. 157 case before the Supreme Court, confronting the validity of the Amnesty Law. See Chapter 4 of this book.

[622] The efforts of the *Frente de Esculacho Popular* and *Levante Popular da Juventude* are described below in section 6.2 of this chapter regarding new strategies and activisms.

[623] Those social movements and organizations have faced persistent denials or low levels of popular support, as previously observed in the 2010 poll which suggested that up to 45% of the population were opposed to the punishment of former police and military personnel found guilty of torture. See: FRANCO, Bernardo Melo, "Punição a Tortura na Ditadura Divide Opiniões no País", *Folha de São Paulo*, June 7, 2010, http://www1.folha.uol.com.br/fsp/poder/po0706201008.htm.

[624] There is no precise information about how many political opponents were buried in the clandestine grave of Perus since the identification of bodies is still not finished. Teles commented that it would be 19 individuals, while media news said it would be around 40 persons. See: PAES, Caio de Freitas, "Como é feito o trabalho de identificar restos mortais de desaparecidos na ditadura", *BBC Brasil*, December 3, 2018, https://www.bbc.com/portuguese/brasil-46429950; TELES, Janaína de Almeida, "A Vala Clandestina de Perus: Entre o Passado e o Presente", *Revista Insurgência*, vol. 4/2018, pp. 300–341.

[625] Probably, between 1978 and 1979, family members of disappeared persons discovered that many opponents of the regime were buried in a mass grave inside the Dom Bosco cemetery, from comments by workers and administrators of the cemetery. However, since the transition was not yet finished, they decided to remain quiet and monitor events. See: TELES, Janaína de Almeida, "A Constituição das Memórias sobre a Repressão da Ditadura: o Projeto Brasil Nunca Mais e a Abertura da Vala de Perus", *Anos 90*, vol. 19/2012, pp. 261–298.

[626] BARCELLOS, Caco, "O Globo Reporter sobre a Vala de Perus", in TELES, Janaína de Almeida, *Mortos e Desaparecidos Políticos: Reparação ou Impunidade?*, São Paulo, Humanitas, 2001.

several bodies marked with a letter "T" in the year 1975 (exactly when the mass grave was created) Later on it was found that the letter "T" stood for "terrorist".

The opening of the Perus mass grave made an impact.[627] For instance, in April of 1991, shortly after the conclusion of a parliamentary investigation of the case, the CFMD and human rights activists organized an expedition to the Araguaia region in order to locate the remains of the guerrilla fighters believed to have died there. They found two skeletons supposedly belonging to Maria Lúcia Petit da Silva and Francisco Manoel Chaves, in the cemetery in Xambioá (in the state of Tocantins). Later on, in 1996, one of these two sets of remains was duly identified as being that of Maria Lúcia and the family finally gave her a funeral, in the city of Bauru (in the state of São Paulo). In fact, during the course of these efforts from 1991 to 1992, a total of five sets of remains were identified.[628] Also, as a consequence of the same movement for the identification of bodies, Bergson Gurjão Farias, whose remains were found in 1991, was finally identified and buried in 2009, in the city of Fortaleza (in the state of Ceará). A second consequence was the opening of the archives of São Paulo State Department of Political and Social Order (*Departamento Estadual de Ordem Política e Social de São Paulo* – DEOPS/SP) in 1992.

However, the process of identifying the remains from the Perus mass grave that are still in boxes has not yet finished, and it is far from a success story even 29 years later. Just to illustrate, in 1990, the University of Campinas (Unicamp) agreed to work to identify the remains and several years later they were placed in boxes and transferred from Campinas to São Paulo, where they were sent to the columbarium of the Araçá Cemetery. Later, the University of São Paulo restarted the analyses in the early 2000s, when the remains of Flavio de Carvalho Molina (in 2005) and of Luiz José da Cunha (in 2006) were identified. This process, however, was interrupted once again.[629] To find out what happened in the previous stages, under the pressure of victims' families, in 2009 the Federal Public Prosecutor's Office initiated a Public Civil Action.[630]

---

[627] TELES, Maria Amélia de Almeida and LISBOA, Suzana Keniger, "A Vala de Perus: Um Marco Histórico na Busca da Verdade e da Justiça!", in CARDOSO, Ítalo and BERNARDES, Laura (eds.), *Vala Clandestina de Perus – Desaparecidos Políticos, Um Capítulo Não Encerrado da História Brasileira*, São Paulo, Ed. Do Autor, 2012, pp. 51–102.

[628] From 1991 up to 1992 the remains of Sônia Maria Morais Angel Jones, Helber José Gomes Goulart, Antônio Carlos Bicalho Lana, Emanuel Bezerra dos Santos, and Maria Lúcia Petit da Silva were identified. See: GONZAGA, Eugênia Augusta, "As Ossadas de Perus e a Atuação do Ministério Público Federal em São Paulo", in CARDOSO, Ítalo and BERNARDES, Laura (eds.), *Vala Clandestina de Perus – Desaparecidos Políticos, Um Capítulo Não Encerrado da História Brasileira*, São Paulo, Ed. Do Autor, 2012, pp. 106–116.

[629] CASTRO, Lanaís, *Brazil's Clandestine Mass Grave in Perus (São Paulo)*, https://www.menschenrechte.org/wp-content/uploads/2018/10/Massengrab_Perus.pdf.

[630] GONZAGA, Eugênia Augusta, "As Ossadas de Perus e a Atuação do Ministério Público Federal em São Paulo", in CARDOSO, Ítalo and BERNARDES, Laura (eds.), *Vala Clandestina de Perus – Desaparecidos Políticos, Um Capítulo Não Encerrado da História Brasileira*, São Paulo, Ed. Do Autor, 2012, pp. 106–116.

Chapter 6. Civil Society and NGOs in the Quest for Truth, Justice, and Memory

Years later, in 2014, under pressure from the CFMD that had continuously denounced the vulnerable conditions in which the remains were being kept, the Secretariat for Human Rights of the Office of the President and the Special Commission on Political Deaths and Disappearances reached an agreement with the São Paulo Municipal Secretariat for Human Rights and Citizenship, the Federal University of São Paulo (Unifesp) and the Human Rights and Minorities Commission of the Chamber of Deputies, to resume the analysis of the remains. To this end, the Perus Working Group (*Grupo de Trabalho Perus*) was created as a forensic anthropology task-force for the identification of the bones from the *Vala de Perus*.[631]

In February of 2018, the Perus Working Group completed the identification of Dimas Antônio Casemiro, who was killed in April 1971 by agents of the military regime. And, in December of 2018, the same group completed the identification of Aluízio Palhano Pedreira Ferreira. In both cases the final confirmation was completed after the Working Group received the results of DNA tests from the first group of biological samples, which were sent for genetic analysis to the International Commission on Missing Persons (ICMP) in The Hague.

Accountability for crimes committed during the dictatorship has being placed in the background in comparison to other social claims for several reasons. Among these were: (a) the control of the political transition by the members of the military (between 1979 and 1985); (b) the emergence of new social demands; and (c) the lack of success of the movement of victims and families of political opponents in securing broader support by the wider society. Overall, the example of the 29 years of ups and downs in the experience of the Perus grave has shown that the lapse of time is a factor, added to a low degree of social coordination, which has created a political obstacle and barred the full implementation of Transitional Justice mechanisms in Brazil.

There is also another aspect of the efforts of relatives of the dead and disappeared seeking Transitional Justice, which is their struggles for judicial mechanisms under the domestic law and before international courts. Locally, one of the disputes began in March 1982, when 22 relatives of the dead and disappeared linked to the *Araguaia Guerrilla Campaign* filed a lawsuit against the federal government in order to locate the remains and determine the fate of the guerrilla fighters. The proceedings lasted more than 20 years, with the final decision being issued in 2007. In the course of this long judicial battle, the relatives of the dead and disappeared continued to mobilize and to organize networks of denunciation and solidarity, activating various international and national human rights institutions and entities.

---

[631] See: *Centro de Antropologia e Arqueologia Forense (CAAF), Grupo de Trabalho Perus*, https://www.unifesp.br/reitoria/caaf/hide-blog-caaf/129-29-anos-da-abertura-da-vala-clandestina-de-perus.

At the beginning of 1990, a group of relatives and lawyers representing international human rights NGOs in Brazil met to study the possibility of presenting such a case before the IACtHR, based on the lack of initiatives by the State, including the slowness of the Judiciary in the resolution of the lawsuit initiated in 1982.[632] Therefore, in 1995, with the mobilization of the relatives of the dead and disappeared and NGOs, and 13 years after the filing of the lawsuit in Brazil, the IACtHR received the petition against the Brazilian State presented by the Brazilian section of the Center for Justice and International Law (CEJIL-Brazil) and Human Rights Watch/Americas, to which the Rio de Janeiro chapter of Torture: Never Again and the CFMD were subsequently added as co-petitioner. The decision of the IACHR was finally handed down in 2010, resulting in the Brazilian State being found liable.[633]

Also worthy of note is the existence of the book called "Dossier Dictatorship: Political Deaths and Disappearances in Brazil – 1964–1985" (*Dossiê Ditadura: Mortos e Desaparecidos Políticos no Brasil – 1964–1985*),[634] which had its origin in 1979, and was derived from a list of political dead and disappeared people organized by the Brazilian Amnesty Committee of Rio de Janeiro. At that time, it was a pioneering document that, subsequently, was improved according to the year of death and/or disappearance of the people in it, regardless the political organization to which each one of them was affiliated. This Dossier was even handed over to Senator Teotônio Vilela, who was responsible for examining the Bill of the Amnesty Law in the National Congress. In 1983, the CFMD produced a new edition of the Dossier and it was finally published in the format of a book, and reprinted in 2009 by the Official Press of the state of São Paulo.

Throughout this period, the Dossier served as a source for the preparation of Annex I of Law 9,140 (1995), which recognized the responsibility of the Brazilian State for the disappearance of militants who fought against the dictatorship. Furthermore, during the opening of the Perus mass grave in São Paulo in 1990, the Dossier was a fundamentally important source of information to start investigating who could ultimately be hidden in that site. In addition, the Dossier was adopted as a base document for research by the São Paulo State Truth Commission and the NTC; and the very same document offered subsidies

---

[632] SANTOS, Cecília MacDowell, "Questões de Justiça de Transição: a Mobilização dos Direitos Humanos e a Memória da Ditadura no Brasil", in SANTOS, Boaventura de Sousa; ABRÃO, Paulo; SANTOS, Cecília Macdowell; and TORELLY, Marcelo D., *Repressão e Memória Política no Contexto Ibero-Brasileiro: Estudos sobre Brasil, Guatemala, Moçambique, Peru e Portugal*, Brasília, Ministério da Justiça, Comissão de Anistia, Coimbra, Universidade de Coimbra, Centro de Estudos Sociais, 2010, pp. 124–151.

[633] The detailed explanation of the *Araguaia Case* before the Inter-American Court of Human Rights is described in Chapter 4 of this book.

[634] *Truth Commission of the State of São Paulo*, Final Report, Volume II, "Dossiê Ditadura: Mortos e Desaparecidos Políticos no Brasil – 1964–1985", http://comissaodaverdade.al.sp.gov.br/relatorio/tomo-ii/.

for national lawsuits and the international *Araguaia Case*, at the Inter-American Court of Human Rights.

6.2. ACTIVISMS AND STRATEGIES DURING THE 2000s: FROM CLAIMS FOR JUSTICE TO THE "*ESCRACHOS*"

Relatives of the dead and disappeared, together with human rights lawyers, constituted a group of social actors who tried to implement the justice pillar of Transitional Justice and who played a crucial role in reinforcing human rights norms by filing civil charges against the State and former torturers. In the course of this litigation strategy, the relatives of the dead and disappeared turned to the courts first to seek symbolic and financial reparations, to obtain official recognition of the crimes that had occurred, and finally, for clarification of the circumstances of the disappearances and rectification of any false information that had been placed in public archives. Furthermore, it should be recognized that the family members made creative use of the judicial mechanisms at their disposal in order to make advances in the process of Brazilian Transitional Justice, despite the obstacles in the path of holding the perpetrators criminally responsible.

The efforts of the victims' family members in filing their civil actions are also significant,[635] as it was through those initiatives that it was possible to collect the testimony of possible witnesses in the presence of a judge, as well as to preserve evidence that might otherwise have been lost over time. This was especially true in the case of witnesses who might no longer have been alive when the State finally showed an interest in hearing them. The families' creativity lay in their use of the litigation to elicit testimony in a public forum (a judicial hearing) which was capable of formally verifying the validity of the evidence collected for use in possible future criminal proceedings, despite the absence of any truth commission or similar body at the time.

The family members of victims of serious human rights violations carried out during the dictatorship used the instrument of private civil suits in their struggle for memory, truth, and justice and thus were able to obtain relevant advances. In those suits which sought damages, they were able to get the courts to acknowledge that no statute of limitations applies to the serious violations suffered by the victims. In addition, in those suits seeking a declaratory judgment, they were able to have the courts declare an agent of the State to be a torturer. Thus, the efforts of the victims' families in the civil law sphere were able to make gains not possible in the criminal law sphere, where actions

---

[635] *Truth Commission of the State of São Paulo*, Report, Volume 1, Part 3, "As Ações Judiciais das Famílias Teles e Merlino".

seeking to have the perpetrators held criminally liable and to apply international human rights law are still being blocked.[636] Thus, their actions illustrate well a civil society Transitional Justice strategy with respect to the Brazilian State. It is in this context that the suit brought against Colonel Carlos Alberto Brilhante Ustra by the Teles family is a pioneering example. That suit sought a judicial declaration that the defendant, acting maliciously and illicitly (through the use of torture), caused the defendants harm, even though the latter did not seek any compensation in the case.

The Teles family, who filed their case in São Paulo, have been key protagonists in urging the State to recognize the torture committed during the dictatorship. In 2005, the family filed a declaratory action seeking recognition of the torture suffered by its members while being held at the São Paulo offices of the Department of Information Operations – Center for Internal Defense Operations (*Departamento de Operações de Informações – Centro de Operações de Defesa Interna* – DOI/CODI) in the early 1970s. In August of 2012, the family won a historic legal fight against Colonel Brilhante Ustra, the former head of the DOI/CODI in São Paulo.[637]

In addition, beginning in the 2000s and culminating in 2014, social mobilization reached the level of compelling the Armed Forces to abandon their former position of literal "denial" of the crimes that had been committed during the dictatorship period. This is because, with the approval of Law no. 10,559 (2002), which provides for official recognition of State accountability in relation to human rights violations committed during the dictatorship, new fronts of mobilization emerged along broad lines of Transitional Justice. Those actions treated the matter as being in the collective interest of democracy, and not just as a private interest only of the victims of the regime and their families.

Furthermore, the legal analysis of the Amnesty Law before the Supreme Court, in 2010, succeeded in uniting forces that had previously been scattered, bringing together initiatives of the OAB, the MPF, the AJD, the ABAP, the ADNAM, and the CEJIL. As a result, the theme of Transitional Justice has become a part of the broader human rights movement, so that, since 2009, it has had its own dedicated chapter in the Brazilian government's National Human

---

[636] OSMO, Carla, "O Judiciário Brasileiro Diante dos Crimes da Ditadura: Entre a Imprescritibilidade Civil e a Anistia Penal", http://conti.derhuman.jus.gov.ar/2016/11/seminario/mesa_18/osmo_mesa_18.pdf.

[637] SCHNEIDER, Nina, "Waiting for a Meaningful State Apology: Has Brazil Apologized for Authoritarian Repression?", *Journal of Human Rights*, vol. 13/2014, pp. 1–16. SANTOS, Cecília MacDowell, "Questões de Justiça de Transição: a Mobilização dos Direitos Humanos e a Memória da Ditadura no Brasil", in SANTOS, Boaventura de Sousa; ABRÃO, Paulo; SANTOS, Cecília Macdowell; and TORELLY, Marcelo D., *Repressão e Memória Política no Contexto Ibero-Brasileiro: Estudos sobre Brasil, Guatemala, Moçambique, Peru e Portugal*, Brasília, Ministério da Justiça, Comissão de Anistia, Coimbra, Universidade de Coimbra, Centro de Estudos Sociais, 2010, pp. 124–151.

Rights Plan. In the same period, with the support of victims' families, the Federal Public Prosecutor's Office began to file more lawsuits against the torturers of the dictatorship.

Although the legal mobilization of human rights activists or the justice pillar were not the only or even the most decisive factors contributing to the recent implementation of Transitional Justice in Brazil, it is an important phenomenon to be observed, as the mobilization by sectors of civil society seems to have played a significant role in bringing political pressure to bear on the formulation of new policies of Transitional Justice in the country.[638]

More recently, new groups of social actors – such as the group known as the Popular Youth Uprising (*Levante Popular da Juventude*) – have called for a new form of intervention through political demonstrations known as "*escrachos*" or "*esculachos*": public protests designed to shame the former oppressors, similar to marches, interventions or theatrical "happenings". In the description of Gready and Robins,[639] *escrachos* are multidimensional, street-based actions, usually targeting a person's home and serve as a means to increase social awareness using artistic interventions, theatre, and educational work against the culture of silence and forgetting. Although the practice of *escrachos* in Brazil did not generate a consolidated tradition of social mobilization, a worthwhile factor in this type of happening is that there is no physical confrontation or violence – for one reason because those are seen as elements that could devalue such actions, but mainly because the idea is to avoid reducing the *escrachos* to mere acts of revenge. Rather, the idea is to treat them as exercises of collective rights-claiming for justice at a time when the judicial paths are still blocked, and mainly because such events are available even to those who were not born at the time when the initial violence was committed.[640]

Through demonstrations and performances, the participants identify torturers and officials of the 1964–1985 regime and protest in front of their houses. In this way they are employing some of the ideas developed years ago in Argentina by the group "Daughters and Sons for Identity and Justice and Against Silence and Forgetting" (*Hijas y hijos por identidad y justicia y contra el olvido y silencio*) or HIJOS. That group mobilized to denounce impunity for

---

[638] SANTOS, Cecília MacDowell, "Memória na Justiça: A Mobilização dos Direitos Humanos e a Construção da Memória da Ditadura no Brasil", *Revista Crítica de Ciências Sociais*, vol. 88/2010, pp. 127–154.

[639] GREADY, Paul and ROBINS, Simon, "Rethinking Civil Society and Transitional Justice: Lessons from Social Movements and "New" Civil Society", *The International Journal of Human Rights*, vol. 21/2017, pp. 956–975.

[640] SOARES, Inês Virgínia Prado and QUINALHA, Renan Honório, "Os Escrachos e a Luta Por Verdade e Justiça: O Que Esperar em 2013?", *Correio da Cidadania*, January 3, 2013, http://www.correiocidadania.com.br/colunistas/dicionario-da-cidadania/7968-03-01-2013-os-escrachos-e-a-luta-por-verdade-e-justica-o-que-esperar-em-2013.

torturers and officials of that country's dictatorship. In Argentina, "*escraches*" (the Argentinian term) have divided public and scholarly opinion,[641] whereas in Brazil, as such manifestations are still a recent phenomenon, it remains to be seen exactly how the Brazilian *esculachos* will interact with and support the existing democratic process.[642]

As a general overview, as observed by Gready and Robins,[643] in such actions, these social actors are not directly making demands on the State. Rather, they are addressing their own society and trying to break the silence within communities, waking entire neighborhoods up to the fact that killers and torturers continue to lead normal lives in their midst. In the case of the movement led by the Popular Youth Uprising group, which started precisely in 2006 in the city of Porto Alegre (in the state of Rio Grande do Sul), their initiatives were focused on the right to memory involving the narratives of victims around the cry of "never again", and in the experiences of these Brazilian young people one may see the importance of new generations getting involved in a process concerning facts that they never personally experienced. Such initiatives raise questions such as what the concept of "never again" means for the young people born after the events in question, especially in a society where there is much more stimulus to live in the present and to forget the past.

In this sense, social mobilization, beyond official and State initiatives, may be seen as a moral duty not just on those who suffered directly from the violence of the dictatorship, but also one that weighs on the shoulders of future generations to mitigate the risk of repetition. In the *escrachos*, a collective trauma may be felt in the present by a generation born within the democratic period. They are often conducted not only by the children or grandchildren of the political opponents of the military regime, but also by young people who until recently were unaware of the facts related to the dictatorship and who are distanced in time and the space from those times.

As a form of festive occupation of the public space, the *escrachos* represent an innovative tactic in a struggle marked by new political symbolism, one in which issues such as physical and psychic violations, the absence of victims' bodies, the lack of trials and punishment of those responsible, the suffering of

---

[641] Regarding the "*escraches*" in Argentina, it is said that while some have acknowledged their role as a kind of catalyst, ushering progress toward criminal trials for torturers, others have been more cautious about the ways that these actions allow protestors to take matters into their own hands without fair trials or due process. See: RYAN, Holly Eva, "From Absent to Present Pasts: Civil Society, Democracy and the Shifting Place of Memory in Brazil", *Journal of Civil Society*, vol. 12/2016, pp. 158–177.

[642] RYAN, Holly Eva, "From Absent to Present Pasts: Civil Society, Democracy and the Shifting Place of Memory in Brazil", *Journal of Civil Society*, vol. 12/2016, pp. 158–177.

[643] GREADY, Paul and ROBINS, Simon, "Rethinking Civil Society and Transitional Justice: Lessons from Social Movements and "New" Civil Society", *The International Journal of Human Rights*, vol. 21/2017, pp. 956–975.

victims and their families, that is, the entire puzzle of the past generation are made universal and contemporary. The denunciations in the squares, in the streets, and in front of the homes of the perpetrators, through noise-making, music, posters, and dramatizations, make audible and visible what had been an undisclosed memory or a private pain.

In 2012, the Popular Youth Upraising carried out 12 manifestations or *escrachos* in 11 Brazilian states: Pernambuco, Pará, Bahia, Ceará, Sergipe, Paraíba, Rio Grande do Norte, São Paulo, Minas Gerais, Rio de Janeiro and Rio Grande do Sul. Among these was the one against Harry Shibata which took place in São Paulo. During the dictatorship, he signed several death certificates and created false accounts regarding the deaths of regime opponents, such as that of the journalist Vladimir Herzog. Another *escracho* was against Lieutenant-Colonel Maurício Lopes Lima, who was recognized as a former torturer linked to Operation *Bandeirantes* (*Operação Bandeirante* – OBAN), a notorious campaign of political repression. Performances continued after 2012 and intensified in April of 2014, on the occasion of the fiftieth anniversary of the 1964 *coup d'état*. One *escracho* took place in Brasilia, against Colonel Carlos Alberto Brilhante Ustra, the former head of the DOI/CODI in São Paulo, but also in São Paulo itself, against the police investigator Aparecido Laertes Calandra (nicknamed "Captain Ubirajara"); and in Belo Horizonte against Colonel Pedro Ivo dos Santos Vasconcelos, an officer of the Minas Gerais State Department of Political and Social Order (*Departamento de Ordem Política e Social* – DOPS). In December 2014, the day after the release of the final report of the NTC, the Popular Youth Uprising group organized a demonstration on the Washington Luiz Highway calling for the punishment of the torturers. Each of these manifestations was filmed and posted on social media, an increasingly creative way of informing the public and keeping memory alive. Thus, in this collective therapeutic process, the losses suffered were recognized not only by those who experienced them, but also by those who came after, allowing for symbolic and ethical reparations.[644]

In December of 2012, on the occasion of the awarding of the eighteenth annual Human Rights Prize, by the Office of the President's National Human Rights Secretariat, the Popular Youth Uprising group was given an Honorable Mention. That tribute was due to the series of collective interventions (*escrachos*) they had organized against torturers and agents of repression during the dictatorship in several Brazilian states. With creativity being the central motif behind their political action, they called attention to the Brazilian State's failure to implement

---

[644] Rovai, Marta Gouveia de Oliveira, "A Memória Herdada: as Comissões da Verdade e os Escrachos Promovidos pela Juventude em Países da América Latina, como Argentina, Chile e Brasil", *Revista Eletrônica da Associação Nacional de Pesquisadores e Professores de História das Américas – ANPHLAC*, vol. 18/2015, pp. 223–250.

the justice pillar of Transitional Justice and the absence of acknowledgment of the truth about the violent events of the dictatorship.

Another group, known as the Popular "*Esculacho*" Front (*Frente de Esculacho Popular* – FEP), was formed with the objective of linking the Brazil of the dictatorship with the country as it is today, since until today Black youth, the poor, and those living in outlying areas are still killed with impunity, often with the same excuses provided as those given for killings of the regime's political opponents during the dictatorship; that is, that the victims offered armed resistance to the police.[645] Among the "*esculachos*" carried out by the FEP were a performance in April of 2012 against Harry Shibata, the same person who used to sign false death certificates hiding the signs of torture and who was targeted in the "*esculachos*" of the Popular Youth Upraising. Another, in 2014, took place in front of the headquarters of the São Paulo State Federation of Industry (*Federação de Indústria do Estado de São Paulo* – FIESP) and Itaú Bank, both of which were linked with Operation *Bandeirantes* and the funding of oppression and torture.[646]

Another important social mobilization, in 2013, was a campaign arguing that contemporary police violence is a product of social inequalities and a standard of public safety inherited from the dictatorship. That campaign used flyers to compare the two types of dead people: the "victims of the dictatorship" (including pictures of opponents of the regime like Manoel Fiel Filho and Honestino Guimarães) and "victims of democracy" (including pictures of Amarildo Dias de Sousa[647] and Douglas Rodrigues[648]). The campaign was called "Sir, why did you shoot me?" ("*Por que o senhor atirou em mim?*"), based on a question asked by a young man of the police officer who had just shot him, ultimately fatally.[649]

---

[645] MOURÃO, Alexandre de A.; FIGUEIREDO, Clara F.; SCHINCARIOL, Rafael (eds.), *Lampejos: Arte, Memória, Verdade, Justiça*, Rio de Janeiro, Synergia, 2016.

[646] For more details about the complicity of corporations during the military regime, see Chapter 9 of this book.

[647] On July 14, 2013, Amarildo Dias de Souza, a 43-year-old bricklayer from the Rocinha slum ("*favela*") in Rio de Janeiro, was taken in for questioning at the local Police Pacification Unit (*Unidade de Polícia Pacificadora* – UPP). Officers there believed that he was connected to drug trafficking activity in the the slum, despite having no prior involvement in illegal activity. Shortly after Souza was brought to the police station, he disappeared and was never seen again. See: CARNEIRO, Julia, "Amarildo: The Disappearance that Has Rocked Rio", *BBC Brasil*, September 18, 2013, https://www.bbc.com/news/world-latin-america-24143780.

[648] On October 27, 2013, Douglas Rodrigues, a 17-year-old student was assassinated by a police officer. His death gave rise to a social movement confronting police violence. See: GOMES, Rodrigo, "Após Dois Anos, Família de Jovem Morto por PM na Zona Norte de SP Ainda Espera Justiça", *Rede Brasil Atual*, October 26, 2015, https://www.redebrasilatual.com.br/cidadania/2015/10/apos-dois-anos-familia-de-jovem-morto-por-pm-na-zona-norte-de-sao-paulo-ainda-espera-justica-1890/.

[649] MOURÃO, Alexandre de A.; FIGUEIREDO, Clara F.; and SCHINCARIOL, Rafael (eds.), *Lampejos: Arte, Memória, Verdade, Justiça*, Rio de Janeiro, Synergia, 2016.

As a strategy, those collective actions targeting past violence also create networks of social support that may transform experiences of victimhood.[650] Social movements like the Popular Youth Uprising, the Popular *"Esculacho"* Front, and the campaign "Sir, why did you shoot me?" exercise the social practice of memory to counter the official amnesia which became widespread following the Amnesty Law of 1979.

There are other cases of collective actions and artists who have been refining struggles to promote a public policy of memory, truth, and justice, and to pressure the State to implement the recommendations made by the NTC. What is worthy of note in these cases is that, through such actions, young people get in touch with initiatives of other young artists who, even though they did not experience the years of the dictatorship, nevertheless desire to live in a country where there are no longer cases of illegal persecution, death by torture inside prisons, or forced disappearances carried out by agents of the State. Thus, these collective actions and performances have applied the popular saying "let it not be forgotten so that it never happens again" (*para que não se esqueça, para que nunca mais aconteça*).

This type of approach may be seen in the collective action of a group of artists known as the Political "Appeared" Collective (*Coletivo Aparecidos Políticos*). Created in 2010, the group was formed by some young artists and art students in the city of Fortaleza (state of Ceará) who witnessed the arrival of the remains of the former opponent of the dictatorship, Bergson Gurjão Farias,[651] on October 6, 2009, and attended his funeral. After that dramatic experience, they decided to carry out popular urban interventions and labeled their group by reference to the Portuguese term for those who went missing due to political violence, the so-called "political disappeared", as if those victims had suddenly shown up again as the "political appeared".

In order to explain the motivation behind their performances one of the members commented that,[652] among people of their generation, this topic of discussion is quite rare and usually their peers are only worried about their future jobs or acquiring material goods (like buying a house or a new car). As a result, often enough their efforts (like gatherings "to change the world") seem old fashioned. However, they believe that the wheels of history do not turn in a single direction towards ever-increasing progress; i.e., past atrocities

---

[650] GREADY, Paul and ROBINS, Simon, "Rethinking Civil Society and Transitional Justice: Lessons from Social Movements and "New" Civil Society", *The International Journal of Human Rights*, vol. 21/2017, pp. 956–975.
[651] For detailed information about Bergson Gurjão Farias, see: http://memoriasdaditadura.org.br/memorial/bergson-gurjao-farias/.
[652] MOURÃO, Alexandre de Albuquerque; SIQUEIRA, Gelirton Almeida; MARTINS, Marcos Venicius Lima; ROCHA, Viviane; MOREIRA, Daniel Bruno, "Os Aparecidos Políticos: Arte Ativista e Justiça de Transição, *Revista Anistia Política*, vol. 6/2011, pp. 148–170.

may happen again. Thus, their interventions serve to question certain types of false consensus present in contemporary society, such as that we are living in a very stable democracy or the premise that the broad, general and unrestricted amnesty of 1979 was extended to the whole population.

Just to illustrate more of these types of interventions, between April and September of 2011, the group known as the Who Political Collective (*Coletivo Político Quem*) stamped printed questions like "Who killed Alexandre Vannuchi Leme?"[653] on circulating notes of Brazilian currency (the *real*) and also placed those same questions on walls of the city of São Paulo. In 2013, the group calling itself the Sabô Collective (*Coletivo Sabô*) place signs on walls and hung from trees in the city of Rio de Janeiro with the phrase "to remember is to (re)exist" ("*lembrar é (re)existir*"), in reference to the dead and disappeared of the dictatorship. In December of 2013, there was a campaign named Occupy DOPS (*Ocupa DOPS*) organized by the Rio de Janeiro Collective for Memory, Truth, and Justice (*Coletivo Rio de Janeiro por Verdade, Memória e Justiça*), whose aim was the transformation of the former Department of Political and Social Order (DOPS) into a center for collective memory.[654] In addition, it should be mentioned the *Paulista* Committee for Memory, Truth and Justice (*Comitê Paulista pela Memória, Verdade e Justiça* – CPMVJ),[655] which was created in 2011 and congregates men and women who fight against the dictatorship, as well as family members of the political dead and disappeared and representatives of civil society movements that are seeking memory, truth and justice, especially because the CPMVJ had expanded and strengthened the communication channels with the NTC and civil society.

6.3. CONCLUSIONS

Using the typologies for civil society interactions with Transitional Justice mechanisms, discussed by Gready and Robins as a guide,[656] in the Brazilian context, civil society has played four different roles over more than three decades. It started with the task of facilitation/consultation (with the pro-amnesty campaign). Then came a data collection and monitoring phase

---

[653] For more information about Alexandre Vannucchi Leme, see: http://memoriasdaditadura.org.br/biografias-da-resistencia/alexandre-vannucchi-leme/.
[654] Mourão, Alexandre de A.; Figueiredo, Clara F.; and Schincariol, Rafael (eds.), *Lampejos: Arte, Memória, Verdade, Justiça*, Rio de Janeiro, Synergia, 2016.
[655] About the activities of the *Comitê Paulista pela Memória, Verdade e Justiça* (CPMVJ) see: https://www.gov.br/mdh/pt-br/sdh/noticias/2014/setembro/comite-paulista-pela-memoria-verdade-e-justica-recebe-representante-da-sdh-pr-para-fortalecer-canais-de-comunicacao.
[656] Gready, Paul and Robins, Simon, "Rethinking Civil Society and Transitional Justice: Lessons from Social Movements and "New" Civil Society", *The International Journal of Human Rights*, vol. 21/2017, pp. 956–975.

(with the 1985 "Brazil: Never More" Report and the efforts towards the excavation of the clandestine mass grave in Perus). Next followed a period of representation and advocacy (with the *Araguaia* and *Herzog Cases* brought before the IACtHR and the civil actions of the Teles and Merlino families before the local courts). Finally, the latest phase has been one of intervention and education (with the *escrachos* and artistic movements). Indeed, these are not insignificant efforts for 30 years of democracy.

In contrast to this record of successful action, it may be argued that these civil movements were not enough, especially in light of the 2010 and 2014 polls,[657] which both demonstrated that Brazilian society is still divided regarding accountability for the years of the dictatorship. Those surveys made clear that large sectors of the Brazilian population have remained indifferent, if not openly hostile, to a formal rewriting of the history of the 1964–1989 period, proving that large-scale civil society action does not by itself guarantee progress toward democracy. Or, as Ryan has commented,[658] it gives cause to question the claims of former administrations that Brazil's recent "turn to memory" was a suitable epilogue to the transition that would help to consolidate democracy in the country.

Another consideration about civil society and the Brazilian case is that most of its advocacy and agency was focused on civil-political rights rather than socio-economic rights. As a result, the latent risk remains that social movements did not serve to mitigate conflict-era identities, but rather reinforced polarized and exclusive understandings of guilt and innocence. And, as Gready and Robins have observed, this type of victims' agency potentially holds the transition hostage to the least flexible agendas, infused with competition over limited political and economic resources, such as has occurred in the long process of identifying the remains from the Perus clandestine mass grave.[659]

While understandings rooted in locating body remains, discovering the fates of the victims, and bringing torturers to justice are hugely important for a democratic transition, there is the threat that a narrow perspective is condemned to remain insular, particularly where a proliferation of human

---

[657] FRANCO, Bernardo Melo, "Punição a Tortura na Ditadura Divide Opiniões no País", *Folha de São Paulo*, June 7, 2010, http://www1.folha.uol.com.br/fsp/poder/po0706201008.htm. MENDONÇA, Ricardo, "Maior Parte da População Quer Anular Lei da Anistia, Aponta DataFolha", *Folha de São Paulo*, March 31, 2014, http://www1.folha.uol.com.br/poder/2014/03/1433374-maior-parte-da-populacao-quer-anular-lei-da-anistia-aponta-datafolha.shtml.

[658] RYAN, Holly Eva, "From Absent to Present Pasts: Civil Society, Democracy and the Shifting Place of Memory in Brazil", *Journal of Civil Society*, vol. 12/2016, pp. 158–177.

[659] GONZAGA, Eugênia Augusta, "As Ossadas de Perus e a Atuação do Ministério Público Federal em São Paulo", in CARDOSO, Ítalo and BERNARDES, Laura (eds.), *Vala Clandestina de Perus – Desaparecidos Políticos, Um Capítulo Não Encerrado da História Brasileira*, São Paulo, Ed. Do Autor, 2012, pp. 106–116.

rights agendas dating back centuries may dilute its focus. These include hunger, domestic and gender-related violence, modern-day slavery, land disputes, the claims of indigenous people, environmental conflicts, and other economic and human rights demands. Perhaps, as Gready and Robins have noted,[660] the social actors in Brazil lack a more universal discourse – one addressing human rights, democracy, transparency, the end to the continued use of torture, just to name a few such issues – which might permit the translation of particular issues into a generally accessible framework that would be relevant to the daily lives of most citizens.

As for future actions, for instance, it remains for social movements to mobilize around the causes of the rights of indigenous people and peasants; the complicity of corporations and private actors in oppression; and violence against gender and racial minorities – all of which are causes which, until now, have been marginal to the Transitional Justice mechanisms found in the Brazilian scenario. Hence, it should be seen that it is not enough to solely blame the State for gaps in the implementation of Transitional Justice mechanisms in Brazil (with so-called "top-down" instruments). For decades, efforts to support the right to memory and truth have been largely restricted to the private domain, meaning that they have been merely discussed by victims and their families, with the support of the Catholic Church, lawyers, and some local and global human rights and non-governmental organizations.

It is true that the Amnesty Commission and the Commission on Political Deaths and Disappearances have launched several symbolic initiatives (i.e. Amnesty Caravans, the funding of documentary films, the release of books like *Direito à Memória e à Verdade* and *Luta, Substantivo Feminino*), that the NTC worked to uncover the past atrocities with its 2014 Report, and that a new kind of social movement has recently emerged in the form of the *escrachos* and in collective and individual artistic interventions and performances. The fact is, despite all of the above, that large sectors of Brazilian society still pay scant attention to issues involving the dictatorship and its direct victims and their families.

While trying to understand this phenomenon of insufficient public interest regarding such subjects, Schneider commented that there are complex causes for this dearth of interest in past human rights abuses and the limited mobilization of civil society for truth-seeking and justice initiatives in Brazil.[661] One factor identified for this lack of public mobilization is the 1979 Amnesty

---

[660] GREADY, Paul and ROBINS, Simon, "Rethinking Civil Society and Transitional Justice: Lessons from Social Movements and "New" Civil Society", *The International Journal of Human Rights*, vol. 21/2017, pp. 956–975.

[661] SCHNEIDER, Nina, "Too Little too Late or Premature? The Brazilian Truth Commission and the Question of Best Timing", *Journal of Iberian and Latin American Research*, vol. 19/2013, pp. 149–162.

Law, since that law continues to be regarded as a settlement between victims, society, and Armed Forces, following the myth of a reciprocal amnesty benefiting both torturers and survivors alike.[662] Another is the total number of people affected, as the number of families directly affected by human rights violations during the regime was considerably lower than in Argentina or Chile. As a result, fewer Brazilian families have insisted on the clarification and remembrance of these crimes, and the issue has come to be seen as declining in importance as democracy has "consolidated". A final factor has been the lack of adequate education about the history of the dictatorship, since many Brazilians know very little about State repression during the period.

Moreover, some institutional factors are worth noting. Over the years, scholars like Pereira[663] and Mezarobba[664] have observed that the controlled nature of the Brazilian transition resulted in a lack of both major institutional reforms and overall clarity. Consequently, supporters of the authoritarian regime continued to dominate the Legislative, Executive and Judicial Branches, and the majority of civilian staff in the authoritarian regime remained in power after Brazil's return to democracy.

Lastly, the analysis of the role of Brazilian civil society in the transition to democracy proves that the metaphor of a "familial reconciliation", which permitted the reintegration of political opponents (the demand of the movement for political amnesty between 1975 and 1979), is a strategy of reconciliation long-entrenched in the collective memory of our nation. As discussed by Ryan,[665] there is a tradition or practice in Brazil – hinged on forgetting – that has been repeatedly called forth to deal with the political conflicts of the day. It constitutes a pattern that consistently limits the ambitions of popular movements and has regulated the means of practicing politics.

Consequently, the analogy to a process of family reconciliation that has permeated the long transitional process in Brazil has deprived local communities of their potential agency. This is because, as Madlingozi has perceived,[666] in such a situation only one, restricted point of view remains: that of victims needing to be rescued and perpetrators needing to be prosecuted. Or, as

---

[662] For more explanations about the Amnesty Law, see Chapter 2 of this book.
[663] PEREIRA, Anthony, "An Ugly Democracy? State and the Rule of Law in Post Authoritarian Brazil", in KINGSTONE, Peter R, and POWER, Timothy J. (eds.), *Democratic Brazil: Actors, Institutions, and Processes*, Pittsburgh PA, Pittsburgh University Press, 2000.
[664] MEZAROBBA, Glenda, *O Preço do Esquecimento: as Reparações Pagas às Vítimas do Regime Militar – uma Comparação entre Brasil, Argentina e Chile*, Ph.D. Thesis, Faculdade de Filosofia, Letras e Ciências Humanas, Universidade de São Paulo (USP), São Paulo, 2007.
[665] Ibid.
[666] MADLINGOZI, Tshepo, "On Transitional Justice Entrepreneurs and the Production of Victims", *Journal of Human Rights Practice*, vol. 2/2010, pp. 208–228.

Lundy and McGovern have noted,[667] that part of the citizenry that engaged in armed conflict with the regime came to be viewed either as traumatized victims, lacking the ability to make decisions about the future, or as people driven by a destructive psychosis that rendered them incapable of positive contributions in the democratic era. Both images do not contribute to the future of any country and should be avoided by society as a whole.

Thus, what is still lacking in the role played by Brazilian social movements and civil actors looking to implement Transitional Justice measures is, in fact, the power of a dominant discourse. As Risse and Ropp have observed,[668] a dominant discourse is an enormously important mechanism leading to compliance with human rights norms and regulations. As those authors go on to state, naming and shaming can only be successful if either the target actors or an audience central to the process of change actually believe in the social validity of the norm.

---

[667] LUNDY, Patricia and McGOVERN, Mark, "Whose Justice? Rethinking Transitional Justice from the Bottom Up", *Journal of Law and Society*, vol. 35/2008, pp. 265–292.

[668] RISSE, Thomas and ROPP, Stephen C., "Introduction and Overview", in RISSE, Thomas; ROPP, Stephen C.; and SIKKINK, Kathryn (eds.), *The Persistent Power of Human Rights – From Commitment to Compliance*, Cambridge, Cambridge University Press, 2013.

CHAPTER 7
REDRESSING VIOLATIONS OF INDIGENOUS RIGHTS

> *"My father told me;*
> *I'll tell my son.*
> *When he dies?*
> *He tells his son.*
> *It's like this: nobody forgets".*[669]

The above sentence is mentioned on the last page of the 1984 Report entitled *Brasil: Nunca Mais* (Brazil: Never Again), which was the first comprehensive document describing human rights violations related to the dictatorship and State repression perpetrated against labor union members, students, politicians, journalists and clerics. The remarkable fact is that, although this epilogue comes from the testimony of an indigenous person named Kele Maxacali, this same report does not contain information on the persecution suffered by indigenous people during the period from 1964–1985 – people who were perhaps the most invisible victims of the Brazilian dictatorship.

7.1. THE INVISIBILITY OF INDIGENOUS PEOPLE

In fact, with regard to the indigenous population of Brazil, the representation of the past has been characterized by a kind of emptiness or silence for a long time. It is necessary to deal with this prolonged absence of an official policy regarding the human rights violations committed against indigenous peoples, since it seems that they have been excluded, not only from national history but also from

---

[669] Free translation of the epilogue contained in the report *Brasil: Nunca Mais*. This epilogue was written by Kelé Maxacali, an indigenous person from the village of Mikael, located in the State of Minas Gerais, in 1984. In Portuguese, the epilogue says: "*Meu pai contou para mim,/ eu vou contar para o meu filho./ Quando ele morrer?/ Ele conta pro filho dele./ É assim: ninguém esquece*", http://www.dhnet.org.br/dados/projetos/dh/br/tnmais/epilogo.html.

the consolidated memory of the dictatorship,[670] as will be shown in this chapter. This emptiness refers to the fact that for a long period of time, at least until 2014 (with the presentation of the final report of the National Truth Commission), indigenous concerns had not been included in the narrative of human rights violations during the Brazilian dictatorial regime, which demonstrates that, even during a democratic era, the rights of the indigenous population are still rarely observed.[671]

7.1.1. INDIGENOUS PEOPLE AND LEGAL PROTECTION DURING THE MID-TWENTIETH CENTURY

One can begin to analyze the twentieth-century legal framework regarding indigenous issues with the 1934 Constitution,[672] which referred to indigenous people only in establishing the authority of the federal government to legislate about the incorporation of such people into the wider nation (following an integration model), as well as establishing that the land where indigenous people were located should be respected and could not be sold or disturbed. Later on, in the 1937 and 1946 Constitutions, the protection of indigenous people was also associated with land occupation,[673] and the 1967 Constitution identified indigenous lands as federal assets, assuring the right of indigenous people to the use of the land (the so-called *usufruct*), including the exploitation of its natural resources, but denying them legal title to the land, which continued to belong to the federal government.[674]

Subsequently and mostly under the influence of Cândido Rondon's ideas (his famous motto related to contact with indigenous people was: "Die if necessary,

---

[670] RESENDE, Ana Catarina Zema de, "O Relatório Figueiredo, as Violações dos Direitos dos Povos Indígenas no Brasil dos anos 1960 e a Justa Memória", in SIQUEIRA, Gustavo Silveira; WOLKMER, Antonio Carlos; and PIERDONÁ, Zélia Luiza (eds.), *História do Direito – XXIV Encontro Nacional do Conselho Nacional de Pesquisa e Pós-Graduação em Direito (CONPEDI)*, Florianópolis, CONPEDI, 2015.

[671] CAPRIGLIONE, Laura, "Como a Ditadura Militar Ensinou Técnicas de Tortura à Guarda Rural Indígena (GRIN)", *Folha de São Paulo*, November 11, 2012, https://www1.folha.uol.com.br/ilustrissima/2012/11/1182605-como-a-ditadura-ensinou-tecnicas-de-tortura-a-guarda-rural-indigena.shtml.

[672] See: 1934 Constitution, article 5, XIX (m) and article 129, http://www.planalto.gov.br/ccivil_03/constituicao/constituicao34.htm.

[673] MAGALHÃES, Juliana Neuenschwander, "A Exclusão da Inclusão dos Índios na Ditadura e a Inclusão da Exclusão dos Índios no Brasil, Hoje", www.sociologyoflaw.com.br/Prof.-Juliana-Magalhães.pdf.

[674] In addition, Constitutional Amendment no. 1 of 1969, article 198, established that indigenous lands would be inalienable, and recognized their permanent (physical) possession by indigenous people, as well as the right to the *usufruct* of its respective natural resources, http://www.planalto.gov.br/ccivil_03/constituicao/Emendas/Emc_anterior1988/emc01-69.htm.

but never kill"),[675] throughout the second half of the twentieth century a new political-juridical treatment for indigenous issues emerged, including the concept of the right to difference.[676] Indeed, according to Ribeiro,[677] beginning with the creation of the indigenous protection service (*Serviço de Proteção aos Índios* – SPI), for the first time, there was the respect for indigenous nations and the understanding that those nations had the right to be themselves, to profess their beliefs and to live according to their own ways. Before that, indigenous populations were considered as a kind of "raw material" ready for compulsory Christianization. Marshal Rondon inspired intellectuals such as Darcy Ribeiro[678]

---

[675] Marshal Rondon or Cândido Mariano da Silva Rondon (1865–1958) was a Brazilian military officer, geographer, explorer and peacemaker, who was well recognized for his attempts to integrate indigenous nations into the wider Brazilian culture without the use of force (without weapons or coercion). In 1890, he was an Army engineer and helped to build the first telegraph line across the state of Mato Grosso. Later, between 1900 and 1906, Rondon was commissioned to lay the telegraph line from Brazil to Bolivia and Peru. During this period, he had his first contact with the *Bororo* nation, and by pacifying them he was able to finish the telegraph line. In 1914, Rondon returned to the same region in a scientific expedition with the American statesman and former US President Theodore Roosevelt. Maybe because Rondon was a descendent of the *Bororo* and *Terena* tribes, indigenous peoples identified him as a great protector and friendly person. Besides his important research and surveys, he also founded the public agency related to indigenous protection (*Serviço de Proteção aos Índios* – SPI), becoming its first director, and he was a supporter for the creation of the indigenous reserve that latter became the Xingu National Park. The Brazilian state of Rondonia is named in his honor. See more: RIBEIRO, Darcy, *Os Índios e a Civilização Brasileira – A Integração das Populações Indígenas no Brasil Moderno*, 7th edn., São Paulo, Global, 2017, pp. 107–116. NASCIMENTO, Marcio Luis Ferreira, "Rondon, Einsten's Letter adn the Nobel Peace Prize", *Ciência e Sociedade*, vol. 4/2016, pp. 27–35.

[676] Such concern about the right to difference *vis à vis* the indigenous population was observed by Rosen while commenting that the desire for a unifying political and moral theory is especially strong when indigenous people are concerned, since they have long been left at the mercy of quite different surrounding states. See: ROSEN, Lawrence, "The Right to Be Different: Indigenous People and the Quest for a Unified Theory", *Yale Law Journal*, vol. 107/1997, pp. 227–259.

[677] RIBEIRO, Darcy, *Os Índios e a Civilização Brasileira – A Integração das Populações Indígenas no Brasil Moderno*, 7th edn., São Paulo, Global, 2017, p. 127.

[678] Darcy Ribeiro proposed a change in the study of indigenous people and their contact with the rest of national society. Before his analysis, anthropologists used to apply acculturation theory to deal with the problem of contact. Ribeiro, however, pointed out that such an approach was necessarily bilateral and based on a selective adoption of foreign cultural elements. As a substitute for the acculturation approach, he proposed to study ethnic transfiguration, which could be defined as the process by which indigenous populations confronting the wider national society develop the ability to survive as ethnic groups through a series of changes in their biological stratum, their culture and the form of the relations they maintain with the society that surrounds them. Based on his research, Ribeiro concluded that none of the indigenous groups were assimilated into the national society as indistinguishable parts of it; rather the majority of indigenous groups that survived remained indigenous, no longer in their habits and customs, but rather in their self-identification as peoples different from other Brazilians and as victims of their domination. To summarize, Ribeiro's conclusions in relation to the destiny of indigenous populations are pessimistic, since he theorized that indigenous culture and languages can survive autonomously only in unexplored areas

and indianists (*sertanistas*) like the Villas Bôas brothers (Orlando, Cláudio and Leonardo) who dedicated their lives to the study of indigenous people and promoting their coexistence with the rest of the nation. In 1961, the creation of the Xingu National Park gave this new paradigm in the treatment of indigenous lands a material form, as it was based on a preservationist principle and focused on the survival of the socio-cultural conditions of the indigenous peoples inhabiting the Xingu region.

Concerning the Xingu National Park and its background, in fact, the cultural geography of the Upper Xingu region reflects the strategic trade-offs of its founding fathers, the Villas Bôas brothers. They formulated a proposal in 1952 for a reserve of about 20 million hectares, comprising much of the northern portion of Mato Grosso state up to the Pará state border. Although the land was almost completely inaccessible, the Mato Grosso state government had sold most of it to speculators and settlers, and opposed the creation of the reserve. Thus, the area that ultimately became the Xingu Park, in 1961, was little over 2 million hectares. From the 1950s through 1975, the Villas Bôas brothers relocated five indigenous groups to this place. Several of these groups had recently been devasted by disease and conflicts with invading miners and ranchers, and the implicit bargain of the contacts was trade in goods and healthcare in exchange for ending raids on non-indigenous Brazilians and other indigenous groups, and settling near assistance posts. This policy of contacting and relocating indigenous groups to the Xingu probably saved several groups from extinction; however, the negative aspects of the reallocations were that most of the newcomers were traditional enemies of the Upper Xingu people. And furthermore, the reallocation left previous indigenous lands open for occupation by outsiders. In fact, most of the traditional territory of the *Panará*, *Kawaiweté*, *Ikpeng*, *Tapayuna* and *Kisedje* tribes was appropriated by goldminers, ranchers and colonization projects once they had vacated it.[679]

Based on the work of Cândido Rondon, Darcy Ribeiro[680] and the Villas Bôas brothers, there was a break with the vision that had been pursued

---

or areas of recent penetration, or under the artificial conditions of protective intervention. See: RIBEIRO, Darcy, *Os Índios e a Civilização Brasileira – A Integração das Populações Indígenas no Brasil Moderno*, 7th edn., São Paulo, Global, 2017.

[679] SCHWARTZMAN, Stephan et al., "The Natural and Social History of the Indigenous Lands and Protected Areas Corridor of the Xingu River Basin", *Philosophical Transactions of the Royal Society B*, vol. 368, June 2013.

[680] Darcy Ribeiro worked for the SPI from 1947 to 1958. During this period, Ribeiro slowly began to advocate different policies for the assimilation and integration of the indigenous people into national society and saw this as an almost inevitable result of inter-ethnic contact. He proposed indigenous reserves as the suitable environment for the slow assimilation of the white culture by the indigenous peoples, and he stated that his main concern was not to maintain indigenous ways of life, but rather simply to save indigenous lives. See: PEIRANO, Mariza Gomes e Souza, "The Anthropology of Anthropology: The Brazilian Case", Ph.D thesis, Department of Anthropology, Harvard University, 1981, p. 81, revistas.cbpf.br/index.php/CS/article/viewFile/199/143.

since the colonial period, which was based on a purely assimilationist policy and that had lasted until the mid-twentieth century.[681] However, there was a serious point to be observed: the preservationist objective contrasted with that adopted by government agencies such as the SPI, which was later taken over by the newly-formed *Fundação Nacional do Índio* – FUNAI (National Indigenous Foundation), created in 1967. Both agencies had a developmentalist perspective with a strongly integrationist model, which continued with the idea of the integration of indigenous people into the wider national community. For instance, according to Ramos,[682] FUNAI would gradually be stripped of its humanistic vision (inherited from Marshal Rondon) to become a "guardianship machine" or an "unfaithful guardian".

According to Peirano,[683] while working for the SPI, one of Darcy Ribeiro's concerns was to understand the role of the SPI as an intermediary between the federal government – representing at a distance the interests of the expansionist frontiers – and the local government, which often expressed economic interests colliding with those of indigenous groups, given that the work of pacifying indigenous people was much more a response to the desire of the non-indigenous population for expansion than true concern for indigenous welfare.

---

[681] The clear assimilationist policy towards indigenous nations until the mid-twentieth century may be explained by two major historical perspectives. First, even though Brazil won the War of the Triple Alliance (1865–1870), the country had performed awfully from a military perspective. Such armed conflict raised fundamental questions about whether Brazilian society was ready to join the modern world, since the war disclosed one of the country's problems as a lack of civic spirit or national pride. At that time, it was argued that Brazilians had no unified set of beliefs which could connect Brazilians as a single people with a shared vision. The nation, then, would have to be refashioned, since there was the idea that a homogeneous identity should replace the panoply of customs, cultures and backgrounds. Secondly, in the 1900s, Brazil was a single country but perhaps not a unified one. As a coastal nation, to federal officials living in Rio de Janeiro, Brazil's vast interior could seem like a foreign country, separated by enormous distances and varied beliefs and loyalties. Also, there was a dramatic change triggered by the expansion of world trade and Brazil's increasing incorporation into the world market as an exporter of tropical agricultural products. The expansion of export agriculture brought those once isolated interior lands into view, and, as a result, economic development (urbanization, immigration, improvements in transportation, an early manufacturing industry and capital accumulation) provoked social dislocations and the emergence of new social groups. See: DIACON, Todd A., *Stringing Together a Nation: Cândido Mariano da Silva Rondon and the Construction of a Modern Brazil (1906–1930)*, Durham, NC and London, Duke University Press, 2004, pp. 10–12.

[682] RAMOS, Alcida Rita, "Os Direitos do Índio no Brasil: na Encruzilhada da Cidadania", *Seminário A proteção dos Direitos Humanos nos Planos Nacional e Internacional: Perspectivas Brasileiras*, Instituto Interamericanao de Direitos Humanos, Fundação Friedrich Naumann, Comitê Internacional da Cruz Vermelha, Brasília, 1991, http://www.dan.unb.br/images/doc/Serie116empdf.pdf.

[683] PEIRANO, Mariza Gomes e Souza, "The Anthropology of Anthropology: The Brazilian Case", Ph.D thesis, Department of Anthropology, Harvard University, 1981, p. 81, revistas.cbpf.br/index.php/CS/article/viewFile/199/143.

In fact, the SPI had acted as a buffer between indigenous societies and the economic frontier activities (such as mining, cattle-raising and agriculture). On many occasions it had attempted to secure the land rights to certain groups and had also capitulated in the face of pressure from political and economic interests when these were in conflict with indigenous rights.[684] Following increasing negative assessments, in 1967 the SPI was replaced by FUNAI, in part due to the denunciation of SPI agents who had acquiesced to atrocities committed against indigenous populations.[685]

Consequently, as regards the State's directives relating to indigenous issues during the period from 1964 to 1985, it is possible to note that the official discourse of integration also contained a "neutralizing" goal: to push aside anyone who might hold back the modernizing projects of the State. This perspective resulted in the impossibility of a public policy that would recognize indigenous groups in all their diversity and, more than that, caused serious violations of the human rights of those who were seen as "undesirable" under the development model.[686]

And this approach is not atypical, since this same pattern was observed by Corntassel and Holder while analyzing the violence committed against indigenous peoples in Peru and Guatemala,[687] where those communities were repeatedly identified as potential threats and were targeted because of worries about what their indigeneity might lead to in terms of self-determination claims and opposition to State-favored modernization programs. These concerns were in part motivated by racialized perceptions of indigenous communities as "backward" and in need of modernization.

7.1.2. INDIGENOUS TRIBES AND THE DICTATORSHIP PERIOD (1964–1985)

It has been seen that the dictatorial regime handled the indigenous population by placing them in reserves, fostering a decrease in the size of their original lands, and by imposing on them a kind of semi-prisoner status. As a consequence of this artificial resettlement, though, the policy led to the maintenance of

---

[684] RIBEIRO, Darcy, *Os Índios e a Civilização Brasileira – A Integração das Populações Indígenas no Brasil Moderno*, 7th edn., São Paulo, Global, 2017, pp. 168–173.
[685] ARAÚJO, Rayane Barreto de, "Imprensa e História: a Crise do SPI e a Violação dos Direitos Indígenas Narrados pelo Jornal do Brasil (1966–1968)", *Anais do XVII Encontro de História da ANPUH*, Rio de Janeiro, 2016, http://www.encontro2016.rj.anpuh.org/resources/anais/42/1466920295_ARQUIVO_ARTIGO-RAYANEBARRETOUFRJ-versaofinal.pdf.
[686] MATTOS, André Borges de and FOLTRAM, Rochelle, "Estado, Indigenismo e a Ditadura Militar no Brasil Pós-64", in MATTOS, André Borges et al. (eds.), *Ciências Humanas em Foco*, Diamantina, UFVJM, 2017, pp. 13–39.
[687] CORNTASSEL, Jeff and HOLDER, Cindy, "Who's Sorry Now? Government Apologies, Truth Commissions, and Indigenous Self-Determination in Australia, Canada, Guatemala and Peru", *Human Rights Review*, vol. 9/2008.

their culture.[688] As mentioned before, paradoxically, during the years of the dictatorship – while the discourse of preservation, respect for cultural diversity and the indigenous people's rights to their lands were all strengthened – beginning with the early decades of the twentieth century, the expropriation and extermination of various indigenous peoples also took place in the name of economic development. There was an ambiguity in this discourse of preservation since under the mantle of this protective doctrine[689] there was also the impulse towards development, which concealed violations of indigenous peoples' rights that remained obscured for many decades. As Lima once said,[690] we probably know much more of the fate of indigenous people during the colonial and imperial periods than we do of what occurred during almost the last 50 years.

This ambiguity may also be observed in the federal government's broad program concerning the economic exploration of the Brazilian Amazon region, beginning in 1966. Although there had previously been a slow and spontaneous process of occupation of the western half of the State, from the mid-fifties on there was a deliberate occupation specifically of the Central West and the North of the country, in which the dictatorial regime decided to accelerate and proliferate the characteristics of said colonization. At that time, objectives were both economic and geopolitical, and the motto was "*integrar para não entregar*" ("integrate to not hand over"), meaning that it would be better to integrate the Amazon region into the nation instead of delivering it to the supposed domination of foreign States.[691] According to Martins,[692] the Armed Forces used the argument that there was a strategical necessity to occupy the country's empty spaces, even though that region was inhabited by dozens of indigenous groups (many of whom had never been contacted by non-indigenous people) and also only very sparsely by peasants who had been in the area at least since the eighteenth century.

Faced with this economic and geopolitical project and as a result of farming (the implementation of agriculture and cattle-raising), indigenous tribes suffered heavy demographic declines in contact with non-indigenous people and their respective diseases.[693] In addition, thousands of peasants were eventually

---

[688] MAGALHÃES, Juliana Neuenschwander, "A 'Exclusão da Inclusão' dos Índios na Ditadura e a 'Inclusão da Exclusão' dos Índios no Brasil, Hoje", www.sociologyoflaw.com.br/Prof.-Juliana-Magalhães.pdf.
[689] See previous notes about Marshal Rondon, Darcy Ribeiro, and the Villas Bôas brothers.
[690] LIMA, Edilene Coffaci de, "Exílios Índios: Sobre Deslocamentos Compulsórios no Período Militar (1964-1985)", *Aceno*, vol. 3/2016, pp. 18–35.
[691] PEIXOTO, Fabrícia, "Linha do Tempo: Entenda como Ocorreu a Ocupação da Amazônia", *BBC Brasil*, July 23, 2009, https://www.bbc.com/portuguese/noticias/2009/07/090722_amazonia_timeline_fbdt.
[692] MARTINS, José de Souza, "A Reprodução do Capital na Frente Pioneira e o Renascimento da Escravidão no Brasil", *Tempo Social Revista de Sociologia da USP*, vol. 6/1994, pp. 1–25.
[693] A significant number of indigenous groups diminished as a result of diseases that they had not previously been exposed to until their contact with non-indigenous people, such as

expelled from their lands too, since livestock require vast spaces for grasslands. Consequently, many natives and peasants eventually migrated to cities where they live in deprivation and inhabit slums.[694]

Moreover, according to the analyses of the National Truth Commission (NTC),[695] the economical and geopolitical projects in the Midwest and the North of the country were based on a myth defined as the "demographic void", which is commonly used by settlers when they are seeking to protect the national sovereignty of a country. According to this point of view, national sovereignty can only be safeguarded if the demographic vacuums existing in border regions are suppressed. Based on this dogma the invasion of indigenous territories was justified under the motto of *"muita terra para pouco índio"* (lots of land for too few Indians)[696] since it would seem to require, according to Ramos,[697] an "almost natural and obligatory" occupation to foster the demographic and economic frontiers.

This so-called mandatory occupation was identified in the NTC Final Report as a policy of extermination and persecution of indigenous people, driven by the ideal of development and expansion of agriculture in the 1970s.[698] According to the NTC Report, within the expansionist paradigm that marked the period (1964–1985), indigenous peoples were identified as an obstacle to development[699] and as a result of this policy at least 8,350 indigenous people were killed[700] – which is almost 20 times more than the total number of non-indigenous dead and disappeared identified by the NTC (434 persons).[701]

Curiously, even though indigenous people could not be tagged as being "communist", "opposition" or "subversive", they were labeled as being against the political project of the State, therefore they were very often designated as

---

influenza, measles, chickenpox, pneumonia and smallpox. See: ALMEIDA, Carina Santos and NÖTZOLD, Ana Lúcia Vulfe, "O Impacto da Colonização e Imigração no Brasil Meridional: Contágios, Doenças e Ecologia humana dos Povos Índigenas, *Tempos Acadêmicos*, no. 6 2010, http://periodicos.unesc.net/historia/article/download/431/440.

[694] MARTINS, José de Souza. "A Reprodução do Capital na Frente Pioneira e o Renascimento da Escravidão no Brasil", *Tempo Social Revista de Sociologia da USP*, vol. 6/1994, pp. 1–25.

[695] *NTC Report*, Volume II, Text 5, item 4, p. 209, http://cnv.memoriasreveladas.gov.br/.

[696] OLIVEIRA, João Pacheco de, "Muita Terra para Pouco Índio? Uma Introdução Crítica ao Indigenismo e a Atualização do Preconceito", in SILVA, Aracy Lopes and GRUPIONI, Luís Donisete Benzi, *A Temática Indígena na Escola*, MEC – UNESCO, 1995, pp. 61–86.

[697] RAMOS, Alcida Rita, "O Papel Político das Epidemias: O Caso Yanomani", *Série Antropologia - Universidade de Brasília*, vol. 153/1993, pp. 2–21.

[698] *NTC Report*, Volume II, Text 5, pp. 214 and 223, http://cnv.memoriasreveladas.gov.br/.

[699] *NTC Report*, Volume II, Text 5, p. 251, http://cnv.memoriasreveladas.gov.br/.

[700] The NTC Report mentions that the actual number of indigenous people killed in the period is likely significantly higher, since only a very restricted portion of the affected indigenous people was analyzed at that time. See: *NTC Report*, Volume II, Text 5, p. 205, http://cnv.memoriasreveladas.gov.br/.

[701] *NTC Report*, Volume III, "Introduction", p. 26, http://cnv.memoriasreveladas.gov.br/.

Chapter 7. Redressing Violations of Indigenous Rights

an "impediment" or an "obstacle" to the nation. In fact, as Lima and Pacheco commented,[702] the very way of living of those groups was the element that transformed them into antagonists of the order imposed by the regime.

While describing different forms of violation of indigenous people's rights during the dictatorship, the NTC Report signals that initially (from 1946 up to 1968) the federal government behaved with a pattern of omission and neglect – which facilitated the annexation of indigenous lands by settlers, at the same time that the regime failed to monitor the corruption of its own public agents who worked for the SPI.[703] It is worth mentioning that said omission (regarding the corruption in agencies like the SPI) was initially pointed out by the so-called "Figueiredo Report of Investigation", which was conducted by the Ministry of the Interior in 1967, and contained more than 7,000 pages in 30 volumes. In addition to widespread corruption, the *Figueiredo Report* identified human rights violations committed against indigenous people, such as torture, ill-treatment, abusive detention, forced labor and misappropriation of the wealth of indigenous territories – all through acts of public agents working at the various levels of the indigenous people protection agency, SPI.[704]

The commission of inquiry members headed by Jader Figueiredo traveled more than 16,000 kilometers within the interior of the country and visited more than 130 indigenous posts in order to map the illegalities within the SPI, but shortly after the report was formally presented, in March 1968, the document suddenly "disappeared". In fact, there was a misunderstanding regarding dates that fostered the idea that the Report had been burned during an accidental fire in the building where the Ministry of the Interior was located, in Brasilia.[705] However, it remained undamaged and decades later, in 2008, FUNAI officers sent to the Indigenous Museum, in Rio de Janeiro, around 150 boxes of documents related to the extinct SPI. Once these documents were all cataloged and scanned, in 2010, the *Figueiredo Report* was found again, suppressing the myth that it had been consumed by the fire.[706]

---

[702] LIMA, Edilene Coffaci de and PACHECO, Rafael, "Povos Indígenas e Justiça de Transição: Reflexões a partir do Caso Xetá", *Aracê – Direitos Humanos em Revista*, vol. 5/2017, pp. 219–241.

[703] *NTC Report*, Volume II, Text 5, p. 204, http://cnv.memoriasreveladas.gov.br/.

[704] *NTC Report*, Volume II, Text 5, p. 207, http://cnv.memoriasreveladas.gov.br/.

[705] RESENDE, Ana Catarina Zema de, "O Relatório Figueiredo, as Violações dos Direitos dos Povos Indígenas no Brasil dos anso 1960 e a Justa Memória", in SIQUEIRA, Gustavo Silveira; WOLKMER, Antonio Carlos; and PIERDONÁ, Zélia Luiza (eds.), *História do Direito – XXIV Encontro Nacional do Conselho Nacional de Pesquisa e Pós-Graduação em Direito (CONPEDI)*, Florianópolis, CONPEDI, 2015.

[706] The *Figueiredo Report* was found at the Indigenous Museum, in Rio de Janeiro, by Marcelo Zelic, vice president of the *Tortura: Nunca Mais* (Torture: Never Again) group from São Paulo, in April 2013. See: Canêdo, Felipe, "Relatório Figueiredo que Mostra Extermínio de Aldeias é Encontrado", Correio Braziliense, April 19, 2013, https://www.correiobraziliense.com.br/app/noticia/politica/2013/04/19/interna_politica,361411/relatorio-figueiredo-que-mostra-exterminio-de-aldeias-e-encontrado.shtml.

In addition to this phase of neglect in relation to human rights violations of indigenous peoples, the NTC also identified a second period – from 1968 (with the issuance of Institutional Act no. 5 – the infamous "AI-5") until 1988 (with the promulgation of the Federal Constitution) – in which the leading role of the federal government in the perpetration of serious violations of human rights against native Brazilians became more evident, although acts of omission and neglect – particularly in the area of health and checks on corruption – did not cease.[707] For instance, it was during this second period when the *Krenak Indigenous Agrarian Reformatory* in the state of Minas Gerais was created. According to the NTC Report, it was a jail or a type of concentration camp where natives were imprisoned on the basis of spurious grounds or with no administrative procedures at all, or were put into forced labor, tortured or exposed to ill-treatment.[708]

And there are also narratives mentioning that inside the *Krenak* Reformatory indigenous people were forbidden to speak in their mother tongue and parents were forbidden to give indigenous names to their children.[709] In this respect, the case of the *Krenak* Reformatory resembles that of the residential schools in Canada, which were first established during the late 1800s and resulted in the forced removal of over 90,000 indigenous children from their families and homelands. One of the major aims of these institutions was to require indigenous children to "unlearn" their languages and cultural teachings in an effort to promote their assimilation into the dominant culture.[710]

The *Krenak* Reformatory was located in the region of Resplendor (in the state of Minas Gerais) and began its operations in 1969, where the former indigenous post named "Guido Marlière" was situated. At least 121 individuals from 23 ethnic groups were imprisoned at this reformatory[711] and they were generally sent there at the request of the local heads of FUNAI posts and under the pretext of being alcoholics, violent, cattle thieves, murderers, or opponents to certain government development projects; but there were also cases vaguely described as vagrancy, and other situations in which natives were detained for years without even knowing about the crime they had supposedly committed.[712]

---

[707] *NTC Report*, Volume II, Text 5, p. 204, http://cnv.memoriasreveladas.gov.br/.
[708] *NTC Report*, Volume II, Text 5, pp. 243–245, http://cnv.memoriasreveladas.gov.br/.
[709] *Federal Public Prosecutor's Office*, "Ação Civil Pública do Reformatório Krenak", http://www.mpf.mp.br/mg/sala-de-imprensa/docs/acp-reformatorio-krenak.pdf/view. GONÇALVES, Bruno Simões, "Parecer Psicossocial da Violência contra os Povos Indígenas Brasileiros: o Caso Reformatório Krenak", *Psicologia: Ciência e Profissão*, vol. 37/2017, pp. 186–196.
[710] CORNTASSEL, Jeff and HOLDER, Cindy, "Who's Sorry Now? Government Apologies, Truth Commissions, and Indigenous Self-Determination in Australia, Canada, Guatemala and Peru", *Human Rights Review*, vol. 9/2008, pp. 465–489.
[711] *NTC Report*, Volume II, Text 5, p. 244, http://cnv.memoriasreveladas.gov.br/.
[712] According to the civil class action proposed by the Federal Public Prosecutor's Office relating to *Krenak* tribe reparations, in 2015, pp. 16 and 20, http://www.mpf.mp.br/mg/sala-de-imprensa/docs/acp-reformatorio-krenak.pdf/view.

In many situations, the *Krenak* Reformatory received those natives who opposed the rules of the indigenous post administration or were considered as social misfits, and they were not only kept in jail but suffered corporal punishment in cases of insubordination.[713]

During that period, another lamentable event occurred in the state of Minas Gerais: the *Krenak* tribe's lands (including the place where the Reformatory was located) were being claimed by squatters that inhabited the region and the state government, so FUNAI decided to exchange these lands for the *Fazenda Guarani* (*Guarani Farm*), located in the region of Carmésia (also in the state of Minas Gerais), so that those unlawful tenants would be able to continue living on the lands they were claiming. Thus, in 1972, the *Krenaks* and all the prisoners of the Reformatory were forcibly displaced to the *Guarani Farm* (a former torture facility for political prisoners and counterguerrilla training center) despite the fact that – as Ciccarone[714] has mentioned – the *Krenaks* had previously won a reintegration suit in 1971 for 4,000 hectares, precisely in their original lands, that is, in Resplendor and not in Carmésia.

According to Resende,[715] in the *Guarani Farm* there was a continuation of the practices implemented in the *Krenak* Reformatory: the imprisonment of indigenous people considered as delinquents and those opponents to the land's occupation, like the *Pataxó, Guarani, Maxakali, Xacriabá, Xavante, Tuxá* and *Pankararu* ethnic groups. And concerning the forced displacement of the *Krenak* people, in 1981, they had decided to leave the *Guarani Farm* and return to their original lands in the region of Resplendor since they used to complain about the poor living conditions present at the *Guarani Farm*. For instance, they asserted that: (a) there was no large river to fish in; (b) the climate was too cold; (c) the soil was already exhausted from over-planting; (d) there was no raw material (clay) for crafts and pottery; and (e) they were forced to coexist either with prisoners of the reformatory or with other ethnic groups that were not too kind to them, such as the *Pataxó* and *Guarani*.[716]

In fact, the *Krenak* people received false promises about the abundance of the place but the supposedly "farmable" lands of the *Guarani Farm* were

---

[713] VALENTE, Rubens, *Os Fuzis e as Flechas – História de Sangue e Resistência Indígena na Ditadura*, São Paulo, Companhia das Letras, 2017, pp. 73–85.

[714] CICCARONE, Celeste, "The Guarani Farm: Indigenous Narratives about Removal, Reclusion and Escapes during the Military Dictatorship in Brazil", *Vibrant Virtual Brazilian Anthropology*, vol. 15/2018, http://dx.doi.org/10.1590/1809-43412018v15n3d511.

[715] RESENDE, Ana Catarina Zema de, "O Relatório Figueiredo, as Violações dos Direitos dos Povos Indígenas no Brasil dos anos 1960 e a Justa Memória", in SIQUEIRA, Gustavo Silveira; WOLKMER, Antonio Carlos; and PIERDONÁ, Zélia Luiza (eds.), *História do Direito – XXIV Encontro Nacional do Conselho Nacional de Pesquisa e Pós-Graduação em Direito (CONPEDI)*, Florianópolis, CONPEDI, 2015.

[716] CICCARONE, Celeste, "The Guarani Farm: Indigenous Narratives about Removal, Reclusion and Escapes during the Military Dictatorship in Brazil", *Vibrant Virtual Brazilian Anthropology*, vol. 15/2018, http://dx.doi.org/10.1590/1809-43412018v15n3d511.

actually arid pastures not suitable for planting and its few forests had little game. As a consequence, in 1981, some *Krenak* families chose to go to the *Vanuíre* indigenous post (in São Paulo state), to cities like Colatina (in Espírito Santo state) and Conselheiro Pena (in Minas Gerais state) and only 26 of the 49 *Krenaks* who arrived at *Fazenda Guarani*, in 1972, returned to their original lands in the municipality of Resplendor nine years later. Consequently, as noted by Paraíso,[717] the *Krenaks*' forced displacement to the *Guarani Farm* resulted in the dispersion of their population and in the risk of a reduction in their social group.

Besides the practices of forced displacement, imprisonment and forced labor, the NTC also mentioned in the list of violations the creation, in 1969, of an Indigenous Rural Guard (*Guarda Rural Indígena* – GRIN), which used to recruit indigenous people from the Araguaia and Tocantins rivers, as well as from the state of Minas Gerais to serve as police officers within the indigenous posts. With regard to this kind of recruitment, there was an episode that exposes the perverse side of turning indigenous people into collaborators in the massacre of their very own people. It occurred on February 5, 1970, during a parade organized to celebrate the graduation of the first GRIN class and held at the Battalion School of the Military Police of Minas Gerais.

The parade included 84 individuals recruited from the *Xerente*, *Maxacali*, *Carajá*, *Krahô*, and *Gaviões* ethnic groups and they demonstrated their abilities in judo, horseback-riding, and the capture of prisoners, with and without guns. But at the end of the parade, two GRIN soldiers appeared carrying an indigenous person hanging from a "macaw's perch" or *pau de arara* (a torture technique in which a person is tied to a pole placed over his biceps and behind his knees, and that had been used since colonial times to punish black slaves who escaped from the sugar cane plantations; the same technique was also employed against opponents of the regime during the dictatorship).[718] As observed by Resende,[719] the scene showing the macaw's perch as a technique of torture represents a very dark chapter of the contact between the Brazilian State and indigenous groups, since it demonstrates that practices of torture were being taught to indigenous

---

[717] Paraíso, Maria Hilda Baqueiro, "Os Krenak do Rio Doce, a Pacificação, o Aldeamento e a Luta pela Terra", in *XIII Encontro Anual da ANPOCS*, 1989, http://www.etnolinguistica.org/biblio:paraiso-1989-krenak.

[718] This parade was filmed by German photographer and documentary filmmaker Jesco von Puttkamer and parts of Puttkamer's documentary named "*Arara*" (macaw) may be found at: https://www.youtube.com/watch?v=H0s4m1WQNmg. The documentary is part of the collection of the Jesco Puttkamer Museum, located in the city of Goiania, and organized by of the Pontific Catholic University of Goiás, http://sites.pucgoias.edu.br/pesquisa/igpa/jesco-puttkamer/.

[719] Resende, Ana Catarina Zema de, "O Relatório Figueiredo, as Violações dos Direitos dos Povos Indígenas no Brasil dos anos 1960 e a Justa Memória", in Siqueira, Gustavo Silveira, Wolkmer, Antonio Carlos and Pierdoná, Zélia Luiza (eds.), *História do Direito – XXIV Encontro Nacional do Conselho Nacional de Pesquisa e Pós-Graduação em Direito (CONPEDI)*, Florianópolis, CONPEDI, 2015.

people expecting that they themselves would inflict ill-treatment on their fellow native Brazilians. Subsequently, GRIN members were constantly accused of committing arbitrary acts like beatings and other acts of cruelty such that, by the late 1970s, the GRIN was demobilized.[720]

The NTC Final Report also identified other violations against indigenous populations, which were related to the State's activities during the dictatorship.[721] These include, among many others, the cases of:

(a) the *Guarani-Kaiowá* and *Ava Guarani* in Mato Grosso do Sul state and western Paraná state;[722]
(b) the *Avá Canoeiro*, in the region of the Araguaia River, who between 1973 and 1974 were captured by government agents, at which time indigenous women suffered sexual abuse and many of them were transferred to the territory of an enemy tribe;[723]
(c) the *Aikewara* or *Suruí do Pará* indigenous group, whose many members were forced to work as forest guides during the capture of guerrilla fighters operating in the Araguaia region;[724]
(d) the expropriation of the *Arara* territory, during the construction of the Trans-Amazonian highway;[725]
(e) the massacre of the *Cinta Larga* people (located in the northwest of Mato Grosso state and the southeast part of Rondônia state), an episode which became known as the "11th Parallel Massacre";[726]
(f) violations committed against the *Waimiri-Atroari* people (who were located in the southeast part of Roraima state and in the northeast portion of Amazonas state), when the BR-174 highway was constructed;[727]
(g) the social fragmentation and extermination of the *Xetá* ethnic group, during the construction of the Itaipu hydroelectric plant (in western part of Paraná state).[728]

The following sections will verify what kind of Transitional Justice mechanisms have been implemented so far in the field of reparations to and reconciliation with indigenous people, and also which are the gaps that remain to be filled in the near future.

---

[720] NTC Report, Volume II, Text 5, p. 212, http://cnv.memoriasreveladas.gov.br/.
[721] To observe in pictures the relationship between indigenous peoples and the dictatorial regime see: "Deslocamentos Forçados", El País, July 25, 2017, https://brasil.elpais.com/brasil/2017/07/23/album/1500833290_860968.html#foto_gal_1.
[722] NTC Report, Volume II, Text 5, p. 214, http://cnv.memoriasreveladas.gov.br/.
[723] Ibid., p. 228.
[724] Ibid., p. 246.
[725] Ibid., p. 230.
[726] Ibid., p. 237.
[727] Ibid., p. 234.
[728] Ibid., pp. 218–219.

7.2. THE CHALLENGES OF COLLECTIVE REPARATIONS

In 2012, the NTC established a working group which was responsible for the investigation of human rights violations related to peasants and indigenous people.[729] Before this measure, the majority of investigations relating to violations committed by the dictatorial regime highlighted crimes committed in urban areas, such as the terrorizing practices of physical elimination and torture, and very little had been documented about the violence suffered by indigenous people during the dictatorship (such as the practices of ethnic extermination and forced dislocation). Certainly, there was a need to revisit such other kinds of past atrocities, mainly because, as observed by Valente,[730] the previous History was characterized by a kind of absenteeism related to the fate of indigenous people during the dictatorial regime. Ciccarone has already pointed out that there is a need to observe multiple actors and situations that occurred during the dictatorship and not only those facts intimately related to political opponents of the regime.[731] In the case of indigenous people and the narrative established through the work of the NTC, in addition to territorial usurpation and environmental devastation, other different faces of State violence emerged. These included persecution and forced displacement, imprisonment, slave labor and abandonment, which should no longer remain invisible to social memory.

In fact, the 2014 NTC Final Report must be recognized as the first and initial attempt towards the symbolic acknowledgment by the Brazilian State that in the past there was a systematic policy of extermination of indigenous people. As a first step, the Commissioners decided to present their recommendations within the specific thematic chapter on indigenous human rights violations[732] and not in the final proposals contained in the Part V of Volume I of the report. Within those specific recommendations, contained in Volume II of the final report, the following are worth noting:

(a) the public apologies;
(b) the creation of a new truth commission to deepen the investigation of the treatment of indigenous people;

---

[729] See: Resolution of NTC no. 5/2012, http://cnv.memoriasreveladas.gov.br/institucional-acesso-informacao/resolucoes.html.
[730] VALENTE, Rubens, *Os Fuzis e as Flechas – História de Sangue e Resistência Indígena na Ditadura*, São Paulo, Companhia das Letras, 2017, pp. 73–85.
[731] CICCARONE, Celeste, "The Guarani Farm: Indigenous Narratives about Removal, Reclusion and Escapes during the Military Dictatorship in Brazil", *Vibrant Virtual Brazilian Anthropology*, vol. 15/2018, http://dx.doi.org/10.1590/1809-43412018v15n3d511.
[732] For those specific recommendations see: *NTC Report*, Volume II, Text 5, pp. 253–254, http://cnv.memoriasreveladas.gov.br/.

Chapter 7. Redressing Violations of Indigenous Rights

(c) the promotion of national campaigns to inform the public about the violations committed against indigenous peoples;
(d) the inclusion of such cases in the curriculum for students in the public education system;
(e) the registry of the cases with the National Archives;
(f) amendment of Law no. 10,559 (2002) concerning the reparations program, in order to include collective reparations to indigenous nations, since that law is based exclusively on individual reparations;
(g) the strengthening of public policies regarding the health of the indigenous population; and
(h) the regularization/demarcation of indigenous territories and the environmental restoration of those lands, etc.

The new official narrative about the Brazilian dictatorship, the fate of indigenous people and the previously mentioned recommendations made by the NTC all represent a historical advance, but there is still a latent and unanswered question: if all the violations revealed in the report were committed within the scope of indigenous people viewed as a single category, how might it be possible to establish a framework for Transitional Justice focused on the specificities of these people? In fact, the Brazilian case seems to repeat the same pattern that Corntassel and Holder have already highlighted in their study of truth commissions in Australia, Canada, Guatemala and Peru *vis à vis* indigenous issues.[733] Although those commissions recommended recognizing communities as victims and establishing the respective reparations, the terms on which reparations were to be made available to individuals were different than those under which reparations were to be made to communities – but the respective truth commission reports did not differentiate the two in detail.

In addition to the NTC's final report, there are other examples of Transitional Justice mechanisms related to violations committed against indigenous peoples in Brazil that are worthy of note, such as:

(a) as an example of a judicial mechanism – the Federal Public Prosecutor's decision to investigate indigenous cases relating to the military period;[734]
(b) as examples of truth-seeking projects – the creation of memory, truth and justice committees that focus on indigenous issues in the states of

---

[733] CORNTASSEL, Jeff and HOLDER, Cindy, "Who's Sorry Now? Government Apologies, Truth Commissions, and Indigenous Self-Determination in Australia, Canada, Guatemala and Peru", *Human Rights Review*, vol. 9/2008, pp. 465–489.
[734] *Ministério Público Federal*, http://www.mpf.mp.br/atuacao-tematica/ccr6/dados-da-atuacao/grupos-de-trabalho/violacao-dos-direitos-dos-povos-indigenas-e-registro-militar. See also section 7.2.3. below.

São Paulo,[735] Amazonas,[736] and Mato Grosso do Sul,[737] and the initiative concerning the truth commission of the *Suruís* people;[738]

(c) as an effort to avoid those violations being repeated – the organization of a virtual collection of documents produced by the State during the dictatorship related to indigenous matters;[739]

(d) as an example of reparations program – the work of the Amnesty Commission regarding the official apology and the granting of pecuniary reparation to 14 *Suruí* indigenous people, in 2014, in recognition of their exploitation by the Army during the *Araguaia Guerrilla War*;[740] and

(e) the making of the documentary film *Guerra Sem Fim* (Endless War), in 2016, regarding the establishment of the *Krenak* Reformatory and the forced displacement of this ethnic group to *Guarani Farm*.[741] However, given the specificities of the violations committed against indigenous peoples and the collective dimension of these damages, there are still obstacles to an effective remedy for the harm that was caused, as will be noted further below.

7.2.1. OBSTACLES TO LAND RECOVERY

According to Corntassel and Holder,[742] the return of indigenous people to their ancestral homeland is critical to any discussion of indigenous restitution and, by extension, reconciliation, but the cultural and physical homeland claims of

---

[735] *Final Report of the Truth Commission of São Paulo State*, Volume I, Part II, Chapter 2: "Violações aos Direitos dos Povos Indígenas", http://comissaodaverdade.al.sp.gov.br/relatorio/tomo-i/parte-ii-cap2.html.

[736] *Truth Committee of Amazonas*, http://comitedaverdade.blogspot.com/2014/06/as-malocas-da-praca-de-maio-por-jose.html.

[737] *Comitê pela Verdade, Memória e Justiça do Mato Grosso do Sul*, https://al.ms.gov.br/Noticias/66857/comite-da-verdade-apura-casos-da-ditadura-militar-no-estado.

[738] BALZA, Guilherme, "Comissão da Verdade apura mortes de índios que podem quintuplicar vítimas da ditadura", *Notícias UOL*, November 12, 2012, https://noticias.uol.com.br/politica/ultimas-noticias/2012/11/12/comissao-da-verdade-apura-mortes-de-indios-que-podem-quintuplicar-vitimas-da-ditadura.htm; BALZA, Guilherme, "Índios do Araguaia Criam Comissão da Verdade Própria para Investigar Crimes da Ditadura", *Notícias UOL*, November 12, 2012, https://noticias.uol.com.br/politica/ultimas-noticias/2012/11/12/indios-do-araguaia-criam-comissao-da-verdade-propria-para-investigar-crimes-da-ditadura.htm.

[739] *Centro de Referência Virtual Indígena*, http://armazemmemoria.com.br/centros-indigena/.

[740] NASCIMENTO, Luciano, "Comissão Concede Anistia à 14 Indígenas Afetados na Guerrilha do Araguaia", *Agência Brasil*, September 19, 2014, http://agenciabrasil.ebc.com.br/direitos-humanos/noticia/2014-09/comissao-concede-anistia-14-indigenas-afetados-na-guerrilha-do.

[741] Documentary Film "*Guerra Sem Fim – Resistência e Luta do Povo Krenak*", https://www.youtube.com/watch?v=DfkGVfkJpAM.

[742] CORNTASSEL, Jeff and HOLDER, Cindy, "Who's Sorry Now? Government Apologies, Truth Commissions, and Indigenous Self-Determination in Australia, Canada, Guatemala and Peru", *Human Rights Review*, vol. 9/2008, pp. 465–489.

indigenous people are rarely addressed by State restitution schemes in other countries, which tend to favor solutions that minimize settler-colonial territorial and material sacrifice, while maximizing political/legal expediency. This situation is no different in the Brazilian experience and the nation's reparations program for indigenous people.

Indeed, while questioning the implementation of Transitional Justice mechanisms for indigenous peoples in the Brazilian case, Demetrio and Kozicki have stated that indigenous peoples and nature are part of a whole,[743] in which the land forms part of the essence of those groups – a fact which demonstrates the vital importance of incorporating a discussion of land rights within any analysis of Transitional Justice instruments. This same understanding has been endorsed by the Inter-American Court of Human Rights (IACtHR), which has stated that States must respect the special relationship that members of indigenous and tribal peoples have with their territory, and in a way that guarantees their social, cultural and economic survival.[744] However, the intricate point in dealing with this perspective is that, whereas individual rights form the basis of human rights in western societies, due to the cultural and anthropological sense of territory that indigenous peoples hold, an individual vision of land rights must be deconstructed.

As pointed out by Walker,[745] the hegemony of western conflict resolution limits indigenous peoples' opportunities to function within their own worldviews and to implement their own methods of processing conflict, since communal societies – such as those found in indigenous cultures – exhibit a collectivist approach to conflict resolution. Thus, conflict is viewed holistically, not analytically or broken into parts. In contrast to communal societies, western societies tend to be individualistic and to require linear and deterministic analysis, and consequently the hegemony of western epistemologies has largely silenced indigenous people's worldviews in regard to conflict resolution and has continued to be one of the major tools of colonization. These cultural differences or worldviews may be observed in the discussion below of the mediation and resolution schemes that have been applied to the land conflict in Brazil during the last three decades.

To begin with, the Federal Constitution of 1988, in article 231, specifies that lands traditionally occupied by indigenous peoples must be set aside for their own permanent possession, which includes the *usufruct* respectively of the soil,

---

[743] DEMETRIO, André and KOZICKI, Katya, "A (In)Justiça de Transição para os Povos Indígenas no Brasil", *Direito e Práxis*, vol. 10/2019, pp. 129–169.
[744] *Inter-American Court of Human Rights*, Case of the Saramaka People vs. Suriname, Preliminary Objections, Merits, Reparations and Costs. Judgment of November 28, 2007, Series C, No. 172, para. 91; Case of the Mayagna (Sumo) Awas Tingni Community vs. Nicaragua, Merits, Reparations and Costs. Judgment of January 31, 2001, Series C, No. 79, para. 149.
[745] WALKER, Polly O., "Decolonizing Conflict Resolution: Addressing the Ontological Violence of Westernization", *American Indian Quarterly*, vol. 28/2004, pp. 527–549.

rivers and lakes located in those spaces. However, in judicial decisions there have been obstacles to the demarcation of these territories, especially the time-limit constraints (the so-called temporal requirement or *"marco temporal"*). That requirement stipulates that, in order to request demarcation of its lands, an indigenous community must prove that it was in physical possession of the claimed territory as of the date of the promulgation of the Federal Constitution – that is, on October 5, 1988.

This understanding of the temporal requirement emerged in the judgment of *Extraordinary Appeal no. 219983-3/1998*, when the Supreme Court decided that the recognition of the rights of indigenous peoples to the lands they inhabited would not be extended to situations that had existed long before but not exactly on the date of the Constitution's enactment.[746] Consequently, in applying the 1988 time-limit requirement, the Supreme Court undermined many of the parameters for Transitional Justice for indigenous people, since violations committed during the dictatorship such as the forced relocations to different territories occurred long before 1988.[747]

In 2009, during its analysis of the demarcation of the *Raposa Serra do Sol* indigenous land case,[748] the Supreme Court confirmed that the date to assess the traditional nature of any given indigenous occupation would be the date of the promulgation of the 1988 Constitution. Subsequently, in 2010, the Supreme Court issued *Precedent no. 650/2010*,[749] which stipulated that extinct settlements or even lands occupied by indigenous peoples since long before there were even records would not be subject to demarcation unless such lands were occupied on the date in question, applying the 1988 time-limit as a legal parameter.

As a matter of fact, although the NTC report documented the systematic practice of forced removals of indigenous communities, *Precedent no. 650/2010* may restrict the possibility of indigenous peoples to recover those territories where they used to live between 1964 and 1988 or earlier if that land was expropriated during the military dictatorship and had not been restored to them before 1988. This time-frame requirement has been criticized by Yamada and Villares[750] as containing an intrinsic defect since it neglects the history of human

---

[746] *Federal Supreme Court*, Recurso Extraordinário n. 219983-3/1998, Judgment of December 9, 1998, http://stf.jus.br/portal/jurisprudencia/listarJurisprudencia.asp?s1=%28219983%2ENUME%2E+OU+219983%2EACMS%2E%29&base=baseAcordaos&url=http://tinyurl.com/yxlmxjwb.

[747] To read more see: DEMETRIO, André and KOZICKI, Katya, "A (In)Justiça de Transição para os Povos Indígenas no Brasil", *Direito e Práxis*, vol. 10/2019, pp. 129–169.

[748] *Federal Supreme Court*, Petição 3388, Judgment of September 25, 2009, http://portal.stf.jus.br/processos/detalhe.asp?incidente=2288693.

[749] *Federal Supreme Court*, Precedent no. 650/2010, http://www.stf.jus.br/portal/jurisprudencia/menuSumarioSumulas.asp?sumula=1634.

[750] YAMADA, Erica Magami and VILLARES, Luiz Fernando, "Julgamento da Terra Indígena Raposa Serra do Sol: Todo Dia Era Dia de Índio", *Revista Direito Getulio Vargas*, vol. 6/2010, pp. 143–158.

relations; and, although there is a certain symbolism in it, the designation of the date of the promulgation of the 1988 Constitution as a time-limit grants an almost divine character to that document, at the same time that it disregards the value of the Indigenous Peoples Act (Law no. 6,001 (1973)) and the long past indigenist tradition in Brazil, dating back to the work of Cândido Rondon, the Villas Bôas brothers, and Darcy Ribeiro, as previously described in this chapter.

Although the 1988 Constitution guarantees indigenous peoples the right to traditionally occupied lands, as well as respect for their social organization, customs, traditions and beliefs, the current scenario demonstrates that the Brazilian State has been unable to establish a new relationship with these original peoples after the end of the dictatorial period. As pointed out by Osowski,[751] this gap in the implementation of Transitional Justice with respect to these peoples makes clear the parameters of the transition implemented in Brazil and the limits on the effective realization of the fundamental rights defined by the 1988 Constitution. Actually, it seems that the Brazilian State – with the collaboration of the Judiciary in the establishment of the so-called temporal requirement – has been executing a policy of conscious forgetting in relation to the violations committed against indigenous peoples, since, under the pretext of pacifying very old social conflicts or of establishing civil peace, the Federal Supreme Court has mandated obliviousness.[752]

Still, there are members of the Federal Supreme Court that had a different point of view concerning the understanding of *Precedent no. 640/2010*,[753] and that rejected the so-called temporal requirement. They argued for recognition of the lands traditionally occupied by indigenous people before 1988 because they were forcibly removed from those places and did not leave their lands voluntarily, in addition to not being allowed to return to those regions. This point of view thus acknowledges that the 1988 time requirement should only be applicable to those cases where the indigenous tribes freely left the territory they were seeking to resettle in, or to cases in which it can be verified that the cultural ties that connected them to the area had been dissolved over the years.

Considering this major topic of lands and indigenous peoples, the work of the Inter-American Court of Human Rights (IACtHR) may serve as a

---

[751] Osowski, Raquel, "O Marco Temporal para Demarcação de Terras Indígenas, Memória e Esquecimento", *Mediações Revista de Ciências Sociais*, vol. 22/2017, pp. 320–346.

[752] Cunha, Manuela Carneiro da, "O STF e os Índios", *Folha de São Paulo*, November 20, 2014, https://www1.folha.uol.com.br/opiniao/2014/11/1550130-manuela-carneiro-da-cunha-o-stf-e-os-indios.shtml.

[753] *Supreme Court*, Ação Cível Originária (ACO) 362, vote of Minister Luís Roberto Barroso, judgment of August 16, 2017. See: Public Prosecutor's Office, "Manual de Jurisprudência dos Direitos Indígenas", 2019, p. 198, http://www.mpf.mp.br/pgr/noticias-pgr/mpf-lanca-manual-de-jurisprudencia-de-direitos-indigenas.

future guideline for Brazil to resolve conflicts related to indigenous territorial claims.[754] In such cases, the IACtHR has explained that members of indigenous peoples who have unwillingly lost possession of their lands, when those lands were lawfully transferred to innocent third parties, are entitled to restitution to obtain other lands of equal extent and quality.[755] The approach also makes quite clear the corollary that third parties who do not hold title in good faith have no legitimate expectations or bona fide property rights. Such is the case, for example, of settlements made to individuals without regard to the indigenous peoples who have always lived there. According to the IACtHR, indigenous peoples' right to property and restitution remains in place even though the claimed lands are in private hands, and it is not acceptable for indigenous territorial claims to be automatically denied. In each case, there must be a process of balancing the competing claims in order to establish limitations on one or the other property rights in conflict, in light of the standards of legality, necessity, proportionality and a legitimate purpose in a democratic society.[756]

For the IACtHR, possession is not a requirement on which the existence of indigenous land restitution rights depends.[757] In fact, the IACtHR has questioned whether the right to restitution of lands has a temporal limit, or if it "lasts indefinitely in time", and has concluded that the right will last for as long as the indigenous people's fundamental relationship with ancestral territory subsists.[758] The IACtHR takes into consideration that the spiritual and material basis for indigenous people's identity is mainly supported by their unique relationship with their traditional lands. So as long as said relationship exists, the right to claim lands is enforceable; otherwise, it will lapse.[759] This unique relationship to traditional territory may be expressed in different ways, depending on the particular indigenous people involved and the specific circumstances surrounding the relationship, and it may include traditional use or presence, be it through spiritual or ceremonial ties; settlements or sporadic cultivation; seasonal or nomadic gathering, hunting and fishing; the

---

[754] *Inter-American Court of Human Rights, Case of the Yakye Axa Indigenous Community versus Paraguay.* Merits, Reparations and Costs. Judgment of June 17, 2005, series C, no. 125, para. 143.
[755] *Inter-American Court of Human Rights, Case of the Sawhoyamaxa Indigenous Community versus Paraguay.* Merits, Reparations and Costs. Judgment of March 29, 2006, series C, no. 146, para. 128.
[756] Ibid., para. 138.
[757] Ibid., para. 128.
[758] Ibid., paras. 126–131.
[759] *Inter-American Court of Human Rights, Case of the Xákmok Kásek Indigenous Community versus Paraguay.* Merits, Reparations and Costs. Judgment of August 24, 2010, series C, no. 214, para. 112.

use of natural resources associated with their customs and any other element characterizing their culture.[760]

Moreover, the IACtHR recognizes that there are situations in which indigenous peoples are not occupying or using their traditional lands for reasons of *force majeure*, whether because of the forced relocation of such peoples – including relocations for reasons related to a health, humanitarian or food crisis – or because of situations, generally associated with internal armed conflicts, which have forced indigenous peoples to abandon their lands because of a well-founded fear of being victims of violence. For instance, in the case of the *Moiwana Community versus Suriname*, the IACtHR held that the members of the Ndjuka Maroon community living in Moiwana could be considered the legitimate owners of their traditional lands, and as a consequence they have the right to use that territory in spite of the fact that they have been deprived of this right to the present day, as a result of the massacre of 1986 and the State's subsequent failure to investigate those occurrences.[761] In a subsequent case, the IACtHR reaffirmed its prior jurisprudence, clarifying that indigenous title to communal property must be made possible, in the sense that it shall not be considered extinguished if the community has been unable to occupy or use its traditional lands because they have been prevented from doing so for reasons beyond their control, which actually hinder them from maintaining such a relationship.[762]

Finally, the IACtHR recognizes that the right to restitution of traditional territories is not an absolute right, and it finds a limit in those exceptional cases in which there exist objective and justified reasons making it impossible for the State to restore the territorial rights of indigenous peoples. In such situations, the communities are nonetheless entitled to redress or to alternative lands of equal extent and quality, which will be chosen by agreement with the members of the indigenous peoples, according to their own consultation and decision procedures.[763] In addition, the remedies of alternative lands and/or an indemnity

---

[760] Inter-American Court of Human Rights, *Case of the Sawhoyamaxa Indigenous Community versus Paraguay*. Merits, Reparations and Costs. Judgment of March 29, 2006, series C, no. 146, para. 131.

[761] Inter-American Court of Human Rights, *Case of the Moiwana Community versus Suriname*. Preliminary Objections, Merits, Reparations and Costs. Judgment of June 15, 2005, series C, no. 124, para. 134.

[762] Inter-American Court of Human Rights, *Case of the Sawhoyamaxa Indigenous Community versus Paraguay*. Merits, Reparations and Costs. Judgment of March 29, 2006, series C, no. 146, para. 132. In the same sense: *Inter-American Court of Human Rights, Case of the Xákmok Kásek Indigenous Community versus Paraguay*. Merits, Reparations and Costs. Judgment of August 24, 2010, series C, no. 214, paras. 113–116.

[763] Inter-American Court of Human Rights, *Case of the Sawhoyamaxa Indigenous Community versus Paraguay*. Merits, Reparations and Costs. Judgment of March 9, 2006, series C, no. 146, para. 135.

in cases where restitution is an objective impossibility must secure the effective participation of the affected indigenous people.[764]

As pointed out by Yamada and Villares,[765] democracy cannot be consolidated without a profound respect for the right to information and participation in political decisions, especially those resolutions that directly affect a given people. Indeed, indigenous people deserve to be informed and to participate in the decisions of the State that affect their lives, through their culture and differentiated understanding of the world, since such consent will result in choices with greater consensus and, therefore, with more legitimacy. In the Brazilian case, this right may be found in a related interpretation of the 1988 Constitution (article 231, paragraph 2), the Indigenous Statute (article 2 of Law no. 6001 (1973)), and ILO Convention 169 (article 6), which was ratified by the Brazilian State in Decree no. 5,051 (2004).

7.2.2. OBSTACLES TO COLLECTIVE REPARATIONS

Lima and Pacheco have noted that there are some commonly employed arguments to deny indigenous peoples any participation in the process of Transitional Justice,[766] such as the argument that those peoples did not politically act or intervene in the dictatorship and that the process of extermination began in 1500 with the arrival of the Portuguese settlers in Brazil and the dawn of the colonial period. Actually, this kind of justification – that indigenous people did not resist the regime in the political sense[767] – reveals the persistence of a superficial understanding of what really occurred in the country between 1964 and 1985; that is, the maintenance of a widespread conception or a historical perspective only centered on the role of armed organizations and opponents of the dictatorial regime, which positions indigenous peoples as passive communities living in a political vacuum. These examples are some of the misunderstandings that still persist in the collective memory of the Brazilian dictatorship and that certainly need to be confronted in the near future.

---

[764] Inter-American Court of Human Rights, *Case of the Yakye Axa Indigenous Community versus Paraguay*. Merits, Reparations and Costs. Judgment of June 17, 2005, series C, no. 125, para. 151.

[765] YAMADA, Erica Magami and VILLARES, Luiz Fernando, "Julgamento da Terra Indígena Raposa Serra do Sol: Todo Dia Era Dia de Índio", *Revista Direito Getulio Vargas*, vol. 6/2010, pp. 143–158.

[766] LIMA, Edilene Coffaci de and PACHECO, Rafael, "Povos Indígenas e Justiça de Transição: Reflexões a partir do Caso Xetá", *Aracê – Direitos Humanos em Revista*, vol. 5/2017, pp. 219–241.

[767] For more examples of this kind of prejudice regarding indigenous people and their resistance against the dictatorship see the interview of Maria Rita Kehl, former member of the NTC by the Agência Pública: *Pública Agência de Jornalismo Investigativo*, "Os Ecos de Itaipu", March 16, 2015, https://apublica.org/2015/03/os-ecos-de-itaipu/.

In addition, as commented by Sharp,[768] the field of Transitional Justice was born out of a recognized need to address legacies of violence in times of political transition, and by doing so, it has also sought to fulfill an impulse to push illiberal, imperfectly liberal, and newly liberal States onto a more democratic path. Particularly, such measures were based on the western liberal paradigm, and consequently many transitional efforts were focused on issues of physical violence, including breach of civil and political rights all committed or restricted by State agents, while questions of economic violence and economic justice were commonly impelled to the margins. Still, based on this framework, it must be considered that many of the violations against indigenous people were not committed by agents of the State, but by settlors (private agents), who were seeking lands. In such cases, although the State was not a direct author of the violations, it was silent or manipulative. So, if we consider Transitional Justice, as related to a liberal conception of human rights, in general, it only focuses on the State (or State agents) as responsible for violations susceptible to criminal liability and/or reparations, which reinforces the invisibility of indigenous cause.

Another paradigm that places the indigenous population in an aura of invisibility and denial, such as that fostered by the above-mentioned arguments, relates to the reparations program that was implemented under Law no. 10,559 (2002), since it does not provide reparations for the collective dimension of human rights violations perpetrated against indigenous peoples, nor does it recognize the connection between these violations and their own ethnic conditions. It took 12 years from the creation of such reparations program for this contradiction to be acknowledged, which occurred when the NTC, in its 2014 Report considered the collective dimension as an essential characteristic of the human rights violations committed against indigenous peoples, since even though the abuses had an impact on each person individually, those violations targeted native populations as a whole.[769]

Despite these legal constrains regarding collective reparations, in 2014, the Amnesty Commission, in applying Law no. 10,599 (2002), recognized that 14 indigenous people from the *Aikewara* tribe (also called *Suruí do Pará*) had been victims of the dictatorship during the *Araguaia Guerrilla War* in 1972, since the Brazilian Army, who were positioned inside the territory of the *Aikewaras*, subjected them to confinement and deprivation and forced them to serve as forest guides in the hunting of the guerrillas in the jungle.[770]

---

[768] SHARP, Dustin N., "Interrogating the Peripheries: The Preoccupations of Fourth Generation Transitional Justice", *Harvard Human Rights Journal*, vol. 26/2013, pp. 149–178.
[769] *NTC Report*, Volume II, Text 5, p. 223, http://cnv.memoriasreveladas.gov.br/.
[770] *Fundação Nacional do Índio (FUNAI)*, "Comissão de Anistia concede indenização a indígenas Suruí do Pará", September 23, 2014, http://www.funai.gov.br/index.php/comunicacao/noticias/3050-comissao-de-anistia-concede-indenizacao-a-indigenas-surui-do-para.

Before this official acknowledgment by the Amnesty Commission, the image of the *Aikewara* tribe as "headhunters of guerrillas"[771] was yet another of the critical misconceptions that had persisted in memories of the dictatorship. Also, this public recognition of the *Aikewaras* as victims of violations proposes another problematic topic – that is the use of indigenous labor by agents of the State within the forests – since the forced use of indigenous expertise about the forest is in fact one of the forms of indigenous slavery that still persisted in the twentieth century.[772]

Despite these achievements brought about by the *Aikewaras*' case in the Amnesty Commission,[773] we should keep in mind that, according to the formula adopted in Brazil, the pecuniary reparation was directed to the individuals and not to the collectivity of the *Aikewara* tribe.[774] Thus, there is a primary condition that must be addressed in the analysis of the violations committed against indigenous peoples, which was already noted in the NTC Final Report: the legal amendment of the reparations program (regulated by Law no. 10,559 (2002)). This is because, the way it is currently designed, it remains focused on the employment prospects of urban workers who lost their jobs during their political persecution. In this way the program provides a single form of reparation: individual and pecuniary – as if everything were reduced to a precise calculation of hours worked, production and loss of profits – thus following the previously mentioned pattern of resolution of conflict based on the perspective of western society, which is individualistic and requires a direct and settled analysis.

The official apology to these 14 indigenous people from the *Aikewara* tribe was supposed to achieve reconciliation by revisiting a past historical injustice.

---

[771] *Opera Mundi*, "Forçados por militares a combater guerrilha, indígenas Aikewara contam em livro versão sobre conflito no Araguaia", January 20, 2015, https://operamundi.uol.com.br/samuel/39199/forcados-por-militares-a-combater-guerrilha-indigenas-aikewara-contam-em-livro-versao-sobre-conflito-no-araguaia.

[772] VALENTE, Rubens, *Os Fuzis e as Flechas – História de Sangue e Resistência Indígena na Ditadura*, São Paulo, Companhia das Letras, 2017, p. 125.

[773] It should be mentioned that one year before the judgment of the *Aikewara case*, in 2013, the Amnesty Commission also granted pecuniary reparation to one indigenous person (named Tiuré Potiguara) who was considered a victim of the dictatorship and had lived many years in Canada as a political refugee. See: *Carta Maior*, "Pela primeira vez, Brasil concede anistia a índio perseguido pela ditadura", December 2, 2013, https://www.cartamaior.com.br/?/Editoria/Direitos-Humanos/Pela-1%25AA-vez-Brasil-concede-anistia-a-indio-perseguido-pela-ditadura/5/29707.

[774] Each one of the 14 *Aikewaras* received the amount of BRL 86,800.00 (equivalent to approximately US$22,371.13 in June 2019). See: *Fundação Nacional do Índio (FUNAI)*, "Comissão de Anistia concede indenização a indígenas Suruí do Pará", September 23, 2014, http://www.funai.gov.br/index.php/comunicacao/noticias/3050-comissao-de-anistia-concede-indenizacao-a-indigenas-surui-do-para.

But, as pointed out by Corntassel and Holder,[775] the risk is that this kind of public apology itself may be treated as sufficient to discharge other State officials of their responsibility, mainly because the work of such commissions tends to focus on reconciling perpetrators and victims as individual citizens within the State, thus limiting the potential for dealing with indigenous peoples.

It seems that, as observed by Vieille,[776] the fact that Transitional Justice mechanisms are steeped in western liberalism may be problematic because it makes it difficult to take account of instruments and approaches that do not fit within its legalistic and individualistic framework. Truly, those traditional instruments conceive the individual as the irreducible unit of society, and find it difficult to accommodate practices that do not correspond to this view, and this principle of individuation has shaped much of existing efforts in transitional societies. Moreover, the implementation of this one-size-fits-all approach lacks the social, historical and cultural connection to the people who are primarily affected by the transition. This formula or set of processes, having been merely imported based on foreign models (and its incorrect dogma that what has worked in a few countries will work elsewhere), has already been severely condemned by the United Nations[777] as well as by scholars.[778]

7.2.3. CHALLENGES TO JUDICIAL AND ADMINISTRATIVE MEASURES

In observing all the limitations related to indigenous reparations for the damage caused by the dictatorship, in 2013, the Federal Prosecutor's Office (*Ministério Público Federal* – MPF) created a working group in charge of the analysis of how indigenous people were affected by the military regime.[779] Its main objectives were: a) to qualify and quantify violations against indigenous people; b) to

---

[775] CORNTASSEL, Jeff and HOLDER, Cindy, "Who's Sorry Now? Government Apologies, Truth Commissions, and Indigenous Self-Determination in Australia, Canada, Guatemala and Peru", *Human Rights Review*, vol. 9/2008.

[776] VIEILLE, Stephanie, "Transitional Justice: A Colonizing Field?", *Amsterdam Law Forum*, vol. 4/2012, pp. 58–68.

[777] United Nations Organization, "Guidance Note of the Secretary-General – United Nations Approach to Transitional Justice", March 2010, p. 5.

[778] LUNDY, Patricia and MCGOVERN, Mark, "Whose Justice? Rethinking Transitional Justice from the Bottom Up", *Journal of Law and Society*, vol. 35/2008, pp. 265–292. DRAGOO, Michelle, "Does One Size Really Fit All? Transitional Justice Process and Commemoration in Post-Conflict Santiago Atitlán Guatemala", *Sociology and Anthropology*, vol. 4/2016, pp. 546–553.

[779] *Federal Public Prosecutor's Office*, "Portaria n. 001/2016-6CCR/MPF", http://www.mpf.mp.br/atuacao-tematica/ccr6/dados-da-atuacao/grupos-de-trabalho/violacao-dos-direitos-dos-povos-indigenas-e-registro-militar.

propose Transitional Justice measures for the particular nature of indigenous cases; c) to support the work of the prosecutors in cases of violations of indigenous rights during the military dictatorship; and d) to assist civil society in the pursuit of memory and truth related to indigenous issues.

This working group of the Federal Public Prosecutor's Office is especially concerned with judicial measures – as a pillar of Transitional Justice – in the following cases:

(a) the *Tenharim* and *Jiahui* nations, for damage caused during the construction of the Trans-Amazonian Highway, which provoked forced displacements of those tribes;
(b) the *Krenak* nation, for the creation of a reformatory for indigenous people, as well as, their forced displacement to *Guarani Farm*, in the state of Minas Gerais, which resulted in forced labor and torture; and
(c) the *Waimiri-Atroari* nation, for damage caused during the construction of Highway BR-174, across the Amazon Rainforest, between the state of Roraima and the Venezuelan border.[780]

In 2015, the Federal Public Prosecutor's Office initiated a civil action seeking historical reparations for the *Krenak* nation and specifically mentioning the extermination, forced labor, torture, forced displacement and social disintegration of several indigenous ethnic groups during the dictatorship period (1964–1985), the result not only of the omission, but also of the direct action of the Brazilian State.[781] The claim is focused on three emblematic cases of serious violations of the rights of indigenous peoples: (a) the creation of the Indigenous Rural Guard (GRIN); (b) the installation of the *Krenak* Reformatory; and (c) the forced displacement of various ethnic groups (mainly *Krenak*) to *Guarani Farm*. In addition, the Federal Prosecutor's Office remarked that indigenous rights established at that time were not respected, resulting in the enhance vulnerability, as well as the cultural and biological destruction, of indigenous communities.[782]

---

[780] *Federal Public Prosecutor's Office*, "Report of the Working Group on Indigenous Tribes and Military Regime", http://www.mpf.mp.br/atuacao-tematica/ccr6/dados-da-atuacao/grupos-de-trabalho/violacao-dos-direitos-dos-povos-indigenas-e-registro-militar/docs-1/docs_relatorios_atividades/relatorio-2014_gt-violacao.pdf.

[781] *Federal Public Prosecutor's Office*, "Ação Civil Pública do Reformatório Krenak", http://www.mpf.mp.br/mg/sala-de-imprensa/docs/acp-reformatorio-krenak.pdf/view.

[782] The civil action was supported by a psychosocial report on political violence committed against *Krenak* indigenous populations during the Brazilian dictatorship which was still virtually unknown and little publicized. For an analysis of the psychological technical input carried out to ascertain the psychosocial effects of the political violence against the *Krenak* population, see: Gonçalves, Bruno Simões, "Parecer Psicossocial da Violência contra os Povos Indígenas Brasileiros: o Caso Reformatório Krenak", *Psicologia: Ciência e Profissão*, vol. 37/2017, pp. 186–196.

In its claim, the Federal Public Prosecutor's Office explained that the *Krenak's* surreal narrative shows how indigenous people, who were the legitimate owners of their traditional territories, became confined, were forbidden to return to their lands, were transformed into a kind of landless indigenous people, and were expelled from their own territory through physical violence and moral brutality. Among the several judicial requests contained in this civil action, it is worth highlighting those that are linked to Transitional Justice measures such as:

(a) the environmental recovery of the indigenous lands that were degraded during the period of the dictatorship;
(b) the translation into the *Krenak* language of some important documents like the 1988 Constitution, ILO Convention no. 169 and the portion of the NTC Final Report related to violations of the human rights of indigenous peoples;
(c) the opening of governmental files related to *Krenak* cases and their systematization in the National Archives;
(d) the implementation of measures in order to promote the teaching and dissemination of the *Krenak* language;
(e) financial support for indigenous initiatives aiming to rescue and preserve *Krenak* culture;
(f) the demarcation of the *Krenak* indigenous territory known as "*Sete Salões*" (in the state of Minas Gerais);[783]
(g) a public and official apology by the State;
(h) the restoration of the *Guarani Farm* headquarters and its transformation into a center of memory;
(i) the inclusion in the public school curriculum of the study of the violations of the human rights of indigenous peoples during the military regime.

In this same civil action, in 2016, there was a Judicial ruling ordering that some of the requests be accepted immediately under a request for injunctive relief,[784] such as the procedure for the demarcation of the *Krenak* indigenous land of "*Sete Salões*"; the creation of a working group to prepare the translation into the

---

[783] The *Krenak* indigenous nation already had another traditional territory demarcated. This first demarcation process started in 1983, shortly after the members of the tribe left *Guarani Farm* and returned to the Resplendor region, when the National Indian Foundation (FUNAI) proposed a claim in order to cancel title to property held by unlawful settlors. In 1993 the Supreme Court ruled in favor of the *Krenak* members. So, in 1997, the indigenous tribe returned to its traditional land once the unlawful settlors were removed. See: *Supreme Court*, Ação Cível Originária (ACO/MG) no. 323, https://stf.jusbrasil.com.br/jurisprudencia/19154638/execucao-na-acao-civel-originaria-aco-323-mg-stf.

[784] *Federal Public Prosecutor's Office*, Civil Action no. 64483-95.2015.4.01.3800, Decision on Injunctive Relief of December 5 2016, http://www.mpf.mp.br/mg/sala-de-imprensa/docs/decisao-liminar-reformatorio-krenak/view.

Krenak language of the documents requested; the opening and systematization of the government archives concerning the *Krenak* people,[785] and the implementation of linguistic workshops to rescue and preserve their culture. However, until the present time, the case is still awaiting final judgment.[786]

Concerning such civil action, on September 13, 2021, the Federal Court of Minas Gerais, condemned the Federal Union, the National Indian Foundation (FUNAI) and the state of Minas Gerais for human rights violations and crimes committed against the *Krenak* indigenous people during the military dictatorship.[787] As expected, according to the judgment, the Federal Union, FUNAI and the state of Minas Gerais must hold a public ceremony in which the serious violations of the rights of indigenous peoples should be properly addressed and recognized, followed by a public apology to the *Krenak* people. In addition, FUNAI must (a) complete the process of delimitation of the *Krenak* Indigenous Land of "*Sete Salões*"; (b) define environmental reparations for the degraded lands belonging to the indigenous people; and (c) together with the state of Minas Gerais, implement actions and initiatives aimed at registering, promoting and teaching the *Krenak* language, in order to rescue and preserve the memory and culture of these indigenous people. The Federal Union, on the other hand, will have to gather and systematize all the documentation related to the serious violations of the human rights of indigenous peoples concerning the creation of the *Krenak* Reformatory and make the files available on the Internet.

Additionally, in 2015, the Federal Prosecutor's Office submitted to the Amnesty Commission a request for collective reparation to the *Krenak* ethnic group.[788] This administrative demand followed the model defined by the Reparations Program (according to Law no. 10,559 (2002)), but it is worth mentioning that the invisibility of the violations perpetrated against indigenous people during the dictatorship period meant that the Transitional Justice model adopted in Brazil was poorly adapted to the specificities of reparations to indigenous communities, so Law no. 10,559 (2002) does not have any provisions for collective reparations.

And this omission is not new. As a matter of fact, in Brazil, the entire method traditionally applied in the adoption of laws shows little concern for ensuring

---

[785] The governmental documents related to the *Krenak* indigenous people were digitalized in 2017, and they are available at the website of the National Archives System of Information, http://arquivonacional.gov.br/br/component/tags/tag/povo-krenak.html.

[786] DANTAS, Dimitrius, "MP Quer Reparação a Índigenas por Mortes em Conflitos durante Ditadura", *O Globo*, April 1, 2019, https://oglobo.globo.com/sociedade/mp-quer-reparacao-indigenas-por-mortes-em-conflitos-durante-ditadura-23563949.

[787] *Correio Braziliense*, "Juíza Condena Funai, União e MG por campo de concentração Krenak na Ditadura", September 16, 2021, https://www.correiobraziliense.com.br/brasil/2021/09/4949862-juiza-condena-funai-uniao-e-mg-por-campo-de-concentracao-krenak-na-ditadura.html.

[788] *Amnesty Commission*, Requirement no. 75002, June 24, 2015, https://sinca.mj.gov.br/sinca/pages/externo/consultarProcessoAnistia.jsf.

the participation of indigenous people in policymaking.[789] The process repeats the logic of oppression employed since colonial times and this restrictive procedure insists on the invisibility of the indigenous people in the wider society. Historically, the relationship between the colonizer and native people was marked by an approach filled with violence (slavery, assimilation, forced displacements, etc.) and, behind the façade of tutelage and the discourse of assimilationism, in many situations, federal state polices caused the extermination of resisting people in order to occupy their lands and to explore the west of the country.

Moreover, once approved by the Amnesty Commission, this emblematic request for collective reparations for the *Krenak* nation proposes that the indigenous people be called to intervene and to suggest how their own financial and symbolic reparation should be carried out, with free, prior and informed consent, which should assist them in renegotiating their relations with the State.[790]

This different approach for dealing with the inclusion of indigenous people in the decision-making process, which requires their culture and knowledge being called upon to meet their needs, is based on the right to prior, free and informed consultation. This protocol, as proposed by Convention no. 169 of the International Labor Organization (ILO),[791] has ensured such consultation whenever legislative or administrative measures are envisaged which may directly affect a collective group. But, until June of 2019, this requirement has not yet been analyzed by the Amnesty Commission.[792]

Concerning the *Waimiri-Atroari* nation, in 2017, the Federal Prosecutor's Office filed a civil action in the Federal Court, seeking reparations for damage caused to this indigenous people during the construction of Highway BR-174 (also called the Manaus–Boa Vista highway). In this claim, the Federal Prosecutor's Office is seeking payment of a pecuniary amount (estimated at BRL 50 million), an official apology made by the State, the inclusion of the facts of human rights violations as part of the national public school curriculum, the creation of a memory center, the opening of the military archives and the

---

[789] Peruzzo, Pedro Pulzatto, "Direito à consulta prévia aos povos indígenas no Brasil", *Direito e Praxis*, vol. 8/2017, pp. 2708–2740.

[790] In 2017, the *Krenak* indigenous nation created its own protocol for consultation, see: http://www.mpf.mp.br/mg/sala-de-imprensa/noticias-mg/povo-indigena-krenak-cria-protocolo-de-consulta-previa.

[791] *International Labour Organization*, Convention concerning Indigenous and Tribal Peoples no. 169, adopted on June 27, 1989, in force since September 5, 1991, https://www.ilo.org/dyn/normlex/en/f?p=NORMLEXPUB:12100:0::NO::P12100_ILO_CODE:C169. Brazil ratified this Convention on April 19, 2004 by Decree no. 5,051 (2004), http://www.planalto.gov.br/ccivil_03/_ato2004-2006/2004/decreto/d5051.htm.

[792] Dantas, Dimitrius, "MP Quer Reparação a Índigenas por Mortes em Conflitos durante Ditadura"; *O Globo*, April 1, 2019, https://oglobo.globo.com/sociedade/mp-quer-reparacao-indigenas-por-mortes-em-conflitos-durante-ditadura-23563949.

systematization in the National Archives of all documentation related to the human rights violations committed against the *Waimiri-Atroari* people.[793]

Until the present time, this civil action has not been concluded, but in January 2018, the indigenous people in question had a partial victory when an injunction was granted that made the implementation of development and infrastructure projects capable of causing major impact on their indigenous land conditional upon the prior and informed consent of the *Waimiri-Atroari* people. That injunction, however, was overturned by the Federal Court of Appeal and the case returned to the court of first instance[794] for continued deliberations.

In February 2019, during the evidence-taking period in the case, a court hearing was held inside the territory of the *Waimiri-Atroari* people in a kind of indigenous meeting house (called a *taba*), where the population used to assemble for celebrations and story-telling. This may be considered a symbolic moment when indigenous people spoke openly about their memories and the violations committed against them between 1970 and 1980.[795] Six survivors of the attacks detailed how the Army entered their land, destroyed sacred sites and caused the death of the children, adolescents and adults of entire villages through the use of poison spills dropped by airplanes, explosives, shooting attacks and stabbings.[796]

However, the possible outburst provoked by the court hearing in February 2019 was eclipsed by the news that a power transmission line project (named *Linhão do Tucuruí*) had been designated by the federal government as a matter of national security and defense,[797] since Roraima is the only state that is not yet part of the National Electric Power System. Currently, its energy comes from neighboring Venezuela, whose power grid has been subject to blackouts. As a

---

[793] *Federal Justice of Amazonas Region*, Civil Action no. 1001605-06.2017.4.01.3200, www.mpf.mp.br/am/sala-de-imprensa/docs/acp-waimiri-atroari-violacoes.

[794] FARIAS, Elaíze, "Waimiri-Atorari Genocide: Survivors Report Attacks During the Work of BR-174", March 6, 2019, http://amazoniareal.com.br/waimiri-atroari-sobreviventes-de-genocidio-relatam-ataques-durante-obra-da-br-174/.

[795] Reports of attacks and deaths of hundreds of *Waimiri-Atroaris* are not new. In 2015, the State Committee for the Right to Truth, to Memory and Justice of the Amazon launched the book "The Military Dictatorship and Genocide Waimiri-Atroari People: Why Kamña Killed Kiña" (*A Ditadura Militar e o Genocídio do Povo Waimir-Atroari: Por que Kamña matou Kiña?*), which was based on documentation and indigenous reports, gathered by researchers Egydio Schwade and Dorothy Schwade – who lived for four years with the *Waimiri-Atroari* tribe in the' 80s and estimated that about 2,000 persons of said ethnic tribe were killed in the course of the BR-174 highway construction. See: SAVARESE, Maurício, "Tribu amazónica acusa de atrocidades al ejército de Brasil", *Associated Press*, March 8, 2019, https://www.apnews.com/f39d5e720d4e43288e6d6097340a6a3e.

[796] SAVARESE, Maurício, "Tribu amazónica acusa de atrocidades al ejército de Brasil", *Associated Press*, March 8, 2019, https://www.apnews.com/f39d5e720d4e43288e6d6097340a6a3e.

[797] FARIAS, Elaíze, "Waimiri-Atorari Genocide: Survivors Report Attacks During the Work of BR-174", March 6, 2019, http://amazoniareal.com.br/waimiri-atroari-sobreviventes-de-genocidio-relatam-ataques-durante-obra-da-br-174/.

result, the Brazilian State decided to accelerate the environmental licensing of the transmission line project, which will extend from the city of Manaus (located in Amazonas state) to the city of Boa Vista (located in Roraima state), parallel to Highway BR-174 and crossing 120 km within the *Waimiri-Atroari* indigenous land.[798]

The Federal Prosecutor's Office issued a formal statement regarding this project which recommended that administrative agencies like FUNAI and the Brazilian Institute of Environment and Natural Resources (IBAMA) guarantee the rights constitutionally given to indigenous people and that the apparent lack of dialogue and the attempt to carry out a work of great impact in an unplanned manner must be prevented from resulting in the repetition of episodes of serious violations, such as those that occurred during the construction of the highway.[799] In addition, the still newly created *Arns Commission for Human Rights Defense*[800] expressed its support and solidarity with the *Waimiri-Atroari* people, and recommended compliance with ILO Convention no.169 concerning the rights of indigenous peoples. It argued that the State needed to conduct an informed consultation prior to the implementation of measures that may affect these peoples. According to the *Arns Commission*, starting the infrastructure work on *Waimiri-Atroaris* lands without this prior consultation (within the proper legal frameworks and according to specific protocols) would represent a serious violation of the human rights of these people.[801] If truth be told, the future decision relating to the *Linhão do Tucuruí* project and the respect for indigenous rights may serve as leading case in the analysis of the effectiveness or otherwise of the non-repetition measures designed by the Transitional Justice mechanisms in Brazil.

---

[798] DAMASIO, Kevin, "Ditadura militar quase dizimou os Waimiri-Atroari e indígenas temem novo massacre", *National Geographic*, April 1, 2019, https://www.nationalgeographicbrasil.com/historia/2019/04/ditadura-militar-waimiri-atroari-massagre-genocidio-aldeia-tribo-amazonia-indigena-indio-governo.

[799] *Federal Public Prosecutor's Office*, "MPF estuda medidas diante da tentativa de aceleração de licenciamento do Linhão de Tucuruí entre Am e RR", March 1, 2019, http://www.mpf.mp.br/am/sala-de-imprensa/noticias-am/mpf-estuda-medidas-diante-de-tentativa-de-aceleracao-do-linhao-de-tucurui-entre-am-e-rr.

[800] The *Arns Commission for Human Rights Defense* was established in February 2019, and congregates human rights advocates like Paulo Sérgio Pinheiro, Belisário dos Santos Jr., Dalmo de Abreu Dallari, Fábio Konder Comparato, José Carlos Dias, José Gregori, Oscar Vilhena Vieira, Paulo Vannuchi, and many others. The aim of the *Arns Commission* is to contribute to the visibility and legal follow-up in national and international instances of serious human rights violations motivated by hatred and intolerance, as well as restrictions on the exercise of civil liberties and participation in political life. See: *Comissão Arns*, https://comissaoarns.org/.

[801] *The Arns Commission for Human Rights Defense*, "Public Statement no. 2", June 5, 2019, https://comissaoarns.org/notas/2019-06-05-nota-p%C3%BAblica-2-apoio-ao-povo-waimiri-atroari/.

7.3. CONCLUSIONS

The repression of indigenous people includes singularities when compared to other groups that were also subjugated during the dictatorship. In fact, it was a kind of violence hidden under the commonplace reasoning of an oppressive historical relation that began during the colonial period (1500–1822). The subjugation of the indigenous population during 1964–1985 was not always recognized as being part of the legal monopoly of State violence because it was occasionally perpetrated by the agents of the State (Armed Forces, Police Forces and public agencies in charge of the indigenous policies like the former SPI and the FUNAI); and, in other cases, it was exercised in the form of private violence, sponsored by settlers who became landowners, companies and capital ventures working in the countryside.[802]

In the long course of Brazilian history, this form of violence in the countryside was often disguised and this has made it difficult not only to identify the crimes but also to repair those past atrocities committed against the indigenous people, resulting in silence, denial, impunity and dissension – all elements that Transitional Justice struggles with and tries to prevent. In addition, another consequence of this silence and lack of recognition of past history lies in the very continuity of conflicts, such as the massacres against indigenous peoples that have occurred even during the democratic period, for example in the cases of the *Yanomani*, near Haximu (in 1993)[803] and the *Akroá-Gamella* (in 2017).[804] Likewise, according to a 2018 report made by the Indian Missionary Council (*Conselho Missionário Indígena* – CIMI), very recent presidential administrations (those of 2011–2016 and 2016–2018) have broken records for negative land demarcations, and have implemented works that affected indigenous rights,

---

[802] NOVAIS, Adriana Rodrigues, "A Memória da Repressão e Violência no Campo em Tempos da Comissão Nacional da Verdade", *Revista Interdisciplinar de Direitos Humanos*, vol. 3/2015, pp. 43–55.

[803] In the Haximu massacre (also known as *Yanomani* massacre) 16 indigenous people were killed by gold miners who were illegally mining inside the *Yanomani*'s land. In 2006, by means of an Extraordinary Appeal (Recurso Extraordinário no. 351487), the Supreme Court confirmed that the crime perpetrated against those indigenous people was genocide. See: *Survival International*, "Remembering the Haximu massacre 20 years on", https://www.survivalinternational.org/articles/3298-haximu-survivors; and Survival International, "Supreme Court upholds genocide ruling", https://www.survivalinternational.org/news/1786.

[804] On April 30, 2017, in Viana in the state of Maranhão, a group of approximately 200 people brutally attacked the indigenous community of *Akroá-Gamella* that has been returning to its traditional territory since 2015 and has reclaimed such area. During this attack, 22 indigenous people were injured by knifes and beaten with stones, two of them were shot and two others had their hands cut off. See: Conselho Indigenista Missionário (CIMI), "Relatório CIMI: violência contra os povos indgígenas no Brasil tem aumento sistêmico e contínuo", September 27, 2018, https://cimi.org.br/2018/09/relatorio-cimi-violencia-contra-os-povos-indigenas-no-brasil-tem-aumento-sistemico-e-continuo/.

such as the *Belo Monte* hydroelectric plant (in Pará state).[805] Furthermore, the NTC Final Report pointed out that many such violations are still occurring at the present time, despite the existence of a different political context.[806] In addition, as Negócio has observed,[807] the violation of the rights of indigenous peoples is not unfamiliar to contemporary Brazilian reality, notwithstanding the efforts to recognize these rights.

Through the overview analysis in this chapter, it is possible to assert that, as indicated by McAuliffe,[808] indigenous norms and State institutions present a "clash of two goods" – respect for local traditions and practices, on the one hand, and the goals of sustainable development and rights-based State reconstruction, on the other. And up to now, against this background and observing the Transitional Justice mechanisms implemented in Brazil, such instruments have not been acclaimed as broadening horizons to include indigenous forms of reparations, especially if we observe cases such as (i) the mere pecuniary reparation made to the *Aikeawara* indigenous people; (ii) the lack of State initiative in seeking changes in legislation capable of contemplating collective reparations and the participation of indigenous peoples in decisions about their own form of reparations (such as the *Krenak* people's case awaiting action under the Amnesty Commission's decision in 2015, related to Law no. 10,559 (2002) and Ordinance (*Portaria*) no. 2,523 (2008)[809]); (iii) the upholding of the judicial approach to regulating the demarcation of indigenous lands which may potentially constrain the recovery of territories that were lost due forced displacements implemented in the dictatorship; and (iv) the need for judicial intervention against the State in order to exert pressure for compliance with the

---

[805] Conselho Indigenista Missionário (CIMI), "Relatório CIMI: violência contra os povos indgígenas no Brasil tem aumento sistêmico e contínuo", September 27, 2018, https://cimi.org.br/2018/09/relatorio-cimi-violencia-contra-os-povos-indigenas-no-brasil-tem-aumento-sistemico-e-continuo/. See also: VALENTE, Rubens, *Os Fuzis e as Flechas – História de Sangue e Resistência Indígena na Ditadura*, São Paulo, Companhia das Letras, 2017, p. 393. BARRIONUEVO, Alexei, "Amazon Dam Project Pits Economic Benefit Against Protection of Indigenous Lands", *The New York Times*, April 16, 2010, https://www.nytimes.com/2010/04/17/world/americas/17brazil.html?src=me.

[806] *NTC Report*, Volume II, Text 5, p. 252, http://cnv.memoriasreveladas.gov.br/.

[807] NEGÓCIO, Carla Daniela Leite, "A Violência Física e Cultural Contra os Povos Indígenas Durante o Regime Militar", *Aracê Direitos Humanos em Revista*, vol. 5/2017, pp. 263–294.

[808] McAULIFFE, Padraig, "Romanticization Versus Integration: Indigenous Justice in Rule of Law Reconstruction and Transitional Justice Discourse", *Goettingen Journal of International Law*, vol. 5/2013, pp. 41–86.

[809] According to the Federal Prosecutor's Office, Ordinance no. 2,523 (2008) is in fact evidence that the Transitional Justice in Brazil, in its genesis, did not consider the serious violations committed against the human rights of indigenous peoples, since it fails to recognize that collectivity is an essential aspect of the indigenous way of life. See: Federal Prosecutor's Office, *Technical Opinion no. 03/2017-6°CCR/MPF*, April 3, 2017, www.mpf.mp.br/atuacao-tematica/ccr6/documentos-e-publicacoes/publicacoes/nota-tecnica/2017/nota-tecnica-no-03-anistia-coletiva.pdf.

recommendations listed in the NTC Final Report (in the case of civil actions related to the *Krenak* and *Waimiri-Atroari* peoples).

Vieille has stated that there is a real danger that Transitional Justice simply serves to promote, maybe even involuntarily, a biased approach to doing justice,[810] which fails to offer an answer to local needs and realities, and this perspective seems to describe the Brazilian framework of Transitional Justice *vis à vis* indigenous matters. Regrettable actions like ignoring local needs and failing to engage indigenous actors is likely to undermine the anchoring of lasting reconciliation, the resumption of dialogue between the parties and the restoration of trust in the society.

In fact, official apologies made by the Amnesty Commission to the *Aikeawaras* and the Final Report of the NTC, both in 2014, did not succeed in transforming existing oppressive relationships with indigenous peoples. Analyzing the Brazilian political strategy in very recent times in an article for *The New Yorker*, Jon Lee Anderson commented that, in the Brazilian interior – a vast area served by few roads or railways, in which there are pitched battles for land and survival among settlers, miners, ranchers, and indigenous groups – everything recalls life on the early American frontier,[811] showing that the historical past is still very fresh. This is so much the case that a song recorded, in 1978, by the Brazilian singer *Djavan*, called *Cara de Índio* ("Face of the Indian"), evoking the North American expression "pale-face", is still quite accurate to this day. That song gave advice to the indigenous population, not only requesting patience, but also criticizing the relationship between indigenous and non-indigenous people[812] by saying:

> Your action is valid, my dear Indian / … When someone is able to plant / He is not an Indian. / Indigenous people want to name themselves, / I doubt it, indigenous people. / It may take time, / Take care of yourself, indigenous people.[813]

---

[810] VIEILLE, Stephanie, "Transitional Justice: A Colonizing Field?", *Amsterdam Law Forum*, vol. 4/2012, pp. 58–68.

[811] ANDERSON, Jon Lee, "Jair Bolsonaro's Southern Strategy – In Brazil, a budding authoritarian borrows from the Trump playbook", *The New Yorker*, March 25, 2019, https://www.newyorker.com/magazine/2019/04/01/jair-bolsonaros-southern-strategy.

[812] FLORÊNCIO, Roberto Remígio, "Índio Cara Pálida ou Cara de Índio: Uma Breve Análise dos Discursos sobre a Temática Indígena das Letras de Música Popular Brasileira", *Opará – Etnicidades, Movimentos Sociais e Educação*, vol. 4/2016, pp. 35–46.

[813] Free translation of the song "*Cara de Índio*": "*Sua ação é válida, meu caro índio. / … Quando alguém puder plantar, / não é índio. / Índio quer se nomear, /duvido índio. / Isso pode demorar, / te cuida índio*". See: DJAVAN, "*Cara de Índio*", Album *Djavan*, 1978, https://djavan.com.br/discografia/djavan/.

CHAPTER 8

A GENDERED APPROACH TO BRAZILIAN TRANSITIONAL JUSTICE[814]

"Silence is what allows people to suffer without recourse, what allows hypocrisies and lies to grow and flourish, crimes to go unpunished. If our voices are essential aspects of our humanity, to be rendered voiceless is to be dehumanized or excluded from one's humanity. And the history of silence is central to women's history".[815]

History is made by men and women, in every single moment, in their daily lives. However, many of these experiences or political battles are lost forever, accumulating silences, which are sometimes historically constructed, because from time to time history has been partial, and has silenced or hidden subjects. But, lately, in an attempt to correct historical gaps, the objects of investigation have been pluralized, admitting as historical subjects the workers, the peasants, the slaves and the women, who before were underestimated. In this aspiration to reverse traditional historical perspectives, scholars[816] began to look at historical events from the perspectives of other subjects. Specifically, in the case of women, we have sought to observe their presence in History, including them not only as object of study, but also as active subjects of History; and to this end, the category of analysis – gender – has been used to theorize the question of sexual difference and of power relations between men and women. In this chapter, we will analyze the History of women and their participation in groups opposed to military dictatorship, and the reparations that Brazilian Transitional Justice has provide to them.

8.1. WOMEN'S PARTICIPATION IN THE ANTI-DICTATORSHIP MOVEMENT

Women were probably the part of the society that most faced changes during the 1960s and 1970s in Brazil, since they had to deal with modifications in everyday

---

[814] The author is thankful to her research colleague Dr. Inês Virgínia Prado Soares, who has been a consistent example of tenaciousness and of inexorable encouragement. Her deep involvement, sustained interest and brain-storming discussions on symbolic reparations have helped the author a lot in bringing this chapter to maturity.
[815] SOLNIT, Rebecca, *The Mother of All Questions*, Chicago, IL, Haymarket Books, 2007.
[816] COLLING, Ana Maria, *As Mulheres e a Ditadura Militar no Brasil*, https://wp.ufpel.edu.br/ndh/files/2017/02/10.-ana_colling.pdf.

life, in the job market, with the reduction of the number of children per family, and so on. In order to answer to those challenges, they had to improve their level of education, which in the long run has altered their relationships not only with men, but also with other women. At that time, this new dynamic of life for women was due to several factors: the expansion of capitalism, the growth of the manufacturing industry, the decline of the rural population, and the increase of urban areas. So, within these new social relations, women obtained independence, at the same time that large cities grew without adequate infrastructure. Without long-term planning slums started to expand as well as the suburban neighborhoods. Adding to that, Brazil dealt with an enlargement of the labor market and a decrease of wages, and with the scenario a parcel of women started to seek paid employment and leave aside household tasks as their main duties.[817]

According to demographic statistics, in 1970, women made up 50.3% of the total Brazilian population and 21% of economically active adults.[818] On the other hand, in terms of politics and the resistance movements, even though some left-wing organizations had a fair number of women members during the 1960s and 1970s, men made up the majority of most of them. As Ridenti has observed,[819] women participated more significantly in urban armed groups, where they represented around 18.3% of members. That is not an insignificant number if we consider an important fact of that period: even though women had had the right to vote since 1932,[820] until the late 1960s, women held only secondary ranks in Brazilian politics and society. And, as Colling has noted,[821] women of that period were customarily not involved in politics, except to reaffirm their social roles as "mothers and wives".

Thus, the average of 18% female participation in urban armed groups reflects the beginning of progress in female liberation and represents a rupture with the generation of women restricted to the private and domestic spheres, since, before this period, to men there was the public space, the political space, where power was centralized; to women there was the private domain and the sanctuary of their home, and the feminine role used to present a unique path – motherhood and marriage.

In general, as reported by Teles,[822] the participation of women in clandestine organizations was related to the infrastructure and organization of political and

---

[817] TELES, Maria Amélia de Almeida, "Violações dos Direitos Humanos das Mulheres na Ditadura", *Estudos Feministas*, vol. 23/2015, pp. 1001–1022.

[818] *Instituto Brasileiro de Geografia e Estatística* (IBGE), "Demographic Census 1970", available at https://biblioteca.ibge.gov.br/visualizacao/periodicos/69/cd_1970_v1_br.pdf.

[819] RIDENTI, Marcelo Siqueira, "As Mulheres na Política Brasileira: Os Anos de Chumbo", *Revista Tempo Social*, vol. 2/1990, pp. 113–128.

[820] See: Electoral Code, Article 2, Decree no. 21,076 (1932).

[821] COLLING, Ana Maria, *A Resistência da Mulher à Ditadura Militar no Brasil*, Rio de Janeiro, Rosa dos Tempos, 1997.

[822] TELES, Maria Amélia de Almeida, "Violações dos Direitos Humanos das Mulheres na Ditadura", *Estudos Feministas*, vol. 23/2015, pp. 1001–1022.

armed actions. They also joined the so-called underground media, authoring newspaper articles and flyers denouncing the regime. Some of them carried guns, mainly in the *Araguaia Guerrilla* movement. Also, they were forced to live clandestine lives, changing their identities and moving to different parts of Brazil or even to other countries. Many of them chose to have children with companions in the resistance movement, facing motherhood while still engaged in the conflict or while under arrest, and others suffered miscarriages brought on by torture during imprisonment.

As Colling asserts,[823] if political history generally portrays a man's point of view, the history of the dictatorship in Brazil may even present the radicalization of the invisibility of the feminine. The political militant woman, engaged in political parties opposed to the dictatorship, was not seen as a subject of history, often being excluded from the power game. Also, for many women, who suffered the most varied acts of violation, be it symbolic, psychological or physical, talking about some aspects and/or remembering certain passages in their lives is still something painful. Thus, many of them preferred anonymity, not only as a way to preserve their emotional integrity, but also to try to overcome the situations experienced. So, considering this obscured historical data concerning women's activities during the dictatorship, it was only after the 1990s that discussions began to arise about the representation of women on the Brazilian left-wing and other movements opposing the dictatorial regime, and in the struggle for gender equality.[824]

In addition, it should be recalled that not all female opposition to the regime was related to left-wing and armed movements, since there were also women who were human rights activists – the mothers, wives, and sisters of the disappeared – and who spoke out against oppression.[825] Also, countless women participated in less visible events not properly explored by History and still barely acknowledged by Brazilian society. As mapped by Rovai,[826] those actions took place behind doors or in the shadows: giving refuge; hiding weapons, objects, and documents; delivering messages to members of clandestine groups;

---

[823] COLLING, Ana Maria and CAVALCANTI, Ary Albuquerque Junior, "Militantes e Guerrilheiras – As Mulheres e a Ditadura Militar no Brasil", *Espacialidades*, vol. 15, 2019, pp. 47–61.

[824] Among such analyses we mention the contributions of Ridenti (1990), Colling (1997), Teles (2015) (see footnotes above), and also FERREIRA, Elizabeth F. Xavier, *Mulheres, Militância e Memória*, Rio de Janeiro, Fundação Getúlio Vargas, 1996; CARVALHO, L.M., *Mulheres que Foram à Luta Armada*, São Paulo, Globo, 1998; and RIBEIRO, Maria Cláudia B., *Mulheres na Luta Armada: Protagonismo Feminino na ALN (Ação Libertadora Nacional)*, São Paulo, Alameda, 2018.

[825] *Portal Memórias da Ditadura*, http://memoriasdaditadura.org.br/biografias-da-resistencia/therezinha-zerbini/index.html.

[826] ROVAI, Marta Gouveia de Oliveira, "O Direito à Memória: A História Oral de Mulheres que Lutaram Contra a Ditadura Militar", *Tempo & Argumento*, vol. 5/2013, pp. 1–17.

and acting as intermediaries between prisoners and their families. The collective transformation carried by them was huge, mainly because of their non-violent and "maternal" behavior, full of solidarity and compassion. Even more, their peaceful participation against the regime made it difficult for the State to fight against them; after all, how could the regime cope with the fact that it felt threatened by a group of unarmed women who did not engage in any violent action?

This peaceful engagement was remembered for instance, in 1979, when some classics of the so-called "openings songs" era emerged,[827] such as: "*O Bêbado e a Equilibrista*" (The Drunk and the Tightrope Walker) composed by João Bosco and Aldir Blanc. Those types of songs were created at a time when many artists still feared producing works that were linked to politics, since they were scared of censorship, torture and exile.[828] In particular, the song "*O Bêbado e a Equilibrista*", recorded by singer Elis Regina,[829] offered a reflection about the social context of that time and also called for the return of political exiles.

While asking for the return of those who were banished, some verses of this song say, of those who were weeping: "our motherland cries / Marias and Clarices cry upon the soil of Brazil". In this case, "Marias" and "Clarices" referred not only to many wives and mothers who lost their loved ones in the fight against the regime, but also to Clarice Herzog, who was the wife of the journalist Vladimir Herzog,[830] who was killed by agents of the State during the military regime. On the other hand, "Maria" – besides being a very common name in Brazil – was the name of Henfil's mother (Mrs. Maria da Conceição Figueiredo Souza). During the 1970s, "Henfil", the nickname of Henrique de Souza Filho, was one of the most important cartoonists in Brazil, and he was also a declared opponent of the dictatorship.[831] In fact, by welcoming the role of women who had lost their

---

[827] The so-called *canções da abertura* (opening songs) indicated a new historical time, which was between the trauma of the dictatorship and the dream of a future democracy. In addition, there were also the canticles of the "amnesty movement", which had just begun at this same time. See: NAPOLITANO, Marcos, "MPB: A trilha Sonora da Abertura Política (1975/1982)", *Revista de Estudos Avançados da USP*, vol. 24/2010, pp. 389–402.

[828] GASPARI, Elio; VENTURA, Zuenir and HOLLANDA, Heloísa Buarque de, *Cultura em Trânsito 70/80: da Repressão à Abertura*, Rio de Janeiro, Aeroplano, 2000, pp. 40–41.

[829] The Elis Regina Official Website, Album: *Elis, Essa Mulher* (1979), http://www.elisregina.com.br/Por-Elis/Albuns/.

[830] The arbitrary imprisonment, torture and consequently death of Vladimir Herzog, in 1975, was recently judge by the Inter-American Court of Human Rights. See: *Inter-American Court of Human Rights, Herzog Case*, judgment of March 15, 2018, series C, no. 353.

[831] At that time, Henfil had a newspaper column named "*Cartas da Mãe*" (Mother's Letters), in the weekly journal "*Isto É* (This is), in which, by writing letters to his mother (Mrs. Maria) in an intimate tone, he used to discuss the political problems of the country, to give local news to his co-religionists and to contribute with some "advice" to the Army – all as if he were exchanging letters with his beloved family in an everyday way. See: FILHO, Henrique de Souza, *Cartas da Mãe*, Rio de Janeiro, Codecri, 1981.

cherished families during the dictatorship, the song gave hope for better days and offered a dream of living in a democratic era.[832]

Such female peaceful opposition to the dictatorship may also be exemplified by the case of a woman called Zuzu Angel, who was an important fashion designer in Brazil during the '60s and '70s, but also a tireless opponent of military regime. In 1971, her son (Stuart Edgar Angel Jones) was tortured and murdered by agents of the dictatorship, and she spent years denouncing the acts of repression against him. For instance, in 1971, shortly after the disappearance of her son, Zuzu held a fashion show at the Brazilian Consulate in New York, where she showed her opposition to the regime by incorporating in her dresses imprints representing war tanks, cannons, caged birds and quiet angels.[833]

Zuzu died in 1976, in what at that time was considered a car accident at the exit of a tunnel in Rio de Janeiro. But in 1998, the Special Commission on Political Deaths and Disappearances recognized that the military regime was the responsible for her death, since evidence showed that the accident was intentionally caused by an agent of the State, who was driving a car near her.[834] This public recognition of the facts surrounding her death is one of the various symbolic reparations that Zuzu received since the 1970s,[835] and nowadays the place of the accident is named "Tunnel Zuzu Angel".

---

[832] SILVA, Fernando Lopes, "O Poético e o Factual na Letra da Canção O Bêbado e a Equilibrista", *Revista Alpha*, vol. 17/2016, pp. 115–127.

[833] ANDRADE, Priscila, "A Marca do Anjo: A Trajetória de Zuzu Angel e o Desenvolvimento da Identidade Visual de sua Grife", *Iara Revista de Moda, Cultura e Arte*, vol. 2/2009, pp. 85–119.

[834] According to testimonies, Zuzu Angel's car was supposedly run off the road by another car driven by agents of repression. See: *Archives of the Special Commission on Political Deaths and Disappearances*, File 237/96, http://cemdp.sdh.gov.br/modules/desaparecidos/acervo/ficha/cid/332.

[835] In 1987, Virgínia Valli, the sister of Zuzu Angel, published the book "*Eu, Zuzu Angel, procuro meu filho – a verdadeira história de um assassinato político*" (I, Zuzu Angel, look for my son – the true story of a political assassination). Afterwards, in 2006, film director Sérgio Rezende transformed this book into the film called "*Zuzu Angel*", which paid a fitting tribute to her story.
In 1988, the writer José Louzeiro published the police novel "*Em Carne Viva*" ("In Living Flesh"). The fictional story takes place in the late 1960s and describes the clashes between the secret police and government opponents. The character "Sebastiana dos Anjos", whose son was killed by agents of repression, was inspired by the life of Zuzu Angel.
In 2001, the fashion designer Ronaldo Fraga launched a collection called "*Quem matou Zuzu Angel?*" (Who killed Zuzu Angel?) and, on the stage, Ronaldo placed big puppets hanging by the neck (as if they were hanged during sessions of torture), which puppets were at the same time hovering above clouds just like angels, and the models had angel's haloes around their heads and many clothes had prints of caged birds, all in reference to the previous fashion collection produced by Zuzu in 1971, denouncing the disappearance of her son. See: Carla Nascimento, "Ronaldo Fraga emociona ao levar os anjos de Zuzu para a passarela", *Jornal Folha de São Paulo*, June 30, 2001, http://www1.folha.uol.com.br/folha/ilustrada/ult90u15007.shtml.
In 2014, when the 1964 *coup d'état* reached its 50th anniversary, there was an exhibition, "Occupation Zuzu Angel", in São Paulo. Said exhibition was organized by her daughter, and showed documents and letters relating to the search for Zuzu's son, as well as dresses

In 1977, one year after Zuzu's death, singers Chico Buarque and Miltinho composed the song "*Angélica*" (Angelic) on her honor.[836] The song tells the story of a mother searching for her son and one of the verses says:

> Who is this woman / Who always sings this lament? / I just wanted to remember the torment / That made my son sigh. Who is this woman / Who always sings the same arrangement? / I just wanted to wrap up my angel / And let his body rest.

In fact, Zuzu Angel's image, her personal and her professional life were all marked by the military dictatorship, devoting herself as mother and as a warrior. In such a way, through her fashion designs and collections, she was looking for justice and her fight was not ignored.[837]

Throughout the Brazilian dictatorship it was possible to identify women not only as combatants, but also as peaceful advocates of human rights, as targets of physical and sexual violence, and as a group in society that was expected to sustain everyday life, even under catastrophic conditions. As Reilly once remarked,[838] Transitional Justice scholars have paid little attention to women's wider experiences of conflict, their extensive contributions to peace initiatives, or the significance of pervasive gender inequalities and biases in limiting women's meaningful participation at every level of post-conflict transition.

For example, in the Brazilian case, one should mention also those movements of human rights activists mainly conducted by women, which protested against the repression. Although these women did not have a radical struggle against the dictatorship, they fought for the restoration of a democratic rule, as the case of Therezinha de Jesus Zerbini, who was a Brazilian lawyer, feminist leader and founder of the *Movimento Feminino pela Anistia* – MFPA (Female Movement for Amnesty),[839] whose goal was to pressure the government for the release of political prisoners and the return of exiles to Brazil.

---

and performances with Zuzu's collections. See: *El País*, "Ocupação Zuzu Angel: quando a moda e a política se encontraram na passarela", April 8, 2014, https://brasil.elpais.com/brasil/2014/04/08/cultura/1396984998_303025.html.

[836] The Chico Buarque official website, http://www.chicobuarque.com.br/construcao/mestre.asp?pg=angelica_77.htm.

[837] SIMILI, Ivana Guilherme, "Memórias da Dor e do Luto: as Indumentárias Político-Religiosas de Zuzu Angel", *Revista Brasileira de História das Religiões*, vol. 6/2014, pp. 165–182. BASTOS, Lucia Elena Arantes Ferreira Bastos and SOARES, Inês Virgínia Prado, "Zuzu Angel: quem é essa mulher que fez da moda sua arma política e da maternidade, sua razão de existir?", in SOARES, Inês Virgínia; PIOVESAN, Flávia; RABELO, Cecilia Nunes; and BARBOUR, Vivian (eds.), *Mulheres, Direito e Protagonismo Cultural*, São Paulo, Almedina, 2022, pp. 551–576.

[838] REILLY, Niamh, "Seeking Gender Justice in Post-Conflict Transitions: Towards a Transformative Women's Human Rights Approach", *International Journal of Law in Context*, vol. 3/2007, pp. 155–172.

[839] Therezinha Zerbini was married to General Euryale Jesus Zerbini, who was one of the four generals to take a legalist position against the *coupe d'état*, in 1964, resulting in the revocation of his political rights. Therezinha Zerbini was required to respond to a military

Another emblematic case was Clara Charf – who was the partner of Carlos Marighella, the founder of *Ação Libertadora Nacional* (National Liberation Action), a Brazilian communist guerilla group – since Clara has had a leading role as a human rights activist and her history is marked by several examples of symbolic reparations.[840] Clara Charf joined the Brazilian Communist Party (PCB) in 1946, and in 1964, due to her political activities, she had her political rights canceled. Later on, in 1969, with the death of her husband, who was murdered by agents of State, she went into exile in Cuba, and only returned 10 years later, in 1979, after the approval of the Amnesty Law. Since then, Clara has fought for the memory of her husband, or the re-democratization of the country and against domestic violence. In 2003, she founded the *Associação Mulheres pela Paz* (Women for Peace Association),[841] and edited a book based on the same project, which was named *Brasileiras – Guerreiras da Paz* (Brazilian Women – Warriors of Peace), and nowadays, this NGO has an important role in the confrontation of domestic violence in Brazil.[842]

As for the tributes paid to Clara Charf, in 2005, she received the "Bertha Lutz Certificate", which was established by the Federal Senate to honor women who have contributed to the defense of women's rights and gender issues in Brazil.[843] Moreover, the Amnesty Commission granted her monthly and lifelong financial compensation payments, in 2008. During the public session of this official apology, in which said reparation was granted, Clara emphasized that the money granted was not relevant and that the most valuable asset for her was the exposure of the violence committed during the dictatorship.[844] Also, in 2014, the Secretary of Human Rights of the Republic awarded to Clara Charf the

---

police investigation into her role in helping students in the organization of a congress opposing the military regime. She was indicted, in December of 1969, and sent to prison for eight months. In 1975, Therezinha Zerbini founded the Female Movement for Amnesty (*Movimento Feminino pela Anistia* – MFPA), which issued a manifesto for general amnesty, managing to gather 16,000 signatures supporting the cause. She died in 2015 with 86 years old. See: *Portal Memórias da Ditadura*, http://memoriasdaditadura.org.br/biografias-da-resistencia/therezinha-zerbini/index.html. See also: *Folha de São Paulo*, "Therezinha Godoy Zerbini (1928–2015): Fundou o Movimento Feminino pela Anisita, March 21, 2015, https://www1.folha.uol.com.br/cotidiano/2015/03/1606122-therezinha-godoy-zerbini-1928-2015---fundou-o-movimento-feminino-pela-anistia.shtml.

[840] In 2012, the Brazilian singer Caetano Veloso released the song "*Um Comunista*" (The Communist) – in honor of Carlos Marighella (Clara's husband) – and she was also quoted in the music with a message of hope for the future, when the singer asks "how" and "who" will help to enlighten the Earth and to "undo" its knots. See: Caetano Veloso, lyrics of "*Um Comunista*", https://som13.com.br/caetano-veloso/um-comunista.

[841] *Associação Mulheres Pela Paz*, http://www.mulherespaz.org.br/.

[842] Pompeu, Fernanda, *Clara Charf de Todas as Lutas*, http://operamundi.uol.com.br/dialogosdosul/clara-charf-de-todas-as-lutas/28072017/.

[843] *Federal Senate*, https://www25.senado.leg.br/web/atividade/conselhos/-/conselho/cdbl/agraciados/.

[844] Andrade, Claudia, *Companheira de Carlos Marighella Recebe Indenização do Governo*, https://noticias.uol.com.br/ultnot/2008/03/07/ult23u1413.jhtm.

"Human Rights Premium of 2014" in the category of gender equality.[845] After that, in 2015, when Clara Charf turned 90 years old, the press described her as a "giant of history" and "as one of Brazil's most fascinating women".[846]

But while observing the dignifying examples of Zuzu Angel, Therezinha de Jesus Zerbini or Clara Charf, it should be said that those Brazilian cases resemble what Ní Aoláin has already noted by commenting that in processes of political change, while women have often been at the forefront of peace initiatives throughout a conflict, subsequently, men predominantly negotiated peace agreements or the next steps of the transition.[847] Furthermore, this disparity is pointed to by Rooney as a problem possibly derived from the gender neutrality of liberal equality norms applied by Transitional Justice methods,[848] since she observed that there is an absence of women amongst negotiating elites and a silence in the course of negotiations on socio-economic matters to do with women's day-to-day lives.

To illustrate the fact the women scarcely participated in the aftermath of the transitional measures in the Brazilian case, it should be recalled that for the 1987 National Assembly, which was responsible for the drafting of the 1988 Constitution, only 26 women were elected from a range of 166 women candidates, which represented 5.3% of the Parliament.[849] Besides the minority representation, the political articulation of women at that time became known as the "Lipstick Lobby" (*Lobby do Batom*); that is to say, such derogatory term was used in first place to discount the efforts of those women.[850]

On the other hand and considering this scenario, it is worth pointing that Brazilian women achieved significant progress with the 1988 Constitution. For example, article 5 promotes equality between men and women; article 7, subparagraph XXX prohibits differences in salaries, the performance of job functions and the criteria for admission to employment on grounds of sex, age, race or marital status and, in subparagraph XXV of the same article, free

---

[845] *Secretaria de Direitos Humanos da Presidência da República*, http://www.sdh.gov.br/noticias/2014/novembro/divulgada-relacao-de-vencedores-do-premio-direitos-humanos-2014.-solenidade-de-entrega-sera-dia-10-de-dezembro.

[846] MAGALHÃES, Mário, "Clara Charf, gigante da história, faz 90 anos", *UOL Notícias*, July 16, 2015, https://blogdomariomagalhaes.blogosfera.uol.com.br/2015/07/16/clara-charf-gigante-da-historia-faz-90-anos/.

[847] NÍ AOLÁIN, Fionnuala, "Political Violence and Gender During Times of Transition", *Columbia Journal of Gender and Law*, vol. 15/2006, pp. 829–849.

[848] ROONEY, Eilish, "Engendering Transitional Justice: Questions of Absence and Silence", *International Journal of Law in Context*, vol. 3/2007, pp. 93–107.

[849] *Congresso em Foco*, "A Bancada do Batom e a Constituição Cidadã", October 31, 2013, https://congressoemfoco.uol.com.br/opiniao/colunas/a-bancada-do-batom-e-a-constituicao-cidada/.

[850] *Arquivo Nacional: Que República é Essa?*, "Lobby das Meninas: A Mulher na Constituinte de 1987/88", http://querepublicaeessa.an.gov.br/temas/213-lobby-das-meninas.html, March 19, 2020.

childcare is provided to children and dependents from birth to five years of age, in daycare centers and pre-schools; article 183 assures the title to land acquired by unopposed occupation and the concession of such land use, both in urban and rural areas, to both men and women, regardless of marital status; article 226 establishes special protection for the family by the State, creating mechanisms to restrain violence in the context of their relationships, and this measure subsequently enabled the development of legislation in the context of domestic violence; and the same article 226, paragraph 7, ends the theory of supreme patriarchal power, by providing that family planning is the couple's free decision.[851]

8.2. OFFICIAL SYMBOLIC REPARATIONS TO WOMEN

8.2.1. THE BOOK *LUTA, SUBSTANTIVO FEMININO* (FIGHT: A FEMININE NOUN)

As part of International Women's Day celebrations, in March 2010, the Special Secretariat for Human Rights and the Special Secretariat for Policies for Women published the book *Luta, Substantivo Feminino*.[852] In addition to recording the lives and deaths of 45 Brazilian women who fought against the dictatorship, this work includes the testimony of 27 women who survived that period of violence. The book incorporates not only an introductory text summarizing the context of each stage of repression, but there is also a chapter entitled "Resistance and Pain" describing the subjective aspects of torture and how women's strength was important to overcome past atrocities.

In the book's introduction, the former Secretary of Human Rights acknowledges that the volume does not include the full number of women who died in that period as victims of political persecution, since the research was exclusively based on the work of the Special Commission on Political Deaths and Disappearances: until now, the exact number of women caught up in the landscape of systematic violence is still undetermined. In almost all reported cases, the victims either died as a result of torture or was executed, or their fate remains unknown to their family and friends. Thus, in order to avoid those episodes being lost to oblivion, the book attempts to clarify some of the cases and to preserve the statements of those women who survived.

---

[851] BARRETO, Ana Cristina Teixeira, "Igualdade entre Sexos: Carta de 1988 é um marco contra discriminação", November 5, 2010, CONJUR, https://www.conjur.com.br/2010-nov-05/constituicao-1988-marco-discriminacao-familia-contemporanea.

[852] *Memórias Reveladas*, Book "Luta Substantivo Feminino" (2010), www.memoriasreveladas.gov.br/administrator/components/com_simplefilemanager/uploads/5851a57ad9db10.32446106/livro_mulheres.pdf.

The book is also important because it counters certain underlying perceptions, for instance, that the women who fought against the State should have stayed at home and taken care of their domestic affairs. In addition, the book helped to confront the stigma associated with rape – since there is still the deeply ingrained perception that rape and other forms of sexual violence are unavoidable aspects of the breakdown in social order that accompanies conflicts – as well as women's own fears of social rejection by their families and communities if they officially report the sexual violence that they suffered.[853]

Besides contributing to an official explanation of the facts, the purpose of the publication is to rescue the role of women during important moments of Brazilian history. Indeed, in terms of symbolic reparations, this book offers visibility to women in the political and cultural construction of their country. However, this kind of approach remains in line with Transitional Justice's traditional focus on reporting only direct violence, which often results in a tendency to spectacularize sexual violence and other forms of direct violence, while failing to analyze what happened to women who did not suffer these specific gendered forms of violence.

The book presents women as a vulnerable group of victims, identifying their sexual subordination as a key aspect of their oppression. According to Weber,[854] these initiatives unhelpfully zoom in on a single aspect of their experience while ignoring the complexity of their lives and their different sorts of agency, resistance, and resilience. Hence, the book tends to ignore social and economic rights violations, as well as not mentioning the historical patterns of structural violence which women experienced on an everyday basis. As a result, gender inequalities were left unaddressed by this particular symbolic and official gesture.

8.2.2. THE WORK OF THE AMNESTY COMMISSION: "AMNESTY CARAVANS" AND THE "STAMPS OF MEMORY" PROJECT

As one of the Transitional Justice measures, the reparations programs are becoming less compensation mechanisms and are introducing more complex schemes that include symbolic measures, such as official apologies offered by government authorities and cultural initiatives to discuss the legacy of past atrocities. These gestures – as well as the disclosure of the fate of loved ones

---

[853] REILLY, Niamh, "Seeking Gender Justice in Post-Conflict Transitions: Towards a Transformative Women's Human Rights Approach", *International Journal of Law in Context*, vol. 3/2007, pp. 155–172.

[854] WEBER, Sanne, "From Victims and Mothers to Citizens: Gender-Just Transformative Reparations and the Need for Public and Private Transitions", *International Journal of Transitional Justice,* vol. 12/2018, pp. 88–107.

or assistance in finding their remains and giving them a proper burial – might be very necessary for many widows, sisters and daughters to feel that they are not betraying or selling out their relatives if they accept material compensation, as commented by Rubio-Marín and De Greiff.[855] So, within the Brazilian transition, besides financial compensation, many of the symbolic reparations were left under the responsibility of the Amnesty Commission, including the implementation of the "Amnesty Caravans".[856]

In 2008, the Amnesty Commission began an educational project in which it held public hearings in the locations where persecutions and torture occurred. The project aimed to recall and clarify the historical facts, rescue the dignity of the victims,[857] and create a broader sense of recognition of their suffering. In fact, as observed by Rosito and Damo,[858] such "Amnesty Caravans" were the precursor vehicle for a public debate on a national Transitional Justice initiative and they fostered recognition and assistance to victims and society by trying to make sense of all those painful events of the past.

Against this background, in 2011, the Amnesty Commission organized a "Cultural Amnesty" project specifically in honor of women[859] who participated in the defense of human rights and defied the regime.[860] One year later, in March of 2012, an "Amnesty Caravan" was specially designed to honor the women who resisted the military dictatorship, and at that time there was a public session of the documentary film funded by the Amnesty Commission called *"Repare Bem"*

---

[855] RUBIO-MARÍN, Ruth and DE GREIFF, Pablo, "Women and Reparations", *The International Journal of Transitional Justice*, vol. 1/2007, pp. 318–337.

[856] It is important to observe that the word "amnesty" as applied in these cases ("Amnesty Commission" and/or "Amnesty Caravans") has acquired a different meaning or effect, since it does not refer to the absence of criminal punishment for the perpetrator, but rather refers to the process of accountability in which the State has accepted its responsibility for the human rights violations committed during the period. In fact, the use of the term to designate such a commission and its projects recalls the initial intention of civil society groups when they first began seeking amnesty, which was reserved for those who were in prison or in exile for opposing the authoritarian regime, but not extending to public agents who committed atrocities in the name of the dictatorship. See: MEZAROBBA, Glenda, "Entre Reparações, Meias Verdades e Impunidade: o Difícil Rompimento com o Legado da Ditadura no Brasil", *SUR – Revista Internacional de Direitos Humanos*, vol. 7/2010, pp. 7–25.

[857] *Comissão de Anistia*, "Projetos de Memória e Reparação", http://www.justica.gov.br/seus-direitos/anistia/projetos/projetos-de-memoria-e-reparacao#caravana.

[858] ROSITO, João Baptista Alvares and DAMO, Arlei Sander, "A Reparação por Perseguição Política e os Relatos de Violência nas Caravanas da Anistia", *Horizontes Antropológicos*, vol. 42/2014, pp. 181–212.

[859] The women honored were: Sônia Hipólito, Denize Crispin, Rose Nogueira, Maria Thereza Goulart, Rita Sipahi, and Damaris Oliveira Lucena. Subsequently, requirements for political amnesties were granted to: Margarita Banina Gaudez, Iracema Maria dos Santos, Helena Jório de Vasconcelos, and Linda Tahyah de Melo. See: *Amnesty Commission*, http://www.abi.org.br/anistia-cultural-em-homenagem-ao-dia-da-mulher/.

[860] *Amnesty Commission*, http://www.abi.org.br/anistia-cultural-em-homenagem-ao-dia-da-mulher/.

(Take Heed),[861] and another seven women were recognized as being political persecuted during the military regime.[862] There were also tributes to women who were protagonists in the country's re-democratization.[863]

Additionally, in 2013, the Amnesty Caravan paid a special tribute to women with the acknowledgement of seven more cases of political persecution.[864] In 2015, there was a similar event in which another seven women were celebrated and received State's apologies.[865] By organizing such tributes to women, the Amnesty Commission demonstrates how apology and forgiveness fit into a project of truth-seeking, mainly because, as noted by Blum,[866] it is not only desirable to establish an accurate record of the history of violations – its victims, its perpetrators, and the role of the State apparatus – but action is also required to develop a method of healing the society.

---

[861] After this public session, the documentary film *"Repare Bem"* (Bacuri's Eyes) was officially released in 2013. The documentary was directed by Maria de Medeiros and presents the history of three real women affected by the Brazilian dictatorship: Encarnación Lopes Perez (mother), Denise Crispim (daughter), and Eduarda Crispim Leite (granddaughter). Denise tells about torture she suffered when she was pregnant and describes the birth of her daughter, who was born in a military hospital. Later on Denise went to Chile, and, following the Pinochet *coup d'état*, escaped to Italy with her daughter. Following all these events, Eduarda grew up without knowing her father, Eduardo Leite (whose nickname was "Bacuri", as seen in the alternative title of the movie in English), who was assassinated by the military regime in 1970. Still, in 2013, the documentary won "Best Foreign Film" at the Gramado Film Festival. See: *Ministério da Justiça*, "Filme sobre anistiadas leva 3 prêmios no festival de Gramado", http://www.justica.gov.br/news/filme-sobre-anistiadas-leva-3-premios-no-festival-de-gramado.

[862] These women were: Maria Niedja de Oliveira, Maria Nadja Leite de Oliveira, Maria Angélica Santos Bacellar, Gilda Fioravanti da Silva, Ida Schrage, Hilda Alencar Gil, and Darci Toshiko Miyaki. See: *Amnesty Commission*, http://memoria.ebc.com.br/agenciabrasil/noticia/2012-03-08/comissao-da-anistia-homenageia-mulheres-com-filmes-e-sessao-de-julgamento.

[863] The women honored for their work in the re-democratization of the country were: Encarnación Lopez Peres, Maria Auxiliadora Arantes, Marina Vieira da Paz, Joana D'Arc Vieira Neto, Clara Charf, Adoração Sanchez, Consuelo de Toledo Silva, Damáris Lucena, Izaura Coqueiro, Josephina Bacariça, and Maria Prestes. See: *Amnesty Commission*, http://memoria.ebc.com.br/agenciabrasil/noticia/2012-03-08/comissao-da-anistia-homenageia-mulheres-com-filmes-e-sessao-de-julgamento.

[864] The women acknowledge as political persecuted were: Thereza Sales Escame, Roseli Fátima Senise Lacreta, Monica Tolipan, Maria de Lourdes Toledo Nanci, Maria Déia Vieira, Lélea Amaral, and Maria Oneide Costa Lima. See: *Amnesty Commission*, http://anistiapolitica.org.br/abap/index.php?option=com_content&view=article&id=2475%3A67o-caravana-da-anistia-homenageia-mulheres-com-julgamento&Itemid=54.

[865] The women who received the State's apology were: Sandra Carnio, Selma Benjamin, Maria Fernanda Vieira, Raira Pena Cardoso, Jocely Regina Sardão, and Selma Bandeira Vale. See: *Amnesty Commission*, http://www.brasil.gov.br/cidadania-e-justica/2015/03/justica-anistia-mulheres-vitimas-de-perseguicao-na-ditadura.

[866] BLUM, Carolyn Patty, "Visions of Justice and Accountability: Transitional Justice and Film", in RAMÍREZ-BARAT, Clara (ed.), *Transitional Justice, Culture, and Society Beyond Outreach*, New York, International Center for Transitional Justice and Social Science Research Council, 2014, pp. 461–488.

Additionally, it is important to mention the so-called "Stamps of Memory" Project, which was created by the Amnesty Commission in 2008, in order to rescue the memory of victims through the construction of a collection of oral and audiovisual resources. This project emerged as an alternative to the concentration of memory initiatives only at the governmental level, since it funds some activities that are directly developed and executed by non-governmental organizations and civil society groups. Such initiatives funded by the State gather testimonies, systematize information, and foster cultural events that allow Brazilian society to know the past and extract lessons for the future. In the specific case of reparations for women, the "Stamps of Memory" Project financed the production of two films.

In 2011, the Amnesty Commission granted funds for the documentary film entitled "*Vou Contar Para Meus Filhos*" (I Will Tell My Children), directed by Tuca Siqueira.[867] This film refers to the history of 24 women who were jailed in the *Bom Pastor* Women's Penal Colony, in Recife (state of Pernambuco), between 1969 and 1979. According to the filmmaker, all those women were fighting for social equality and democracy during the military dictatorship, and, 40 years later, they were brought together in order to reflect on their history of solidarity in prison.

As a memoir film, it reinforces the ideal of the strength needed to change the authoritarian regime, a historical period that must be preserved in memory across generations. The title of the documentary already states its purpose: the act of narrating and witnessing, especially for the generations that came after the 1980s. The term "children", used in the title of the film, refers to parenthood, in this case motherhood, which could imply that the women are primarily concerned with providing an explanation about the past for their own children, but it may also function as a metaphor for youth and future generations in general.

In fact, though Siqueira presents experiences and memories about the military period which aid the process of truth-telling – which should be considered one of the main goals of conventional Transitional Justice – the film does not deal with the ways in which the legacy of the past continues to linger into and affect the present and succeeding generations of women. Thus, it does not raise questions for the audience about their actual relationships to the dynamics of transition and transformation in gender-based discrimination.

Later on, in 2013, the documentary film "*Repare Bem*" (Bacuri's Eyes), directed by Maria de Medeiros, was released to the public. The film was a co-production between France, Italy and Brazil, and it was supported by the Amnesty Commission with funding through the "Stamps of Memory" Project,

---

[867] *Amnesty Commission*, "Projeto Marcas da Memória 2010", http://www.justica.gov.br/seus-direitos/anistia/projetos/marcas-da-memoria-i-2010.

as previously described. The film is focused on the testimony of the three female protagonists of the same family (a mother, a daughter, and a granddaughter) and it describes their acts of resistance and resilience during the dictatorship.

The psychological wounds left by torture are noticeable with every word of this family, and the memories of gender relations can also be clearly found in the daughter's speech when she recalls a conversation with her father – who suggested that her role as a rebel was more important than her duties as a mother. But, in fact, the daughter concluded that what made her able to survive all the violence of the period was her own perspective as a mother, which required a tremendous effort on her part to stay alive and to raise her child. The film undeniably portrays the Brazilian military regime's systematic policy of forced disappearances and denial of its human rights violations, thus supporting the process of acknowledgement of the facts of the past during the post-conflict transition.

There is no doubt that the film pays powerful tribute to the memory of those three women of the same family by exploring the legacies of the dictatorship. As a tool for raising general awareness, the film is of immense value. But does it have the capacity to cross the lines of the inequality so strongly instilled in Brazilian history? More specifically, does the film confront viewers with something more radical? What can one say about transformative gender justice regarding *"Repare Bem"*? Can a fact-based human rights film narrative like this one capture the imagination and provoke the empathy of its viewers?

If truth be told, as previously pointed out by Simic and Volcic,[868] in an atmosphere where the narrative of victimhood is dominant, films about violence during the dictatorship have mostly failed to challenge conventional patriarchal assumptions about rape, sex, and gender roles, and continued to reinforce clear-cut narratives of victims and perpetrators in a time of conflict. Thus, the capacity of *"Repare Bem"* to promote and catalyze possibilities for structural change remains very limited.

8.2.3. THE FINAL REPORT OF THE NATIONAL TRUTH COMMISSION (NTC) AND GENDER

The Brazilian National Truth Commission's work was concluded in 2014 with the publication of a Report consistent with its findings, and Chapter 10, Volume 1 of the NTC Report states that sexual violence was a widespread practice of the dictatorial period. In addition, it notes that such violence affected women and men differently, which represents symbolic recognition for those women who challenged the regime.

---

[868] SIMIC, Olivera and VOLCIC, Zala, "In the Land of Wartime Rape: Bosnia, Cinema and Reparation", *Griffith Journal of Law & Human Dignity*, vol. 2/2014, pp. 377–401.

The sexual violence reported by survivors of the dictatorship to the NTC demonstrated that torture had become a way of exercising power and domination, as stated by Borges, Silva and Albuquerque;[869] that is, the gender hierarchy and female sexuality had been mobilized for the purpose of perpetrating violence and breaking the limits of human dignity against women.[870] As proof of this domination, the NTC Report mentioned that some women were identified pejoratively as prostitutes, adulteresses, and deviants – labels seen as inconsistent with their expected roles of wives and mothers. According to their torturers, as a result, those labels made them "deserving" of the sexual violence they suffered. Also, violence was not only restricted to the rape of women in prison, but also extended to threats of rape against the daughters and wives of opponents of the regime while they were interrogated or under torture.

Similarly, specific violence was used as a form of humiliation, depending on whether the victim was pregnant or had recently given birth or was breastfeeding, since the NTC concluded that there were special "experts" in charge of the torture of pregnant women, so that those State actors used specific techniques and care when they wished to either prevent or cause a miscarriage or when they intended to make their victims sterile for life.[871]

Chapter 10 of the NTC Report presents several narratives of women who officially reported the torments they suffered and, based on those statements, the NTC concluded that the repetitive nature of sexual violence committed against women represented an instrument of subjugation that the regime used against female political opponents.[872] Through these narratives, the NTC's work has the merit of removing the social invisibility of the female victims, especially for those still dealing with the stigma that surrounds sexual crimes.[873]

Notwithstanding the merits of its Report, the NTC did not present any specific gender-related recommendations or non-repetition of violence proposals specially linked to gender issues. In fact, the NTC Report is similar to other major reconciliation initiatives that focus on murders, disappearances, torture, deprivation of liberty, kidnappings, illegal detention, and so on. Of course, these are important questions for any Truth Commission, but despite exposing the reality of sexual violence, this type of effort does not represent an advance in

---

[869] BORGES, Rosa Maria Zaia; SILVA, Simone Schuck da; and ALBUQUERQUE, Laura Gigante, "Crimes Sexuais na Ditadura Civil-Militar Brasileira (1964–1985) – Perspectivas das Violências Institucional e de Gênero", *Sistema Penal & Violência*, vol. 8/2016, pp. 3–15.

[870] *NTC Report*, Chapter 10, p. 404, http://cnv.memoriasreveladas.gov.br/images/documentos/Capitulo10/Capitulo%2010.pdf.

[871] *NTC Report*, Chapter 10, p. 411, http://cnv.memoriasreveladas.gov.br/images/documentos/Capitulo10/Capitulo%2010.pdf last.

[872] JOFILLY, Mariana, "Sexual Violence in the Military Dictatorships of Latin America: Who Wants to Know?", *SUR – International Journal on Human Rights*, vol. 13/2016, pp. 165–176.

[873] *NTC Report*, Chapter 10, item 39, p. 422, http://cnv.memoriasreveladas.gov.br/images/documentos/Capitulo10/Capitulo%2010.pdf.

relation to the breadth of women's experiences under authoritarian regimes, as Nesiah has previously observed.[874]

Other aspects of human rights related to women were also not discussed by the NTC Report, such as their extreme vulnerability or how the repressive system affected women forced into exile, those who were made the sole supporters of their households while their husbands were involved in the conflict, or those struggling to locate their disappeared family members, etc. Consequently, while sexual violence is the most critical point, it alone does not capture the complex and multidimensional ways in which women have experienced abuse.

In addition, the NTC should have provided recommendations in the area of education in order to increase society's recognition of gender history and the roles performed by women during the period of repression. In this context, the concept of transformative reparations constitutes a combination of this kind of direct healing, through truth-telling, and wider social support measures. Those measures – such as education, skills training, and access to land and financial resources – are crucial for women, as transformative justice recommends the construction of a "bridge" between corrective and distributive justice.[875]

The public education curriculum could contribute to changing conceptions about gender relations and identities, since, according to Vianna and Ridenti,[876] the school space in Brazil ends up reflecting the sexism that permeates the rest of society by reproducing stereotypes and prejudices that represent girls as "nice, quiet and organized". In that space, they are expected to have neat notebooks and never get dirty or sweaty on the playground, while boys are allowed to be more "agitated and undisciplined", have less organized notebooks, incomplete materials, and are expected to enjoy football. Thus, education could be used to contradict the simplistic explanation of female or male roles at school, as described above. More generally, education could play an important role in instilling citizenship and teaching young people how to claim their rights and participate as citizens in society.

Rubio-Marín and De Greiff have already identified an increasing interest in how to make truth-telling mechanisms sensitive to the specific needs and concerns of women. They claim that there is now a growing sense of the need to "genderise" reparations.[877] What should not be done is to emphasize the

---

[874] NESIAH, Vasuki, "Truth Commissions and Gender: Principles, Policies and Procedures", *Gender Justice Series of International Center for Transitional Justice*, ICTJ, 2006.

[875] WEBER, Sanne, "From Victims and Mothers to Citizens: Gender-Just Transformative Reparations and the Need for Public and Private Transitions", *International Journal of Transitional Justice*, vol. 12/2018, pp. 88–107.

[876] VIANNA, Cláudia and RIDENTI, Sandra, "Relações de Gênero e Escola: das Diferenças ao Preconceito", in AQUINO, Julio G. (ed.), *Diferenças e Preconceito na Escola: Alternativas Teóricas e Práticas*, São Paulo, Summus, 1998, pp. 93–105.

[877] Rubio-Marín and De Greiff cite, by way of illustration that the reparations program recommended in the final report of the Timor Leste Commission for Reception, Truth, and Reconciliation (CAVR) lists gender equity as one of five guiding principles underlying its

violence perpetrated by the State against its political opponents, while allowing the everyday violence perpetrated against women – notably domestic and community violence – to be ignored and overlooked.

Otherwise, this discourse will reduce women to the sum of their injuries, centering their identities on the violations they suffered – and on the perpetrators of that violence – rather than discussing the gendered power relations that lead to the violations in the first place. What should be considered is that physical violence against women in times of conflict and violence is intimately linked to cultures that limit women's rights in peacetime.[878] The "holistic approach" to violence against women takes into account the violence of structural discrimination and analyses social and economic hierarchies through a complex understanding of identity, equality and power. None of those elements were addressed by the NTC in its Transitional Justice initiative.

8.2.4. THE SYMBOLIC REPARATION TO WOMEN AT THE MEMORIAL OF THE RESISTANCE OF SÃO PAULO

The connection between individuals and objects (buildings and artifacts) surrounding them is noticeable, and such association may mark everyone's memories. This symbolism can be further potentialized when these objects, buildings, etc. are linked to a period of fear, repression, torture, suffering, imprisonment, as in a dictatorial background. Consequently, using memories of the people who were imprisoned during the dictatorship and analyzing those reminiscences in relation to buildings and artifacts is an important tool to analyze that historical moment and the social relations that were established in that period.[879] These studies have led to a line of research called archeology of repression and resistance,[880] which was influenced by the paradigmatic work of Argentine professionals who created, in 1984, a forensic archeology group (*Equipo Argentino de Antropología Forense* – EAFF) that was one of the

---

overall conception. Moreover, Morocco's Equity and Reconciliation Commission (IER) made gender mainstreaming one of the priorities in its reparations policy. In addition, the authors also describe that Colombia's National Commission for Reparation and Reconciliation (CNRR) has established a specific unit to ensure that all policies and recommendations of the Commission take into account the specific needs of women and other marginalized groups. See: Rubio-Marín, Ruth and de Greiff, Pablo, "Women and Reparations", *The International Journal of Transitional Justice*, vol. 1/2007, pp. 318–337.

[878] Gready, Paul and Robins, Simon, "Rethinking Civil Society and Transitional Justice: Lessons from Social Movements and 'New' Civil Society", *The International Journal of Human Rights*, vol. 21/2017, pp. 956–975.

[879] Sousa, Priscila Paula de, "Memória, Objetos e Edifícios – Uma Análise Arquológica Sobre o Edifício Que Sediou o DEOPS/SP", *Revista de Arqueologia Pública*, vol. 10/2014, pp. 177–194.

[880] Funari, Pedro Paulo and Zarankin, Andres, *Arqueología de la Represión y Resistência em América Latina (1960–1980)*, Catamarca, Encuentro, 2006.

pioneering groups to apply forensic science to the documentation of human rights violations.[881]

So it was, based on the reflections of the archeology of repression and resistance – that is, from the collection of testimonies of violations of human rights and the understanding of how the occupation of a building took place – that the research for the assembly of the *Memorial of the Resistance of São Paulo* was started. In fact, as pointed out by Soares,[882] a place that has harbored terror and suffering can be transformed into a memorial for the purpose of providing the community with a space for human rights education, and at the same time it can be observed as a form of collective reparation for society. Moreover, the Memorial functions as a physical, tangible, concrete vehicle for revealing the truth and strengthening the memory of the victims, which serves to give voice to those who have suffered torture and other cruelties and to tackle the denial surrounding the facts linked to the dictatorial period.

In the assembly of such a Memorial, the importance of counting on the collaboration of emotional memory of persons who were directly involved in human rights violations is due to the fact that the building was not built for the purpose of becoming a prison and, consequently, a space of political repression during the dictatorship. In fact, the place was adapted to house a jail by means of the creation of cells in the ground floor, since this building was originally constructed, in 1914, as a warehouse and office of the Sorocabana Railway Station. However, in 1942, it started to be used by the State Department of Political and Social Order of São Paulo (Deops/SP), and during the dictatorial period the building was used to keep and interrogate prisoners considered subversive by the regime.

Since 2009, by the initiative of the government of the state of São Paulo, it hosts the *Memorial of the Resistance*, which is dedicated to the preservation of the memories of political repression that occurred in the Brazilian republican period.[883] And among those testimonies that assisted with the preparation of the Memorial are those of two women who were imprisoned in this building during the dictatorship: Rose Nogueira and Elza Lobo. The journalist Rose Nogueira was arrested, in 1969, on the grounds that she and her husband used to provide their home as a meeting point for opponents of the regime.[884]

---

[881] For more information about the Argentine Forensic Anthropology Team see: https://eaaf.typepad.com/founding_of_eaaf/.
[882] SOARES, Inês Virgínia Prado, "Novas Perspectivas Para a Arqueologia da Repressão e da Resistência no Brasil Depois da Comissão Nacional da Verdade", *Revista de Arqueologia Pública*, vol. 10/2014, pp. 177–194.
[883] *Memorial of Resistance of São Paulo*, http://memorialdaresistenciasp.org.br/memorial-en/.
[884] See more about Rose Nogueira at http://memoriasdaditadura.org.br/biografias-da-resistencia/rose-nogueira/index.html.

Elza Lobo was working for the Treasury Department of São Paulo State when she joined an opposition group to the dictatorship; due to her involvement with this movement called *Ação Popular* (Popular Action) she was arrested on November 10, 1969. When Elza Lobo left prison, in 1971, she went into exile and only returned to Brazil in 1979.[885]

Although the whole history of this building is important, we call attention to the symbolic tribute paid to the political prisoner Elza Lobo. This tribute refers to a red carnation which is placed in one of the jail cells. In that chamber, where dozens of political prisoners were jailed during the dictatorship, the red carnation contrasts with the coolness of the environment. This is because, according to Elza Lobo's testimony, at Christmas in 1969, while she was detained, she asked her family to bring flowers for her. Then, Elza's family delivered her several red carnations. Feeling compassion towards others prisoners, Elza distributed the red carnations among them and, according to her memories, she wanted to give them "the smell of freedom".[886]

Today, symbolically, cells where the combatants of the dictatorship have stayed are filled with their memories. And, in one of them, the most visited of all, lies an always fresh red carnation in honor of Elza Lobo and her act of solidarity. In this case, as Rago has noted,[887] it is not a matter of victimizing women once more, crying indefinitely for their pain, or naively constructing heroic and idealized figures. Rather, it is a question of allowing the plurality of History not to be obliterated by the supposedly universal narrative, which always excludes and stigmatizes; the exhibition of the cell with the red carnation in honor of a woman is, indeed, a matter of creating space for the differentiated expression of the memory within all social sectors.

8.3. STRUGGLES TO BE FACED

8.3.1. EMBLEMATIC SETBACK: THE *INÊS ETIENNE CASE*

Once these remarks about gender and symbolic reparations have been made, it will be observed that there are still gaps to be remedied. This is because, while social transformation has created conditions for women to become empowered and to report sexual violence they have suffered, there are still sectors which

---

[885] *Memorial da Resistência do Estado de São Paulo*, http://www.memorialdaresistenciasp.org.br/memorial/default.aspx?c=entrevistados&idEntrevista=126&idEntrevistado=70&mn=56.

[886] For the testimony of Elza Lobo at the Memorial of Resistance see: http://www.memorialdaresistenciasp.org.br/memorial/default.aspx?c=entrevistados&identrevistado=70&identrevista=12&mn=56.

[887] RAGO, Margareth, "Desejo de Memória", *Revista Labrys*, vol. 15/2009, https://www.labrys.net.br/labrys15/sumarioditadura.htm.

seems detached from the Transitional Justice goals,[888] and this theory may be observed according to the history of a woman named Inês Etienne Romeu and the failure of the Judicial System in dealing with past atrocities committed against her during the dictatorship.[889]

It is a fact that, by the end of 2017, the Federal Public Prosecution Office had already filed about 30 criminal proceedings related the violations of human rights committed during the Brazilian dictatorship, but none of these criminal cases have been concluded yet. Some of these cases were refused as soon as they were proposed (as in the *Inês Etienne Case*) and others have been analyzed, but they still have not reached a final judgment.[890] So, among these cases, there was the criminal complaint related to the torture and rape of Inês Etienne Romeu, which action mostly emphasized sexual violence and rape. Certainly, within the range of the dictatorship's criminal actions, this was the most emblematic action on gender violence (illegal detention, torture and rape of a woman).

Regarding Inês Etienne Romeu, she joined the armed struggle against the military dictatorship and participated in organizations opposing the regime such as the *Vanguarda Armada Revolucionária – Palmares* (VAR-Palmares) and the *Organização Revolucionária Marxista Política Operária* (POLOP). On May 5, 1971, Inês was arrested in São Paulo accused of participating in the kidnapping of the Swiss ambassador Giovanni Bucher, which occurred months earlier in Rio de Janeiro. She became only survivor of the clandestine torture center named *Casa da Morte* (The House of Death), located in the city of Petrópolis (Rio de Janeiro state), where she was held in illegal detention for 96 days and suffered from torture and rape. Later in 1971, she was sentenced to life imprisonment, and was only released in 1979, as the Amnesty Law came into force.[891]

After her release, Inês Etienne started to focus on denouncing and illuminating crimes committed during the military dictatorship, and her presence in the post-dictatorship landscape has always been relevant due to her resistance, but mainly because she did not accept remain silent and worked hard to identify the exact location of the secret center where she was tortured. But, her testimony[892] was not enough to bring her rapist and torturer to justice.

---

[888] JOFILLY, Mariana, "Sexual Violence in the Military Dictatorships of Latin America: Who Wants to Know?", *SUR – International Journal on Human Rights*, vol. 13/2016, pp. 165–176.

[889] REGO, Tânia, "Juiz Federal rejeita denúncia contra militar acusado de estuprar presa política", *Último Segundo*, March 9, 2017, https://ultimosegundo.ig.com.br/brasil/2017-03-09/juiz.html.

[890] 2017 Report of the Transitional Justice Working Group of the Federal Public Prosecutor's Office, http://www.mpf.mp.br/atuacao-tematica/ccr2/publicacoes/roteiro-atuacoes/005_17_crimes_da_ditadura_militar_digital_paginas_unicas.pdf.

[891] For more information see: *Memórias da Ditadura, Biografias da Resistência*, Inês Etienne Romeu, http://memoriasdaditadura.org.br/biografias-da-resistencia/ines-etienne-romeu/index.html.

[892] On March 25, 2014, Inês Etienne Romeu recognized six of her torturers and jailers during an audience of the National Truth Commission, held specifically on the subject of the

Following the previous perceptions of the Brazilian Supreme Court,[893] once again the Judiciary deduced that crimes related to the dictatorship should be forgotten since the Brazilian Amnesty Law is still in force, and also because the great majority of judges still refute the idea that those were crimes against humanity. So, by applying rules applied to ordinary crimes, they have been constantly closing down such cases based on statutes of limitations combined with the effects of the Amnesty Law. But, for the Inter-American Court of Human Rights – which convicted Brazil expressly because of the impunity of the crimes committed during the dictatorship (the *Gomes Lund Case* in 2010 and the *Herzog Case* in 2018) – these same offenses are not covered by statutes of limitation or by the amnesty precisely because they are considered crimes against humanity.

This judicial's setback arrived exactly on International Women's Day of 2017, and the judgment was issued by the Federal Court of Petrópolis (Rio de Janeiro) in the criminal action related to the torture and rape of Inês Etienne. Symbolically, such rejection of the criminal complaint represents an outrage to the rights of all women who were victims of violence, since Inês Etienne was treated as a dangerous terrorist, and her testimony, as a victim, was not valued as evidence of crime.[894] On the other hand, much of the evidence brought before the court in this criminal action came from the 2014 NTC Report and constitutes official evidence collected by the Brazilian State and, therefore, benefits from the presumption of being the endorsed truth.

The decision causes perplexity: why are gender stereotypes and prejudices still so prevalent? The case proves that many judges often adopt rigid standards of behavior that they consider appropriate for women, and penalize those who do not act according to these categories. In such a way, these stereotypes also affect the credibility of women's voices, arguments and testimonies. Regarding stereotypes, it is remarkable that even during the dictatorship those women who became political opponents to the military regime were seen as "deviant" beings or as unusual persons, because "normal" women were in the space meant for them: at home, taking care of their husbands and children.[895] Unfortunately, this

---

clandestine center of torture named "*Casa da Morte*" (House of Death), which was located in Petrópolis/Rio de Janeiro. See: *Memórias da Ditadura, Biografias da Resistência*, Inês Etienne Romeu, http://memoriasdaditadura.org.br/biografias-da-resistencia/ines-etienne-romeu/index.html. She died aged 72 in 2015.

[893] Reference is made to the judgment of ADPF no. 153, which in 2010 ruled that the Amnesty Law should continue to be applied in Brazil. For more information, see Chapter 4 of this book.

[894] NITHAHARA, Akemi, "O Terceiro Estupro de Inês Etienne Romeu: Justiça Rejeita a Denúncia de Presa Política", *HuffPost Brasil*, March 9, 2017, http://www.huffpostbrasil.com/2017/03/09/o-terceiro-estupro-de-ines-etienne-romeu-justica-rejeita-denu_a_21878754/.

[895] COLLING, Ana Maria, *A Resistência da Mulher à Ditadura Militar no Brasil*, Rio de Janeiro, Rosa dos Tempos, 1997.

same stereotype from the former times came to light on the occasion of the Inês Etienne judgment, in 2017.

Indeed, regarding those stereotypes, the UN Committee on the Elimination of All Forms of Discrimination against Women (the CEDAW Committee) has recognized that the discrimination of women based on sex and gender is inextricably linked with other factors that affect women, such as race, ethnicity, religion or belief, health, status, age, class, caste and sexual orientation and gender identity, which all have negative impacts on women.[896] And it is not new that gender stereotypes are among the root causes of violence against women; in fact, the CEDAW Committee recognizes that wrongful stereotypes perpetuate and justify gender-based violence against women.[897] Finally, this regrettable decision in 2017 shows that women's right to justice in cases of violations committed during the dictatorship has not progressed. The Brazilian judicial system failed in what could have been a powerful example of symbolic reparation, that is, a judgment that could recognize the singularities surrounding human rights violations committed against women.

Later on, the Public Prosecutor's Office responsible for the *Etienne Case* refused to accept this previous judgment and proposed an appeal and, in August of 2019, the Regional Federal Court reconsidered the arguments initially provided about the sexual violence, so, at the current time the crime continues under judicial investigation and it is still pending a decision by.[898] The presiding judge of this second judgment was a female judge and she based her decision on the jurisprudence of the Inter-American Court of Human Rights (the *Araguaia Case* and the *Herzog Case*) and in the international theory of crimes against humanity,[899] which supersedes the understanding that a national amnesty law would block the analysis and judgment of such cases.[900]

Although this Judiciary's loophole, which still requires time to be resolved and according to Meyer and Carvalho reflects a precarious application of concepts and categories of international law, but also a political and ideological position, Inês Etienne was well-recognized for her efforts towards the protection of human rights in Brazil. In 2009, the Secretary of Human Rights of the Republic granted

---

[896] CEDAW, "General Recommendation no. 28 on the Core Obligations of State Parties under Article 2 of the Convention on the Elimination of All Forms of Discrimination against Women", CEDAW/G/GC/28 (2010), para. 18.
[897] CEDAW, "General Recommendation no. 19: Violence against Women", A/47/38 (1992).
[898] *Tribunal Regional Federal*, "TRF2 recebe denúncia e torna réu sargento acusado de tortura na década de 1970", August 14, 2019, https://www10.trf2.jus.br/portal/trf2-recebe-denuncia-e-torna-reu-sargento-acusado-de-tortura-na-decada-de-1970/.
[899] *El País*, "Em Caso Inédito, Militar será Julgado por Estupro de Presa Política na Ditadura", August 15, 2019, https://brasil.elpais.com/brasil/2019/08/14/politica/1565802126_256909.html.
[900] For detailed information about the Amnesty Law blocking criminal investigations in Brazil, see Chapter 4 of this Book.

her the "Human Rights Premium of 2009" in the category of right to truth and memory.[901] And, in 2016, just one year after her death, the Truth Commission of São Paulo organized an event in her honor.[902]

8.3.2. NORMALIZATION OF VIOLENCE AGAINST WOMEN: CONTINUUMS AND INEQUALITIES

In order to observe these denials of past atrocities related to women (as in the *Inês Etienne Case*) and the normalization of violence against women during the dictatorship as well as in the present day, we would like to mention that, during the 2016 Brazilian election campaign, a candidate for São Paulo city council was told that, as she was a feminist, she deserved to be raped and tortured, as used to happen during the military regime.[903] Also, in 2016, a poll carried out by *Datafolha* identified that 37 per cent of those interviewed agreed with the statement "a woman who wears provocative clothing cannot complain if she is raped", meaning that one-third of Brazilians blame women who are raped.[904] Even after 30 years of democratic rule in Brazil, all these insights demonstrate the ongoing connection between political torture, sexual crime, and rape as a weapon in political combat and reveal the continued existence of the conservatism that marked the military dictatorship.

On the other hand, in recent years, Brazil has achieved success in reducing poverty and income equality, since, according to World Bank data,[905] the poverty headcount ratio (the number of people living on less than international poverty line) has fallen markedly, from 21.6% of the population in 1990 to 4.8% in 2017. Also, Brazil made progress in reducing gender inequality; according to the results of a 2018 study by the Brazilian Institute of Geography and Statistics (IBGE),[906]

---

[901] Agência Brasil, "Morre Única Sobrevivente da Casa da Morte de Petrópolis, no Rio", April 27, 2015, http://www.ebc.com.br/cidadania/2015/04/morre-unica-sobrevivente-da-casa-da-morte-de-petropolis-no-rio.

[902] *Prefeitura de São Paulo*, http://www.prefeitura.sp.gov.br/cidade/secretarias/direitos_humanos/comissao_da_memoria_e_verdade/noticias/?p=215906.

[903] BERGAMO, Mônica, "Feministas Merecem Tortura, Ouve Candidata à Câmara Municipal em SP", *Folha de São Paulo*, 02 October 2016, https://www1.folha.uol.com.br/colunas/monicabergamo/2016/10/1818623-feministas-merecem-tortura-ouve-candidata-a-camara-municipal-em-sp.shtml.

[904] MENA, Fernanda, "Um Terço dos Brasileiros Culpa Mulheres por Estupros Sofridos", *Folha de São Paulo*, 21 September 2016, https://www1.folha.uol.com.br/cotidiano/2016/09/1815301-um-terco-dos-brasileiros-culpa-mulheres-por-estupros-sofridos.shtml.

[905] *The World Bank*, Poverty & Equity Data Portal, http://povertydata.worldbank.org/poverty/country/BRA.

[906] *Instituto Brasileiro de Geografia e Estatística* (IBGE), "Estatísticas de Gênero – Indicadores Sociais das Mulheres no Brasil", June 8, 2018, https://www.ibge.gov.br/estatisticas-novoportal/multidominio/genero/20163-estatisticas-de-genero-indicadores-sociais-das-mulheres-no-brasil.html?=&t=publicacoes.

in 2016, the school attendance rate for boys aged from 15 to 17 years old was 63.2%, while the same rate for girls was 73.5%. And in terms of education, the highest percentage difference by sex is at the tertiary level of schooling, in which the percentage of men who completed tertiary education was 15.5%, while the percentage of women reached 21.5%; that is, an indicator 37.9% higher for women than that of men. So, there is no doubt that at the current time Brazilian women are generally more educated, with participation in tertiary education significantly exceeding male participation. Likewise, the ratio of female to male labor force participation rate increased from 52.2% in 1990 to 63.9% in 1995, 66.7% in 2000 and 73.3% in 2010.

Despite these achievements, however, inequality remains at relatively high levels.[907] For instance, gender pay gaps still persist in Brazil since, according to this same 2018 study by the IBGE, in 2016, in the category of workers who had completed tertiary education, women received 63.4% of men's wages. As for the indicator of the participation of women in managerial positions – that is, the insertion of women into leadership positions in both the public and private sectors in Brazil – 60.9% of managerial positions were occupied by men and 39.1% by women, in 2016.[908]

According to the Gender Gap Index (GGI) developed by the World Economic Forum, in 2018, Brazil was ranked 95 out of 149 countries.[909] Also, on most social indicators, Brazilian women continue to bear the brunt of time allocated to family chores; in 2016, they devoted an average of 18.1 hours per week to caring for their families and housekeeping, whereas men devoted an average of 10.5 hours per week to such tasks (thus, women spent about 73% more time on care and household chores than men).[910]

But what could explain the gender gap in Brazil? According to a study related to women's work and employment in Brazil,[911] the gap appears to reflect

---

[907] AGÉNOR, Pierre-Richard and CANUTO, Otaviano, "Gender Equality and Economic Growth in Brazil: A Long-Run Analysis", *The World Bank Policy Research Working Paper no. 6348*, 2013, https://openknowledge.worldbank.org/bitstream/handle/10986/13174/wps6348.pdf?sequence=1.

[908] *Instituto Brasileiro de Geografia e Estatística* (IBGE), "Estatísticas de Gênero – Indicadores Sociais das Mulheres no Brasil", June 8, 2018, https://www.ibge.gov.br/estatisticas-novoportal/multidominio/genero/20163-estatisticas-de-genero-indicadores-sociais-das-mulheres-no-brasil.html?=&t=publicacoes.

[909] *The World Economic Forum*, "The Global Gender Gap Report 2018", https://www.weforum.org/reports/the-global-gender-gap-report-2018.

[910] *Instituto Brasileiro de Geografia e Estatística* (IBGE), "Estatísticas de Gênero – Indicadores Sociais das Mulheres no Brasil", June 8, 2018, https://www.ibge.gov.br/estatisticas-novoportal/multidominio/genero/20163-estatisticas-de-genero-indicadores-sociais-das-mulheres-no-brasil.html?=&t=publicacoes.

[911] VAN KLAVEREN, Maarten; TIJDENS, Kea; HUGHIE-WILLIAMS, Melanie; and RAMOS MARTIN, Nuria, "An Overview of Women's Work and Employment in Brazil", *Amsterdam Institute of Advanced Labour Studies (AIAS) Working Paper no. 83*, University of Amsterdam, 2009, https://dare.uva.nl/search?identifier=99daf4ba-e84d-4b48-a3c4-fb60a53be0cb.

Chapter 8. A Gendered Approach to Brazilian Transitional Justice

discriminatory practices and social norms. In fact, attitudes among many Brazilians are still very traditional and conservative, with many in public opinion surveys supporting the notion that men hold public power and control over the domestic space, and men have control over women and their bodies. Thus, even though there have been great social transformations in the last decades, the patriarchal order remains very present in Brazilian culture and it is found on a daily basis, in the devaluation of all feminine characteristics, in domestic violence, and in the acceptance of sexual violence.[912]

In the political sphere, there remains a contrast between the success of women seeking national office, and their struggles in lower level contests. While women have made progress in Presidential elections,[913] they continue to lag behind men in legislative and local elections.[914] Regarding women's participation in the political sphere, although they represented half of the population during the 1980s, 1990s, and until 2010 (the date of the last demographic census conducted by IBGE[915]), it is still far from the level it should be at compared with their numbers in terms of population. Based on the 2018 elections for the National Congress, women made up 52% of the country's electorate, however, only 15% of federal deputies[916] and 13% of senators.[917] With these results, the percentage of Brazilian women in political office[918] is below the world average of 24.9% combined for the lower (federal deputies) and upper (senators) houses of the legislature and below the average for the Americas of 30.6 per cent.[919] Although there has been legislation in force in Brazil since 1995 that aims to reduce the under-representation of women in politics through legally-mandated gender quotas stipulated for the candidate list of each party,[920] these percentages constitute an imbalance that, in fact, denies women effective participation

---

[912] *Instituto de Pesquisas Econômicas Aplicadas* (IPEA), "Tolerância Social à Violência contra as Mulheres", April 4, 2014, http://www.ipea.gov.br/portal/index.php?option=com_content&view=article&id=21971.

[913] Reference is made to tenure of Ms. Dilma Rousseff as President of Brazil, from 2011 to 2016.

[914] AGUILAR, Rosario; CUNOW, Saul; and DESPOSATO, Scott, "Choice Sets, Gender, and Candidate Choice in Brazil", *Electoral Studies*, vol. 39/2015, pp. 230–242.

[915] *Instituto Brasileiro de Geografia e Estatística* (IBGE), "Censo Demográgico 2010", https://ww2.ibge.gov.br/home/estatistica/populacao/censo2010/default.shtm.

[916] See: http://www2.camara.leg.br/camaranoticias/noticias/POLITICA/564035-BANCADA-FEMININA-NA-CAMARA-SOBE-DE-51-PARA-77-DEPUTADAS.html.

[917] See: https://g1.globo.com/politica/eleicoes/2018/eleicao-em-numeros/noticia/2018/10/08/no-de-mulheres-eleitas-se-mantem-no-senado-mas-aumenta-na-camara-e-nas-assembleias.ghtml.

[918] According to the 2019 Inter-Parliamentary Union data, Brazil was ranked 133 out of 191 countries, http://archive.ipu.org/wmn-e/ClaSSif.htm.

[919] *Inter-Parliamentary Union*. "Women in National Parliaments 2019", http://archive.ipu.org/wmn-e/arc/world010119.htm.

[920] This refers to the so-called "legislative quotas", which focus on the candidate stage and requires that all parties nominate a certain proportion of women, first introduced by Law 9,100 (1995), then by Law 9,504 (1997), Law 12,034 (2009), and Law 13,165 (2015).

in the decision-making inherent to the political process in a representative democracy.[921]

This persistent disproportion has also been denounced by researchers arguing that this gender gap in the political sphere is linked to social and cultural problems that discourage women in this domain, like the vestiges buried deep in the female subconscious of a thousand-year-old culture of women's inferiority.[922] In addition, as previously stated, there are issues related to the patriarchal culture of the country, which is marked by sexism and where the "double shift" for women (one at work and another at home) is still criticized.[923]

In fact, as observed by Gruneich and Cordeiro,[924] political gender violence is one of the causes of the underrepresentation of women in parliament, since these women suffer violence before they even launch their candidacy, and they are exposed to political violence when they are holding a public career, when they are leaders of professional associations, State-owned companies and so on. Also, when a woman is elected, the political violence becomes more evident, when for instance she is not appointed as a member of a commission, or as a leader of her party or as a coordinator of an important project. They are also constantly interrupted and questioned about their clothes, physical appearance or weight, as if these characteristics influenced the exercise of their mandate or function.

Facing this reality, the recently enacted Law no. 14,192 (2021) may bring encouragement to those women in politics since it defines political violence against women as any action, conduct or omission aimed at preventing, hindering or restricting women's political rights. In order to address these harmful practices, the new law aims to prevent, repress and combat political violence against women in spaces and activities related to the exercise of their political rights and public functions, and to ensure the participation of women in debates.

On the other hand, in addition to the official recognition of sexual and gender violence committed by State agents during the dictatorship, as granted by the NTC, it is crucial to consider policies to fight against sexual and gender violence in the future. This is because – as Borges, Silva and Albuquerque[925]

---

[921] RODRIGUES, Ricardo José Pereira, "A Evolução da Política de Cotas de Gênero na Legislação Eleitoral e Partidária e a Sub-representação Feminina no Parlamento Brasileiro", *Revista Eletrônica Direito e Política*, vol. 12/2017, pp. 27–51.
[922] MASCHIO, Jane, "Eficácia/Ineficácia do Sistema de Cotas para Mulheres", *Resenha Eleitoral*, vol. 10/2003, pp. 46–62.
[923] BOLOGNESI, Bruno, "A Cota Eleitoral de Gênero: Política Pública ou Engenharia Eleitoral?", *Paraná Eleitoral Revista Brasileira de Direito Eleitoral e Ciência Política*, vol. 1/2012, pp. 113–129.
[924] GRUNEICH, Danielle and CORDEIRO, Iara, "Violência Política de Gênero: das Violências Invisíveis aos Aspectos Criminais", *Boletim CONJUR*, November 3, 2020, https://www.conjur.com.br/2020-nov-03/gruneich-cordeiro-violencia-politica-genero.
[925] BORGES, Rosa Maria Zaia; SILVA, Simone Schuck da; and ALBUQUERQUE, Laura Gigante, "Crimes Sexuais na Ditadura Civil-Militar Brasileira (1964–1985) – Perspectivas das Violências Institucional e de Gênero", *Sistema Penal & Violência*, vol. 8/2016, pp. 3–15.

have already stated – the risk of not looking at the violent procedures of the past is that this practice may be repeated in a democratic State, perpetuating the techniques of an androcentric and violent culture. Hence, the consequence of failure to confront a specific past period related to gender inequality – which slowly started to be addressed during the 2000s with the work of the Amnesty Commission and later with the NTC – may be observed in the increasing rates of domestic violence in Brazil, which we address below.

During the last three decades there have been important transformations in the social perception of sexual violence[926] – mainly because of the creation of women's police stations to provide specific assistance in such cases (in 1985); the creation of the Maria da Penha Act (in 2006), which is a landmark piece of legislation responding to domestic violence with a multidisciplinary approach (prevention, protection, and criminalization); and the creation of the crime of femicide (in 2015) and the crime of sexual harassment (in 2018). All these legal frameworks demonstrate that gender violence has been identified as a social problem in Brazil.

However, despite all these great achievements, a 2018 survey conducted by the *Fórum Brasileiro de Segurança Pública* concluded that the country is still very violent for women, since in 2017, on a daily basis, 606 women suffered from domestic violence (for a total of 221,238 reported cases) and 60,018 rapes were reported for the year (an index which increased by 8.4 per cent when compared with 2016).[927] Also, in a 2019 survey which evaluated the victimization of women in Brazil, the *Fórum Brasileiro de Segurança Pública* confirmed that 3 in every 10 women still suffer violence (including verbal offense, threats, beating, chasing, pushing, sexual offenses, gun threat, strangulation, shooting, and stabbing) in the country.[928]

And why are we presenting these critical overviews based on gender inequalities and gender violence? Because, as pointed out by Weber,[929] in terms of Transitional Justice, beyond compensation or immediate relief, women most desire structural change in their position within society. Moreover, when we consider gender transformative reparations, we not only seek recognition, but

---

[926] SANTOS, Cecília MacDowell, "De Delegacia da Mulher à Lei Maria da Penha: Absorção/ Tradução de Demandas Feministas pelo Estado", *Revista Crítica de Ciências Sociais*, vol. 89/2010, pp. 153–170.

[927] *Fórum Brasileiro de Segurança Pública*, "12° Anuário Brasileiro de Segurança Pública 2018", http://www.forumseguranca.org.br/publicacoes/anuario-brasileiro-de-seguranca-publica-2018/.

[928] *Fórum Brasileiro de Segurança Pública*, "2019 Report Visível e Invisível: A Vitimização de Mulheres no Brasil", http://www.forumseguranca.org.br/publicacoes/visivel-e-invisivel-a-vitimizacao-de-mulheres-no-brasil-2-edicao/.

[929] WEBER, Sanne, "From Victims and Mothers to Citizens: Gender-Just Transformative Reparations and the Need for Public and Private Transitions", *International Journal of Transitional Justice*, vol. 12/2018, pp. 88–107.

we are also interested in reinforcing women's role as social and economic actors; we are aiming to enhance their autonomy.

This is definitely a long-term process which cannot be expected to produce results only by the initiatives described in this chapter, since they are part of a much broader goal linked to the so-called right to development[930] and the millennium development goals (MDGs).[931] But, viewing those symbolic reparations (emerging from official mechanisms of Transitional Justice as described here) as a part of a wider strategy to transform gender inequality, if we look at the rates of participation of Brazilian women in education, in the labor force, and in the political sphere and the levels of increasing domestic violence, in the recent democratic period, the conclusion is that there is still much to be done. In this sense, the Brazilian scenario points to what Boesten and Wilding previously observed: that it would be inadequate to talk of "transition" – moving from a context of chronic violence to a more "peaceful" society – if these results are more of the same, just under different circumstances.[932]

8.3.3. GENDER IDENTITY AND TRANSITIONAL JUSTICE: BEYOND THE BINARY PERSPECTIVE

Although Transitional Justice was initially silent on gender identity, lately, as observed above, there has been an increasing application of gender lenses in the field, as presented by researchers like Nesiah; Rubio-Marín and De Greiff; Reilly; and Boesten and Wilding.[933] However, diverse gendered experiences

---

[930] The right to development can be found in the provisions of the Charter of the United Nations, the Universal Declaration on Human Rights and the two International Human Rights Covenants. In 1986, the United Nations proclaimed the Declaration on the Right to Development as "an inalienable human right by virtue of which every human person and all peoples are entitled to participate in, contribute to, and enjoy economic, social, cultural and political development, in which all human rights and fundamental freedoms can be fully realized" (article 1). *United Nations Human Rights Office of the High Commissioner*, https://www.ohchr.org/EN/Issues/Development/Pages/Backgroundrtd.aspx.

[931] Among the eight millennium development goals are: to promote gender equality and empower women, see: *2000 The United Nations Millennium Declaration*, http://www.un.org/millenniumgoals/.

[932] BOESTEN, Jelke and WILDING, Polly, "Transformative Gender Justice: Setting an Agenda", *Women's Studies International Forum*, vol. 51/2015, pp. 75–80.

[933] NESIAH, Vasuki, "Discussion Lines on Gender and Transitional Justice: An Introductory Essay Reflecting on the ICTJ Bellagio Workshop on Gender and Transitional Justice", *Columbia Journal of Gender and Law*, vol. 15(3)/2006.; RUBIO-MARÍN, Ruth and DE GREIFF, Pablo, "Women and Reparations", *The International Journal of Transitional Justice*, vol. 1/2007, pp. 318–337; REILLY, Niamh, "Seeking Gender Justice in Post-Conflict Transitions: Towards a Transformative Women's Human Rights Approach", *International Journal of Law in Context*, vol. 3/2007, pp. 155–172; BOESTEN, Jelke and WILDING, Polly, "Transformative Gender Justice: Setting an Agenda", *Women's Studies International Forum*, vol. 51/2015, pp. 75–80.

remain unaccounted for, and existing Transitional Justice processes have largely disappointed in advancing important approaches. Maybe this is because, as Schulz said,[934] the increasing discussion about gender and Transitional Justice is largely the one about whether or not, and how, Transitional processes are to promote rapid gender justice for female victims of violence.

As an outcome, such assessment has in many cases resulted in severely limited and reductionist accountability for gendered victimhood, since they are mostly based on women as vulnerable victims who are in need of external protection. At the same time, those evaluations envisage men as the naturally violent perpetrators or as custodians of peace. In addition, the male character has frequently been associated with certain types of masculinity like "the warrior", "the General", "the revolutionary", "the peacemaker". Consequently, all these perspectives tend only to reinforce a hetero-normative binary point of view.

Indeed, as Fobear and Baines recently verified,[935] the field and practice of Transitional Justice remains relatively silent on questions of sexuality and gendered hypotheses of power and violence, and it has failed to deepen the investigation of the intersection of gender identities and other dimensions of persecution. Therefore, intersectional analytical lenses urgently need to be applied to mechanisms of Transitional Justice to guarantee the full rights of LGBTI persons,[936] and this approach is not different in the Brazilian case.

In fact, in Brazil, this hetero-normative binary point of view finds implications even during the dictatorship and within the armed groups opposing the regime, since as examined by Green, the revolutionaries who were caught up in desires for their fellow comrades or other people of the same sex had to face manifestations of hate, hostility, rejection, and so on.[937] Besides, Green described that during

---

[934] SCHULZ, Philipp, "Towards Inclusive Gender in Transitional Justice: Gaps, Blind-Spots and Opportunities", *Journal of Intervention and Statebuilding*, October 21, 2019.

[935] FOBEAR, Katherine and BAINES, Erin, "Pushing the Conversation forward: the Intersections of Sexuality and Gender Identity in Transitional Justice", *The International Journal of Human Rights*, vol. 24/2020, pp. 307–312.

[936] We use the concept of LGBTI for lesbian, gay, bisexual, transgender and intersex people. In addition, we follow the definition presented by Bueno-Hansen: "Gender and sexual minorities refers to individuals that do not fit into the cisgender and/or heterosexual majorities or norms. Cisgender indicates those individuals that identify with their sex assigned at birth ... In contrast, transgender names those individuals that do not fit, or care to fit, the normative male-female binary". See: BUENO-HANSEN, Pascha, "The Emerging LGBTI Rights Challenge to Transitional Justice in Latin America", *International Journal of Transitional Justice*, vol. 12/2018, pp. 126–145.

[937] To explain such context, James Green wrote: "As a whole, the revolutionary Left considered homosexuality inappropriate and unacceptable sexual behavior ... Dozens of former Brazilian revolutionaries who joined the armed struggle in the 1960s and early 1970s have written accounts of this period, but most authors maintain silence about sexuality, and especially homosexuality. The noted exception is Herbert Daniel, whose memoir, "*Passagem paao o próximo sonho*" (Ticket to the Next Dream), deals extensively with his experiences as an urban guerrilla and his repressed homosexuality". See: GREEN, James N., "Who Is the Macho Who Wants to Kill Me?" Male Homosexuality, Revolutionary Masculinity, and the

the 1960s the discourse about morality was deeply rooted in ideological frameworks like: (i) the link of homosexuality to bourgeois behavior; (ii) the medical and psychiatric ideas that homosexuality was a type of physical and emotional degeneration; (iii) the traditional Catholic teachings that considered homosexuality to be a moral abomination; (iv) anti-imperialist sentiment associating homosexual behavior and criticisms of homophobia with foreign (U.S.) influences; and (v) popular notions that rejected male homosexuality because it implied the feminization of masculinity and disrupted a pervasive construction of revolutionary masculinity.

On the other hand, considering Transitional Justice measures in Brazil and homosexuality, there are some landmarks that must be highlighted,[938] such as the public hearing of the São Paulo State Truth Commission on November 26, 2013, on the subject of dictatorship, homosexuality, and resistance by the LGBT movement, in which researchers presented important explanations of how individuals experienced such realities and how they were repressed because of their dissident sexualities.[939] Later, on March 29, 2014, the National Truth Commission in partnership with the Resistance Memorial (*Memorial da Resistência*) also held a public hearing on the topic, which was attended by different sectors of the human rights and LGBT social movements and researchers.[940]

As a result of these public hearings, the final reports of the São Paulo State Truth Commission[941] and the National Truth Commission[942] presented chapters on dictatorship and homosexuality. In this same sense, the National Truth Commission elaborated Recommendation number 23, which is specifically against discrimination of LGBTI people, by advocating for the suppression, in any legislation, of discriminatory references to homosexuals, such as article 235 of the Military Penal Code (of 1969), which used to define as a crime "to practice, or allow the military to engage in a libidinous act, homosexual or not, in places under the military administration". In fact, this recommendation was accepted and implemented by means of a lawsuit filed by the Attorney General's Office, in which the constitutionality of that particular legal provision was questioned,

---

Brazilian Armed Struggle of the 1960s and 1970s", *Hispanic American Historical Review*, vol. 92/2012, pp. 437–469.

[938] For more information, see: GREEN, James N. and QUINALHA, Renan (eds.), *Ditadura e homossexualidades: repressão, resistência e a busca pela verdade*, São Carlos, EdUFSCar, 2014.

[939] *Memórias da Ditadura*, "CNV e LGBT", http://memoriasdaditadura.org.br/cnv-e-lgbts/.

[940] *National Truth Commission*, "CNV e CEV-SP realizam audiência pública Ditadura e homossexualidade no Brasil", http://cnv.memoriasreveladas.gov.br/index.php/outros-destaques/455-cnv-e-cev-sp-realizam-audiencia-publica-ditadura-e-homossexualidade-no-brasil, March 25, 2014.

[941] *São Paulo State Truth Commission Report*, Volume I, Part II, "Ditadura e Homossexualidades: Iniciativas da Comissão da Verdade do Estado de São Paulo Rubens Paiva".

[942] *NTC Report*, "Ditadura e Homossexualidades", Volume 2, Text 7, pp. 300–311, cnv. memoriasreveladas.gov.br/images/pdf/relatorio/Volume%202%20-%20Texto%207.pdf.

and in October 2015, the Supreme Federal Court (STF) judged the case and declared that the expression inserted in article 235 of Military Penal Code (the expression "homosexual or not") was unconstitutional.[943]

Certainly, those are initiatives representing an initial step towards the recognition of the violence suffered by LGBTI people due to their sexual orientations and gender identities during the dictatorship. However, in the Brazilian case, as already verified in Chapter 5 of this book, despite the remarkable initiative to address the situation of violations committed against the LGBTI population during the dictatorship, none of the Transitional Justice measures seek to promote more structural changes and more egalitarian democracy in any depth.

And following this assumption, as observed by Schulz,[944] while recognizing and remedying the structurally-embedded victimization and discrimination of women has already required us to challenge prevailing notions about victimhood, in the near future we also need to recognize the existence of different structural levels of discrimination, as well as a number of additional categories of victims, including sexual and gender minorities alongside women and girls. Contrarily, the failure to acknowledge the abuses done to LGBTI people, along with the lack of promotion of accountability, will deepen their exclusion.

In the Brazilian case, later on, beginning in 2020 and running until May 2021, at the Resistance Memorial (located in São Paulo city), it is valuable to mention the exhibition "Pride and Resistance: LGBT in the Dictatorship" (*Orgulho e Resistências: LGBT na Ditadura*),[945] which revealed how gays, lesbians and trans people were portrayed during the '60s, '70s and '80s and how this group sought to express themselves, even under the threat of being hunted down, arrested, and murdered. Thus, by means of such exhibition, which recalled the aspect of a symbolic reparation to LGBTI community, the public had access to literary works, posters of plays, music, films, photographs, magazines, and materials that confronted censorship at the time, in addition to official documents of the dictatorship.

Consequently, an artistic exhibition on such theme confirms the expectation that the time has come and Transitional Justice measures need to go beyond the gender binary. In addition, the exhibition should be praised as innovative, not only as a symbolic reparation, but also bearing in mind that in the Brazilian

---

[943] The insertion of the term homosexual was judged as unreasonable and prejudiced, because if the punishment relates to any libidinous act inside the barracks, it can obviously be homosexual or heterosexual. See: *Brazilian Federal Court*, "STF mantém no Código Penal Militar crime de ato libidinoso", October 28, 2015, http://www.stf.jus.br/portal/cms/verNoticiaDetalhe.asp?idConteudo=302782.

[944] SCHULZ, Philipp, "Towards Inclusive Gender in Transitional Justice: Gaps, Blind-Spots and Opportunities", *Journal of Intervention and Statebuilding*, October 21, 2019.

[945] *Memorial da Resistência*, "Orgulho e Resistências: LGBT na Ditadura", http://memorialdaresistenciasp.org.br/memorial/default.aspx?mn=38&c=444&s=0.

context, many of the claims of the LGBTI movement were achieved quite recently, such as, in 2011, with the official recognition of same-sex marriage,[946] in 2018, with the regulation concerning the change of first name and sex in the records,[947] and, in 2019, with the criminalization of LGBTI phobia.[948]

8.4. CONCLUSION: THE NEED FOR MORE CRITICAL INTERVENTIONS AND FEWER REPRESENTATIONS OF SUFFERING

In this chapter about gender and Transitional Justice in Brazil it was possible to observe that those women who challenged the dictatorship claimed visibility from a historical perspective, and their efforts have been acknowledged in many symbolic ways. In particular, this research revealed that symbolic initiatives were conducted by the State (commissions' reports, official apologies, memoir books, and documentary films) so that, during the past decades, women have gained a voice in the landscape of claims for justice, truth, and reparation in the country. In most cases, the common element that permeated such demands was the peculiarity of women's experience in contexts of violence and authoritarianism; and the importance of a gendered point of view in studies about the Brazilian dictatorship and its transition was based on the recognition of the fundamental role played by women during the resistance.

In this case, gender, as an analytical category, exposes a fundamental dimension of Transitional Justice: the achievement of equality between men and women as one of the objectives of the Rule of Law,[949] mainly because the notion of gender refers to the social construction of what it means to be men or women

---

[946] According to the judgment provided by the Federal Supreme Court, on May 5, 2011. See: CONJUR, "Supremo Tribunal Federal reconhece união estável homoafetiva", May 5, 2011, https://www.conjur.com.br/2011-mai-05/supremo-tribunal-federal-reconhece-uniao-estavel-homoafetiva.

[947] On June 29, 2018, the National Council of Justice enacted Provision 73/2018 regulating the procedures to require a change of first name and sex in the official civil records. See: CONJUR, "*CNJ regulamenta alterações de nome e sexo no registro civil de pessoas transexuais*", June 29, 2018, https://www.conjur.com.br/2018-jun-29/cnj-regulamenta-alteracoes-nome-sexo-registro-transexuais.

[948] On June 13, 2019, the Federal Supreme Court (STF) approved the criminalization of homophobia and transphobia in Brazil by 8 votes to 3. And, with such decision, prejudiced acts against homosexuals and transsexuals began to constitute a crime with a penalty of imprisonment ranging from one to three years, in addition to the imposition of a fine. See: *BBC*, "STF aprova a criminalização da homofobia", June 13, 2019, https://www.bbc.com/portuguese/brasil-47206924.

[949] ROESLER, Claudia Rosane and SENRA, Laura Carneiro de Mello, "Gênero e Justiça de Transição no Brasil", *Revista Jurídica da Presidência*, vol. 15/2013, pp. 35–67.

and their respective relations to power.[950] Hence, incorporating the history of women in official processes, giving voice to their narratives through books and movies, and considering the importance of their struggle are symbolic aspects that are seeking to fulfill the demand for inclusion and recognition of women in Brazilian society.

In summary, by observing these specific cases, it can be seen that those women who challenged the dictatorship obtained a degree of visibility in recent history that has kept their work alive and remembered. However, we shall go deep and explore whether political and cultural interventions such as official apologies, public acknowledgements, books, and films are able to do more than give visibility to women who were victims of violence.

Moreover, despite their increased awareness, this Chapter has shown that the status of women in Brazilian society has not changed to the degree expected by the Transitional Justice mechanisms, mainly considering topics like the labor market, domestic violence and democratic participation. These gaps in the Brazilian society confirm some previous understandings[951] according to which a continuum of violence is also a characteristic of transitional societies, since most of these societies pass through a rupture with the past while at the same time they are enduring conflicts around the distribution of wealth, structural poverty, inequality, and discrimination.

As a set of preliminary assumptions, the research for this chapter centered on the arguments of Gready and Robins that,[952] although Transitional Justice has expanded to encompass State-led practices such as trials, truth-telling, institutional reform, and reparations, the impact of such mechanisms has been disappointing in several cases, mainly because they have treated the symptoms rather than the causes of conflict. Consequently, the investigation here on gender and past atrocities in Brazil was based on the concept of Transformative Justice,[953] which addresses concerns such as structural and everyday violence

---

[950] LANGLOIS, Léa Lemay, "Gender Perspective in UN Framework for Peace Processes and Transitional Justice: The Need for a Clearer and More Inclusive Notion of Gender", *International Journal of Transitional Justice*, vol. 12/2018, pp. 146–167.

[951] BOESTEN, Jelke and WILDING, Polly, "Transformative Gender Justice: Setting an Agenda", *Women's Studies International Forum*, vol. 51/2015, pp. 75–80. See also: GODOY, Angelina Snodgrass, "La Muchacha Respondona: Reflections on the Razor's Edge Between Crime and Human Rights", *Human Rights Quarterly*, vol. 27/2005, pp. 597–624.

[952] GREADY, Paul and ROBINS, Simon, "From Transitional to Transformative Justice: A New Agenda for Practice", *The International Journal of Transitional Justice*, vol. 8/2014, pp. 339–361.

[953] According to Gready and Robins, "transformative justice is defined as transformative change that emphasizes local agency and resources, the prioritization of process rather than preconceived outcomes and the challenging of unequal and intersecting power relationships and structures of exclusion at both local and global level ... Transformative justice entails a shift in focus from the legal to the social and political, and from the state and institutions to communities and every day concerns". See: GREADY, Paul and ROBINS, Simon,

also during the post-conflict period, since the research involved looking for social and political changes that symbolic reparations may have produced within Brazilian society regarding gender standards.

Focusing on the Brazilian background, the importance of a gendered approach in Transitional Justice is based on three main reasons. First is the need to recognize the fundamental role of women during the resistance to the dictatorship. Second is the contribution that feminist criticism offers to transform the limits and to question practices of Transitional Justice. Third is the perception that questioning the violence perpetrated against women in periods of conflict implies a reflection on present day gender violence and inequalities, because even though they occur at distinct moments, both of them find their origin in the gender imbalance.

Although women and men have shared spaces in the struggle against the previous authoritarian regime – whether in armed guerrilla movements, or in organizations that have adopted other strategies of fighting oppression, such as student associations and political parties – the experience of women during the conflict represents something else; because the violence practiced has surpassed the attack on physical integrity to achieve the female subjectivity of the victims, that is to say, the kind of violence they suffered shifted their identity and their role in society. So, sexual violence against women as well as threats to their children or family members have specific consequences for the female victim, as they are deeply connected to what "being a woman" means culturally.[954]

A significant step would be the recognition of the uniqueness of women's experience during conflict or, as suggested by Langlois,[955] in order to effectively tackle the root causes of gender-based violence, an "expansive gender lens" should be applied. In this way, the scope of Transitional Justice would be related not only to the understanding of the gender dimension present in the conflict, but also to questioning the need for transformation of that hierarchy. Otherwise, if Transitional Justice mechanisms are employed without reference to the disadvantages of women, the effectiveness of reparation will be highly limited. It cannot be expected that the consequences of the atrocities will be remedied only with financial measures and without addressing cultural and social roots that are related to the facts.

In fact, Transitional Justice mechanisms adopted in Brazil regarding the female universe until now have failed to adequately deal with the multidimensional

---

"From Transitional to Transformative Justice: A New Agenda for Practice", *The International Journal of Transitional Justice*, vol. 8/2014, pp. 339–361.

[954] ROESLER, Claudia Rosane and SENRA, Laura Carneiro de Mello, "Gênero e Justiça de Transição no Brasil", *Revista Jurídica da Presidência*, vol. 15/2013, pp. 35–67.

[955] LANGLOIS, Léa Lemay, "Gender Perspective in UN Framework for Peace Processes and Transitional Justice: The Need for a Clearer and More Inclusive Notion of Gender", *International Journal of Transitional Justice*, vol. 12/2018, pp. 146–167.

issue of gender justice, and this has partly to do with the way women were treated during the conflict itself, but also with women's roles in the Brazilian society in general. That's the reason why Hellsten has observed that even in countries at peace – the current situation in Brazil – and where women's rights are largely defined,[956] gender inequality remains prevalent; women are under-represented in both politics and business, and are regularly paid less than men in the same positions.

Transitional Justice must be both backward and forward-looking in nature,[957] so Transitional Justice mechanisms must seek not only to address and recognize the wrongs of the past, but also to arrange the foundations for a more just and peaceful future. And one of the key issues facing women seeking justice during a transitional period stems from these two opposite directions, which are complementary and should both be achieved.

In the Brazilian context of gender and Transitional Justice, although much of the work done until now has created the narrative of human suffering and transmitted the painful process of traumatization, in most cases they failed to disorient and disturb the audience in a more profound way that would leave citizens embarrassed by the gender stereotypes hidden underneath those facts. That is to say, those State apologies ("*Caravanas da Anistia*"), that final report of the NTC, those films ("*Vou Contar Para Meus Filhos*" and "*Repare Bem*"), and the memoir book ("*Luta, Substantivo Feminino*") achieved the goals of acknowledging and remembering, but the question about how to transform, how to challenge the existing ways of dealing with gender and reconciliation, remained unaddressed, since there was no critical intervention regarding the underlying and persisting gender inequalities in Brazil.

In addition, this chapter raised the question of the violence against sexual minorities and LGBTI rights, which has recently challenged the practice of Transitional Justice employing binary logic. It was explained that, in the Brazilian case, there has been some initial effort to acknowledge the harm committed against LGBTI people, mainly in the form of public hearings and special chapters in the final reports of the NTC and the State of São Paulo Truth Commission. Certainly, such efforts break a historic silence on the prevailing perception of gender violence with an assumption of heterosexuality. But it remains to be seen whether the future initiatives will avoid the reduction of gender and sexual minorities to a one-dimensional victim status and redirect it to a more transformative justice, including, as well, structural and institutional reforms able to build a more sex-egalitarian democracy.

---

[956] Hellsten, Sirkku K., "Transitional Justice and Aid", *United Nations University (UNU-WIDER) Working Paper no. 6/2012*, https://www.wider.unu.edu/publication/transitional-justice-and-aid.

[957] Stewart, James, "Gender and Transitional Justice", *United Nations University*, March 25, 2013, https://unu.edu/publications/articles/gender-and-transitional-justice.html#info.

CHAPTER 9

THE COMPLICITY OF CORPORATIONS AND PRIVATE ACTORS DURING THE DICTATORSHIP

"*Stephen (springing up again): I am sorry, sir, that you force me to forget the respect due to you as my father. I am an Englishman; and I will not hear the Government of my country insulted.* (He thrusts his hands in his pockets, and walks angrily across to the window).

Undershaft (with a touch of brutality): *The government of your country! I am the government of your country: I, and Lazarus. Do you suppose that you and half a dozen amateurs like you, sitting in a row in that foolish gabble shop, can govern Undershaft and Lazarus? No, my friend: you will do what pays us. You will make war when it suits us, and keep peace when it doesn't. You will find out trade requires certain measures when we have decided on those measures. When I want anything to keep my dividends up, you will discover that my want is a national need. When other people want something to keep my dividends down, you will call out the police and military. And in return you shall have the support and applause of my newspapers, and the delight of imagining that you are a great statesman*".[958]

With the above dialogue between son and father (the latter being a rich and successful munitions maker named Andrew Undershaft), featured in the play *Major Barbara* (1907), Bernard Shaw revealed to us a crucial reality that has not lost its relevance in the present time: the compelling force with which private actors interfere in a country's destiny. This chapter will analyze how this game of power and influence played a role in the Brazilian dictatorship and how the transitional process has dealt with this issue.

9.1. INTRODUCTION

Although the traditional view of human rights law concerns the relationship between the State and the individual, increasing attention has been focused on private actors and their effects on human rights violations.[959] In fact, the very idea

---

[958] SHAW, George Bernard, *Major Barbara*, London, Times Book Club, 1907.
[959] John Ruggie, a leading academic authority on business and human rights and the former UN Secretary-General's Special Representative for Business and Human Rights identified

that private actors who contributed to past atrocities must be held accountable for their actions started with the distinguished efforts of the post-Holocaust Nuremberg Trials, which included the recognition of the role businesses had played in human rights violations during World War II, resulting in the so-called "industrialist trials" (carried out mainly by the United States Military Tribunal and the British Military Court).[960]

Moreover, after Germany's defeat, the Allied powers (The United States, Great Britain, France, and the former Soviet Union) held war crimes trials in various occupied zones. For instance, the Americans conducted 12 trials and three of them involved the prosecution of German industrialists. In these specific prosecutions, German industrialists who collaborated with the Nazi regime were held responsible for their financial or material assistance (as in the *IG Farben Case*) and for profiting from slave labor in the concentration camps (as in the *Krupp Case*).[961] In addition, there was the trial of businessman Bruno Tesch by the British Military Court, in Hamburg, which was related to the supplying of the lethal gas used in concentration camps (the so-called "*Zyklon B Case*").[962]

In history of this long path towards holding accountable non-State actors for violations of human rights, over the decades, other firms have had to answer for their actions. By way of example, there are BMW and Volkswagen which were held accountable for employing slave labor during the Nazi regime.[963] In addition, Swiss banks[964] and insurance companies[965] came under investigation for failing to pay out assets and claims to Holocaust victims. The International Criminal Tribunal for Rwanda convicted three businessmen for their complicity in the 1994 genocide (the so-called "*Media Case*"), since these media executives

---

this topic as follows: "Human rights traditionally have been conceived as a set of norms and practices to protect individuals from threats by the State, attributing to the State the duty to secure the conditions necessary for people to live a life of dignity. The postwar international human rights regime, a remarkable achievement in a world of self-regulating States, was premised on this conception. The idea that business enterprises might have human rights responsibilities independent of legal requirements in their countries of operation is relatively new and still not universally accepted". See: RUGGIE, John Gerard, *Just Business. Multinational Corporations and Human Rights*, New York, W.W. Norton, 2013, pp. xxv.

[960] See: *The Subsequent Nuremberg Trials*, https://museums.nuernberg.de/memorium-nuremberg-trials/the-nuremberg-trials/the-subsequent-nuremberg-trials/.

[961] RAMASASTRY, Anita, "Corporate Complicity: From Nuremberg to Rangoon – An Examination of Forced Labor Cases and Their Impact on the Liability of Multinational Corporations", *Berkeley Journal of International Law*, vol. 20/2002, pp. 91–159.

[962] SKINNER, Gwynne, "Nuremberg's Legacy Continues: The Nuremberg Trial's Influence on Human Rights Litigation in U.S. Courts", *Albany Law Review*, vol. 71/2008, pp. 321–367.

[963] CNN Money, "Nazi-era Slaves Sue Firms", August 31, 1998, https://money.cnn.com/1998/08/31/companies/holocaust/.

[964] *The New York Times*, "Switzerland and Banks Agree to a Fund for Holocaust Victims", 24 January 1997, https://www.nytimes.com/1997/01/24/world/switzerland-and-banks-agree-to-a-fund-for-holocaust-victims.html.

[965] *Swiss Info*, "Swiss Insurers to Compensate Holocaust Victims", May 11, 2000, https://www.swissinfo.ch/eng/swiss-insurers-to-compensate-holocaust-victims/1483632.

used a radio station and a bi-monthly newspaper to inflame ethnic hatred that eventually led to massacres at churches, schools, hospitals, and roadblocks.[966] Also, foreign civil proceedings against businesses engaged in complicity with repressive authoritarian regimes have been held in US federal courts, such as that brought by the Khulumani Support Group from South Africa against companies' complicity in Apartheid.[967]

On the other hand, observing the specific field of Transitional Justice mechanisms, although its objectives do not prevent the inclusion of businesses in accountability efforts, initially, the past abuses carried out by private actors during periods of repression and/or armed conflict have not formally received attention in Transitional Justice mandates. As a consequence, research conducted for the Corporate Accountability and Transitional Justice (CATJ) database[968] ascertained that, in 39 final reports of truth commissions around the world, just half of them (22 reports or 56%) acknowledged the role of economic actors in human rights violations.[969]

Nonetheless – despite this lack of effort to include past involvement of economic actors in human rights violations as an integral part of Transitional Justice – beginning in 2009, the Argentinean case of Transitional Justice started including jurisdictional claims regarding so-called "corporate complicity" in the human rights violations of a repressive regime.[970] In fact, as pointed out by Bohoslavsky and Opgenhaffen,[971] economic factors must be added to any discussion of human rights abuses, even though transitional mechanisms have long neglected to take into account the economic factors behind a repressive

---

[966] *The New York Times*, "Court Finds Rwanda Media Executives Guilty of Genocide", December 3, 2003, https://www.nytimes.com/2003/12/03/international/africa/court-finds-rwanda-media-executives-guilty-of-genocide.html.

[967] *Business & Human Rights Resource Centre*, "Apartheid Reparations Lawsuits (re So. Africa)", https://www.business-humanrights.org/en/apartheid-reparations-lawsuits-re-so-africa?page=1.

[968] The CATJ database includes cases where business have been named in non-judicial and judicial Transitional Justice mechanisms as being complicit with abuses committed in the course of an authoritarian regime or an armed conflict. The CATJ includes 874 observations of companies identified for their involvement in human rights violations in 37 countries that underwent transitions to democratic regimes between 1945 and 2017. The research mentioned in the text was conducted by the University of Oxford with the human rights organizations Andhes, Cels and Dejusticia. See: http://www.tjdbproject.com/#.

[969] PAYNE, Leigh A.; PEREIRA, Gabriel; COSTA, Josefina Doz; and BERNAL-BERMÚDEZ, Laura, "Can a Treaty on Business and Human Rights Help Achieve Transitional Justice Goals?", *Homa Publica International Journal on Human Rights and Business*, vol. 1/2017, pp. 3–33.

[970] VERBITSKY, Horacio and BOHOSLAVSKY, Juan Pablo (ed.), *The Economic Accomplices to the Argentine Dictatorship – Outstanding Debits*. New York, Cambridge University Press, 2016.

[971] BOHOSLAVSKY, Juan Pablo and OPGENHAFFEN, Veerle, "The Past and Present of Corporate Complicity: Financing the Argentinean Dictatorship", *Harvard Human Rights Journal*, vol. 23/2010, pp. 157–203.

regime. The failure to address the economic factors that have helped to maintain a dictatorship constitutes a dangerous example of historical blindness.

To be precise, a discussion focused only on the political conflict and/or one which neglects the economic aspects of that conflict may foster the risk that the same episodes could emerge once again in the near future. Following this theory – as an instrument to avoid repeating the hideous acts of the past – the Argentinean prosecution of non-State actors for the human rights violations perpetrated during the dictatorship provides a prime example of viewing economic factors as an essential part of a holistic assessment of Transitional Justice.

In the Brazilian case, three recent and reprehensible events demonstrate the importance of truly effective non-repetition mechanisms. They endorse the proposition that a past filled with atrocities which have not been duly disclosed can be repeated, and just like an unhealed wound, may be exacerbated. The first of these events refers to the re-emergence of the slogan "*Brasil, ame-o ou deixe-o*" (Brazil, love it or leave it), which in the past was directed against the opponents of the dictatorship. That slogan was seen again on broadcast television in the year 2018,[972] which means that, more than 30 years after the end of the dictatorial regime in Brazil, a broadcasting company is still evoking the campaign of the former military President Emílio Garrastazu Médici, who was responsible for a period of great repression against the political resistance (from 1969 to 1974). One day later, surrendering to pressure from public opinion, the channel removed the advertisement, saying that it had not intended to stir up memories of the early repressive era[973] and acknowledging that it was a mistake.[974] What is remarkable about this episode is the fact that the slogan was re-used by a massive broadcasting company, which apparently did not take into account its ethical responsibility in preserving the democratic values of the country.

Likewise, at the end of 2018, during a convention organized by the *Movimento Brasil Livre* – MBL (Free Brazil Movement),[975] the owner of a huge

---

[972] *Jornal Folha de São Paulo*, "SBT ressucita e mata "Brasil, ame-o ou deixe-o"em vinheta relâmpago", November 6, 2018, https://www1.folha.uol.com.br/ilustrada/2018/11/sbt-ressuscita-brasil-ame-o-ou-deixo-o-em-nova-vinheta.shtml.

[973] *Revista Isto É*, "SBT tira do ar slogan 'Brasil, ame-o ou deixe-o"utilizado na ditadura, November 7, 2018, https://istoe.com.br/sbt-tira-do-ar-slogan-brasil-ame-o-ou-deixe-o-utilizado-na-ditadura/.

[974] *Jornal O Estado de São Paulo*, "SBT admite equívoco e tira do ar slogan "Brasil, ame-o ou deixe-o" utilizado na ditadura", November 7, 2018, https://emais.estadao.com.br/noticias/tv,apos-repercussao-sbt-admite-equivoco-e-tira-do-ar-slogan-brasil-ame-o-ou-deixe-o-utilizado-no,70002592263.

[975] The *Movimento Brasil Livre* (Free Brazil Movement) was founded in 2014 and was mainly responsible for the public demonstrations against the government of Dilma Rousseff, which occurred during March and April of 2015. The movement has been described as liberal concerning its economic ideas, but conservative in respect of gender-equality efforts and women's reproductive rights, for instance. See: https://www.economist.com/the-americas/2015/02/26/niche-no-longer; https://brasil.elpais.com/brasil/2017/09/26/politica/1506459691_598049.html.

department store in Brazil supported the existence of a military government for the country.[976] That speech is also good cause for reflection, since, without any seeming embarrassment, a private actor publicly defended dictatorial ideals in apparently disregard of all the work that has been done through State initiatives aimed at fostering political memory and a sense of recent history. With such talk, it seems that the right to truth and memory and the impact of the reparations made for past atrocities – through the work of many years by agencies like the National Truth Commission (NTC), the Amnesty Commission, and the Commission on Political Deaths and Disappearances – have begun to fade away.

The last example occurred in 2014, when one of the biggest private banks in Brazil distributed a calendar, in which the day of March 31 was marked as the anniversary of the "revolution" of 1964.[977] The term "revolution" – used in reference to the establishment of the dictatorship – was of course the word applied by marshals, generals and torturers at the time of that previous regime to describe some of the events of that year. However, as has been recognized by the National Truth Commission,[978] what occurred was not a "revolution" but a "*coup d'état*" that involved both military and civilian sectors of society. Fortunately, some days later, the same bank decided to recall those calendars, claiming that it was a misunderstanding and that the institution praises democracy.[979]

It is undeniable that businesses have obligations corresponding to human rights, since they are in a position to protect and promote human rights in places where human rights are routinely violated. As has been pointed out by Ruggie,[980] "respecting" rights means not only not violating them, but also not facilitating or being otherwise involved in their violation. Taken together these three episodes lead to the conclusion that the "never again" ideal[981] may be quite fragile in

---

[976] *Revista Forum*, "Vamos defender o governo militar, diz dono da Havan, durante evento do MBL", November 23, 2018, https://www.revistaforum.com.br/vamos-defender-o-governo-militar-diz-dono-da-havan-durante-evento-do-mbl/.

[977] MAGALHÃES, Mário, "50 Anos Depois, Agenda do Itaú Ainda Trata Golpe como Revolução de 1964", February 12, 2014, https://blogdomariomagalhaes.blogosfera.uol.com.br/2014/02/12/50-anos-depois-agenda-do-itau-ainda-trata-golpe-como-revolucao-de-1964/.

[978] *National Truth Commission*, "2014 Final Report", Volume 1, Part II, Chapter 3, "Contexto Histórico das Graves Violações entre 1946 e 1988", pp. 86–110.

[979] *Folha de São Paulo*, "Itaú Recolherá Agenda que Cita Revolução de 64", February 21, 2014, https://www1.folha.uol.com.br/poder/2014/02/1415455-itau-recolhera-agenda-que-cita-revolucao-de-64.shtml.

[980] RUGGIE, John Gerard, *Just Business. Multinational Corporations and Human Rights*, New York, W.W. Norton, 2013.

[981] The reference is to the investigations conducted by Argentina's National Commission on the Disappearance of Persons (CONADEP) and the resulting "*Nunca Más*" (Never Again) Report, which had a significant influence on the course of Transitional Justice policies not only in Argentina, but also internationally in the context of the democratization processes of the region. Governments and human rights movements viewed the *Never Again Report* as a model to deal with the human rights violence committed during the 1970s and 1980s in Latin America. See: CRENZEL, Emilio, "Argentina's National Commission on the Disappearance

Brazilian democracy,[982] and they raise worries about the achievement of the non-repetition guarantee measures currently implemented in the Brazilian scenario.[983] So, in furtherance of these considerations, the following sections will observe the current stage of assessing corporate complicity in relation to the human rights violations committed during the Brazilian dictatorship, as well as the main struggles and future issues to be discussed.

9.2. THE LINKS BETWEEN REPRESSION AND ITS FINANCING

9.2.1. THE *OBAN CASE*

It is recognized that authoritarian regimes combine various strategies of repression, co-optation and legitimation to remain in power,[984] and one of those combinations of strategy which facilitate authoritarian survival is by touting the regime in terms of its economic success and buying loyalties through economic instruments. According to Bohoslavsky and Torelly,[985] this was exactly what had happened in Brazil during the dictatorship, where the economy came to rely on foreign finance, with a huge number of State-owned industrial corporations and by having banks as the biggest borrowers, followed by the support of large local industrial firms and affiliates of multinational corporations. Certainly, the restricted legitimacy of the Brazilian dictatorship was deeply connected with guaranteeing the *status quo* required by economic elites while promoting economic growth and clientelist policies.[986] However, to remain in power,

---

of Persons: Contributions to Transitional Justice", *The International Journal of Transitional Justice*, vol. 2/2008, pp. 173–191.

[982] *The Guardian*, "Bolsonaro's pledge to return Brazil to past alarms survivors of dictatorship", October 22, 2018, https://www.theguardian.com/world/2018/oct/22/after-what-i-lived-through-survivors-of-brazils-dictatorship-fear-bolsonaro.

[983] Assis, Emerson Francisco de, "Das Estranhas Catedrais da Ditadura Civil-Militar à Operação Lava Jato: A Repercussão da Ineficácia do Eixo Memória e Verdade na Justiça de Transição Brasileira", *Contemporânea – Revista de Ética e Filosofia Política*, vol. 3/2017, pp. 36–60.

[984] Maerz, Seraphine, "The Many Faces of Authoritarian Persistence: A Set Theory Perspective on the Survival Strategies of Authoritarian Regimes", *Government and Opposition*, https://www.cambridge.org/core/journals/government-and-opposition/article/many-faces-of-authoritarian-persistence-a-settheory-perspective-on-the-survival-strategies-of-authoritarian-regimes/7FCA47E0A5C484EB18A0744E04641886.

[985] Bohoslavsky, Juan Pablo and Torelly, Marcelo D., "Financial Complicity: The Brazilian Dictatorship Under the Macroscope", in Sharp, D.N. (ed.), *Justice and Economic Violence in Transition* (Springer Series in Transitional Justice vol. 5), New York, Springer, 2014, pp. 233–262.

[986] The "Brazilian miracle" – as the increase of growth from the late 1960s to the 1970s was labeled – was the economic strategy to manage expansion from a position of agrarian stagnation to a stage of industrialization. However, during the 1980s, the country that once was the world banking system's ideal borrower was pleading for loans just to pay the interest on its

Chapter 9. Complicity of Corporations and Private Actors During the Dictatorship

this kind of regime faces a crucial dilemma: the debt undertaken to pursue the regime's economic strategies was also related to the financing of a broad repressive bureaucracy, meaning that the dictatorship also needed means to subdue insurgents and to counter its urban opponents through the use of State terror.

A clear example of this method of financing of repressive bureaucracy, where there was a link between private funds and human rights abuses, may be found in the so-called *Operação Bandeirante* (OBAN), which was a multi-agency military operation in charge of repressing people during the Brazilian dictatorship. Actually, OBAN was considered a prototype of the military coordination of repressive actions,[987] mainly because, until 1968, the repression against political dissidents was carried out by local *Delegacias da Ordem Política e Social* – DOPS (Police Divisions for Political and Social Order), which were agencies managed by each state of the federation.

Later on, as a result of the issuance of Institutional Act no. 5 ("AI-5"), in December 1968, there was increasing cooperation between federal and state governments in terms of repression of the political opposition, and such "teamwork" started to be coordinated – and largely executed – by the federal government through the Armed Forces. Hence, OBAN was the first experience of the Army undertaking repressive operations, and it was implemented in São Paulo as a project in the shadows of official structures.

Based on the "results" achieved by OBAN, its model was replicated throughout the country and led to the creation of new units named *Destacamentos de Operações de Informações dos Centros de Operações de Defesa Interna* – DOI/CODI (Information Operation Units of Internal Defense Operation Centers). Installed in several Brazilian state capitals, these were similar to task forces or operations centers specialized in the internal defense of the country. In this way, as the Report of the São Paulo State Truth Commission observed,[988] OBAN brought about two innovations in the dictatorship's control system: (a) it combined security or repression activities with information and espionage operations; and (b) it brought together members of the various police forces with representatives of the Armed Forces.

---

debts. See: *The New York Times*, "Brazil's Economic Miracle and Its Collapse", November 26, 1983, https://www.nytimes.com/1983/11/26/business/brazil-s-economic-miracle-and-its-collapse.html. See: *El País*, "O Lado Obscuro do Milagre Econômico da Ditadura: O Boom da Desigualdade", November 28, 2017, https://brasil.elpais.com/brasil/2017/09/29/economia/1506721812_344807.html.

[987] WEICHERT, Marlon Alberto, "O Financiamento de Atos de Violação de Direitos Humanos por Empresas Durante a Ditadura Brasileira. Responsabilidade e Verdade", *Acervo*, vol. 21/2008, pp. 181–190.

[988] *Truth Commission of the State of São Paulo*, Report, Volume 1, Part 1, "O Financiamento da Repressão", p. 6.

Part III. Complex Forms of Reparations, Accountability, and Truth-Seeking

The connection with OBAN and private actors evolved because, initially, OBAN did not have its own budget or financial arrangements within the Army, and there are historical[989] and journalistic[990] sources affirming that many businessmen were asked to contribute, not only to the formation, but also to the operation of OBAN. Some are said to even have effectively engaged in the practice of torture and in support of repression.[991] Others were allegedly pressured to contribute with money.[992] There was a rationale for this collaboration: in a society dominated by fear, the contribution would serve as protection against regime arbitrariness.[993] And collaboration could take a variety of forms.[994] Financial contributions, donations of goods in kind (vehicles, food, and equipment), and provision of information (for example, lists of employees with political opinions differing from those of the government, who were spied on and eventually reported by their employers) were all forms of assistance.

---

[989] *National Truth Commission*, "2014 Final Report", Volume 2, Text 8, "Civis que Colaboraram com a Ditadura", pp. 313–338. *Truth Commission of the State of São Paulo*, Report, Volume 1, Part 1, "O Financiamento da Repressão", pp. 7–13.

[990] CONTREIRAS, Helio, "Segredos do Porão. Documentos Secretos da OBAN Mostram como a Tortura Foi Consentida e Financiada Durante o Regime Militar", *Isto É*, January 21, 2001.

[991] The most well-known figure in this process of corporate complicity with political repression was the entrepreneur Henning Albert Boilesen, who worked for the company Ultragás and is said to have coordinated the collection of financial contributions from businesses and to have attended some torture sessions. Boilesen's complicity ended up provoking the anger of the regime's opponents, and a joint action by two armed left-wing organizations – the Tiradentes Revolutionary Movement (*Movimento Revolucionário Tiradentes* – MRT) and the National Liberation Action (*Ação Libertadora Nacional* – ALN) – executed him in São Paulo, in April 1971. See: *Truth Commission of the State of São Paulo*, Report, Volume 1, Part 1, "O Financiamento da Repressão", Item 3 "A Participação dos Empresários no Financiamento da OBAN", p. 12. *National Truth Commission*, "2014 Final Report", Volume 2, Text 8, "Civis que Colaboraram com a Ditadura", pp. 329–331.

[992] For instance, during a gala dinner at the São Paulo Club, it is said that Delfim Netto, the former Minister of Finance, received the amount of US$110,000 from each banker that attended the gathering. The total amount was said to have been donated to strengthen OBAN operations. Bankers like Amador Aguiar (from Bradesco) and Gastão Eduardo de Bueno Vidigal (from Banco Mercantil de São Paulo), among others, attended this event. See: *National Truth Commission*, "2014 Final Report", Volume 2, Text 8, "Civis que Colaboraram com a Ditadura", p. 330. See also the documentary named "Cidadão Boilesen" (Citizen Boilesen), 2009, by Director Chaim Litewski.

[993] There are several reasons to explain the involvement of businesses in financing repressive agencies, since many of them felt threatened and wanted to join the fight in the defense of their own interests, while others were frightened by the violent actions practiced by the urban guerrilla. See: *Truth Commission of the State of São Paulo*, Report, Volume 1, Part 1, "O Financiamento da Repressão", p. 8.

[994] Along with the bankers, several companies financed the formation of OBAN, such as Ultra, Ford, General Motors, Camargo Corrêa, Objetivo, and Folha. Also, multinationals like Nestlé, General Electric, Mercedes Benz, Siemens, and Light were associated with the financing of OBAN. In addition, an unknown number of São Paulo entrepreneurs also contributed, since the collection of resources counted on the active support of the Federation of Industries of the State of São Paulo (FIESP). See: *National Truth Commission*, "2014 Final Report", Volume 2, Text 8, "Civis que Colaboraram com a Ditadura", p. 330.

9.2.2. THE *"BLACK LISTS" CASE*

Usually, there is a recurrent pattern regarding business complicity with human rights violations during authoritarian regimes, which is directed against specific groups like workers and union leaders, since it is understood that these groups pose a threat to the operation of companies by asking for increased labor guarantees and salaries[995] or by disseminating left-wing political ideas. Thus, under repressive regimes, business and State interests to silence these groups often coincide, which may be seen when, for example, businesses provide lists of union leaders to State forces, as was recently discovered to have occurred in the Brazilian case.[996] One consequence of such "black lists" was the subsequent kidnapping, torture, and assassination of labor leaders.[997]

After the *NTC Report* in 2014 expressly mentioned the name of the company Volkswagen (VW) as a collaborator of the previous regime, in December 2017, the company itself also published a Report,[998] written by professor Dr. Christopher Kopper, from the University of Bielefeld (Germany), in which it recognized that, although the management board of VW was aware of the political and social repression by the Brazilian military dictatorship, it accepted and trivialized the situation as being inevitable, based on a colonialist perspective. Indeed, it was acknowledged that, in 1969, the Works Security Department of *VW do Brasil* began a collaboration with the regime's Political Police (DEOPS) which only ended in 1979. As a result, the Works Security Department monitored opposition activities by the company's employees and, through its conduct, aided in the arrest of at least seven members of *VW do Brasil*'s staff.

According to the statement by the imprisoned former worker Lucio Bellentani, which was analyzed by the *VW Report*, the Works Security Department enabled him to not only be arrested but also mistreated by the Political Police on the plant's own premises. Such voluntary collaboration with the regular policing organs of the dictatorship persisted until the first large-scale strike of 1979, although *VW do Brasil* was still dismissing employees because of their trade union activities until 1980.

---

[995] The reference here is to the 1979 metalworkers' strike, in which some 200,000 workers participated in order to obtain salary adjustments and, defying the dictatorship, employees from companies such as Volkswagen, Ford, Mercedes-Benz, and Scania all were involved. See: *Memorial da Democracia*, "A Grande Greve dos Trabalhadores do ABC", http://memorialdademocracia.com.br/card/a-grande-greve-dos-trabalhadores-do-abc.

[996] *El País*, "Empresas Passavam Listas Negras de Trabalhadores a Órgãos de Repressão", December 10, 2014, https://brasil.elpais.com/brasil/2014/12/10/politica/1418237519_479087.html.

[997] *Agência Brasil*, "Ex-funcionário Relata Tortura dentro de Fábrica da Volkswagen durante Ditadura", December 14, 2017, http://agenciabrasil.ebc.com.br/direitos-humanos/noticia/2017-12/ex-funcion%C3%A1rio-relata-tortura-dentro-de-fabrica-da-volkswagen-durante-ditadura.

[998] KOPPER, Christopher, *VW do Brasil in the Brazilian Military Dictatorship 1964–1985: A Historical Study*, https://www.volkswagenag.com/en/group/history.html.

The report also stated that no clear evidence has been found to support the conjecture that *VW do Brasil* provided material assistance to the operation of military torture centers (DOI/CODI), however it was possible that an indirect financial contribution was made through the company's membership dues paid to the industrial confederation (FIESP), and by the provision of vehicles free of charge. The *VW Report* even claimed that *VW do Brasil* likely benefited economically from related military policy measures which weakened labor benefits, stating that government wage controls and restriction on trade unions kept wage levels lower than they would have been in a pluralistic democracy with free salary negotiations and the right to strike, so that *VW do Brasil*, and ultimately VW AG, profited from the suppression of fundamental workers' rights.[999]

Upon the release of the *VW Report*, in December 2017, the company also installed a plaque in honor of the victims in its plant, on which was written: "In memory of all the victims of the military dictatorship in Brazil, for human rights, democracy, tolerance and humanity".[1000] Considering Transitional Justice measures and symbolic reparations, the *VW Report* and its respective plaque represent a public acknowledgment of the company's involvement and, to a certain extent, an official admission of conduct that indirectly led to the violation of human rights and may serve to demonstrate the existence of a causal link between businesses' conduct and acts of repression.

However, the positive action of the company in revisiting its past and in acknowledging violations only has meaning and legitimacy if there has been participation and recognition by the victims. But the opposite happened; that is, there was no interaction between the company and the victims, and this led the victims to criticize the unilateral nature of the measure.[1001] That's because an effective apology takes into account what victims are likely to feel and think about

---

[999] KOPPER, Christopher, *VW do Brasil in the Brazilian Military Dictatorship 1964–1985: A Historical Study*, pp. 112–114, https://www.volkswagenag.com/en/group/history.html.

[1000] *Isto É Dinheiro*, "A Volks e os Anos de Chumbo", December 15, 2017, https://www.istoedinheiro.com.br/volks-e-os-anos-de-chumbo/.

[1001] According to Sebastião Neto, former coordinator of the São Paulo State Truth Commission group that analyzed the repression of workers and unions, the *VW Report* did not meet the expectations of the victims and was considered disappointing and contradictory, since the document states that security officials acted autonomously, although at the same time company managers had tacit knowledge of their actions. See: *El País*, "Volkswagen admite laços com a ditadura, mas falha ao não detalhar participação, diz pesquisador", December 18, 2017, https://brasil.elpais.com/brasil/2017/12/15/politica/1513361742_096853.html. According to one of the victims (Lucio Bellentani), Volkswagen took on the task of analyzing its past by itself, without considering the investigation opened by the Federal Prosecutor's Office in 2015, and without engaging in a dialogue with the victims. See: *Deutsche Welle*, "Relatório da Volkswagen não satisfaz vítimas da ditadura no Brasil", December 14, 2017, https://www.dw.com/pt-br/relat%C3%B3rio-da-volkswagen-n%C3%A3o-satisfaz-v%C3%ADtimas-da-ditadura-no-brasil/a-41803773.

Chapter 9. Complicity of Corporations and Private Actors During the Dictatorship

what is being said. In fact, the most successful apologies are arguably those that have been agreed on with survivors, families of victims, or their representatives, and which address the future and not just the past.[1002]

But it has to be observed that two years before VW's announcements and acknowledgment, in 2015 a civil law investigation had been initiated by the Federal Public Prosecutor's Office in São Paulo concerning the claim that former VW's employees were blacklisted and tortured.[1003] In fact, this civil investigation seeks to examine the case of 12 former employees who claim to have been arrested and tortured in Volkswagen's factory in São Bernardo do Campo, near São Paulo. Much of the evidence was collected in the 2014 NTC Final Report. The investigation examines some illicit conduct by the company, such as: giving permission to arrest employees inside its plant, harassment of workers for political and union activities, creating "black lists" to prevent the hiring of these professionals by other companies, provision of information to agencies of repression, financial collaboration with the regime, and permission to conduct torture at the company's headquarters.

The civil investigation case is paradigmatic for Brazilian Transitional Justice,[1004] since it deals with the elimination of the limitation period protecting legal entities. The only existing precedent to do so refers to cases in which the State is found civilly liable for illegal acts committed during the dictatorship, but there is no similar precedent for a private actor or legal entity. Nonetheless, this subject regarding the statute of limitation protecting legal entities will be further explored in the following section concerning the challenges for corporate complicity in Transitional Justice measures.

So far, concerning this leading case related to VW and Transitional Justice measures, on January 15, 2021, the Federal Prosecutor's Office closed the investigations, since it agreed with the terms of a financial reparation offered by VW.[1005] According to such proposal, VW will pay the amount of BRL 36,300,000 (thirty-six million, three hundred thousand reais or a sum equivalent to

---

[1002] CARRANZA, Ruben; CORREA, Cristián; and NAUGHTON, Elena, "Report Reparative Justice: More than Words. Apologies as a Form of Reparation", *International Center for Transitional Justice*, 2015, https://www.ictj.org/publication/more-than-words-apologies-form-reparation.

[1003] *Federal Public Prosecutor's Office*, Civil Investigation no. 1.34.001.006706/2015-26, http://apps.mpf.mp.br/aptusmpf/index2#/detalhe/100000000000067513810?modulo=0&sistema=portal.

[1004] *Correio Braziliense*, "MPF: Investigação sobre atuação da Volkswagen na ditadura é inédita no país", December 14, 2017, https://www.correiobraziliense.com.br/app/noticia/politica/2017/12/14/interna_politica,648057/mpf-investigacao-sobre-atuacao-da-volkswagen-na-ditadura-e-inedita-no.shtml.

[1005] *CONJUR*, "Volkswagen vai pagar R$36,3 milhões por ter colaborado com a ditadura brasileira", January 15, 2021, https://www.conjur.com.br/2021-jan-15/volkswagen-pagar-36-milhoes-colaborar-ditadura.

US$6,849,056), of which resources will be allocated to the Fund for the Defense of Diffuse Rights (*Fundo de Defesa dos Direitos Difusos – FDDD*), the State Fund for the Defense of Diffuse Interests (*Fundo Estadual de Defesa dos Interesses Difusos*), the Memorial for Justice maintained by the Brazilian Bar Association of the State of São Paulo (*Memorial de Luta por Justiça da OAB/SP*), the Federal University of São Paulo (*Universidade Federal Paulista – Unifesp*),[1006] and to the former workers of VW in Brazil with a donation to the Volkswagen Workers' Association (*Associação dos Trabalhadores e Trabalhadoras da Volkswagen*).[1007]

Initially the decision to close the investigations and accept the financial reparation in place of a potential criminal prosecution was criticized by members of the civil society and/or former workers of VW, mainly because part of the funds would be distributed to the *Memorial de Luta por Justiça da OAB/SP*, to the Federal University of São Paulo (Universidade Federal Paulista – Unifesp), the Fund for the Defense of Diffuse Rights (*Fundo de Defesa dos Direitos Difusos – FDDD*), and the State Fund for the Defense of Diffuse Interests (*Fundo Estadual de Defesa dos Interesses Difusos*),[1008] whose main objectives are not primarily linked to the events surrounding the violations of rights perpetrated inside the VW factory, and consequently the use of reparations would not be connected to the claim itself.[1009]

[1006] Part of the funds, around BRL 10.5 million, will serve to reinforce Transitional Justice measures, such as projects aiming to preserve the right to memory, like the initiatives coordinated by the *Memorial da Luta por Justiça*, whose project will receive BRL 6 million, in order to complete the implementation of its headquarters, located at a former military unit in São Paulo city (for information about the Memorial, see: https://www.oabsp.org.br/noticias/2015/11/memorial-da-luta-pela-justica-ja-pode-sair-do-papel.10499). The remaining BRL 4.5 million will go to the Federal University of São Paulo (Unifesp) to finance new research on the collaboration of corporations with the dictatorship and to identify the bones of political prisoners found in the clandestine mass grave of Perus cemetery. See: *Federal Prosecutor's Office of São Paulo*, "Ministérios Públicos assinam acordo com Volkswagen sobre represessão na ditadura", September 23, 2020, http://www.mpf.mp.br/sp/sala-de-imprensa/noticias-sp/ministerios-publicos-assinam-acordo-com-volkswagen-sobre-repressao-na-ditadura.

[1007] Of the total amount fixed by the agreement, BRL 16.8 million will be donated to the Henrich Plagge Association, which is formed by Volkswagen workers. The amount will be shared among former employees who were harassed for their political beliefs, according to a criterion defined by an independent arbitrator. See: *Federal Public Prosecutor's Office of São Paulo*, "Ministérios Públicos assinam acordo com Volkswagen sobre represessão na ditadura", September 23, 2020, http://www.mpf.mp.br/sp/sala-de-imprensa/noticias-sp/ministerios-publicos-assinam-acordo-com-volkswagen-sobre-repressao-na-ditadura.

[1008] *Opera Mundi*, "Acordo da VW de Indenização por atos na Ditadura não é Legítimo, diz ex-coordenadora da CNV", September 29, 2020, https://operamundi.uol.com.br/memoria/66908/acordo-da-vw-de-indenizacao-por-atos-na-ditadura-nao-e-legitimo-diz-ex-coordenadora-da-cnv.

[1009] SOARES, Inês Virgínia Prado and BASTOS, Lucia Elena Arantes Ferreira, "Caso Volkswagen: entre violações pretéritas aos direitos humanos e dilemas sobre uma reparação coletiva atual e efetiva", *Working Paper*, 2021.

Chapter 9. Complicity of Corporations and Private Actors During the Dictatorship

Such case illustrates what Teitel has said when she advocates for a more expansive view of the question of punishment in criminal justice,[1010] when the response may be compromised or limited, especially considering that alternatives like the financial reparation may be a way to respond to the predecessor regime's repressive rule at the same time that it can develop capacities for advancing the Rule of Law. Hence, we should consider that the justice pillar of Transitional Justice may not reflect the expected standard and Law operates differently in certain concrete situations, and sometimes it is incapable of meeting all of the traditional expectations.

In this sense, it is worthwhile to reflect on the thoughts of Teitel based on the evolution of Transitional Justice over the last decades, since for said author the historical "punishment–impunity" debate has given way to a call for complex forms of accountability associated with the rise of private actors – as is the case of VW – who are implicated in the conflict as well, and yet, she says, we should have a broader lens through which we appreciate the justice pillar, which goes beyond any strict retributive or deterrent effect. Or, as once stated by Garapon while analyzing the class actions initiated by Jewish associations against Swiss Banks and the spoils of the Second World War as well as the cases of the indigenous tribes of Canada and Australia,[1011] the goal of a pecuniary reparation in such historical crimes is further more than the findings of wrongdoings, it leans to the civilization of the world, in the sense of preventing barbarism and fostering the Rule of Law.

Also, concerning symbolic reparations for the violations of human rights linked to *VW do Brasil* during the dictatorship, in 2017, the same year that the *VW Report* was issued, *Deutsche Welle/DW* (the German public broadcaster) produced a documentary called "Accomplices? Volkswagen and the Military Dictatorship in Brazil",[1012] directed by Stefanie Dodt and Thomas Aders, which tells the story of Lúcio Bellentani, a *VW do Brasil* employee at the time of the dictatorship and a member of the Brazilian Communist Party (PCB), who was arrested and tortured inside VW's plant, and then remained in jail for eight months.[1013] The arguments and documents presented in the film were derived from the work of the NTC in 2014, and the investigations conducted by the Federal Prosecutor's Office (which started in 2015). The film also features

---

[1010] TEITEL, Ruti G., *Globalizing Transitional Justice – Contemporary Essays*, New York, Oxford University Press, 2014.
[1011] GARAPON, Antoine, *Peut-on Réparer L'Histoire? Colonisation, Esclavage, Shoah*, Paris, Odile Jacob, 2008.
[1012] The documentary "Accomplices? Volkswagen and the Military Dictatorship in Brazil" is available at: https://www.youtube.com/watch?v=feJsXRP_nYw.
[1013] *Rede Brasil Atual*, "Documentário na Alemanha: evidências de cumplicidade da Volks com a repressão", July 26, 2017, https://www.redebrasilatual.com.br/cidadania/2017/07/documentario-alemao-traz-evidencias-de-cumplicidade-da-volks-com-repressao.

interviews with victims, company directors, and a former president of the company.

Such a documentary, produced by an international broadcaster, must be acclaimed, since extra-judicial mechanisms like artworks and documentary films can play an important role in addressing questions of reconciliation.[1014] Indeed, the ways in which intellectuals forge new narratives about the legacies of violence become relevant components for understanding the social resonance of Transitional Justice processes.[1015]

9.3. THE PROPOSITIONS OF THE TRUTH COMMISSIONS REGARDING CORPORATE COMPLICITY

Payne et al.[1016] have already praised the work of truth commissions in relation to corporate complicity by saying that they perform an important task by identifying the names of those private actors who were engaged in human rights violations, and by holding them at least symbolically accountable for their role, for example, in financing repression, arbitrary detention, kidnapping, torture, extrajudicial killing, forced disappearances, and so on. On the other hand, Bohoslavsky and Torelly have argued that in those few instances where truth commissions have dealt with questions of economic violence,[1017] they have done so in a sadly limited way. So, for them, financial complicity is one of the areas of Transitional Justice that has received the least amount of attention.

Proving this lack of concentration on the issue of corporate complicity, when analyzing the responsibility of banks that did business with the Apartheid regime in South Africa, Sarkin[1018] reasoned that the Report of the Truth and Reconciliation Commission (TRC Report) appeared to place banks in the

---

[1014] SIMIC, Olivera and VOLCIC, Zala, "In the Land of Wartime Rape: Bosnia, Cinema and Reparation", *Griffith Journal of Law & Human Dignity* vol. 2(2)/2014, pp. 377–401.

[1015] RAMÍREZ-BARAT, Clara, "Transitional Justice and the Public Sphere", in RAMÍREZ-BARAT Clara (ed.), *Transitional Justice, Culture, and Society Beyond Outreach*, New York, International Center for Transitional Justice and Social Science Research Council, 2014, pp. 27–45.

[1016] PAYNE, Leigh A.; PEREIRA, Gabriel; COSTA, Josefina Doz; and BERNAL-BERMÚDEZ, Laura, "Can a Treaty on Business and Human Rights Help Achieve Transitional Justice Goals?", *Homa Publica International Journal on Human Rights and Business*, vol. 1/2017, pp. 3–33.

[1017] BOHOSLAVSKY, Juan Pablo and TORELLY, Marcelo D., "Financial Complicity: The Brazilian Dictatorship Under the Macroscope", in SHARP, D.N. (ed.), *Justice and Economic Violence in Transition* (Springer Series in Transitional Justice vol. 5), New York, Springer, 2014, pp. 233–262.

[1018] SARKIN, Jeremy, "The Coming of Age of Claims for Reparations for Human Rights Abuses Committed in the South", *SUR – International Journal on Human Rights*, vol. 1/2004, pp. 66–125.

second and third categories of degrees of culpability. Furthermore, although the TRC Report cited the involvement of banks with gross violations of human rights, it did not take the extra step of analyzing any particular relationship between a bank and an apartheid institution to ascertain: (1) to what extent lending activities aided and abetted oppression; and (2) to what extent banks should have foreseen or known that their lending activities would aid and abet oppression.

All three above-mentioned considerations made by Payne et al., Bohoslavsky and Torelly, and Sarkin may help us to reflect on the work of the National Truth Commission (NTC) in Brazil in examining corporate complicity. In the work of the NTC there was a symbolic recognition of the direct and indirect connection of companies with the violations of human rights; however, there was no deeper examination of those oppressive ties, nor of any consequences arising from them, as will be analyzed below.

By beginning with symbolic recognition and a "naming names" strategy, the NTC Report made a noble effort to affirm that a dictatorship of more than two decades could not have sustained itself without the support of sectors of civil society, in addition to the military itself. Thus, the NTC Report determined that the participation of civilian sectors (a) in the *coup d'état* of 1964, (b) in the implementation of the authoritarian regime, and (c) in the assembly of the very structures of repression, were all crucial dimensions of the Brazilian historical process. Definitely, Commissioners understood that the dictatorship was not an exclusively military phenomenon, although the Armed Forces took a front and center position in that regime.[1019]

Additionally, the NTC Report asserted that in the conspiracy that culminated in the overthrow of President João Goulart, the role of the local and foreign private sector was decisive, through the mobilization of class associations and civil society entities created in that context, such as the *Instituto Brasileiro de Ação Democrática* – IBAD (Brazilian Institute for Democratic Action) and the *Instituto de Pesquisas e Estudos Sociais* – IPES (Institute for Social Studies Research), which, in an coordinated manner, elaborated the guidelines to be followed by the military regime and which were implemented in the country from 1964 until 1985.[1020]

Specifically, regarding corporate complicity, the NTC Report established that in São Paulo, the final preparations for the *coup d'état* had the participation of businesses from the industrial sector, both foreign and domestic, and of various sizes, with at least 53 companies having some kind of active collaboration with

---

[1019] *National Truth Commission*, "2014 Final Report", Volume 2, Text 8, "Civis que Colaboraram com a Ditadura", p. 314.
[1020] *National Truth Commission*, "2014 Final Report", Volume 2, Text 8, "Civis que Colaboraram com a Ditadura", p. 316.

the rise of the military regime.[1021] However, nothing can be more outrageous than the collaboration of large businessmen in financing the structure of repression itself, and in this particular field, in addition to the case of OBAN as mentioned above, the NTC Report also mentioned that private properties served as centers for the torture of opponents of the regime and as illegal prisons, as occurred in the Cambahyba plant belonging to the Ribeiro Gomes family, in Campos dos Goytacazes (state of Rio de Janeiro), and in the "*Casa da Morte*" (House of Death), in Petrópolis (Rio de Janeiro), which was the property of German businessman Mario Lodders.[1022]

After an extensive description of cases of such collaboration, nonetheless, the work of the NTC followed the general rule of other truth commissions, which, as Payne et al. have already observed,[1023] have not tended to include judicial investigations as a follow-up to their findings on corporate complicity and have not established specific recommendations regarding corporate complicity. In the Brazilian case, Commissioners addressed in vague or blurred language the need for businesses to comply with human rights standards, for instance, as in recommendation number 26, which refers to the establishment of a permanent body or agency responsible for the follow-up of the recommendations of the NTC. In item "b" of that recommendation, the need to continue the "investigation" of events and conduct that could not be concluded by the NTC was made clear, as in the case of companies and businesses which collaborated

---

[1021] The *NTC Report* named the following companies that collaborated with the *coup d'état*, on March 31, 1964: A. Queiróz Lugó, Acumuladores Vulcânia, Antônio Maurício Wanderley e Cia. Ltda., Armações de Aço Probel S/A, Atlantic, Auto Asbestos S/A, B.F. Goodrich, Brasital S/A, Cia. Carlos Guedes, Cia. Comercial de Madeiras Kirali, Cia. De Acumuladores Prest-O-Lite, Cia. De Cigarros Souza Cruz, Cia. Fiação e Tecidos Lanifício Plástico, Cia. Madeireira Nacional, Dunlop, Duratex S/A Indústria e Comércio, Duratex S/A, Esso Brasileira de Petróleo, Eucatex S/A Indústria e Comércio, Johnson & Johnson, F. Slaviero, Fábrica de Cigarros Caruso, Fábrica de Cigarros Flórida, Fábrica de Cigarros Sudan S/A, Fábrica de Gases Medicinais Cremer, Firestone S/A, Good Year, Indústria Brasileira de Eletricidade, Indústria de Ataduras Gessadas Cristal, Indústria de Feltros Lua Nova S/A, Irmãos Justa Transportes, Irmãos Nocera, João Batista Antonio Alário, M. Lipper S/A, Madeireira Miguel Forte, Moinhos Santista S/A, Moreira Lima e Cia., Ousei Peceniski (Colchoaria Francisco), P. Barelle Ltda, Pfizer Corporation do Brasil, Pirelli S/A, Pneus General, S/A Brasileira de Tabacos Industrializados, Saturnia Acumuladores Elétricos, Serraria Água Branca, Serraria Americana Salim F. Maluf, Serraria Azevedo Miranda, Serraria Bandeirantes, Serrarias Almeida Porto, Serrarias F. Lameirão, Texaco do Brasil S/A, V. Foreinete, Vicari S/A Indústria e Comércio, Volkswagen do Brasil. See: National Truth Commission, "2014 Final Report", Volume 2, Text 8, "Civis que Colaboraram com a Ditadura", p. 321.

[1022] See: National Truth Commission, "2014 Final Report", Volume 2, Text 8, "Civis que Colaboraram com a Ditadura", p. 329.

[1023] Payne, Leigh A.; Pereira, Gabriel; Costa, Josefina Doz; and Bernal-Bermúdez, Laura, "Can a Treaty on Business and Human Rights Help Achieve Transitional Justice Goals?", *Homa Publica International Journal on Human Rights and Business*, vol. 1/2017, pp. 3–33.

Chapter 9. Complicity of Corporations and Private Actors During the Dictatorship

in repression and violations of human rights during the dictatorship,[1024] but it was not clear whether said investigation should be conducted by the courts or by an administrative agency.

Another weak point was that the NTC placed no demands on economic actors to make payments to the reparations program. In recommendation number three,[1025] there was a remark stating that the Government should propose administrative and judicial claims against public employees or agents of the Public Administration who were identified as responsible for violations of human rights, in order to seek reimbursement of the costs derived from the reparations program that the State has financially supported over the years.[1026] But Commissioners did not suggest that those same compensation claims could be brought against corporations that collaborated with the repression, not to mention that the statutes of limitation should also not be applicable to cases of corporate complicity.

Such a gap in recommendation number three recalls what Bohoslavsky and Torelly have said about the Brazilian process of Transitional Justice,[1027] explaining that the country has mostly focused on abstract forms of accountability, in which the State as a whole (rather than individuals) has assumed responsibility for the repression carried out by State officials. Consequently, the State has undertaken the responsibility of providing reparations through a program of moral and economic redress for the victims, without looking for specific kinds of individual or corporate accountability. As a result, economic factors fostering or contributing to human rights abuses have not been addressed in this context, even with reasonable public knowledge about the different kinds of economic cooperation given to the regime.

Also, the engagement of private actors with repression and military rule, although mentioned without going into any great depth in the NTC Report, was not referred to in the list of the 377 perpetrators of gross human rights violations committed during the dictatorship: collaborating businesses were not officially included as the direct or indirect authors of such atrocities.[1028]

[1024] *National Truth Commission*, "2014 Final Report", Volume 1, Part V, Chapter 18, "Conclusões e Recomendações", p. 967.

[1025] *National Truth Commission*, "2014 Final Report", Volume 1, Part V, Chapter 18, "Conclusões e Recomendações", p. 973.

[1026] The 1988 Constitution (article 37, paragraph 6) stipulates the right of compensation against a public official when it is demonstrated that his/her personal responsibility was linked with the commitment of an unlawful or illegal act.

[1027] BOHOSLAVSKY, Juan Pablo and TORELLY, Marcelo D., "Financial Complicity: The Brazilian Dictatorship Under the Macroscope", in SHARP, D.N. (ed.), *Justice and Economic Violence in Transition* (Springer Series in Transitional Justice vol. 5), New York, Springer, 2014, pp. 233–262.

[1028] *National Truth Commission*, "2014 Final Report", Volume 1, Part IV, Chapter 16, "A Autoria das Graves Violações de Direitos Humanos", pp. 842–931.

Besides the "name and shame" approach,[1029] in terms of recommendations, the São Paulo State Truth Commission (also known as the "Rubens Paiva Commission") presented a more detailed explanation concerning the expectations of future accountability for corporate complicity[1030] by asserting, for example, that companies which contributed to the practice of human rights violations should be held liable as accomplices under international law. In addition, the Rubens Paiva Commission proposed that the legal provision allowing for companies to be held criminally liable in the case of environmental crimes[1031] should be amended in order to include legal entity liability in cases of gross violations of human rights. Lastly, São Paulo State Commissioners were concerned with symbolic reparations by stating that companies that contributed in any way to the practice of human rights violations during the dictatorship should insert a plaque in front of their plants clarifying their participation in such violations.

9.4. THE INTRICATE WAY TO CONNECT CORPORATE COMPLICITY WITHIN THE TRANSITIONAL JUSTICE FRAMEWORK

The difficulty in incorporating corporate complicity into Transitional Justice measures may result from the very approach itself that scholars have taken in the analysis of business and human rights, since for a long time these two areas of study (Transitional Justice *versus* business and human rights) have progressed in different ways. On the one hand, business and human rights studies have looked at more contemporary controversies and violations,[1032] such as freedom of association; the abolition of slavery, forced labor, and child labor; the right to

---

[1029] The classic human rights approach is characterized by three actions: (a) to document abuses, (b) to work to prevent further abuse; and (c) to hold accountable those responsible for abuses. But, because these actions often fail to vindicate the rights of the oppressed, practitioners and law consultants also seek to intervene on a systemic level to improve the capacity of those remedies to operate more effectively. So, looking beyond the legal system, human rights advocates have employed the "shame" aspect; that is, a movement to embarrass abusers and thus stop violations, while forcing investigations and prosecutions of those responsible. So, the essence of human rights work would be the "name and shame" approach, which comprises a methodology to investigate the misconduct and to expose it to public shaming. See: SONNENBERG, Stephan and CAVALLARO, James L, "Name, Shame, and Then Build Consensus? Bringing Conflict Resolution Skills to Human Rights", *Washington University Journal of Law & Policy*, vol. 39/2012, pp. 261–262.
[1030] *Truth Commission of the State of São Paulo*, Report, Volume 1, Part 1, Chapter 8 "O Financiamento da Repressão", pp. 26–27. Available at: http://comissaodaverdade.al.sp.gov.br/relatorio/tomo-i/parte-i-cap8.html.
[1031] The criminal responsibility of legal entities in cases of environmental crimes is defined by Law no. 9,605 (1998), article 3.
[1032] RUGGIE, John Gerard, *Just Business. Multinational Corporations and Human Rights*, New York, W.W. Norton, 2013.

social security; protection of the environment; the fight against corruption; and so on. On the other side, Transitional Justice scholars and practitioners have been scrutinizing the accountability for past atrocities carried out by State forces and their opponents, barely considering the role of businesses in those human rights violations.[1033] This missing dialogue has led to a gap in the establishment of elementary links between these sets of dilemmas. Consequently, societies have failed to acknowledge persistent patterns: the sequence that links past and current abuses by businesses. For this reason, Bohoslavsky and Opgenhaffen state that accountability for corporate complicity in authoritarian and civil conflict situations has been the "missing piece of the puzzle",[1034] in order to pursue the full spectrum of justice and the necessary remedies for periods of authoritarian and civil conflict.

In the Brazilian case, this trend started to be developed in 2014, with the revelation[1035] that many of the large construction companies involved in the current anti-corruption investigation called "Car Wash"[1036] had already benefited from special relations with the State since their launch, in the 1930s and 1950s, and that the payment of bribes ended up consolidating even during the dictatorship (1964–1985). Ironically, this link, exposed in the book *"Estranhas Catedrais"* (Strange Cathedrals, 2014), evokes a verse from Chico Buarque and Francis Hime's song *"Vai Passar"* (It Will Go Away) of 1984,[1037] in which it is said:

> Our motherland was sleeping so distractedly, without realizing that it was subtracted from tenebrous transactions. Your children erred blindly across the continent, carrying stones like penitents, erecting strange cathedrals.

[1033] Reference is made to the CATJ database, which includes cases where businesses have been named in non-judicial and judicial Transitional Justice mechanisms as being complicit in violations of human rights. See: http://www.tjdbproject.com/#.

[1034] BOHOSLAVSKY, Juan Pablo and OPGENHAFFEN, Veerle, "The Past and Present of Corporate Complicity: Financing the Argentinean Dictatorship", *Harvard Human Rights Journal*, vol. 23/2010, pp. 157–203.

[1035] Said connection between construction companies and the authoritarian regime was addressed by a doctoral thesis that was later published in 2014. See: CAMPOS, Pedro Henrique Pedreira, *Estranhas Catedrais. As Empreiteiras Brasileiras e a Ditadura Civil-Militar (1964–1985)*, Niterói, Eduff, 2014.

[1036] Beginning in 2014, the investigation named *"Lava Jato"* (Car Wash) was about to uncover an unprecedented web of corruption in Brazil. The case would go on to discover illegal payments of more than US$5 billon to company executives and political parties, put billionaires in jail, drag a former President into court and cause irreparable damage to the finances and reputations of some of the world's biggest companies. It would also expose a culture of systemic corruption in Brazilian politics, and provoke a backlash from the establishment fierce enough to bring down one government and leave another on the brink of collapse. See: *The Guardian*, "Operation Car Wash: Is this the biggest corruption scandal in history?", June 1, 2017, https://www.theguardian.com/world/2017/jun/01/brazil-operation-car-wash-is-this-the-biggest-corruption-scandal-in-history.

[1037] In 1984, the song *"Vai Passar"* had spread over the country as a symbol of the transition to the first civilian regime after 21 years of military dictatorship. It represented a critical allegory of

At that time (1984), the construction of those "strange cathedrals" referred to projects like the *Rodovia Transamazônica* (Trans-Amazonian Highway),[1038] the Itaipu hydroelectric dam,[1039] the Rio-Niterói bridge,[1040] and the Angra nuclear power plant.[1041]

Although the circumstances mentioned above are notorious,[1042] it remains the fact that judicial corporate accountability has been marginal in Transitional Justice contexts,[1043] that is, the corporate accountability for cooperation with the violations of human rights committed during the dictatorship still remains as topic that is barely discussed.[1044] And although the contributions of Transitional Justice have given a direction in how to deal with this subject, it is still crucial to identify the appropriate methods and tactics to ensure corporate responsibility within the Brazilian legal system and its jurisprudence.

So, the question on how to legally attribute criminal and civil responsibility to those individuals on account of corporate crimes remains barely answered. In fact, the challenge in terms of criminal responsibility of both, corporations and company executives, is the establishment of the connection of the individual crimes with broader and systematic character of human rights violations which occurred during the conflict.

Specifically, in the Brazilian scenario, both the criminal and the civil responsibility of corporations still have to face an obstacle: statutes of limitations.

---

those dark years of the authoritarian regime and, at the same time, it celebrated the resistance and the hope for a democratic future. See: http://memorialdademocracia.com.br/card/vai-passar-a-noite-da-ditadura-militar.

[1038] *New Internationalist*, "From Nothing to Nowhere – The Transamazonian Highway", October 2, 1980, https://newint.org/features/1980/10/01/brazil.

[1039] *The New York Times*, "Brazil's Hydroelectric Project", November 14, 1983, https://www.nytimes.com/1983/11/14/business/brazil-s-hydroelectric-project.html.

[1040] See: http://www.bestourism.com/items/di/7868?title=The-Rio-Niteroi-Bridge&b=343. According to the Report of the National Truth Commission, "State support" for business viability was granted to the most active sponsors of the repressive structure, for example, the company Camargo Corrêa, one of the largest backers of OBAN's repressive operation, won contracts for the construction of large public works, such as the bridge Rio-Niterói. See: *National Truth Commission*, "2014 Final Report", Volume 2, Text 8, "Civis que Colaboraram com a Ditadura", p. 333.

[1041] See: http://www.world-nuclear.org/information-library/country-profiles/countries-a-f/brazil.aspx.

[1042] *Folha de São Paulo*, "Ditadura abafou apuração de corrupção dos anos 70, revelam documentos britânicos", June 2, 2018, https://www1.folha.uol.com.br/poder/2018/06/ditadura-abafou-apuracao-de-corrupcao-dos-anos-70-revelam-documentos-britanicos.shtml.

[1043] PAYNE, Leigh A.; PEREIRA, Gabriel; COSTA, Josefina Doz and BERNAL-BERMÚDEZ, Laura, "Can a Treaty on Business and Human Rights Help Achieve Transitional Justice Goals?", *Homa Publica International Journal on Human Rights and Business*, vol. 1/2017, pp. 3–33.

[1044] SOARES, Inês Virgínia Prado and FECHER, Viviane, "Empresas e Cooperação com a Ditadura Brasileira: Novas Possibilidades para a Responsabilização Empresarial", in FACHIN, Melina Girardi and PAMPLONA, Danielle Anne (eds.), *Direitos Humanos e Empresas*, Curitiba, Íthala, 2019, pp. 323–354.

This procedural problem raises a fundamental question on how far back plaintiffs are entitled to bring a claim. Actually, the length of time between the damage and the judicial petition is fundamental, and in the Brazilian case this time-line factor would not be favorable for the victims, since the dictatorship ended more than 30 years ago. This is also the case because, in terms of criminal responsibility, the Brazilian Judiciary has not yet accepted that the systematic violations of human rights committed during the dictatorship should be described as crimes against humanity[1045] and that, as consequence, no statute of limitations should apply to those crimes, as has been argued by the United Nations since 1968.[1046]

Moreover, concerning private law and civil liability, there is a grey zone that has yet to be clarified, as civil liability expires after three years according to the Brazilian Civil Code.[1047] However, there has been a debate about the exact starting date of this limitation period, and the vast majority of jurisprudence has understood that this period begins from the moment the victim becomes unequivocally aware of the violation, bearing in mind good faith and objective information. As if the violation itself were not enough, it requires the victim's indisputable knowledge of the illicit fact.[1048]

Thus, if we apply this rule to cases of corporate civil liability for human rights violations during the dictatorship, what would the starting date be? If, for example, we consider that knowledge of the damage caused by the companies that collaborated with the military regime – dismissals of politically active employees for political reasons and inclusion of their names on black lists that led to their arrest and torture by the State, among other violations – was only forthcoming upon publication of the Final Report of the NTC, in December 2014, the time period for initiating civil claims seeking reparation for the losses caused by said companies would have expired in December 2017 – the time limit prescribed by the three-year rule to bring an action.

[1045] Until the present time, the Brazilian Judiciary has not shown any intention to prosecute perpetrators of State violence, as the Judiciary Power follows the Amnesty Act and fails to identify the violence committed during the dictatorship as crimes against humanity. So, the Brazilian Judiciary chooses to treat these past atrocities as common crimes subjected to statutes of limitation. Paradoxically, the *Inter-American Court of Human Rights* condemned Brazil because of the impunity of the crimes committed during the dictatorship (Gomes Lund Case, in 2010 and Herzog Case, in 2018) as these offenses are not subject to limitation periods and should not be covered by amnesty because they are crimes against humanity. For more details, see Chapter 4 on criminal justice and judicial accountability.

[1046] See: Convention on the Non-Applicability of Statutory Limitations to War Crimes and Crimes Against Humanity, November 26, 1968, article 1, "b".

[1047] The Brazilian Civil Code, Law no. 10,406 (2002), article 206, §3, V.

[1048] This understanding is based on jurisprudence, the Judicial Summary no. 278 of the *Superior Court of Justice* (STJ). See: GONDIM, Cláudia Gama, "A Teoria da Actio Nata e o Termo A Quo da Contagem de Prazo Prescricional perante o STJ", http://www.ambito-juridico.com.br/site/?n_link=revista_artigos_leitura&artigo_id=18302&revista_caderno=7.

Another possibility would be to apply the same rule that has been imposed against the State in the case of human rights violations perpetrated during the authoritarian regime. In such cases, the *Superior Tribunal de Justiça* (High Court of Justice) has a solid understanding (through its jurisprudence) that civil liability claims may disregard the statute of limitations for such actions as illegal arrests with the objective of restraining the political activity of a person during the military rule.[1049] Therefore, one legal strategy would be to seek an extension of this interpretation to also cover the losses caused by companies that worked in complicity with the State. However, this complicity theory has not yet been scrutinized by the Judiciary. As has previously been noted, the Federal Prosecutor's Office is focusing on this strategy in the case of the Volkswagen civil liability investigation for human rights violations committed during the dictatorship.[1050]

Certainly, corporate complicity and cooperation with repression are linked not only to the losses suffered by political opponents of the regime – like torture, death, forced disappearance, illegal imprisonment, exile, and illegal dismissal – but they are also connected with losses suffered by society as a whole, especially as a result of the dissemination of fear, the imposition of silence, and the propagation of terror by the State. Hence, beyond the protection of human rights and the quest for truth, memory, and justice, ensuring accountability for private actors regarding their past atrocities may reinforce the perception that there is no forgetting or impunity for crimes against humanity. Even if such crimes occurred in the past, these companies must continue to bear the stain and the reprehensible mark on their records, confirming that the lapse of time does not blot out this kind of systematic illegality.

Another argument for holding these companies civilly liable is the deterrent function, that is: accountability emerges as one of the guarantees of non-recurrence that might dissuade other companies from collaborating with governments that do not protect human rights or respect democratic standards. Thus, corporate responsibility may be held up as a measure demonstrating the current commitment of a company to the defense of human rights. Holding companies accountable supports the idea that they no longer tolerate the past atrocities. But until now, these are all theories that must still be discussed by the

---

[1049] According to the Legal Opinion of the Attorney General of the Union (*Parecer da Advocacia Geral da União*) no. 45/2015. See also: *Migalhas*, "É imprescritível reparação por tortura ocorrida no regime militar", August 23, 2018, https://www.migalhas.com.br/Quentes/17,MI286173,41046-E+imprescritivel+reparacao+por+tortura+ocorrida+no+regime+militar.

[1050] *Correio Braziliense*, "MPF: Investigação sobre atuação da Volkswagen na ditadura é inédita no país", December 14, 2017, https://www.correiobraziliense.com.br/app/noticia/politica/2017/12/14/interna_politica,648057/mpf-investigacao-sobre-atuacao-da-volkswagen-na-ditadura-e-inedita-no.shtml.

Brazilian courts before we may have a concrete answer regarding the efficiency of these different points of view.

9.5. CONCLUSIONS

Beyond the challenges that have to be faced by the Brazilian legal framework, another obstacle to holding a company accountable for its complicity linked to violations of human rights lies in the very fact that the structural conditions facilitating this impunity still exist. As indicated by Shaw[1051] and also by Payne et al.,[1052] in many countries, corporate elites are part of the ruling structure. This means that the economic sustainability and development of some States depends on corporate actors who are at the same time linked to massive human rights violations. And, consequently, corporations try to use their economic power to influence the justice system in some way so as to secure impunity for themselves.[1053] Indeed, Sarkin has observed that the involvement of corporations in violations of human rights has often resulted in substantial influence on governments,[1054] and that pressure has not always served the welfare of society.

Thus, seeking economic accountability through the courts is sometimes not possible due to the various procedural factors mentioned above, or it is simply not suitable from a *realpolitik* perspective based on the influence the companies continue to exercise through their economic power. As Bassiouni has explained,[1055] the human rights arena is defined by a constant tension between the attraction of *realpolitik* and the demand for accountability, making impunity commonly the outcome of such *realpolitik*. Therefore, we must look for innovative perspectives that can sustain the collective world pledge of "never again".

Furthermore, there is another complicated factor: businessmen have resources to hire expensive law firms and legal teams that can extend the duration of cases

---

[1051] SHAW, George Bernard, *Major Barbara*, London, Times Book Club, 1907.
[1052] PAYNE, Leigh A.; PEREIRA, Gabriel; COSTA, Josefina Doz; and BERNAL-BERMÚDEZ, Laura, "Can a Treaty on Business and Human Rights Help Achieve Transitional Justice Goals?", *Homa Publica International Journal on Human Rights and Business*, vol. 1/2017, pp. 3–33.
[1053] This influence through economic power has been allegorically demonstrated in the words that Bernard Shaw, in *Major Barbara*, attributes to Undershaft, the munitions manufacturer, as mentioned at the beginning of this chapter.
[1054] SARKIN, Jeremy, "The Coming of Age of Claims for Reparations for Human Rights Abuses Committed in the South", *SUR – International Journal on Human Rights*, vol. 1/2004, pp. 66–125.
[1055] BASSIOUNI, M. Cherif, "Justice and Peace: The Importance of Choosing Accountability Over Realpolitik", *Case Western Reserve Journal of International Law*, vol. 35/2003, pp. 191–204.

for many years and/or engage in jurisdictional forum-shopping,[1056] while these same resources are usually unavailable to the victims. As a matter of fact, there is recognition that companies, unlike many other defendants, have money and experience to litigate fully and use all the advantages available to them to avoid litigation on the merits.[1057]

Due to all of the above, innovative perspectives for accountability for financial complicity are urgently needed and can contribute to overcoming the obstacles that criminal and civil claims may face. In this sense, memory projects and public spaces related to the process of reconciliation should consider the role of private actors in repression, or should describe how private corporations supported the dictatorial regime, especially the policies of blacklists against the leaders of labor unions and the financial assistance given to the repressive system. Although the theme of memory spaces has been in evidence in recent years, in Brazil, there has been no significant discussion about the possibility of the funding of such sites, such as memorials by private actors who cooperated with the dictatorship.[1058] Hence, we should have high hopes concerning the very recent initiative of VW about the pecuniary reparation agreed with the Federal Prosecutor's Office, whose resources will in the near future be allocated to the different Funds, as explained in this chapter.

In fact, museums and memorials related to Transitional Justice are usually one element of a government initiative, which tends to disseminate a version of past atrocities that conforms to the preferences of those in power. In this sense, what is or is not included in the space is often a strategic decision.[1059] Therefore, an initiative begun by a non-governmental actor could add new points of view and foster a dialogue aiming at the right to truth and memory, which would not constitute a top-down approach but could allow for "voices from below" to be heard (a bottom-up truth-telling strategy).[1060]

[1056] Forum shopping is a plaintiff's decision to file a lawsuit in one court rather than another potentially available court, so that by comparing potentially available courts, a plaintiff can determine the court in which they prefer to pursue their claim. In this way, forum shopping is a strategic behavior. See: WHYTOCK, Christopher, "The Evolving Forum Shopping System", *Cornell Law Review*, vol. 96/2011, pp. 481–534.

[1057] ZIA-ZARIFI, Saman, "Suing Multinational Corporations in the U.S. for Violating International Law", *The UCLA Journal of International Law & Foreign Affairs*, vol. 4/1999, pp. 81–147, at 120–121.

[1058] SOARES, Inês Virgínia Prado and FECHER, Viviane, "Empresas e Cooperação com a Ditadura Brasileira: Novas Possibilidades para a Responsabilização Empresarial", *Manuscript in Preparation*, 2019, https://www.academia.edu/23003189/Empresas_privadas_e_viola%C3%A7%C3%B5es_aos_direitos_humanos_possibilidades_de_responsabiliza%C3%A7%C3%A3o_pela_cumplicidade_com_a_ditadura_no_Brasil.

[1059] BALCELLS, Laia; PALANZA, Valeria; and VOYTAS, Elsa, "Do Museums promote reconciliations? A Field Experiment on Transitional Justice", 2018, paper presented at the *International Studies Association Annual Convention*, http://web.isanet.org/Web/Conferences/San%20Francisco%202018-s/Archive/d263dc13-0674-4cd5-8c6a-724cb3d2de69.pdf.

[1060] LUNDY, Patricia and McGOVERN, Marky, "Whose Justice? Rethinking Transitional Justice from the Bottom Up", *Journal of Law and Society*, vol. 35/2008, pp. 265–292.

Also, regarding the axis of symbolic reparation and a different approach concerning Transitional Justice measures, it should be mentioned that, in 2014, the *Frente de Esculacho Popular* (Popular Front for Denunciation) organized an *escracho* protest, denouncing the São Paulo State Federation of Industries' participation in financing the military *coup* of 1964 and the apparatus of repression against opponents of the regime. As a form of public protest, such *escrachos* combine elements of a march, a theatrical "happening", and a public shaming event in front of the headquarters of the Federation, on Paulista Avenue, the main commercial boulevard of the City of São Paulo.[1061]

In addition, there is still a lot of room to launch symbolic initiatives regarding accountability for companies that were complicit in repression. In a survey conducted in 2015, it was identified that just in the City of São Paulo there were approximately 20 places (including streets, squares and avenues) bearing the names of businessmen who supported the dictatorship.[1062] At the same time, there is a specific provision among the recommendations of the NTC for the revocation of measures aimed at honoring perpetrators of human rights violations.[1063] Promoting name changes for streets, public buildings, and public spaces that refer to private actors would be a remarkable mechanism to be implemented.

Another suggestion raised by Bohoslavsky and Torelly is the idea of a claim with the exclusive objective of getting to know the truth or the details of how corporations assisted the authoritarian regime.[1064] Such a legal strategy recalls the "truth trials" which were conducted in Argentina during the late 1990s,[1065] where judicial procedures were implemented to uncover the past based on the fact that learning the truth about their loved one's fate was an essential right of a victim's family which would assist the mourning process. During that period in Argentina, those trials were an innovation particularly because the judicial system of the country was still blocked by amnesty laws. The same truth trial

---

[1061] *Viomundo*, "Esculacho na Fiesp: Denunciados nas Ruas os que Bancaram Golpistas", April 10, 2014, https://www.viomundo.com.br/denuncias/esculacho-na-fiesp-finalmente-alguem-da-nome-aos-que-bancaram-golpistas.html.

[1062] MONTELEONE, Joana, "Ruas de São Paulo homenageiam empresários que apoiaram o golpe e a ditadura", *Painel Acadêmico*, August 11, 2015, https://painelacademico.uol.com.br/painel-academico/4876-ruas-de-sao-paulo-homenageiam-empresarios-que-apoiaram-o-golpe-e-a-ditadura.

[1063] *National Truth Commission*, "2014 Final Report", Volume 1, Part V, Chapter 18, "Conclusões e Recomendações", Recommendation 28, p. 974.

[1064] BOHOSLAVSKY, Juan Pablo and TORELLY, Marcelo D., "Financial Complicity: The Brazilian Dictatorship Under the Macroscope", in SHARP, D.N. (ed.), *Justice and Economic Violence in Transition* (Springer Series in Transitional Justice vol. 5), New York, Springer, 2014, pp. 233–262.

[1065] *Equipo Argentino de Antropologia Forense* (EAAF), "The Right to Truth in Argentina – 2006 EAAF Annual Report", https://eaaf.typepad.com/annual_report_2006/.

proposition was already tried in Brazil, in 2005, by a family of five which had been imprisoned between 1972 and 1973. They filed a civil action against a torturer and the verdict amounted to a formal declaration of his responsibility for torture.[1066]

Finally, in conclusion, as Payne and Pereira have previously asserted,[1067] the inclusion of corporate responsibility in the list of Transitional Justice mechanisms is within the objectives of that form of justice; that is, as a means to promote peace, reconciliation, and democracy. The inclusion of corporate responsibility as one aspect of Transitional Justice is grounded on the recognition of the universality of human rights: companies are not above the law. The idea is not, however, to merely punish companies for their past behavior, but rather to help build a democratic future on a truly solid basis of respect for and protection of human rights. The observations made in this chapter on the Brazilian case and the complicity of non-State actors in the perpetration of human rights violations form a baseline from which there has been some initial movement in relation to the subject, but it has not yet satisfied all the expectations proposed by the principles of Transitional Justice.

[1066] *Truth Commission of the State of São Paulo Report*, vol. 1, Part III, "As Ações Judiciais das Famílias Teles e Merlino", http://comissaodaverdade.al.sp.gov.br/relatorio/tomo-i/parte-iii-cap3.html.

[1067] PAYNE, Leigh A and PEREIRA, Gabriel, "La Complicidad Corporativa en las Violaciones de Derechos Humanos: Una Innovación en la Justicia Transicional de Argentina?", in Instituto Interamericano de Direitos Humanos, *Derechos Humanos Y Empresas: Reflexiones Desde América Latina*, 2017, pp. 293–310.

CHAPTER 10

FINAL REMARKS

The Limits and Possibilities of Transitional Justice in Brazil

In studying the Brazilian case of Transitional Justice, it can be seen that the end of a dictatorial regime and its political repression comprises a multilayered process of changes or shifts. These moves entail the development of a democratic institutional apparatus at the same time that the country is actually discovering and implementing ways to deal with past crimes and human rights abuses that correspond to its specific political and social context – a context which has been permeated by an authoritarian pattern since the colonial times and republican era.[1068] Consequently, as Jelin has stated,[1069] the task of settling accounts with the past must converge at the same time with the need to build a different future. In Brazil, although there have been efforts to develop the institutional apparatus of democracy since 1985, the truth is that the exceptionally long and devious process of settling accounts with the past over 30 years is still subject to question and under evaluation by a society which is unsure of and divided about the moral value of remembering over forgetting.

The most general observation possible from the history of the democratic opening process in Brazil is that the revocation of a dictatorial political regime and the restoration of democratic forms of government are not necessarily achieved by an overthrow, or by a *coup d'état*, or by the rise of a popular movement. As Codato has noted,[1070] a democratic opening can also result, as in the case of Brazil, from an evolutionary process of changes. Hence, this approach to transition to democracy implies two possibilities: (i) either there is a "transfer

---

[1068] To understand the roots of the authoritarian past in Brazil, from the colonial era with slavery, passing into the Republic Period with practices like clientelism and corruption, see: SCHWARCZ, Lilia Moritz, *Sobre o Autoritarismo Brasileiro*, São Paulo, Companhia das Letras, 2019.

[1069] JELIN, Elizabeth, "Public Memorialization in Perspective: Truth, Justice and Memory of Past Repression in the Southern Cone of South America", *The International Journal of Transitional Justice*, vol. 1/2007, pp. 138–156.

[1070] CODATO, Adriano Nervo, "Uma História Política da Transição Brasileira: Da Ditadura Militar à Democracia", *Revista de Sociologia Política*, vol. 25/2005, pp. 165–175.

of power" from the military to the politicians allied with the regime; (ii) or there is a (negotiated) submission by the military to moderate politicians in opposition to the regime. Indeed, in the Brazilian case, there was a modest dose of both options. The military did not transfer all their power to the ruling party (first with the *Aliança Renovadora Nacional* – ARENA, and later with the *Partido Democrático Social* – PDS); rather, they retained strategic positions inside the State organization and could negotiate their withdrawal according to their own ideas.[1071] Consequently, as Stepan has concluded,[1072] political change (rather than political transformation) eventually led to a liberalization of the dictatorial regime, but not necessarily the democratization of the political system.

What is clear from the Brazilian example is that the path to political change was sequential, with certain classical liberal rights being reintroduced[1073] according to a gradual and moderate strategy,[1074] while Transitional Justice measures were implemented in a very fragmented way. As a result, we barely see anything like a transition which is coordinated, coherent, and planned so as to avoid the risk of the return of authoritarian rule. That is to say, even though there have been efforts towards the removal of laws and decrees dating from the dictatorship – the so-called "authoritarian debris" (*entulhos autoritários*),[1075] which are legacies from the 1964–1985 dictatorship and also from an even more remote past dating from the colonial, imperial and even republican era – the three decades of the 1988 Federal Constitution led us to realize that the authoritarian debris are much bigger than the mere wreckage from the dictatorship waiting for its annihilation. Indeed they are a stockpile that constantly renews the forms

---

[1071] Freire, Américo, "A Via Partidária da Transição Política Brasileira", *Varia História*, vol. 30/2014, pp. 287–308.

[1072] Stepan, Alfred C.,"Introdução", in Stepan, Alfred C and Fishlow, Albert (eds.), *Democratizando o Brasil*, Rio de Janeiro, Paz e Terra, 1988.

[1073] For instance, the 1988 Constitution assured equality between men and women, prohibited torture, and determined the inviolable character of intimacy, private life and honor.

[1074] The Constitutional Assembly of 1987–1988 organized a draft so promising to individual rights and civil liberties that it was nicknamed by Ulysses Guimarães, the Assembly's president, as the "Citizen's Constitution" (*Constituição Cidadã*). See: *Educacional*, http://www.educacional.com.br/reportagens/20AnosConstituicao/cidada.asp.

[1075] The expression "authoritarian debris" began to be used in 1979 by the opposition to then President João Baptista Figueiredo to designate the chaotic Brazilian legal order after the revocation of many institutional acts and decrees of exception, which were imposed by the dictatorship. The denunciation of the "authoritarian debris" pointed out that, despite such revocations, some laws (i.e. the Amnesty Law) and institutions persisted in the legal order with the authoritarian tone of the military dictatorship. See: Mendes, Conrado Hübner, "O entulho autoritário era estoque: o regime nascido da Constituição de 1988 não apenas incorporou práticas da ditadura, mas criou formas novas de autoritarismo", *Quatro Cinco Um*, March 1, 2020, https://www.quatrocincoum.com.br/br/artigos/d/o-entulho-autoritario-era-estoque.

of authoritarianism, as observed by Schwarcz,[1076] which so far the Transitional Justice methods were also unable to dismantle.

In order to understand the Brazilian context, we have to admit that the Brazilian political transition, beginning in 1974 and ending along with the Sarney administration (1985–1990), was very peculiar: ironically, it lasted longer than the regime itself (1964–1974), and its main feature was the continuity of authoritarianism in the institutions of civil government that should, after all, have been in "transition".[1077] Linz and Stepan have already suggested that the unusual length of the Brazilian transition is related to the fact that the authoritarian regime was hierarchically controlled by a military organization,[1078] which had sufficient power to manage the pace of the transition and to extract a high price for withdrawing from power.

As a result, if it were possible to extract a lesson from the Transitional Justice measures applied in Brazil in just a few words, one might dare to say that there are some States less inclined to revisit the painful experiences of authoritarian repression, and, in those cases, they may seek to implement policies of oblivion, usually through a discourse of reconciliation. Hence, it is not unusual to find people in Brazil looking at the past in order to glorify the "order and progress" that the dictatorship supposedly secured,[1079] at the same time that there are competing and conflicting understandings and memories of that past, as occurred in the recent debate on the celebration (or not) of the 1964 *coup d'état*.[1080] Curiously, this point of view was reinforced when Power cautioned his readers to avoid a superficial assessment of the country in the sense that Brazil has firmly dissociated itself from the legacy of 1964–1985 dictatorship;[1081] a closer inspection of the country's politics would demonstrate that contemporary Brazilian democracy since 1985 has been, and continues to be, profoundly shaped by legacies of military rule.[1082]

[1076] Schwarcz, Lilia M., *Sobre o Autoritarismo Brasileiro*, São Paulo, Companhia das Letras, 2019.

[1077] CODATO, Adriano Nervo, "Uma História Política da Transição Brasileira: Da Ditadura Militar à Democracia", *Revista de Sociologia Política*, vol. 25/2005, pp. 165–175.

[1078] LINZ, Juan J. and STEPAN, Alfred, *A Transição e Consolidação da Democracia: a Experiência do Sul da Europa e da América do Sul*, São Paulo, Paz e Terra, 1999.

[1079] See: *Revista Forum*, "Vamos defender o governo militar, diz dono da Havan, durante evento do MBL", November 23, 2018, https://www.revistaforum.com.br/vamos-defender-o-governo-militar-diz-dono-da-havan-durante-evento-do-mbl/. *Jornal Folha de São Paulo*, "SBT ressucita e mata 'Brasil, ame-o ou deixe-o'em vinheta relâmpago", November 6, 2018, https://www1.folha.uol.com.br/ilustrada/2018/11/sbt-ressuscita-brasil-ame-o-ou-deixo-o-em-nova-vinheta.shtml.

[1080] *Revista Veja*, "Maioria dos Brasileiros Rejeita Comemorar Golpe de 1964, Diz DataFolha", April 6, 2019, https://veja.abril.com.br/politica/maioria-dos-brasileiros-rejeita-comemorar-golpe-de-1964-diz-datafolha/.

[1081] POWER, Timothy J., "The Brazilian Military Regime of 1964–1985: Legacies for Contemporary Democracy", *Iberoamericana*, vol. 62/2016, pp. 13–26.

[1082] Power (2016, ibid.) affirms that even though for twenty years Brazilians had been governed by leaders of three factions of opposition to military rule – first the intellectual wing by the

Summing up the historical context of the Brazilian experience in Transitional Justice, it is possible to articulate some findings. First, as part of the Armed Forces' tactics, the military regime suggested that there was an equivalency between crimes committed by the State and the crimes of those who opposed the dictatorship, resulting in a level of impunity that reduced and delayed the opportunities for reparations, truth, memory, and justice for a very long time. Secondly, in the period from the adoption of the 1988 Constitution to the 2014 Final Report of the National Truth Commission, several circumstances have challenged this initial strategy. The commissions in charge of promoting reparations policies were instrumental – beginning in 1995 with the SCPDD and continuing in 2002 with the Amnesty Commission – in breaking the cycle of denial that had endured within society and government;[1083] and the human rights activists and family members of the disappeared persons stepped up and initiated successive lawsuits claiming that the 1979 Amnesty Law protected torturers.

Nevertheless, Bohoslavsky and Torelly have identified the initiatives leading to the formation of these commissions as creating an "abstract model" of accountability,[1084] where the State officially recognized the crimes identified through the work of the 1995 and 2002 commissions, assuming both moral and economic responsibility, but at the same time completely avoided the investigation or prosecution of the individual criminals and their accomplices. Hence, the Brazilian Transitional Justice framework is founded on a model of abstract or of nonfigurative accountability, which has hardly been judged as an appropriate response to past atrocities.

Fernando Henrique Cardoso administration, then the social movement wing during the Lula administration, and finally the armed resistance wing with the Dilma Rousseff administration – the country seemed changed only at its surface. See also: ZAVERUCHA, Jorge, "Relações Civil-Militares: o legado autoritário da Constituição Brasileira de 1988", in TELES, Edson & SAFATLE, Vladimir (orgs.), *O que Resta da Ditadura*, São Paulo, Boitempo, 2010.

[1083] In fact, in 1995, the Cardoso administration formally recognized the accountability of the Brazilian State for human rights violations committed after 1964. Consequently, this initial step made it legally possible for the State to pay reparations to former political prisoners and also to family members of disappeared people. After 2002, the Lula administration expanded the reparations program and offered official pardons. Meanwhile, human rights activists stepped up their efforts to revisit past abuses, filing repeated lawsuits claiming that the 1979 Amnesty Law protected torturers. In May 2010, the Supreme Court held in a vote that the Amnesty Law was bilateral, that it had been negotiated during the dictatorship, and that torture was in fact a political crime covered by such statute.

[1084] BOHOSLAVSKY, Juan Pablo and TORELLY, Marcelo D., "Financial Complicity: The Brazilian Dictatorship Under the Macroscope", in SHARP, D.N. (ed.), *Justice and Economic Violence in Transition* (Springer Series in Transitional Justice vol. 5), New York, Springer, 2014, pp. 233–262.

In fact, the root cause of this abstract accountability – or one might say of this "never ending process" of healing the past that Brazil has faced for three decades – is that the emergence or non-emergence of Transitional Justice methods is less a moral question and more one related to the distribution of power during and after any type of transition.[1085] Consequently, only in those countries where political authority collapsed and was replaced by the opposition did the possibility of prosecution, truth-telling, and reparations present themselves as expected.[1086] On the other hand, in transitions through reform, such as that which occurred in Brazil during the '80s, in which an authoritarian pattern was a powerful partner in the transitional process, the scope for the introduction of meaningful Transitional Justice measures is exceptionally limited. Hence, in observing such limitations, Galindo even remarked that the struggles of carrying forward genuine Transitional Justice are likely to have a considerable influence on the institutional and social fragility of the democratic culture and respect for human rights,[1087] which for that author still seems to be an unfinished venture in Brazil.

After reading the experiences summarized in this book, the reader will undoubtedly come to feel frustrated at the stymieing of the several existing Transitional Justice measures in Brazil, mainly because the everyday life of its citizens has changed little or even gotten worse. This is especially true if one looks to, for instance, the chapters dedicated to indigenous people and gender-related problems. In reality, the Brazilian case of Transitional Justice was too "top-down", too elite-driven and too content with simple the restoration of civil and political rights. It gave those rights the high priority they receive in Western rights discourse, but it failed to acknowledge that the underlying causes of any conflict tend to be structural and resource-related. Certainly, part of this frustration is due to the continuing fragility of post-dictatorship Brazil, where economic and social marginalization continues to spark violence, with a political system characterized by clientelism/patronage and bribery/corruption. All these factors combined drastically reduce enthusiasm for any democratic reform duly implemented.[1088]

Indeed, Baggio has signaled that the Brazilian transition has been marked by several contradictions that reflect a dispute of values regarding the historical

---

[1085] HUNTINGTON, Samuel P., *The Third Wave: Democratization in the Late Twentieth Century*, Norman, OK, University of Oklahoma Press, 1991.

[1086] PINTO, António Costa and MORLINO, Leonardo, *Dealing with the Legacy of Authoritarianism – The Politics of the Pat in Southern European Democracies*, New York, Routledge, 2011, p. 5.

[1087] GALINDO, Bruno, "Transitional Justice in Brazil and the Jurisprudence of the Inter-American Court of Human Rights: A Difficult Dialogue with the Brazilian Judiciary", *Sequência*, vol. 79/2018, pp. 27–44.

[1088] ROHT-ARRIAZA, Naomi, "Measures of Non-Repetition in Transitional Justice: The Missing Link?", *Legal Studies Research Paper Series*, University of California Hastings College of the Law, https://papers.ssrn.com/sol3/papers.cfm?abstract_id=2746055.

facts that marked the end of the dictatorship as well as the disagreements relating to the Transition Justice measures that have been implemented to date. In fact, as demonstrated in the chapter about the commissions, there is a strong criticism concerning the reparations model that was carried out in Brazil, alleging that such model was reduced to a merely financial approach and it ended up diminishing those who receive such reparations to "treasure hunters" who aim to live at the expense of public funds. On the other hand, as explained, there are those who perceive reparation as something that goes far beyond the purely financial issue, reaching a moral and symbolic dimension that cannot be overlooked. The challenge is that these disputes lead us to a chaotic analysis framework, which prevents the perception of what are the best strategies for advancing the consolidation of a Transitional Justice for the Brazilian country.

To illustrate such a blurred scenario, let's say that at the beginning Brazil had chosen a process of "forgetting", which started with the 1979 Amnesty Law and was reinforced by the 2010 judgment of the Federal Supreme Court, but in the same country it was also possible to observe some steps towards the process of "remembering", which was mainly coordinated by the three different commissions (the SCPDD, the Amnesty Commission, and the NTC). Consequently, it may be seen that the collective memory of the country is still an on-going strategic action, where different interests have been pursued, often in contradiction to a clearly defined and unique politics of memory. In reality, by observing the Brazilian case, this author tends to agree with Mutua and accepts that the Transitional Justice corpus is not a creed or a set of normative principles suspended in outer space.[1089] The matters that it affects are earthbound and concern the immediate routine of politics and a diverse range of disappointments.

A close reading of the Brazilian example suggests that, as Linz and Stepan previously observed, democracy is not yet "the only game in town",[1090] and it remains unclear just how much – if at all – the NTC's efforts and other related memory initiatives can really boost public confidence in democracy.[1091]

Unfortunately, in some instances, post-conflict initiatives or Transitional Justice measures in Brazil have appeared to become yet just another box to tick on the long "post-conflict checklist". In fact, one should not deny that many initiatives are not a set of culture-neutral or apolitical practices. Whether or not past measures were effective, the real transformation that remains to be seen is

---

[1089] MUTUA, Makau, "The Ideology of Human Rights", *Virginia Journal of International Law*, vol. 36/1996, pp. 589–657.
[1090] LINZ, Juan J. and STEPAN, Alfred, *Problems of Democratic Transition and Consolidation. Southern Europe, South America and Post-Communist Europe*, Baltimore MD, Johns Hopkins University Press, 1996.
[1091] RYAN, H.E., "From Absent to Present Pasts: Civil Society, Democracy and the Shifting Place of Memory in Brazil", *Journal of Civil Society*, vol. 12/2016, pp. 158–177.

if it will be possible to remove the friction surrounding the topic of Transitional Justice measures in Brazil. In order to reach a more coherent, unique, and consistent view of the past and the outcomes of democracy and the Rule of Law, there must be a closing of the fissures in the divided and polarized society that remain until today,[1092] and that have led Brazil to continue walking the tightrope.[1093]

[1092] FRANCO, Luiza, "Mais da Metade dos Brasileiros Acham que Direitos Humanos Beneficiam Quem Não Merece, Diz Pesquisa", *BBC News Brasil*, August 11, 2018, https://www.bbc.com/portuguese/brasil-45138048.

[1093] An example of the Brazilian polarized society may be observed when, in October 31, 2022, leftist former president Luiz Inácio Lula da Silva defeated rightwing incumbent Jair Bolsonaro. Lula obtained 50.90% of the votes to Bolsonaro's 49.10%.

BIBLIOGRAPHY

ABRÃO, Paulo and TORELLY, Marcelo D., "As dimensões da Justiça de Transição no Brasil, a Eficácia da Lei de Anistia e as Alternativas para a Verdade e a Justiça", in PAYNE, Leigh A.; ABRÃO, Paulo; and TORELLY, Marcelo D. (eds.), *A Anistia na Era da Responsabilização: o Brasil em Perspectiva Internacional e Comparada*, Oxford, Oxford University Press, 2011.

—— "The Reparations Program as the Lynchpin of Transitional Justice in Brazil", in REÁTEGUI, Félix (ed.), *Transitional Justice: Handbook for Latin America*, New York, Ministry of Justice and International Center for Transitional Justice, 2011, pp. 443–485.

—— "Mutações do Conceito de Anistia na Justiça de Transição Brasileira – A Terceira Fase de Luta pela Anistia", *Revista de Direito Brasileira*, vol. 3/2012, pp. 357–379.

—— "Resistance to Change. Brazil's Persistent Amnesty and its Alternatives for Truth and Justice", in LESSA, Francesca and PAYNE, Leigh A. (eds.), *Amnesty in the Age of Human Rights Accountability: Comparative and International Perspectives*, New York, Cambridge University Press, 2012, pp. 152–181.

ABRÃO, Paulo; RAMPIN, Talita Tatiana Dias; and FONSECA, Lívia Gimenes Dias da, "Direito à Justiça e Reforma das Instituições", in SOUSA, José Geraldo de, Jr.; SILVA FILHO, José Carlos Moreira da; PAIXÃO, Cristiano; FONSECA, Lívia Gimenes Dias da; and RAMPIN, Talita Tatiana Dias (eds.), *O direito achado na rua: introdução crítica à justiça de transição na América Latina*, Brasília, UnB, vol. 7, 2015.

ADORNO, Sérgio, "Criminal Violence in Modern Brazil: The Case of the State of São Paulo", in SHELLEY, Louise and VIGH, József (eds.), *Social Changes, Crime and Police: International Conference*, Amsterdam, Harwood, 1995.

—— "Insegurança versus Direitos Humanos: entre a Lei e a Ordem", *Tempo Social*, vol. 11/1999.

—— "História e Desventura: O 3° Programa Nacional de Direitos Humanos", *Novos Estudos CEBRAP*, vol. 86/2010, pp. 5–20.

AGAMBEN, Giorgio, *Estado de Exceção*, São Paulo, Boitempo, 2004.

AGÉNOR, Pierre-Richard and CANUTO, Otaviano, "Gender Equality and Economic Growth in Brazil: A Long-Run Analysis", *The World Bank Policy Research Working Paper no. 6348*, 2013, https://openknowledge.worldbank.org/bitstream/handle/10986/13174/wps6348.pdf?sequence=1.

AGUILAR, Rosario; CUNOW, Saul; and DESPOSATO, Scott, "Choice Sets, Gender, and Candidate Choice in Brazil", *Electoral Studies* vol. 39/2015, pp. 230–242.

AGUIRRE, Daniel, "Multinational Corporations and the Realisations of Economic, Social and Cultural Rights", *California Western International Law Journal*, vol. 35/2004, pp. 53–82.

AGUIRRE, Luis Pérez, "The Consequences of Impunity in Society", International Commission of Jurists, *Justice Not Impunity, International Meeting, November 2-5, 1992*, Geneva, International Commission of Jurists, 1993.

Bibliography

ALMEIDA, Eneá de Stutz e and TORREÃO, Marcelo Pires, "O Papel Institucional do Poder Judiciário nas Quatro Dimensões do Sistema de Justiça de Transição", *Revista de Movimentos Sociais e Conflitos*, vol. 3/2017, pp. 20–41.

ALMEIDA, Lucilia Neves Delgado de, "O Governo João Goulart e o Golpe de 1964: Memória, História e Historiografia", *Tempo*, vol. 14/2010, pp. 125–145.

AMANN, Edmund and BAER, Werner, "Neoliberalism and its Consequences in Brazil", *Journal of Latin American Studies*, vol. 34/2002, pp. 945–959.

ANDRADE, Priscila, "A Marca do Anjo: A Trajetória de Zuzu Angel e o Desenvolvimento da Identidade Visual de sua Grife", *Iara Revista de Moda, Cultura e Arte*, vol. 2/2009, pp. 85–119.

ANDRADE, Regis de Castro, "Política e Pobreza no Brasil", *Lua Nova*, vol. 19/1989, pp. 107–121.

APOLINÁRIO, Silvia Menicucci O.S. and BASTOS, Lucia Elena Arantes Ferreira, "Ensaio sobre a Impunidade: Os Crimes Contra a Humanidade Cometidos no Brasil", *Universitas Jus*, vol. 27/2016, pp. 33–47.

AQUINO, Maria Aparecida de, "Brasil: 1964–2014 – Uma Comemoraçãp Possível", *Cadernos de História*, vol. 15/2014, pp. 190–207.

ARAÚJO, Rayane Barreto de, "Imprensa e História: a Crise do SPI e a Violação dos Direitos Indígenas Narrados pelo Jornal do Brasil (1966–1968)", *Anais do XVII Encontro de História da ANPUH*, Rio de Janeiro, 2016, http://www.encontro2016.rj.anpuh.org/resources/anais/42/1466920295_ARQUIVO_ARTIGO-RAYANEBARRETOUFRJ-versaofinal.pdf.

ARENDT, Hannah, *Responsabilidade e Julgamento*, São Paulo, Companhia das Letras, 2004.

ARGUELHES, Diego Werneck and HARTMANN, Ivar A., "Timing Control without Docket Control: How Individual Justices Shape the Brazilian Supreme Court's Agenda", *Journal of Law and Courts*, vol. 5/2017, pp. 105–140.

ARTHUR, Paige, "How Transitions Reshaped Human Rights: A Conceptual History of Transitional Justice", *Human Rights Quarterly*, vol. 31/2009, pp. 321–367.

ASH, Timothy Garton, *The Truth About Dictatorship*, New York Review Books, February 19, 1998, available at https://www.nybooks.com/articles/1998/02/19/the-truth-about-dictatorship/.

ASSIS, Emerson Francisco de, "Das Estranhas Catedrais da Ditadura Civil-Militar à Operação Lava Jato: A Repercussão da Ineficácia do Eixo Memória e Verdade na Justiça de Transição Brasileira", *Contemporânea – Revista de Ética e Filosofia Política*, vol. 3/2017, pp. 36–60.

BAGGIO, Roberta Camineiro, "Anistia e Reconhecimento: o Processo de (Des)integração Social da Transição Política Brasileira", in PAYNE, Leigh A.; ABRÃO, Paulo; and TORELLY, Marcelo D. (eds.), *A Anistia na Era da Responsabilização: o Brasil em Perspectiva Internacional e Comparada*, Oxford, Oxford University Press, 2011, pp. 250–277.

BAGGIO, Roberta Camineiro and MIRANDA, Lara Caroline, "Poder Judiciário e estado de exceção no Brasil: as marcas ideológicas de uma cultura jurídica autoritária", *Revista do Instituto de Hermenêutica Jurídica*, vol. 8/2010, pp. 149–179.

BAK, Joan L., "Cartels, Cooperatives, and Corporatism: Getúlio Vargas in Rio Grande do Sul on the Eve of Brazil's 1930 Revolution", *Hispanic American Historical Review*, vol. 63/1983, pp. 255–275.

BARRETO, Ana Cristina Teixeira, "Igualdade entre Sexos: Carta de 1988 é um marco contra discriminação", November 5, 2010, *CONJUR*, https://www.conjur.com.br/2010-nov-05/constituicao-1988-marco-discriminacao-familia-contemporanea.

BARROS, Alexandre, "Problemas de Transição Democrática na Frente Militar: a Definição do Papel dos Militares, a Mudança da Doutrina e a Modernização do País", *Política e Estratégia*, vol. VI/1988, pp. 206–214.

BASSIOUNI, M. Cherif, *Crimes Against Humanity in International Criminal Law*, The Hague, Kluwer Law International, 1999.

—— "Justice and Peace: The Importance of Choosing Accountability Over Realpolitik", *Case Western Reserve Journal of International Law*, vol. 35/2003, pp. 191–204.

—— "Universal Jurisdiction for International Crimes: Historical Perspectives and Contemporary Practice", *Virginia Journal of International Law*, vol. 42/2001, pp. 81–162.

BASTOS, Lucia Elena Arantes Ferreira, "A Lei de Anistia Brasileira: Os Crimes Conexos, a Dupla Via e Tratados de Direitos Humanos", *Revista da Faculdade de Direito da Universidade de São Paulo*, vol. 103/2008, pp. 593–628.

—— "Anistia e o Direito Internacional", *O Estado de São Paulo – Caderno Aliás*, November 9, 2008, p. 7.

—— *Anistia: As Leis Internacionais e o Caso Brasileiro*, Curitiba, Juruá, 2009.

BASTOS, Lucia Elena Arantes Ferreira and SOARES, Inês Virgínia Prado, "The Challenges of Symbolic Reparations for Gender Justice in Brazil", in BOESTEN, Jelke and SCANLON, Helen (eds.), *Gender, Transitional Justice and Memorial Arts – Global Perspectives on Commemoration and Mobilisation*, New York, Routledge, 2021.

—— "Zuzu Angel: quem é essa mulher que fez da moda sua arma política e da maternidade, sua razão de existir?", in SOARES, Inês Virgínia; PIOVESAN, Flávia; RABELO, Cecilia Nunes; and BARBOUR, Vivian (eds.), *Mulheres, Direito e Protagonismo Cultural*, São Paulo, Almedina, 2022, pp. 551–576.

BATISTA, Nilo, "Aspectos Jurídico-Penais da Anistia", *Revista Encontros com a Civilização Brasileira*, vol. 19/1980, pp. 195–206.

BERNSTEIN, Anita, "Pecuniary Reparations Following National Crisis: A Convergence of Tort Theory Microfinance, and Gender Equality", *University of Pennsylvannia Journal of International Law*, vol. 31/2009, pp. 1–51.

BIANCHI, Andrea, "Immunity versus Human Rights: The Pinochet Case", *European Journal of International Law*, vol. 10/1999, pp. 237–277.

BINDER, Christina, "The Prohibition of Amnesties by the Inter-American Court of Human Rights", *German Law Journal*, vol. 12/2011, pp. 1203–1230.

BLUM, Carolyn Patty, "Visions of Justice and Accountability: Transitional Justice and Film", in RAMÍREZ-BARAT, Clara (ed.), *Transitional Justice, Culture, and Society Beyond Outreach*, New York, International Center for Transitional Justice and Social Science Research Council, 2014, pp. 461–488.

BOESTEN, Jelke and WILDING, Polly, "Transformative Gender Justice: Setting an Agenda", *Women's Studies International Forum*, vol. 51/2015, pp. 75–80.

BOGDANDY, Armin von, "Pluralism, Direct Effect, and the Ultimate Say: on the Relationship Between International and Domestic Constitutional Law", *International Journal of Constitutional Law*, vol. 6/2008, pp. 397–413.

BOHOSLAVSKY, Juan Pablo and OPGENHAFFEN, Veerle, "The Past and Present of Corporate Complicity: Financing the Argentinean Dictatorship", *Harvard Human Rights Journal*, vol. 23/2010, pp. 157–203.

BOHOSLAVSKY, Juan Pablo and TORELLY, Marcelo D., "Financial Complicity: The Brazilian Dictatorship Under the Macroscope", in SHARP, D.N. (ed.), *Justice and Economic Violence in Transition* (Springer Series in Transitional Justice vol. 5), New York, Springer, 2014, pp. 233–262.

BOLLEN, K.A., "Issues in the Comparative Measurement of Political Democracy", *American Sociological Review*, vol. 45/1980, pp. 370–390.

BOLOGNESI, Bruno, "A Cota Eleitoral de Gênero: Política Pública ou Engenharia Eleitoral?", *Paraná Eleitoral Revista Brasileira de Direito Eleitoral e Ciência Política*, vol. 1/2012, pp. 113–129.

BORAINE, Alexander L., "Transitional Justice: A Holistic Interpretation", *Journal of International Affairs*, vol. 60/2006, pp. 17–27.

BORGES, Rosa Maria Zaia; SILVA, Simone Schuck da; and ALBUQUERQUE, Laura Gigante, "Crimes Sexuais na Ditadura Civil-Militar Brasileira (1964–1985) – Perspectivas das Violências Institucional e de Gênero", *Sistema Penal & Violência*, vol. 8/2016, pp. 3–15.

BÖRZEL, Tanja A. and RISSE, Thomas, "Human Rights in Areas of Limited Statehood: The New Agenda", in RISSE, Thomas; ROPP, Stephen C.; and SIKKINK, Kathryn (eds.), *The Persistent Power of Human Rights – From Commitment to Compliance*, Cambridge, Cambridge University Press, 2013.

BRETT, Sebastian; BICKFORD, Louis; SEVCENKO, Liz; and RIOS, Marcela, *Memorialization and Democracy: State Policy and Civic Action*, New York, International Center for Transitional Justice, 2007.

BUCCI, Eugênio, "A Letra da Verdade", *Revista de Estudos Avançados da USP*, vol. 30/2016, pp. 297–302.

BUENO-HANSEN, Pascha, "The Emerging LGBTI Rights Challenge to Transitional Justice in Latin America", *International Journal of Transitional Justice*, vol. 12/2018, pp. 126–145.

BURGORGUE-LARSEN, Laurence and TORRES, Amaya Ubeda de, *Les Grandes Décision de la Cour Interaméricaine des Droits de L'Homme*, Brussels, Bruylant, 2008.

CABRILLAC, Rémy; FRISON-ROCHE, Marie-Anne; and REVET, Thierry (eds.), *Libertés et Droits Fondamentaux*, Paris, Dalloz, 2006.

CAMPOS, Pedro Henrique Pedreira, *Estranhas Catedrais. As Empreiteiras Brasileiras e a Ditadura Civil-Militar (1964–1985)*, Niterói, Eduff, 2014.

CARNEIRO, Ana and CIOCCARI, Marta, *Retrato da Repressão Política no Campo (1962–1985) – Camponeses Torturados, Mortos e Desaparecidos*, Brasília, MDA, 2010.

CARRANZA, Ruben, "Plunder and Pain: Should Transitional Justice Engage with Corruption and Economic Crimes?", *The International Journal of Transitional Justice*, vol. 2/2008, pp. 310–330.

CARRANZA, Ruben; CORREA, Cristián; and NAUGHTON, Elena, "Reparative Justice: More than Words. Apologies as a Form of Reparation", New York/Nairobi, International Center for Transitional Justice, December 2015.

CARRASCO, Jorge Catala; DRINOT, Paulo; and SCORER, James, *Comics and Memory in Latin America*, Pittsburgh PA, University of Pittsburgh Press, 2017.

CARVALHO FILHO, Aloysio, *Comentários ao Código Penal*, vol. IV, Rio de Janeiro, Forense, 1958.

CARVALHO, L.M., *Mulheres que Foram à Luta Armada*, São Paulo, Globo, 1998.

CASSESE, Antonio, *International Criminal Law*, New York, Oxford University Press, 2003.

Castro, Paulo Rabello de Castro and Ronci, Marcio, "Sixty Years of Populism in Brazil", in Dornbusch, Rudiger and Edwards, Sebastian (eds.), *The Macroeconomics of Populism in Latin America*, Chicago IL, University of Chicago Press, 1991, pp. 151–173.

Catela, Ludmila da Silva, "Em Nome da Pacificação Nacional: Anistias, Pontos Finais e Indultos no Cone Sul", in Castro, Celso and D'araújo, Maria C. (eds.), *Democracia e Forças Armadas no Cone Sul*, Rio de Janeiro, Editora Fundação Getúlio Vargas, 2000, pp. 301–315.

—— "Staged Memories: Conflicts and Tensions in Argentine Public Memory Sites", *Memory Studies*, vol. 8/2014, pp. 9–21.

Cavallaro, James L., "Toward Fair Play: A Decade of Transformation and Resistance in International Human Rights Advocacy in Brazil", *Chicago Journal of International Law*, vol. 3/2002, pp. 481–492.

Cavallaro, James L. and Brewer, Stephanie Erin, "Reevaluating Regional Human Rights Litigation in the Twenty-First Century: The Case of the Inter-American Court", *The American Journal of International Law*, vol. 102/2008, pp. 768–827.

Chueiri, Vera Karam de and Camara, Heloisa Fernandes "(Des)ordem Constitucional: Engrenagens da Máquina Ditatorial no Brasil Pos-64", *Lua Nova*, vol. 95/2015, pp. 259–289.

Choukr, Fauzi Hassan, "Diálogos Possíveis entre o Supremo Tribunal Federal e a Corte Interamericana de Direitos Humanos no Caso Araguaia: uma Defesa Ampla, Geral e Irrestrita dos Direitos Humanos?", *Revista Brasileira de Direito Processual Penal*, vol. 2/2016, pp. 269–299.

Ciccarone, Celeste, "The Guarani Farm: Indigenous Narratives about Removal, Reclusion and Escapes during the Military Dictatorship in Brazil", *Vibrant: Virtual Brazilian Anthropology*, vol. 15/2018, http://dx.doi.org/10.1590/1809-43412018v15n3d511.

Cioccari, Marta, "Narrativas da Repressão: Trabalhadores do Campo e das Minas durante o Regime Militar no Brasil", *Teoria e Cultura*, vol. 6/2011, pp. 25–44.

Codato, Adriano Nervo, "Uma História Política da Transição Brasileira: Da Ditadura Militar à Democracia", *Revista de Sociologia Política*, vol. 25/2005, pp. 165–175.

Colling, Ana Maria, *As Mulheres e a Ditadura Militar no Brasil*, https://wp.ufpel.edu.br/ndh/files/2017/02/10.-ana_colling.pdf.

—— *A Resistência da Mulher à Ditadura Militar no Brasil*, Rio de Janeiro, Rosa dos Tempos, 1997.

Colling, Ana Maria and Cavalcanti, Ary Albuquerque Junior., "Militantes e Guerrilheiras – As Mulheres e a Ditadura Militar no Brasil", *Espacialidades*, vol. 15, 2019, pp. 47–61.

Collins, Cath, "Human rights defense in and through the courts in (post) Pinochet Chile", *Radical History Review*, vol. 124/2016, pp. 129–140.

Corntassel, Jeff and Holder, Cindy, "Who's Sorry Now? Government Apologies, Truth Commissions, and Indigenous Self-Determination in Australia, Canada, Guatemala and Peru", *Human Rights Review*, vol. 9/2008, pp. 465–489.

Costa, Emilia Viotti da, *The Brazilian Empire: Myths and Histories*, Chicago/London, University of Chicago Press, 1985, p. 233.

Crane, Susan, "Memory, Distortion and History in the Museum", *History and Theory*, vol. 36/1997, pp. 44–63.

CRENZEL, Emilio, "Argentina's National Commission on the Disappearance of Persons: Contributions to Transitional Justice", *The International Journal of Transitional Justice*, vol. 2/2008, pp. 173–191.

CUNHA, Manuela Carneiro da, "O STF e os Índios, *Folha de São Paulo*, November 20, 2014, https://www1.folha.uol.com.br/opiniao/2014/11/1550130-manuela-carneiro-da-cunha-o-stf-e-os-indios.shtml.

DE GREIFF, Pablo, "On Making the Invisible Visible: The Role of Cultural Interventions in Transitional Justice Processes", in RAMÍREZ-BARAT, Clara (ed.), *Transitional Justice, Culture, and Society Beyond Outreach*, New York, International Center for Transitional Justice and Social Science Research Council, 2014, pp. 11–24.

DEL VECCHIO, Angelo, "A Lei e a Força no Regime Militar Brasileiro: da Proscrição da Frente Ampla à Edição do Ato Institucional n. 5", *Revista Espaço de Diálogo e Desconexão*, vol. 6/2013.

DELMAS-MARTY, Mireille, *Le Pluralisme Ordonne: Les Forces Imaginantes Du Droit*, Paris, Seuil, 2006.

DEMETRIO, André and KOZICKI, Katya, "A (In)Justiça de Transição para os Povos Indígenas no Brasil", *Direito e Práxis*, vol. 10/2019, pp. 129–169.

DERRIDA, J, *Mal de Arquivo. Uma Impressão Freudiana*, Rio de Janeiro, Relume Dumará, 2005.

DIACON, Todd A., *Stringing Together a Nation: Cândido Mariano da Silva Rondon and the Construction of a Modern Brazil (1906–1930)*, London, Duke University Press, 2004.

DICKINSON, Emily, "Compensation", *The Poems of Emily Dickinson: Series Two*, Boston, Roberts Brothers, 1896.

DINIZ, Eli, "A Transição Política no Brasil: Uma Reavaliação da Dinâminca da Abertura", *Dados*, vol. 28, 1985, pp. 329–346.

DRAGOO, Michelle, "Does One Size Really Fit All? Transitional Justice Process and Commemoration in Post-Conflict Santiago Atitlán Guatemala", *Sociology and Anthropology*, vol. 4/2016, pp. 546–553.

DUARTE, Ana Rita Fonteles, "O Movimento Feminino pela Anistia na Luta contra a Ditadura no Brasil: Entrevista com Therezinha Zerbini", *Revista Estudos Feministas*, vol. 27/2019, pp. 1–7.

DURAN, Maria Renata da Cruz and BENTIVOGLIO, Julio, "Paul Ricoeur e o Lugar da Memória na Historiografia Contemporânea", *Dimensões*, vol. 30/2013, pp. 213–244.

ELSTER, Jon, *Closing the Books: Transitional Justice in Historical Perspective*, Cambridge, Cambridge University Press, 2004.

ENGSTROM, Par, "Brazilian Post-Transitional Justice and the Inter-American Human Rights System", *Conference on Post-Transitional Justice in Brazil*, Brazil Institute, King's College, London, 2013.

FABRIZ, Daury Cesar, "Cidadania, democracia e acesso à justiça", in ALMEIDA, Eneá de Stutz e (ed.), *Direitos e Garantias Fundamentais*, Florianópolis, Fundação Boiteux, 2006.

FAUSTO, Boris, "A revolução de 1930", in MOTA, Carlos Guilherme (ed.), *Brasil em Perspectiva*, São Paulo, Difel, 1981.

—— *A Revolução de 1930: História e Historiografia*, São Paulo, Companhia das Letras, 1997.

—— *História Concisa do Brasil*, São Paulo, EDUSP, 2015.

FAVERO, Eugenia Augusta Gonzaga, "Crimes da Ditadura: Iniciativas do Ministério Público Federal em São Paulo", in SOARES, Inês Virgínia Prado and SHIMADA, Sandra Akemi (eds.), *Memória e Verdade – A Justiça de Transicão no Estado Democrático de Direito Brasileiro*, Belo Horizonte, Forum, 2009, pp. 213–232.

FEIJÓ, Sara Duarte, "Em Teu Nome e Batismo de Sangue: Formas Cinematográficas de Representar o Exílio na Ditadura Brasileira", *Projeto História*, vol. 43/2011, pp. 481–495.

FERNANDES, Florestan and MARTINS FILHO, J.R. (eds.), *Florestan Fernandes: a Força do Argumento*, São Carlos, EDUFSCar, 1997.

FERNANDES, Pádua, "Justiça de Transição e o Fundamento nos Direitos Humanos: Perplexidades do Relatório da Comissão Nacional da Verdade Brasileira", in KASHIURA, Celso Naoto Jr.; AKAMINE, Oswaldo Jr.; and MELO Tarso de (eds.), *Para a Crítica do Direito: Reflexões sobre Teorias e Práticas Jurídicas*, São Paulo, Editorial Dobra, 2015, pp. 717–745.

FERREIRA, Elizabeth F. Xavier, *Mulheres, Militância e Memória*, Rio de Janeiro, Fundação Getúlio Vargas, 1996.

FERREIRA, Marcos Alan S.V., "Peace and Conflict in Brazil", in RICHMOND O. and VISOKA, G. (eds.), *The Palgrave Encyclopedia of Peace and Conflict Studies*, London, Palgrave Macmillan, 2020.

FICO, Carlos, "A Negociação Parlamentar da Anistia de 1979 e o Chamado Perdão aos Torturadores", *Revista Anistia Política e Justiça de Transição*, vol. 4/2010, pp. 318–333.

FILHO, Henrique de Souza Filho, *Cartas da Mãe*, Rio de Janeiro, Codecri, 1981.

FLEISCHER, David, *Countries at the Crossroads 2012: Brazil*, available at https://freedomhouse.org/sites/default/files/Brazil%20-%20FINAL.pdf.

FLORÊNCIO, Roberto Remígio, "Índio Cara Pálida ou Cara de Índio: Uma Breve Análise dos Discursos sobre a Temática Indígena das Letras de Música Popular Brasileira", *Opará – Etnicidades, Movimentos Sociais e Educação*, vol. 4/2016, pp. 35–46.

FOBEAR, Katherine and BAINES, Erin, "Pushing the Conversation forward: the Intersections of Sexuality and Gender Identity in Transitional Justice", *The International Journal of Human Rights*, vol. 24/2020, pp. 307–312.

FRANCO, Bernardo Melo, "Punição a Tortura na Ditadura Divide Opiniões no País", *Folha de São Paulo*, June 7, 2010http://www1.folha.uol.com.br/fsp/poder/po0706201008.htm.

FRANCO, Shirley Carvalhêdo, "The Notion of Ramification of Archival Documents: The Example of the 'Fonds' Related to the Brazilian Political Movement Araguaia Guerrilla", *The American Archivist*, vol. 78/2015, pp. 133–153.

FREIRE, Américo, "A Via Partidária da Transição Política Brasileira", *Varia História*, vol. 30/2014, pp. 287–308.

FREYRE, Gilberto, *Casa-Grande e Senzala*, São Paulo, Global, 2006.

FRIEDMAN, Elisabeth Jay and HOCHSTETLER, Kathryn, "Assessing the Third Transition in Latin American Democratization: Representational Regimes and Civil Society in Argentina and Brazil", *Comparative Politics*, vol. 35/2002, pp. 21–42.

FUNARI, Pedro Paulo and ZARANKIN, Andres, *Arqueología de la Represíon y Resistência em América Latina (1960–1980)*, Catamarca, Encuentro, 2006.

GALINDO, Bruno, "Transitional Justice in Brazil and the Jurisprudence of the Inter-American Court of Human Rights: A Difficult Dialogue with the Brazilian Judiciary", in *Sequência*, vol. 79/2018, pp. 27–44.

GALLO, Carlos Artur, "Do Luto à Luta: Um Estudo sobre a Comissão de Familiares de Mortos e Desaparecidos Políticos no Brasil", *Anos 90*, vol. 19/2012, pp. 323–355.

GANDSMAN, Ari Edward, "Retributive Justice, Public Intimacies and the Micropolitics of the Restitution of Kidnapped Children of the Disappeared in Argentina", *The International Journal of Transitional Justice*, vol. 6/2012, pp. 423–443.

GARAPON, Antoine, *Des Crimes Qu'on Ne Peut Ni Punir Ni Pardoner. Pour Une Justice Internationale*, Paris, Odile Jacob, 2002.

—— *Peut-on Réparer L'Histoire? Colonisation, Esclavage, Shoah*, Paris, Odile Jacob, 2008.

GASPARI, Elio, *A Ditadura Escancarada*, São Paulo, Companhia das Letras, 2002.

—— *A Ditadura Envergonhada*, São Paulo, Companhia das Letras, 2002.

GASPARI, Elio; VENTURA, Zuenir; and HOLLANDA, Heloísa Buarque de, *Cultura em Trânsito 70/80: da Repressão à Abertura*, Rio de Janeiro, Aeroplano, 2000.

GIORDANI, Marco Pollo, *Brasil Sempre*, Porto Alegre, Tchê, 1986

GODOY, Angelina Snodgrass, "La Muchacha Respondona: Reflections on the Razor's Edge Between Crime and Human Rights", *Human Rights Quarterly*, vol. 27/2005, pp. 597–624.

GOMES, Luis Flavio and MAZZUOLI, Valerio de Oliveira, "Crimes da Ditadura Militar e o Caso Araguaia: Aplicação do Direito Internacional dos Direitos Humanos pelos Juízes e Tribunais Brasileiros", *Revista Brasileira de Direito da Comunicação Social e Liberdade de Expressão*, vol. 2/2011, pp. 199–234.

GONÇALVES, Bruno Simões, "Parecer Psicossocial da Violência contra os Povos Indígenas Brasileiros: o Caso Reformatório Krenak", *Psicologia: Ciência e Profissão*, vol. 37/2017, pp. 186–196.

GONÇALVES, Raquel Cristina Possolo and MEYER, Emilio Peluso Neder, "Responsabilização Individual de Perpetradores de Crimes Contra a Humanidade em Regimes Autoritários: Importância de sua Implementação no Contexto Brasileiro", in MEYER, Emilio Peluso Neder (ed.), *Justiça de Transição em Perpsectiva Transnacional*, Belo Horizonte, Initia Via, 2017, pp. 273–297.

GONZAGA, Eugênia Augusta, "As Ossadas de Perus e a Atuação do Ministério Público Federal em São Paulo", in CARDOSO, Ítalo and BERNARDES, Laura (eds.), *Vala Clandestina de Perus – Desaparecidos Políticos, Um Capítulo Não Encerrado da História Brasileira*, São Paulo, Ed. Do Autor, 2012, pp. 106–116.

GRAY, David C., "A No-Excuse Approach to Transitional Justice: Reparations as Tools of Extraordinary Justice", *Washington University Law Review*, vol. 87/2010, pp. 1043–1103.

GREADY, Paul and ROBINS, Simon, "From Transitional to Transformative Justice: A New Agenda for Practice", *The International Journal of Transitional Justice*, vol. 8/2014, pp. 339–361.

—— "Rethinking Civil Society and Transitional Justice: Lessons from Social Movements and "New" Civil Society", *The International Journal of Human Rights*, vol. 21/2017, pp. 956–975.

—— "Transitional Justice and Theories of Change: Towards Evaluation as Understanding", *International Journal of Transitional Justice*, vol. 14/2020, pp. 280–299.

GREEN, James N., "Clerics, Exiles, and Academics: Opposition to the Brazilian Military Dictatorship in the United States, 1969–1974", *Latin American Politics and Society*, vol. 45/2003, pp. 87–117.

—— "Who Is the Macho Who Wants to Kill Me? Male Homosexuality, Revolutionary Masculinity, and the Brazilian Armed Struggle of the 1960s and 1970s", *Hispanic American Historical Review*, vol. 92/2012, pp. 437–469.

GREEN, James N. and QUINALHA, Renan, *Ditadura e Homossexualidades: Repressão, Resistência e a Busca da Verdade*, São Carlos, Edufscar, 2014.

GRUNEICH, Danielle and CORDEIRO, Iara, "Violência Política de Gênero: das Violências Invisíveis aos Aspectos Criminais", *Boletim CONJUR*, November 3, 2020, https://www.conjur.com.br/2020-nov-03/gruneich-cordeiro-violencia-politica-genero.

GUILLÉN, Ana Laura Zavala, "Argentinian Transitional Justice Process: Women Behind", *Journal of Peace, Conflict & Development*, vol. 20/2013, pp. 52–60.

GUIMARAES, Maria, "Uma Luta Contra o Desaparecimento", *Pesquisa Fapesp*, vol. 250/2016, pp. 76–81.

HAMBER, Brandon, "Living with the Legacy of Impunity: Lessons for South Africa about Truth, Justice and Crime in Brazil", *Latin American Report*, vol. 13/1998, pp. 4–16.

—— "Repairing the Irreparable: Dealing with the Double-Binds of Making Reparations for Crimes of the Past", *Ethnicity and Health*, vol. 5/2000, pp. 215–226.

HAMBER, Brandon; MOSIKARE, Ntombi; FRIEDMAN, Maggie; and MAEPA, Traggy, "Speaking Out. The Role of the Khulumani Victim Support Group in Dealing with the Past in South Africa", *Psychosocial Programmes after War and Dictatorship Conference*, Frankfurt, Germany, June 17–21, 2000, http://www.brandonhamber.com/publications/pap_khulumani.doc.

HASKINS, Ekaterina, "Between Archive and Participation: Public Memory in a Digital Age", *Rhetoric Society Quarterly*, vol. 37/2007, pp. 401–422.

HAYNER, Priscilla, *Unspeakable Truths – Transitional Justice and the Challenge of Truth Commissions*, New York, Routledge, 2002.

HAZAN, Pierre, "Measuring the Impact of Punishment and Forgiveness: A Framework for Evaluating Transitional Justice", *International Review of the Red Cross*, vol. 88/2006, pp. 19–47.

HELLSTEN, Sirkku K., "Transitional Justice and Aid", *United Nations University (UNU-WIDER) Working Paper* no. 6/2012, https://www.wider.unu.edu/publication/transitional-justice-and-aid.

HITE, Katherine and COLLINS, Cath, "Memorials Fragments, Monumental Silences and Reawakenings in 21st-Century Chile", *Millennium Journal of International Studies*, vol. 38/2009, pp. 379–400.

HOCHSTETLER, Kathryn, "Democratizing Pressures from Below? Social Movements in New Brazilian Democracy", *XX International Congress of Latin American Studies Association*, Mexico, 1997.

HOLLANDA, Cristina Buarque de and ISRAEL, Vinícius Pinheiro, "Panorama das Comissões da Verdade no Brasil: uma reflexão sobre novos sentidos de legitimidade e representação democrática", *Revista de Sociologia e Política*, vol. 27/2019, pp. 2–21.

HOWE, Sara Eleanor, "The Madres de la Plaza de Mayo: Asserting Motherhood; Rejecting Feminism?", *Journal of International Women's Studies*, vol. 7/2006, pp. 43–50.

HTUN, Mala, "From Racial Democracy to Affirmative Action: Changing State Policy on Race in Brazil", *Latin American Research Review*, vol. 39/2004, pp. 60–98.

HUNTINGTON, Samuel P., *The Third Wave: Democratization in the Late Twentieth Century*, Norman OK, University of Oklahoma Press, 1991.

JELIN, Elizabeth, "Public Memorialization in Perspective: Truth, Justice and Memory of Past Repression in the Southern Cone of South America", *The International Journal of Transitional Justice*, vol. 1/2007, pp. 138–156.

JOFFILY, Mariana, "Direito à Informação e Direito à Vida Privada: Os Impasses em Torno do Acesso aos Arquivos da Ditadura Militar Brasileira", *Estudos Históricos*, vol 25/2012, pp. 129–148.

────── "Sexual Violence in the Military Dictatorships of Latin America: Who Wants to Know?", *SUR – International Journal of Human Rights*, vol. 13/2016, pp. 165–176.

JOINET, Louis, *Report of the Special Rapporteur on the Study on Amnesty Laws and their Role in the Safeguard and Promotion of Human Rights*, U.N. Doc. E/CN.4/Sub.2/1985/16 (21 June 1985).

KALIL, Isabela Oliveira, "Gender Ideology Incursions in Education", *SUR – International Journal of Human Rights*, vol. 29/2019.

KINZO, Maria D'Alva G., "A Democratização Brasileira: Um Balanço do Processo Político desde a Transição", *São Paulo em Perspectiva*, vol. 15/2001, pp. 1–12.

KOPPER, Christopher, *VW do Brasil in the Brazilian Military Dictatorship 1964–1985: A Historical Study*, https://www.volkswagenag.com/en/group/history.html.

KRITZ, Neil, *Transitional Justice: How Emerging Democracies Reckon with Former Regimes*, Washington, United States Institute of Peace Press, 1995.

KROETZ, Flávia Saldanha, "Reflexos da Impunidade dos Agentes Estatais por Graves Violações aos Direitos Humanos Cometidas Durante a Ditadura Militar no Brasil", *Revista Jurídica da Procuradoria-Geral do Distrito Federal*, vol. 39/2014, pp. 175–196.

LANGLER, Johannes, "Are Truth Commissions Just Hot-Air Balloons? A Reality Check of the Impact of Truth Commission Recommendations", *Desafíos*, vol. 29/2017.

LANGLOIS, Léa Lemay, "Gender Perspective in UN Framework for Peace Processes and Transitional Justice: The Need for a Clearer and More Inclusive Notion of Gender", *International Journal of Transitional Justice*, vol. 12/2018, pp. 146–167.

LAPLANTE, Lisa, "Transitional Justice and Peace Building: Diagnosing and Addressing the Socioeconomic Roots of Violence through a Human Rights Framework", International Journal of Transitional Justice, Vol. 2/2008, pp. 331–355.

────── "On the Indivisibility of Rights: Truth Commissions, Reparations, and the Rights to Development", *Yale Human Rights & Development Law Journal*, vol. 10/2007, pp. 141–177.

────── "The Plural Justice Aims of Reparations", in BUCKLEY-ZISTEL, Susanne; BECK, Teresa Koloma; BRAUN, Christian; and MIETH, Friederike (eds.), *Transitional Justice Theories*, New York, Routledge, 2014, pp. 66–84.

LAPLANTE, Lisa J. and THEIDON, Kimberly, "Truth with Consequences: Justice and Reparations in Post-Truth Commission Peru", *Human Rights Quarterly*, vol. 29/2007, pp. 228–250.

LEAL, Victor Nunes, *Coronelismo, Enxada e Voto: Município e o Regime Representativo No Brasil*, São Paulo, Alfa-Omega, 1978.

LEGOUX, Jules, *Droit de Grâce en France Comparé avec les Législations Étrangères*, Paris, Librarie du Conseil D'État, 1865.

LEMOS, Renato, "Anistia e Crise Política no Brasil pós-1964", *Topoi*, vol. 3/2002, pp. 287–313.

LEVITSKY, Steven and ZIBLATT, Daniel, *How Democracies Die*, New York, Crown Publishing, 2018.

LIGHT, Duncan and YOUNG, Craig, "Public Memory, Commemoration and Transitional Justice: Reconfiguring the Past in Public Space", in STAN, Lavinia and NEDELSKY, Nadya (eds.), *Post-Communist Transitional Justice: Lessons from 25 Years of Experience*, Cambridge, Cambridge University Press, 2015, pp. 233–251.

LIMA, Edilene Coffaci de, "Exílios Índios: Sobre Deslocamentos Compulsórios no Período Militar (1964–1985)", *Aceno*, vol. 3/2016, pp. 18–35.

LIMA, Edilene Coffaci de and PACHECO, Rafael, "Povos Indígenas e Justiça de Transição: Reflexões a partir do Caso Xetá", *Aracê – Direitos Humanos em Revista*, vol. 5/2017, pp. 219–241.

LINZ, Juan J. and STEPAN, Alfred, *Problems of Democratic Transition and Consolidation. Southern Europe, South America and Post-Communist Europe*, Baltimore MD, Johns Hopkins University Press, 1996.

—— *A Transição e Consolidação da Democracia: a Experiência do Sul da Europa e da América do Sul*, São Paulo, Paz e Terra, 1999.

LUNDY, Patricia and MCGOVERN, Marky, "Whose Justice? Rethinking Transitional Justice from the Bottom Up", *Journal of Law and Society*, vol. 35/2008, pp. 265–292.

MADLINGOZI, Tshepo, "On Transitional Justice Entrepreneurs and the Production of Victims", *Journal of Human Rights Practice*, vol. 2/2010, pp. 208–228.

MAGALHÃES, Juliana Neuenschwander, "A Exclusão da Inclusão dos Índios na Ditadura e a Inclusão da Exclusão dos Índios no Brasil, Hoje", www.sociologyoflaw.com.br/Prof.-Juliana-Magalhães.pdf.

MAGGIORE, Giuseppe, *Derecho Penal*, vol. 2, Bogotá, Temis, 1972.

MARSCHALL, Sabine, *Landscape of Memory: Commemorative Monuments, Memorials and Public Statuary in Post-Apartheid South Africa*, Leiden, Brill, 2009.

MARTIN-CHENUT, Kathia and ABDELGAWAD, Elisabeth Lambert (eds.), *Reparer les Violations Graves et Massives des Droits de L'Homme: La Cour Interaméricaine, Pionnière et Modèle?*, Paris, Société de Législation Comparée, 2010.

MARTINS, André Saboia and ISHAQ, Vivien, "O Legado da Comissão Nacional da Verdade: Dois Anos Depois da Publicação do Relatório, o Reconhecimento Judicial do Direito à Verdade Desafia a Falta de Justiça Efetiva", in WESTHROP, Amy Jo; GARRIDO, Ayra Guedes; PARREIRA, Carolina Genovez; and SANTOS, Shana Marques Prado dos, *As Recomendações da Comissão Nacional da Verdade: Balanços sobre a Sua Implementação Dois Anos Depois*, Rio de Janeiro, ISER, 2016, pp. 42–65.

MARTINS, José de Souza. "A Reprodução do Capital na Frente Pioneira e o Renascimento da Escravidão no Brasil", *Tempo Social Revista de Sociologia da USP*, vol. 6/1994, pp. 1–25.

MASCHIO, Jane, "Eficácia/Ineficácia do Sistema de Cotas para Mulheres", *Resenha Eleitoral*, vol. 10/2003, pp. 46–62.

MATTOS, André Borges de and FOLTRAM, Rochelle, "Estado, Indigenismo e a Ditadura Militar no Brasil Pós-64", in MATTOS, André Borges et al. (eds.), *Ciências Humanas em Foco*, Diamantina, UFVJM, 2017, pp. 13–39.

MAUÉS, Antonio Moreira, "Supra-legality of International Human Rights Treaties and Constitutional Interpretation", *SUR – International Journal of Human Rights*, vol. 18/2013, pp. 205–223.

MAY, John D., "Democracy, Organization, Michels", *The American Political Science Review*, vol. 59/1965, pp. 417–429.

McAuliffe, Padraig, "Romanticization Versus Integration: Indigenous Justice in Rule of Law Reconstruction and Transitional Justice Discourse", *Goettingen Journal of International Law*, vol. 5/2013, pp. 41–86.

McSherry, J. Patrice, "Tracking the Origins of a State Terror Network: Operation Condor", *Latin American Perspectives*, vol 29/2002, pp. 38–60.

Melo, Carolina de Campos and Martins, André Saboia, "The National Truth Commission (NTC) – Truth and Responsibility", in Schneider, Nina, *The Brazilian Truth Commission: Local, National and Global Perspectives*, New York, Berghahn Books, 2019, pp. 111–125.

Mello, Felipe Correa and Baccega, Maria Aparecida, "Imprensa e Discurso Histórico: A Comissão Nacional da Verdade na Folha de São Paulo e no Estado de São Paulo", *Comunicação e Educação* vol. 20(1)/2015, pp. 105–116.

Mera, Jorge. "Chile: Truth and Justice under the Democratic Government", in Arriaza, Naomi Roth (ed.), *Impunity and Human Rights in International Law and Practice*, New York, Oxford University Press, 1995, pp. 171–184.

Mesquita Neto, Paulo de, "Crime, Violence and Political Uncertainty in Brazil", *Crime and Policing in Transitional Societies Conference*, Johannesburg, August 30–September 1, 2000.

Meyer, Emilio Peluso Neder and Carvalho, Claudia Paiva, "Sexual Crimes and Transitional Justice before Courts in Brazil – Accountability for Crimes Against Humanity", in Ciocchini, Pablo and Radics, George (eds.), *Criminal Legalities in the Global South. Cultural Dynamics, Political Tensions, and Institutional Practices*, London, Routledge, 2019.

Mezarobba, Glenda, *Um Acerto de Contas com o Futuro – a Anistia e suas Conseqüências – um Estudo do Caso Brasileiro*, Dissertação (Mestrado), Faculdade de Filosofia, Letras e Ciências Humanas, Universidade de São Paulo (USP), São Paulo, 2003.

—— *Um Acerto de Contas com o Futuro: a Anistia e suas Conseqüências: um Estudo do Caso Brasileiro*, São Paulo, Humanitas Fapesp, 2006.

—— *O Preço do Esquecimento: as Reparações Pagas às Vítimas do Regime Militar – uma Comparação entre Brasil, Argentina e Chile*, Ph.D Thesis, Faculdade de Filosofia, Letras e Ciências Humanas, Universidade de São Paulo (USP), São Paulo, 2007.

—— "Entre Reparações, Meias Verdades e Impunidade: o Difícil Rompimento com o Legado da Ditadura no Brasil", *SUR – Revista Internacional de Direitos Humanos*, vol. 7/2010, pp. 7–25.

Michels, Robert, *Political Parties: A Sociological Study of the Oligarchical Tendencies of Modern Democracy*, New York, Heart's International Library Co., 1915.

Michener, Gregory and Pereira, Carlos, "A Great Leap Forward for Democracy and the Rule of Law? Brazil's Mensalão Trial", *Journal of Latin American Studies*, vol. 48/2016, pp. 477–507.

Miles, William F.S., "Auschwitz: Museum Interpretation and Darker Tourism", *Annals of Tourism Research*, vol. 29/2002, pp. 1175–1178.

Motta, Marly, "Teotônio das Alagoas: O Menestrel da Abertura", *Maracanan*, vol. 8/2012, pp. 259–282.

Mourão, Alexandre de Albuquerque; Figueiredo, Clara F.; and Schincariol, Rafael (eds.), *Lampejos: Arte, Memória, Verdade, Justiça*, Rio de Janeiro, Synergia, 2016.

Mourão, Alexandre de Albuquerque; Siqueira, Gelirton Almeida; Martins, Marcos Venicius Lima; Rocha, Viviane; and Moreira, Daniel Bruno, "Os

Aparecidos Políticos: Arte Ativista e Justiça de Transição, *Revista Anistia Política*, vol. 6/2011, pp. 148–170.

Mutua, Makau, "The Ideology of Human Rights", *Virginia Journal of International Law*, vol. 36/1996, pp. 589–657.

Nascimento, Marcio Luis Ferreira, "Rondon, Einsten's Letter and the Nobel Peace Prize", *Ciência e Sociedade*, vol. 4/2016, pp. 27–35.

Napolitano, Marcos, "MPB: A trilha Sonora da Abertura Política (1975/1982)", *Revista de Estudos Avançados da USP*, vol. 24/2010, pp. 389–402.

Negócio, Carla Daniela Leite, "A Violência Física e Cultural Contra os Povos Indígenas Durante o Regime Militar", *Aracê Direitos Humanos em Revista*, vol. 5/2017, pp. 263–294.

Nesiah, Vasuki, "Discussion Lines on Gender and Transitional Justice: An Introductory Essay Reflecting on the ICTJ Bellagio Workshop on Gender and Transitional Justice", *Columbia Journal of Gender and Law*, vol. 15(3)/2006.

—— "Truth Commissions and Gender: Principles, Policies and Procedures", *Gender Justice Series of International Center for Transitional Justice*, ICTJ, 2006.

Ní Aoláin, Fionnuala, "Political Violence and Gender During Times of Transition", *Columbia Journal of Gender and Law*, vol. 15/2006, pp. 829–849.

Nino, Carlos S., "Transition to Democracy, Corporatism and Constitutional Reform in Latin America", *University of Miami Inter-American Law Review*, vol. 44/1989, pp. 129–136.

Nora, Pierre, "Between Memory and History: Les Lieux de Mémoire", *Representations*, vol. 26/1989, pp. 7–24.

Novais, Adriana Rodrigues, "A Memória da Repressão e Violência no Campo em Tempos da Comissão Nacional da Verdade", *Revista Interdisciplinar de Direitos Humanos*, vol. 3/2015, pp. 43–55.

O'Donnell, Guillermo, "On the State, Democratization and Some Conceptual Problems – A Latin American View with Glances at Some Post-Communist Countries", *Working Paper no. 192, The Helen Kellogg Institute for International Studies*, April 1993.

Oliveira, João Pacheco de, "Muita Terra para Pouco Índio? Uma Introdução Crítica ao Indigenismo e a Atualização do Preconceito", in Silva, Aracy Lopes and Grupioni, Luís Donisete Benzi, *A Temática Indígena na Escola*, MEC – UNESCO, 1995, pp. 61–86.

Oliveira, Luciano, *Do Nunca Mais ao Eterno Retorno – Uma Reflexão sobre a Tortura*, São Paulo, Brasiliense, 1994.

Olson, Laura M., "Provoking the Dragon on the Patio. Matters of Transitional Justice: Penal Repression vs. Amnesties", *International Review of the Red Cross*, vol. 88/2006, pp. 275–294.

Osiel, Mark, *Juger les Crimes de Masse – La Mémoire Collective et le Droit*, Paris, Seuil, 2006.

Osmo, Carla. "O Judiciário Brasileiro Diante dos Crimes da Ditadura: Entre a Imprescritibilidade Civil e a Anistia Penal", http://conti.derhuman.jus.gov.ar/2016/11/seminario/mesa_18/osmo_mesa_18.pdf.

Osowski, Raquel, "O Marco Temporal para Demarcação de Terras Indígenas, Memória e Esquecimento", *Mediações Revista de Ciências Sociais*, vol. 22/2017, pp. 320–346.

Ost, François, *O tempo do Direito*, Lisboa, Piaget, 1999.

Paraíso, Maria Hilda Baqueiro, "Os Krenak do Rio Doce, a Pacificação, o Aldeamento e a Luta pela Terra", in *XIII Encontro Anual da ANPOCS*, 1989, http://www.etnolinguistica.org/biblio:paraiso-1989-krenak.

Payne, Leigh A and Pereira, Gabriel, "La Complicidad Corporativa en las Violaciones de Derechos Humanos: Una Innovación en la Justicia Transicional de Argentina?", in Instituto Interamericano de Direitos Humanos, *Derechos Humanos Y Empresas: Reflexiones Desde América Latina*, 2017, pp. 293–310.

PAYNE, Leigh A.; PEREIRA, Gabriel; COSTA, Josefina Doz; and BERNAL-BERMÚDEZ, Laura, "Can a Treaty on Business and Human Rights Help Achieve Transitional Justice Goals?", *Homa Publica International Journal on Human Rights and Business*, vol. 1/2017, pp. 3–33.

PEIRANO, Mariza Gomes e Souza, "The Anthropology of Anthropology: The Brazilian Case", Ph.D thesis, Department of Anthropology, Harvard University, 1981, p. 81, revistas.cbpf.br/index.php/CS/article/viewFile/199/143.

PEREIRA, Anthony W., "An Ugly Democracy? State and the Rule of Law in Post Authoritarian Brazil", in KINGSTONE, Peter R. and POWER, Timothy J. (eds.), *Democratic Brazil: Actors, Institutions, and Processes*, Pittsburgh PA, Pittsburgh University Press, 2000.

—— "The US Role in the 1964 Coup in Brazil: A Reassessment", *Bulletin of Latin American Research*, vol. 37/2018, pp. 5–17.

PERUZZO, Pedro Pulzatto, "Direito à consulta prévia aos povos indígenas no Brasil", *Direito e Praxis*, vol. 8/2017, pp. 2708–2740.

PETERSON, Trudy Huskamp, *Final Acts: A Guide to Preserving the Records of Truth Commissions*, Woodrow Wilson Center Press with The Johns Hopkins University Press, 2005.

PICCONE, Theodore J., "Transitional Justice", *American Journal of International Law*, vol. 90/1996, pp. 540–541.

PILLAY, Navi, "Brazil's Indigenous and Afro-Brazilian Populations face Serious Discrimination", *The Huffington Post*, November 18, 2009, https://www.huffingtonpost.com/navi-pillay/brazils-indigenous-and-af_b_362183.html.

PINHEIRO, Paulo Sérgio, "Autoritarismo e Transição", *Revista da Universidade de São Paulo*, vol. 9/1991, pp. 45–56.

—— "The Legacy of Authoritarianism in Democratic Brazil", in NAGEL, Stuart S. (ed.), *Latin American Development and Public Policy*, New York, St Martin Press, 1994.

—— "Democracy without Citizenship: Democratization and Human Rights", *International Conference on Democratic Transitions in Latin America and in Eastern Europe: Rupture and Continuity*, Paris, 1996.

—— "Passado não está morto: nem passado é ainda … [Prefácio]", in DIMENSTEIN, Gilberto (ed.), *Democracia em Pedaços: Direitos Humanos no Brasil*, São Paulo, Companhia das Letras, 1996.

PINTO, António Costa and MORLINO, Leonardo, *Dealing with the Legacy of Authoritarianism – The Politics of the Pat in Southern European Democracies*, New York, Routledge, 2011.

PIOVESAN, Flavia and VIEIRA, Renato Stanziola, "Justiciabilidade dos Direitos Sociais e Econômicos no Brasil: Desafios e Perspectivas", *Araucaria Revista Iberoamericana de Filosofia, Política y Humanidades*, vol. 15/2006, pp. 128–146.

POMPEU, Fernanda, *Clara Charf de Todas as Lutas*, http://operamundi.uol.com.br/dialogosdosul/clara-charf-de-todas-as-lutas/28072017/.

POWER, Jonathan, *Amnesty International: The Human Rights Story*, Oxford, Pergamon Press, 1981.

POWER, Timothy J., "The Brazilian Military Regime of 1964–1985: Legacies for Contemporary Democracy", *Iberoamericana*, vol. 62/2016, pp. 13–26.

PRZEWORSKI, Adam; ALVAREZ, Michael; CHEIBUB, José Antonio; LIMONGI, Fernando, "O que mantém as democracias?", *Lua Nova*, vols. 40–41/1997.

QUINALHA, Renan Honório, "Com Quantos Lados se Faz uma Verdade? Notas sobre a Comissão Nacional da Verdade e a Teoria dos Dois Demônios", *Revista Jurídica da Presidência*, vol. 15/2013, pp. 181–204.

RAGO, Margareth, "Desejo de Memória", *Revista Labrys*, vol. 15/2009, https://www.labrys.net.br/labrys15/sumarioditadura.htm.

RAMASASTRY, Anita, "Corporate Complicity: From Nuremberg to Rangoon – An Examination of Forced Labor Cases and Their Impact on the Liability of Multinational Corporations", *Berkeley Journal of International Law*, vol. 20/2002, pp. 91–159.

RAMÍREZ-BARAT, Clara, "Transitional Justice and the Public Sphere", in RAMÍREZ-BARAT, Clara (ed.), *Transitional Justice, Culture, and Society Beyond Outreach*, New York, International Center for Transitional Justice and Social Science Research Council, 2014, pp. 27–45.

RAMOS, Alcida Rita, "Os Direitos do Índio no Brasil: na Encruzilhada da Cidadania", *Seminário A proteção dos Direitos Humanos nos Planos Nacional e Internacional: Perspectivas Brasileiras*, Instituto Interamericanao de Direitos Humanos, Fundação Friedrich Naumann, Comitê Internacional da Cruz Vermelha, Brasília, 1991, http://www.dan.unb.br/images/doc/Serie116empdf.pdf.

—— "O Papel Político das Epidemias: O Caso Yanomani", *Série Antropologia – Universidade de Brasília*, vol. 153/1993, pp. 2–21.

RAMOS, André de Carvalho, "A ADPF 153 e a Corte Interamericana de Direitos Humanos", in GOMES, Luiz Flavio and MAZZUOLI, Valerio Oliveira (eds.), *Crimes da Ditadura Militar*, São Paulo, Revista dos Tribunais, 2011, pp. 174–225.

—— "Pluralidade das Ordens Jurídicas: Uma Nova Perspectiva na Relação entre o Direito Internacional e o Direito Constitucional", *Revista da Faculdade de Direito da Universidade de São Paulo*, vols. 106–107/2011–2012, pp. 497–524.

RANGELOV, Iavor and TEITEL, Ruti, "Global Civil Society and Transitional Justice", in ANHEIER, H.; GLASIUS, M.; KALDOR, M.; PARK, GS.; and SENGUPTA, C. (eds.), *Global Civil Society*, London, Palgrave Macmillan, 2011, p. 162.

RAUSCHENBACH, Mina; SCAGLIOLA, Stef; PARMENTIER, Stephan; and DE JONG, Franciska, "The Perfect Data-Marriage: Transitional Justice Research and Oral History Life Stories", *Transitional Justice Review*, vol. 1/2016, pp. 7–58.

REILLY, Niamh, "Seeking Gender Justice in Post-Conflict Transitions: Towards a Transformative Women's Human Rights Approach", *International Journal of Law in Context*, vol. 3/2007, pp. 155–172.

REINA, Eduardo, *Cativeiro Sem Fim – As Histórias dos Bebês, Crianças e Adolescentes Sequestrados pela Ditadura Militar no Brasil*, São Paulo, Alameda, 2019.

REIS FILHO, Daniel Aarão, "As Organizações Comunistas e a Luta de Classes – 1961–1968", Ph.D thesis, *Faculdade de Filosofia, Letras e Ciências Humanas da Universidade de São Paulo*, 1987, http://caph.fflch.usp.br/node/4265.

RESENDE, Ana Catarina Zema de, "O Relatório Figueiredo, as Violações dos Direitos dos Povos Indígenas no Brasil dos anos 1960 e a Justa Memória", in SIQUEIRA, Gustavo Silveira; WOLKMER, Antonio Carlos and PIERDONÁ, Zélia Luiza (eds.), *História do Direito – XXIV Encontro Nacional do Conselho Nacional de Pesquisa e Pós-Graduação em Direito (CONPEDI)*, Florianópolis, CONPEDI, 2015.

Resende, Pâmela de Almeida, "Da Abertura Lenta, Gradual e Segura à Anistia Ampla, Geral e Irrestrita: A Lógica do Dissenso na Transição para a Democracia", *Revista Sul-Americana de Ciência Política*, vol. 2/2014, pp. 36–46.

Ribeiro, Darcy, *Os Índios e a Civilização Brasileira – A Integração das Populações Indígenas no Brasil Moderno*, 7th edn., São Paulo, Global, 2017.

Ribeiro, Maria Cláudia B., *Mulheres na Luta Armada: Protagonismo Feminino na ALN (Ação Libertadora Nacional)*, São Paulo, Alameda, 2018.

Ridenti, Marcelo Siqueira, "As Mulheres na Política Brasileira: Os Anos de Chumbo", *Revista Tempo Social*, vol. 2/1990, pp. 113–128.

Risse, Thomas and Ropp, Stephen C., "Introduction and Overview", in Risse, Thomas; Ropp, Stephen C.; and Sikkink, Kathryn (eds.), *The Persistent Power of Human Rights – From Commitment to Compliance*, Cambridge, Cambridge University Press, 2013.

Robertson, Geoffrey, *Crimes Against Humanity – the Struggle for Global Justice*, New York, The New Press, 2000.

Robinson, Darryl, "Serving the Interests of Justice: Amnesties, Truth Commissions and the International Criminal Court", *European Journal of International Law*, vol. 14/2003, pp. 481–505.

Rodeghero, Carla Simone, "Pela Pacificação da Família Brasileira: Uma Breve Comparação entre as Anistias de 1945 e de 1979", *Revista Brasileira de História*, vol. 34/2014.

Rodrigues, Ricardo José Pereira, "A Evolução da Política de Cotas de Gênero na Legislação Eleitoral e Partidária e a Sub-representação Feminina no Parlamento Brasileiro", *Revista Eletrônica Direito e Política*, vol. 12/2017, pp. 27–51.

Rodrigues, Oswaldo Lima, *Verdade e Realidade*, Cantagalo, Jornal da Região, 1987.

Roesler, Claudia Rosane and Senra, Laura Carneiro de Mello, "Gênero e Justiça de Transição no Brasil", *Revista Jurídica da Presidência*, vol. 15/2013, pp. 35–67.

Roht-Arriaza, Naomi, "Reparations Decisions and Dilemmas", *Hastings International and Comparative Law Review*, vol. 27/2004, pp. 157–219.

—— "After Amnesties Are Gone: Latin American National Courts and the New Contours of the Fights Against Impunity", *Human Rights Quarterly*, vol. 37/2015, pp. 341–382.

—— "Measures of Non-Repetition in Transitional Justice: The Missing Link?", *Legal Studies Research Paper Series*, University of California Hastings College of the Law, https://papers.ssrn.com/sol3/papers.cfm?abstract_id=2746055.

Rooney, Eilish, "Engendering Transitional Justice: Questions of Absence and Silence", *International Journal of Law in Context*, vol. 3/2007, pp. 93–107.

Rosito, João Baptista Alvares and Damo, Arlei Sander, "A Reparação por Perseguição Política e os Relatos de Violência nas Caravanas da Anistia", *Horizontes Antropológicos*, vol. 42/2014, pp. 181–212.

Rouquié, Alain, *O Estado Militar na América Latina*, São Paulo, Alfa-Omega, 1984.

Rovai, Marta Gouveia de Oliveira, "O Direito à Memória: A História Oral de Mulheres que Lutaram Contra a Ditadura Militar", *Tempo & Argumento*, vol. 5/2013, pp. 1–17.

Rubio-Marín, Ruth and de Greiff, Pablo, "Women and Reparations", *The International Journal of Transitional Justice*, vol. 1/2007, pp. 318–337.

Ruggie, John Gerard, *Just Business. Multinational Corporations and Human Rights*, New York, W.W. Norton, 2013.

RYAN, Holly Eva, "From Absent to Present Pasts: Civil Society, Democracy and the Shifting Place of Memory in Brazil", *Journal of Civil Society*, vol. 12/2016, pp. 158–177.

SAAD FILHO, Alfredo, "Neoliberalism, Democracy, and Development Policy in Brazil", *Development and Society*, vol. 39/2010, pp. 1–28.

SALES, Camila Maria Risso and MARTINS FILHO, João Roberto, "The Economist and Human Rights Violations in Brazil During the Military Dictatorship", *Contexto Internacional*, vol. 40/2018, pp. 203–227.

SALLUM, Brasílio Jr., *Labirintos. Dos Generais à Nova República*, São Paulo, Hucitec, 1996.

SALOMÃO, Ivan, "Da Distensão Política à Nova República: Apontamentos sobre a Vitória Oposicionista no Colégio Eleitoral", *Textos e Debates*, vol. 32/2019, pp. 53–74.

SANTOS, Cecília MacDowell, "De Delegacia da Mulher à Lei Maria da Penha: Absorção/ Tradução de Demandas Feministas pelo Estado", *Revista Crítica de Ciências Sociais*, vol. 89/2010, pp. 153–170.

—— "Memória na Justiça: A Mobilização dos Direitos Humanos e a Construção da Memória da Ditadura no Brasil", *Revista Crítica de Ciências Sociais*, vol. 88/2010, pp. 127–154.

—— "Questões de Justiça de Transição: a Mobilização dos Direitos Humanos e a Memória da Ditadura no Brasil", in SANTOS, Boaventura de Sousa; ABRÃO, Paulo; SANTOS, Cecília Macdowell; and TORELLY, Marcelo D., *Repressão e Memória Política no Contexto Ibero-Brasileiro: Estudos sobre Brasil, Guatemala, Moçambique, Peru e Portugal*, Brasília, Ministério da Justiça, Comissão de Anistia, Coimbra, Universidade de Coimbra, Centro de Estudos Sociais, 2010, pp. 124–151.

SANTOS, Cecília MacDowell; TELES, Edson; and TELES, Janaína de Almeida (eds.), *Desarquivando a Ditadura: Memória e Justiça no Brasil*, vol. 1, São Paulo, Hucitec, 2009.

SANTOS, José Vicente Tavares dos, "As Lutas Sociais contra as Violências", *Política e Sociedade*, vol. 11/2007, pp. 71–100.

SARKIN, Jeremy, "The Coming of Age of Claims for Reparations for Human Rights Abuses Committed in the South", *SUR – International Journal of Human Rights*, vol. 1/2004, pp. 66–125.

SCHABAS, William, *Unimaginable Atrocities – Justice, Politics, and Rights at the War Crimes Tribunals*, Oxford, Oxford University Press, 2012.

SCHINKE, Vanessa Dorneles, *Judiciário e Autoritarismo: Regime Autoritário (1964–1985), Democracia e Permanências*, Rio de Janeiro, Lumen Juris, 2016.

SCHMID, Evelyne, *Taking Economic, Social and Cultural Rights Seriously in International Criminal Law*, Cambridge, Cambridge University Press, 2015.

SCHNEIDER, Nina, "Breaking the Silence of the Military Regime: New Politics of Memory in Brazil", *Bulletin of Latin American Research*, vol 30/2010, pp. 198–212.

—— "Impunity in Post-authoritarian Brazil: The Supreme Court's Recent Verdict on the Amnesty Law", *European Review of Latin American and Caribbean Studies*, vol. 90/2011, pp. 39–54.

—— "Too Little too Late or Premature? The Brazilian Truth Commission and the Question of Best Timing", *Journal of Iberian and Latin American Research*, vol. 19/2013, pp. 149–162.

—— "Waiting for a Meaningful State Apology: Has Brazil Apologized for Authoritarian Repression?", *Journal of Human Rights*, vol. 13/2014, pp. 1–16.

SCHNEIDER, Nina and ALMEIDA, Gisele Iecker de, "The Brazilian National Truth Commission (2012–2014) as a State-Commissioned History Project", in BEVERNAGE, B. and WOUTERS, N. (eds.), *The Palgrave Handbook of State-Sponsored History After 1945*, London, Palgrave Macmillan, 2018, pp. 637–652.

SCHWARCZ, Lilia M., *Sobre o Autoritarismo Brasileiro*, São Paulo, Companhia das Letras, 2019.

SCHWARCZ, Lilia M. and STARLING, Heloisa M., *Brasil: Uma Biografia*, São Paulo, Companhia das Letras, 2015.

SCHWARTZMAN, Stephan et al., "The Natural and Social History of the Indigenous Lands and Protected Areas Corridor of the Xingu River Basin", *Philosophical Transactions of the Royal Society B*, vol. 368, 2013.

SCHWINN, Simone Andrea and SCHMIDT, João Pedro, "Da Ditadura à Democracia: a Inacabada Transição Brasileira", *Reflexão e Ação*, vol. 23/2015, pp. 25–53.

SCHULZ, Philipp, "Towards Inclusive Gender in Transitional Justice: Gaps, Blind-Spots and Opportunities", *Journal of Intervention and Statebuilding*, October 21, 2019.

SEIXAS, Ivan Akselrud de and SOUZA, Silvana Aparecida, "Comissão Nacional da Verdade e a Rede de Comissões Estaduais, Municipais e Setoriais: A Trajetória do Brasil", *Revista Estudos de Sociologia*, vol. 20/2015, pp. 347–364.

SERBIN, Kenneth P., "The Anatomy of a Death: Repression, Human Rights, and the Case of Alexandre Vannucchi Leme in Authoritarian Brazil", *Working Paper no. 248, The Helen Kellogg Institute for International Studies*, 1998, https://kellogg.nd.edu/documents/1543.

SHARP, Dustin N., "Interrogating the Peripheries: The Preoccupations of Fourth Generation Transitional Justice", *Harvard Human Rights Journal*, vol. 26, 2013, pp. 149–178.

SHAW, George Bernard, *Major Barbara*, London, Times Book Club, 1907.

SILVA, Amanda Romanelli, "Brasil: Nunca Mais – Imprensa, Memória da Ditadura e Transição Democrática", *Seminário História & Democracia: Precisamos Falar Sobre Isso*, UNIFESP– Campos Guarulhos, September 2018.

SILVA, Fernando Lopes, "O Poético e o Factual na Letra da Canção O Bêbado e a Equilibrista", *Revista Alpha*, vol. 17(1)/2016, pp. 115–127.

SIMIC, Olivera and VOLCIC, Zala, "In the Land of Wartime Rape: Bosnia, Cinema and Reparation", *Griffith Journal of Law & Human Dignity*, vol. 2/2014, pp. 377–401.

SIMILI, Ivana Guilherme, "Memórias da Dor e do Luto: as Indumentárias Político-Religiosas de Zuzu Angel", *Revista Brasileira de História das Religiões*, vol. 6/2014, pp. 165–182.

SLAUGHTER, Anne-Marie, "Global Community of Courts", *Harvard International Law Journal*, vol. 44/2003, pp. 191–219.

SLYE, Ronald C, "The Legitimacy of Amnesties under International Law and General Principles of Anglo-American Law: Is a Legitimate Amnesty Possible?", *Virginia Journal of International Law*, vol. 43/2002, pp. 173–247.

SKIDMORE, Thomas E., "The Historiography of Brazil, 1889–1964 – Part 1", *Hispanic American Historical Review*, vol. 55/1975, pp. 716–748.

SKIDMORE, Thomas, *Brasil: de Getúlio a Castelo*, Rio de Janeiro, Paz e Terra, 1988.

SKINNER, Gwynne, "Nuremberg's Legacy Continues: The Nuremberg Trial's Influence on Human Rights Litigation in U.S. Courts", *Albany Law Review*, vol. 71/2008, pp. 321–367.

SOARES, Inês Virgínia Prado, "Novas Perspectivas Para a Arqueologia da Repressão e da Resistência no Brasil Depois da Comissão Nacional da Verdade", *Revista de Arqueologia Pública*, vol. 10/2014, pp. 177–194.

―― "Um Pouco da Vasta Atuação do Ministério Público Federal no Tema da Ditadura", in GONÇALVES, Oksandro; HACHEM, Daniel Wunder and SANTANO, Ana Claudia (eds.), *Desenvolvimento e Sustentabilidade*, Curitiba, Íthala, 2015, pp. 59–83.

―― "Uma é pouco, duas … bom, sete nem é demais: as ações do MPF pelos crimes da ditadura militar", *Correio Cidadania*, December 20, 2013, available at: https://www.correiocidadania.com.br/colunistas/dicionario-da-cidadania/9205-20-12-2013-uma-e-pouco-duasbom-sete-nem-e-demais-as-acoes-do-mpf-pelos-crimes-da-ditadura-militar?.

SOARES, Inês Virgínia Prado and BASTOS, Lucia Elena Arantes Ferreira, "Direito à Verdade na Corte Interamericana de Direitos Humanos: as Perspectivas no Julgamento do Brasil – Caso Araguaia", *Revista Anistia Política e Justiça de Transição*, vol. 3/2010, pp. 288–305.

―― "A Verdade Ilumina o Direito ao Desenvolvimento? Uma Análise da Potencialidade dos Trabalhos da Comissão Nacional da Verdade no Cenário Brasileiro", *Revista Anistia Política e Justiça de Transição*, vol. 6/2011, pp. 44–69.

―― "Caso Volkswagen: entre violações pretéritas aos direitos humanos e dilemas sobre uma reparação coletiva atual e efetiva", *Working Paper*, 2021.

SOARES, Inês Virgínia Prado and FECHER, Viviane, "Empresas e Cooperação com a Ditadura Brasileira: Novas Possibilidades para a Responsabilização Empresarial", in FACHIN, Melina Girardi and PAMPLONA, Danielle Anne (eds.), *Direitos Humanos e Empresas*, Curitiba, Íthala, 2019, pp. 323–354.

SOARES, Inês Virgínia Prado and QUINALHA, Renan Honório, "A Memória e Seus Abrigos: Considerações sobre os Lugares de Memória e seus Valores de Referência", *Revista da Anistia Política e Justiça de Transição*, vol. 4/2010, pp. 250–279.

―― "Os Escrachos e a Luta Por Verdade e Justiça: O Que Esperar em 2013?", *Correio da Cidadania*, January 3, 2013, http://www.correiocidadania.com.br/colunistas/dicionario-da-cidadania/7968-03-01-2013-os-escrachos-e-a-luta-por-verdade-e-justica-o-que-esperar-em-2013.

SOLNIT, Rebecca, *The Mother of All Questions*, Chicago IL, Haymarket Books, 2007.

SONNENBERG, Stephan and CAVALLARO, James L, "Name, Shame, and Then Build Consensus? Bringing Conflict Resolution Skills to Human Rights", *Washington University Journal of Law & Policy*, vol. 39/2012, pp. 257–308.

SOUSA, José Geraldo de Jr., *Ideias para a Cidadania e para a Justiça*, Porto Alegre, Sergio Antônio Fabris Editor, 2008.

SOUSA, Priscila Paula de, "Memória, Objetos e Edifícios – Uma Análise Arquológica Sobre o Edifício Que Sediou o DEOPS/SP", *Revista de Arqueologia Pública*, vol. 10/2014, pp. 177–194.

STAVENHAGEN, Rodolfo, "América Latina: Derechos Humanos y Desarrollo", *International Foundation for Development Alternatives – IFDA Dossier*, vol. 79/1990, pp. 41–52.

STEPAN, Alfred C., "Introdução", in STEPAN, Alfred C and FISHLOW, Albert (eds.), *Democratizando o Brasil*, Rio de Janeiro, Paz e Terra, 1988.

STEWART, James, "Gender and Transitional Justice", *United Nations University*, March 25, 2013, https://unu.edu/publications/articles/gender-and-transitional-justice.html#info.

STOPPINO, Mário, "Ditadura", in BOBBIO, Norberto; MATTEUCCI, Nicola; and PASQUINO, Gianfranco (eds.), *Dicionário de Política*, Brasília, UnB Press, 1991.

STRECK, Lênio Luiz, "A lei de anistia e os limites interpretativos da decisão judicial: o problema da extensão dos efeitos à luz do paradigma do Estado Democrático de Direito", *Revista do Instituto de Hermenêutica Jurídica*, vol. 8/2010, pp. 171–181.

SVEAASS, Nora and SONNELAND, Anne Margrethe, "Dealing with the Past: Survivors' Perspectives on Economic Reparations in Argentina", *International Perspectives in Psychology: Research, Practice, Consultation*, vol. 4/2015, pp. 223–238.

TANG, Yi Shin, "International Justice Through Domestic Courts: Challenges in Brazil's Judicial Review of the Amnesty Law", *International Journal of Transitional Justice*, vol. 9/2015, pp. 259–277.

TEITEL, Ruti G., "Transitional Justice Genealogy", *Harvard Human Rights Journal*, vol. 16/2003, pp. 69–94.

—— *Globalizing Transitional Justice – Contemporary Essays*, New York, Oxford University Press, 2014.

TEKLIK, Joanna and MESNARD, Phillipe. "El Viaje a Auschwitz:Turismo de la Memoria o Turismo Cultural?", in FLEURY, Beatrice and JACQUES, Walter, *Memorias de la Piedra: Ensayos em Torno a Lugares de Detención y Massacre*, Buenos Aires, Ejercitar la Memoria, 2011.

TELES, Edson and QUINALHA, Renan, "Lógica da Governabilidade como Escolha da Democracia – O Trabalho de Sísifo da Comissão Nacional da Verdade", *Le Monde Diplomatique Brasil*, September 2, 2013, https://diplomatique.org.br/o-trabalho-de-sisifo-da-comissao-nacional-da-verdade/.

TELES, Janaína de Almeida, "A Constituição das Memórias sobre a Repressão da Ditadura: o Projeto Brasil Nunca Mais e a Abertura da Vala de Perus", *Anos 90*, vol. 19/2012, pp. 261–298.

—— "A Vala Clandestina de Perus: Entre o Passado e o Presente", *Revista Insurgência*, vol. 4/2018, pp. 300–341.

—— "Entre o Luto e a Melancolia: a Luta dos Familiares de Mortos e Desaparecidos no Brasil", in SANTOS, Cecília MacDowell; TELES, Edson and TELES, Janaína de Almeida (eds.), *Desarquivando a Ditadura: Memória e Justiça no Brasil*, vol. 1, São Paulo, Hucitec, 2009, pp. 151–176.

TELES, Maria Amélia de Almeida, "Violações dos Direitos Humanos das Mulheres na Ditadura", *Estudos Feministas*, vol. 23/2015, pp. 1001–1022.

TELES, Maria Amélia de Almeida and LISBOA, Suzana Keniger, "A Vala de Perus: Um Marco Histórico na Busca da Verdade e da Justiça!", in CARDOSO, Ítalo and BERNARDES, Laura (eds.), *Vala Clandestina de Perus – Desaparecidos Políticos, Um Capítulo Não Encerrado da História Brasileira*, São Paulo, Ed. Do Autor, 2012, pp. 51–102.

TESSITORE, Viviane, "Projeto Brasil Nunca Mais: Reconstrução, História, Recuperação e Aplicação da Metodologia", *Revista Projeto História*, vol. 50/2014, pp. 275–288.

THEODORO, Mário (ed.), *Desigualdades Raciais, Racismo e Politicas Públicas: 120 Anos após a Abolição*, Brasília, Instituto de Pesquisa Econômica Aplicada (IPEA), 2008.

TORELLY, Marcelo D., "Das Comissões de Reparação à Comissão da Verdade: Contribuições da Comissão sobre Mortos e Desaparecidos Políticos (1995) e da Comissão de Anistia

(2001) para a Comissão Nacional da Verdade", in TOSI, Giuseppe; FERREIRA, Lúcia de Fátima Guerra; TORELLY, Marcelo D.; and ABRÃO, Paulo (eds.), *Justiça de Transição: Direito à Justiça, à Memória e à Verdade*, João Pessoa, Editora da UFPB, 2014, pp. 215–232.

—— "Gomes Lund vs. Brasil Cinco Anos Depois: Histórico, Impacto, Evolução Jurisprudencial e Críticas", PIOVESAN, Flavia and SOARES, Inês Virgínia Prado (eds.), *Impacto das Decisões da Corte Interamericana de Direitos Humanos na Jurisprudência do STF*, Salvador, Jus Podivm, 2016, pp. 525–560.

URIBE, Camila, "Do Amnesties Preclude Justice?", *International Law Revista Colombiana de Derecho Internacional*, vol. 21/2012, pp. 297–359.

USTRA, Carlos Alberto Brilhante, *Rompendo o Silêncio*, São Paulo, Thesaurus, 1987.

VALENÇA, Márcio M., "Patron-Client Relations and Politics in Brazil – An Historical Overview", *Research Papers in Environmental and Spatial Analysis*, vol. 58, 1999.

VALENTE, Rubens, *Os Fuzis e as Flechas – História de Sangue e Resistência Indígena na Ditadura*, São Paulo, Companhia das Letras, 2017.

VAN KLAVEREN, Maarten; TIJDENS, Kea; HUGHIE-WILLIAMS, Melanie; and RAMOS MARTIN, Nuria, "An Overview of Women's Work and Employment in Brazil", *Amsterdam Institute of Advanced Labour Studies (AIAS) Working Paper no. 83*, University of Amsterdam, 2009, https://dare.uva.nl/search?identifier=99daf4ba-e84d-4b48-a3c4-fb60a53be0cb.

VENTURA, Deisy, "A Interpretação Judicial da Lei de Anistia Brasileira e o Direito Internacional", *Revista Anistia Política e Justiça de Transição*, vol. 4/2010, pp. 196–227.

VERBITSKY, Horacio and BOHOSLAVSKY, Juan Pablo (eds.), *The Economic Accomplices to the Argentine Dictatorship – Outstanding Debits*, New York, Cambridge University Press, 2016.

VERDEJA, Ernesto, "A Normative Theory of Reparations in Transitional Democracies", *Metaphilosophy*, vol. 37/2006, pp. 449–468.

VIANNA, Cláudia and RIDENTI, Sandra, "Relações de Gênero e Escola: das Diferenças ao Preconceito", in AQUINO, Julio G. (ed.), *Diferenças e Preconceito na Escola: Alternativas Teóricas e Práticas*, São Paulo, Summus, 1998, pp. 93–105.

VIDAL, Nicolás Alfredo and CASALECCHI, Gabriel Avila, "Legitimidade Democrática no Brasil e na Argentina em Perspectiva Comparada: Difernetes Transições Democráticas e Suas Consequências", *Teoria & Pesquisa – Revista de Ciência Política*, vol. 27/2018, pp. 54–74.

VIEILLE, Stephanie, "Transitional Justice: A Colonizing Field?", *Amsterdam Law Forum*, vol. 4/2012, pp. 58–68.

VILLA, Marco Antonio, "Coup Brazilian Style", *The Brazilian Economy*, vol. 6, 2014.

VIZENTINI, Paulo Gilberto Fagundes, "A Experiência Histórica do Brasil e da Argentina Contemporâneos: Autoritarismo e Desenvolvimento (1964–1985)", in LLADÓS, José Maria and GUIMARÃES, Samuel Pinheiro (eds.), *Perspectivas: Brasil e Argentina*, Brasília, IPRI, 2000, pp. 435–485.

VRIEZEN, Vera, *Amnesty Justified? The Need for a Case by Case Approach in the Interests of Human Rights*, Cambridge, Intersentia, 2012.

WALKER, Polly O., "Decolonizing Conflict Resolution: Addressing the Ontological Violence of Westernization", *American Indian Quarterly*, vol. 28/2004, pp. 527–549.

Weber, Sanne, "From Victims and Mothers to Citizens: Gender-Just Transformative Reparations and the Need for Public and Private Transitions", *International Journal of Transitional Justice*, vol. 12/2018, pp. 88–107.

Weichert, Marlon Alberto, "O Financiamento de Atos de Violação de Direitos Humanos por Empresas Durante a Ditadura Brasileira. Responsabilidade e Verdade", *Acervo*, vol. 21/2008, pp. 181–190.

—— "O Relatório da Comissão Nacional da Verdade: Conquistas e Desafios", *Projeto História*, vol. 50/2014, pp. 86–137.

Weschler, Lawrence, *Um Milagre, Um Universo: O Acerto de Contas com os Torturadores*, São Paulo, Companhia das Letras, 1990.

—— *A Miracle, a Universe: Settling Accounts with Torturers*, Chicago IL, The University of Chicago Press, 1998.

Westhrop, Amy Jo; Peluzio, Luciana and Simi, Gustavo, *Comissão Nacional da Verdade: Balanços e Perspectivas da Finalização de seu Processo Político-Institucional*, Rio de Janeiro, ISER, 2015.

Westhrop, Amy Jo; Garrido, Ayra Guedes; Parreira, Carolina Genovez; and Santos, Shana Marques Prado dos, *As Recomendações da Comissão Nacional da Verdade: Balanços sobre a Sua Implementação Dois Anos Depois*, Rio de Janeiro, ISER, 2016.

Whytock, Christopher, "The Evolving Forum Shopping System", *Cornell Law Review*, vol. 96/2011, pp. 481–534.

Wilcken, Patrick, "The Reckoning", *New Left Review*, vol. 78/2012, pp. 63–78.

Wilke, Christine, "Remembering Complexity? Memorials for Nazi Victims in Berlin", *The International Journal of Transitional Justice*, vol. 7/2013, pp. 136–156.

Williams, Daryle, *Cultural Wars in Brazil – The First Vargas Regime (1930–1945)*, Durham NC and London, Duke University Press, 2001, pp. 1–5.

Yamada, Erica Magami and Villares, Luiz Fernando, "Julgamento da Terra Indígena Raposa Serra do Sol: Todo Dia Era Dia de Índio", *Revista Direto Getúlio Vargas*, vol. 6/2010, pp. 143–158.

Zaverucha, Jorge, *Rumor de Sabres: Tutela Militar ou Controle Civil?*, São Paulo, Ática, 1994.

—— "Relações Civil-Militares: o legado autoritário da Constituição Brasileira de 1988", in Teles, Edson and Safatle, Vladimir (eds.), *O que Resta da Ditadura*, São Paulo, Boitempo, 2010.

Zia-Zarifi, Saman, "Suing Multinational Corporations in the U.S. for Violating International Law, *The UCLA Journal of International Law & Foreign Affairs*, vol. 4/1999, pp. 81–147, at 120–121.

INDEX

A
accountability   50, 102, 108, 157
   abstract accountability   270–271
   accountability for past atrocities
      259
   nonfigurative accountability   270
agency   214
amnesty
   double-handed amnesty   92
   white   92
Amnesty Caravans (*Caravanas da Anistia*)
   62–63
Amnesty Law   27–29, 33, 35, 38, 47
   Law n. 6.683/1979   27–28
   two-sided law   41
apology, official   211, 214
archaeology of repression and resistance
   221–222
archives   73
assimilationism   199
assimilationist policy   175
authoritarianism   135, 137
   authoritarian debris   268
   authoritarian repression   269
   socially rooted   135

B
blood crimes   36
"Brazil: Never Again"   148

C
civil society   145–146, 148, 150, 160–161,
   167–168
commissionism   117
complicity   243, 249, 262–263,
   265–266
conciliatory character   101
conflicting understandings and memories
   269
connected crime   36–38
conservatism   227, 229
continuism   135, 137
continuity (*continuísmo*)   134
   continuity of authoritarianism   269
conventionality control   95, 99
corporate accountability   257, 260
corporate civil liability   261
corporate complicity   243, 246, 251, 254–255,
   257–259, 262

corporate responsibility   266
crime of forced disappearance   83
crimes against humanity   41, 57, 87–88,
   91, 98–100, 104, 122, 135, 226,
   261–262
   impossibility of granting amnesty for   83
   the prohibition of amnesty for   98
crimes committed by agents of the State   82
criminal justice   29, 44

D
demarcation   188
demographic void   178
deterrence   102, 132, 253
dignity of the victims   215
domestic affairs   214
domestic violence   231–232

E
economic actors   243
enforceability of international precedents by
   local courts   84
escrachos   161–163, 167–168
ESCR violations   122, 134
experiences of conflict, women's   210

F
female or male roles   220
   feminine role   206
   political militant woman   207
Figueiredo Report of Investigation   179
financial complicity   254, 264
financial contributions   248
financial reparation   252–253
financing of repressive bureaucracy,
   method of   247
forced disappearance   88–90
forced displacement   182, 184, 186
forgiveness   138

G
gender-based violence   119, 226, 230–231,
   238–239
   normalization of violence against women
      227
   political violence against women   230
   reductionist accountability for gendered
      victimhood   233
   social invisibility of the female victims   219

Index

gender
    gender gap   228, 230
    gender identities   233, 235
    gender inequality   214, 232, 238–239
    gender justice, multidimensional issue of   239
    gender minorities   235
    gender-related recommendations   219
    visibility of women   214
Guarani Farm   181–182

H
holistic approach   221
household chores   228
human rights law   241
human rights movement   146
human rights organizations   147
human rights violations   50, 241–242, 246, 249, 254, 258
    committed against indigenous peoples   171, 184
    mass   29
    of economic, social and cultural rights   122
    of human rights   93, 102, 114, 134, 242
    of socioeconomic rights   125

I
impunity   135, 137
Inter-American Court of Human Rights   27
international human rights   42, 110
    international human rights treaties   83–84

K
Krenak Reformatory   180–181

L
legacies
    of military rule   270
    of past atrocities   214
LGBTI population, effects of Brazilian dictatorship   118

M
macaw's perch   182
mandatory occupation   178
mass grave, clandestine   155, 167
memorials   74
    and monuments   67
memory   74
    collective   102, 138, 169, 272
    of gender relations   218
    politics of   272
    sites of   74
minority representation   212
missing persons   50

N
name and shame approach   170, 258
naming of names   113, 255
    strategy of   90

narratives of victims and perpetrators   218
National Truth Commission   48
network of truth commissions   116, 118
non-recurrence, guarantees of   76
non-repetition   111, 114, 132
non-State actors   242, 244

O
oblivion   138, 213, 269
opposition to the regime, female   207

P
pardon   131
participation, female   206
past atrocities   262
patriarchal culture   230
peaceful opposition, female   209
political crimes   29–30, 41
political opponents, female   219
private actor   241–243, 245, 248, 254, 257, 262, 264
private and domestic spheres   206
process of "forgetting"   272
process of "remembering"   272
psychological wounds   218
public hearings   113, 117, 234

R
reconciliation   82, 91, 138, 186, 239, 254, 266, 269
reparation   47, 50, 52, 57–58, 60, 65, 73, 237, 245, 271–272
    collective   203, 222
    reparations for LGBTI victims   120
    reparations programs   76–77, 81
Rule of Law   29, 74, 100, 102, 114, 236, 273

S
self-amnesty   92
settling accounts with the past   267
sexual violence   214, 218–220, 224, 226, 229–230, 238; *see also* gender-based violence
social mobilization   161
social movements   170
social pacification   101
social rights   124
social roles   206
statute of limitations   260–261
stereotype   225–226
structural socioeconomic violence   123–124
structural violence, historical patterns of   214
symbolic reparation   235, 238, 250, 253, 258, 265
symbolic tribute   223

T
temporal requirement   188
theory of the lesser evil   40

transformation, collective 208
transformative justice 220, 239
transformative reparations 220, 231
truth-seeking 168, 216
truth-telling 52, 132, 217, 220, 237, 271
    truth-telling process 108
    truth-telling program 114

V
violence
    against sexual minorities 119
    in rural areas 133

W
war crimes trials 242

ABOUT THE AUTHOR

Lucia Elena Arantes Ferreira Bastos is a Brazilian lawyer who has a Ph.D in International Law from the Faculty of Law of the University of São Paulo (USP), Brazil. Lucia concluded her Ph.D thesis in 2007 and her research was related to International Human Rights, Transitional Justice, Amnesty Laws, and Dictatorships in Latin America. For the period from 2004 to 2007, she received a scholarship from the National Council for Scientific and Technological Development of Brazil (CNPq). After the conclusion of her Ph.D, she authored a book related to amnesties and international law in 2009, named "*Anistia. As Leis Internacionais e o Caso Brasileiro*" (Amnesty. International Law and the Brazilian Case), published by Juruá, as well as various articles and book chapters about her main area of research.

From 2007 to 2011, Lucia held a post-doctoral researcher position in the Center for the Study of Violence in the University of São Paulo (NEV/USP). NEV/USP is a well-known center that promotes interdisciplinary studies in the fields of violence, democracy and human rights. While engaged at NEV/USP, she was granted a scholarship from the State of São Paulo Research Foundation (FAPESP) to pursue research comprising Human Rights and Restorative Justice in Latin America.

She was born in Brazil, but also lived in New York (2009–2010) for academic research, and moved to Basel (2016–2019) on sabbatical leave, during which she wrote this book.

Printed in the USA
CPSIA information can be obtained
at www.ICGtesting.com
LVHW080455240524
780636LV00004B/44